Project Bible Truth

A Minister Turns Atheist and Tells All

By Joe E. Holman

Copyright 2008

ISBN: 978-0-6152-3722-0

Dedication

This work is dedicated to all freethinkers everywhere who have gone through the pain of losing a deeply cherished faith.

Special thanks going out to...

Those wonderful souls who have participated and encouraged me in the production and editing of this book, especially the Ionian Spirit team. Special thanks go out to Perry Spiller for heading up the editing process. Special thanks to John W. Loftus for his critical eye, and to Paul Cabby for his technical insights. Your ideas, criticisms, and exhortations will never be forgotten.

Table of Contents

Preface
Introduction

Chapter 1 The Long Journey Begins: My Early Years and Conversion to Christianity.
p. 1

Chapter 2 From Preaching School to the Ministry: The Beginning of the End.
p. 15

Chapter 3 The Faith Fall-off: The End Approaches.
p. 27

Chapter 4 Faking Faith: The Minister Turns Atheist.
p. 46

Chapter 5 The Chips Fall: Reactions to My Change.
p. 56

Chapter 6 Against Inspiration-I: Hints of the Non-inspiration of the Bible.
p. 69

Chapter 7 Against Inspiration-II: On the Nature of Biblical Contradictions.
p. 83

Chapter 8 Against Inspiration-III: On the Morality of the God of the Bible.
p. 109

Chapter 9 Earth in the Scriptures: What the Bible Really Teaches about our Planet.
p. 119

Chapter 10 Messiah Matters: The Truth about the Old Testament Messiah.
p. 127

Chapter 11 Puppets on a String: The Bible's Teaching on Predestination.

p. 156

Chapter 12 Lost Hope: Jesus Christ, the Deserter.
p. 169

Chapter 13 The Cruel Commission: Why Christ's "Great Commission" isn't so Great.
p. 181

Chapter 14 Evil Never Dies: The Problem of Evil is Still a Problem.
p. 196

Chapter 15 Stolen Goods: From Tantalizing Tall Tales to Mythologically Morphed Messiahs.
p. 218
- The Making of a Mighty Myth p. 219
- Where Have I Seen That Before? p. 230

Chapter 16 Corrupt and Scandalous: A look at the Oppressive Church of Jesus Christ Throughout the Ages.
p. 250

Chapter 17 God's Shrinking Living Room: A Journey Through Time.
p. 260

Chapter 18 A Spooky Kooky World: My Experiences Investigating the Paranormal.
p. 272

Chapter 19 On Morality: Morality from a Godless Standpoint.
p. 286

Chapter 20 God's Little Shop of Horrors: The Biblical Message of Eternal Damnation.
p. 303

Chapter 21 What if I'm Wrong?: Blaise Pascal's Bad Wager and Death through the Eyes of an Atheist.
p. 309
- Pascal's Bad Wager p. 310
- Facing Death as an Atheist p. 317

Chapter 22 Articles of Anti-Faith: An Assortment of Godless Articles.
p. 322

- Jesus and the End of the World p. 323
- Why Does the Universe Bother to Exist? p. 329
- The Line Must Be Drawn Here! p. 332
- Good Old Christian Morals p. 336
- The Dangers of Fundamentalism-I p. 338
- The Dangers of Fundamentalism-II p. 341
- The Dangers of Fundamentalism-III p. 345
- The Dangers of Fundamentalism-IV p. 348
- The Follies of Faith-I p. 351
- The Follies of Faith-II p. 355
- A Response to "You were never really saved!" p. 357

Chapter 23 The Sacred Writings of Saint Sarcasticus: Bizarre, Ironic, and Humorous Reflections from the Word of God.
p. 360

- Questions for God p. 361
- A Petition to Reinstate Heretic Burning p. 369
- The Charlatan Letter: a manipulation manual for psychics and televangelists p. 376
- Christian McDumb Takes a Stand! p. 381
- Give Me The Secular Nation! p. 383

Chapter 24 Hats Off to the Real Jesus: A Final De-conversion Milestone.
p. 385

Preface

"Conspiracy," "classified," "cover-up," "top secret," these buzzwords are enough to get anyone's attention. Some of the best dramas and bestselling novels contain the conspiracy motif, the idea that someone or some organization in a powerful position has something they don't want us to know. The trained reporter knows how to have a hay-day when a cover-up story of any type comes along. Whether it's Watergate, Enron, or the U.S. government's alleged recovery and storage of alien bodies from Roswell, New Mexico in 1947, we are intrigued at the possibility of suspicious activity. We immediately begin to wonder how conspiracies might affect our families, our nation, and ourselves. We take profound interest at the very thought of some taboo activity going on under our noses. This can be a good or a bad thing.

Upon selecting a title for this book, I decided against "The Bible's X Files," preferring "Project Bible Truth: A Minister Turns Atheist and Tells All," in place of it due to potential copyright and trademark issues that might have arisen from its use. A very successful TV show bears a big chunk of this title. But the decision to leave it behind was still difficult, partly because of the association of "X files" with the ever-popular and attention-getting conspiracy motif—just say "conspiracy" somewhere in the title and you stand a better chance of someone else picking up a book who otherwise wouldn't have.

Another reason I decided against this title was because of the things I didn't like about The X Files television show. This is where the negative aspects of conspiracy thinking come out. I watched with vigor about two or three episodes of the show when it first came on the scene in 1993. After that, I would catch an episode a couple times a year or so, or if I was up late at night and happened to come across a rerun on television. What I hated about it was that almost every episode was a blow-up of every farfetched myth and hoax in existence. Never did I find that Mulder and Scully ran into pranksters, con men, scam artists, or legend explained away on scientific analysis. Never did Scully prove to Mulder that werewolves don't exist, or that vampires are unreal. It was always the hard-nosed skeptic getting put in her place by a believer in the fantastic. The show continually went the route of crowd-pleasing Hollywood by giving our nation's many new-agers and mystics exactly what they wanted. When it comes to entertainment, sugar is great, but sugar all the time doesn't taste as good. Some science fiction (preferably thinkable science fiction) is fine—it is, after all, entertainment, but continual paranormal and extraterrestrial encounters ruin the value. What makes good science fiction good is the occasional ability to "fudge" the laws of physics and make things a little more fun, but taken too far, this goes sour, as did the show.

But there were some redeeming qualities about it. Take, for instance, the show's slogan: **"The Truth is Out There!"** Mulder and Scully were after the truth, trying to answer the big questions of life, amidst cover-ups and lies. I felt the same way about my struggle as I moved from believer to atheist. I became a Christian in an effort to find ultimate truth. I was compelled to leave Christianity and expose it, not only because I did not find truth in it, but also because I saw how badly a Christian-dominated culture wanted to cover up the falsehoods it contained. So you could say I was an agent on the investigating team of *The Bible's* X Files.

As stated, while I did not like the pseudo-scientific angle of The X Files, I was rather enamored with the publicity and attention such a title would bring. And, of course, we can only spend so much time pointing out the nutcases and crackpots who go off the deep end, making up alien abduction stories and claims of healing from crystals, and those endless tales of séance contacts from the spirit world. We must also acknowledge that conspiracies can be and often are genuine claims *not* fueled by paranoia and the alarmist's drive for attention. In fact, conspiracies will exist; human nature dictates as much.

One such conspiracy is the suppression of the truth about Christianity by the fundamentalist religious elite of America. It *is not* the case that the religious segment of America knows Christianity to be false and then suppresses it. People are generally sincere about their beliefs. It *is* the case, however, that a critical look at the religion is made impossible by the overwhelming bias of a Christian country. The truth is that the Bible contains glaring contradictions within its pages. The truth is that the Bible contains no true prophecies, but actually contains prophecies that failed to materialize, robbing it of credibility. The truth is that the word of God is steeped in error and mythology. The truth is that a mature knowledge of science has bankrupted the Bible with its archaic claims. The truth is that America has no longer a need to follow a deity to find meaning, morality, and purpose in life. The truth is that the church has no monopoly on truth whatsoever. These things the church and her many conservative associates won't tell you. Rooted in ignorance, the church seeks to preserve fear, power, and financial stability.

One can very easily fail to realize just how much Christian influence you are bombarded with each and every day in America and in many other places around the world. How many crosses have you seen people wearing this week? How many times have you laid eyes on a religious T-shirt that said something like "Because He cared" with an accompanying picture of bloody nails? How many times have you driven by a church and seen an enormous steeple pointing to heaven? What about a huge sign and a billboard resting out on the front lawn? Perhaps they said something like, "God is Pro-life," or "How do you prefer eternity? Smoking or non?"

Or maybe the billboard had a more inviting question like, "Dusted off your Bible lately?" Maybe you saw an even bigger sign downtown with a colorful picture of a dove next to handsome Pastor Steve's face, with a message printed in a large, fancy, gold-colored font at the bottom of the sign, saying, "A Pastor Who Cares." How many times have you seen a graphically detailed and decorated crucifix on a wall in the lobby of an established business or restaurant? How many Christian emailed newsletters do you find cluttering up your inbox at home, and maybe even at work? How many of your co-workers subscribe to these newsletters? How many times have you been subjected to a public prayer by employees in your workplace? How many times have you been listening to the radio and heard a portion of a sermon or church invitation with beautiful, imploring organ music in the background?

How about Christian music stations or conservative talk radio stations funded by Christian Churches that feature sermons and widely broadcasted worship services of mega-churches on the weekends? How about TV stations like The Word and Trinity Broadcasting Network? How about the passing references to God, Jesus, and the Virgin Mary in non-religious songs you hear on a favorite CD, tape, or radio station? How many times have you caught the last portion of a televised Billy Graham tour while flipping through channels? How many newspaper articles did you run across in your local paper where a whole section was dedicated to weekly articles from church pastors? Maybe one of them had the title, "By grace are ye saved." How many bumper stickers have you come upon that said "Real men love Jesus"? How many Latter Day Saint infomercials have you seen in the last several months where two unusually beautiful white women sit down together and discuss "another Testament of Jesus Christ," and describe how complete and warm they feel while reading the Book of Mormon?

What about the religious tracts and flyers you found stuck in your screen door or door crevice, promoting the religious beliefs of the Watchtower Bible and Tract Society, the Jehovah Witnesses? How many neighbors have invited you to church services? What about bookstores? How many times have you seen the religious section of Barnes & Noble packed with people scanning the shelves for the newest gushy discourse on Jesus and his grace? How many Christian bestsellers have you seen promoted in the grocery stores in your area? How many cardboard cutout mini-signs have you seen advertising these books next to the checkout line? Think about those annoying evangelical doorknockers, the bench signs that say something like, "Jesus Loves You," or those "Eternal Life Insurance Policy" pamphlets anonymously left under one of your windshield wiper blades one day.

The by-now-all-too-obvious point is that we live in a Christian-dominated society. We have no idea how powerful of an influence Christianity is to us unless we benefit from it or have been hurt by it. It has desensitized us to its presence and lessoned our reactions to certain religious leaders taking power and claiming that it was God who put them there. Christianity maintains a chokehold on the world, particularly America, and shows no signs of letting go of its own accord. We have become blind to Christendom's influences because they are all around us, drowning us in formidable propaganda.

The purpose of my work here is to provide a look at the other side of the coin, the one you never hear about, the side your pastor, preacher, priest, rabbi, church cell leader, youth minister, elders and deacons, monsignor, coach, camp counselors, and community leaders won't tell you about.

Far too often, we simply take what we are given from our culture and upbringing. Mom and dad's habits become our own and so does mom and dad's religion. We take what life gives us, no questions asked, and in effect, live in this prison of limited influence. Sometimes it takes some prodding to get us to seriously question what we've been taught about our origins, and sometimes this prodding comes in the form of negative experiences with Christianity which cause us to question its validity. Sometimes it is merely the nature of the individual that prompts them to begin their own search for meaning and individuality. In my case, my own experiences in the ministry afforded me the time and opportunity to see the problems that many others cannot, or else refuse to see.

Scattered amongst the masses of America, there are a few who are not afraid to march to the beat of a different philosophical drum. They are not afraid to think for themselves, to disagree with the status quo, to question the validity of what they've been taught. To them, the *against* has just as much an obligation to be heard as the *for* of an issue. For so very long, Christianity has had a great many voices giving her endless praise. That's all fine and good, but now it's time for the underdog's voice, the voice of the critic, to be heard once again. Now is our time. Now you will hear our voice.

Introduction

I began this work back in May of 2002. Even though I was not an "out" atheist at the time, I began making a word document list of the issues I was facing, like a diary for myself. It didn't take long until that humble list was transformed into the outline for a book, and then on into the work you presently hold in your hands.

Those who have known me have always chided me for being a person of extremes. Whatever I would do, I would do it to the extreme. I would always be between some extreme (hot or cold, lazy or motivated, for or against, etc.). I was a fundamentalist, firebrand Christian minister and am now an avid atheist! I was writing church bulletin articles and pieces for Christian journals, and now for humanist and atheist publications. If a person of extremes is how I am to be characterized, so be it! Some might well see this as a fault. I see it as a trait of a determined perfectionist's intricate mind. Having made that little comment of praise about my person, I will now criticize myself and this work.

First, I will accept that the thrust of this work is not original. So many competent freethought authors have carried the torch before me, touching on these matters, or else dealing with them far more exhaustively than I have. I have set forth, not to reveal hidden, or as of yet undiscovered information on the flaws of god-belief and Christianity, but to bring these formerly known facts to the table again, this time from an ex-minister's perspective—from my own perspective and experiences. Many unbelievers have been believers, but not many have been Christian professionals (ministers). My knowledge of Christianity, together with my life's work as a minister, gives me a certain credibility on the subject matter.

Second, I will accept that my book leans heavily towards the layman's point of view. It is not my intent to delve into super deep detail on the science and/or biblical issues I will deal with. Such writing loses the average reader very quickly. I want to make my point in such a way that everyone, even the casual, undedicated reader can come away with a simple, working understanding of why I made the decisions I did in leaving the ministry and rejecting Christian theism. I will try at times to aim in writing for my ideal audience (learned skeptics and freethinkers), but I cannot forget about my real audience (consisting of average people who may not have any college degrees). I have aimed to gel down the truths presented for the sake of practicality and clarity.

I pride myself on Bible knowledge and my ability to draw sound conclusions from a wide variety of sources spanning many disciplines. I graduated after two years at a well-respected seminary among Churches of Christ. I spent six years at four different churches as pulpit minister, after three years as a personal evangelist, including my time as a minister in training. These experiences should more than qualify me to be considered competent in dealing with the subject of this work. But like most ministers, my expertise is in the all-round art and work of the ministry. In no particular area of expertise do I represent myself to be an accredited, degreed authority or expert. I turn to the experts in every major scholastic division…in the fields of biblical archeology, Greek, Hebrew, hermeneutics, and textual criticism. I have aimed to do the best research I could possibly do, and I leave it up to the reader to determine the fidelity of my research.

I see my work being of exceptionally practical use, perhaps even as an unbeliever's de-conversion manual in tabletop discussions between infidels and Christians. I have labored to make this work as concise and straightforward as I possibly could, coming right down to the point in every segment of every chapter.

Thirdly, I am willing to accept that while this work effectively overturns the validity of all major schools of Christian thought, it is more hard-hitting against the literalist or fundamentalist's understanding of Christianity. I did, after all, come from a fundamentalist sect of Christianity, and much of my material impacts that outlook the hardest. If you are a more progressive or liberal Christian and don't subscribe to a global flood, a six thousand year old Earth, Bible miracles, and virgin-born saviors, then you will not be too taken by my stand. However, most contemporary believers firmly hold onto most miraculous Bible claims, and therefore, have as much to lose in seeing them demolished. Should a reader subscribe to any of the major faith tenants of mainline Christianity, this book will serve as a strike against their faith just the same.

Fourthly, I am willing to accept that this work is not extremely anticipatory when it comes to the responses of theist objectors. That is, I am not in the game of trying to anticipate and respond to every conceivable theistic response to a naturalist's claims.

As a debater and public speaker, I understand clearly the meaning of the phrase, "Don't go there!" Of course, I want to be able to do away with as many theistic responses as I can in my material, but this method of anticipatory argument only goes so far. One simply cannot answer adequately every conceivable response. Beyond a practical point, the amateur student of debate soon realizes that for every point he makes in a controversial claim, an opponent can misunderstand or misconstrue these points, fail to get the point of analogies made, or contest every little component of each fact presented, so that a mere ten page debate by correspondence demands a fifteen page reply. The same is true of an oratory exchange—only so much material can be argued for or against within a given time limit. So it is futile to think that any one book can deal with the broad topic of believer vs. unbeliever in such a way that they could answer all contentions and silence all theistic future gainsaying. I am going to present my case and defend it as best I can. I believe the facts I present successfully refute Christianity. I am confident that the average, open-minded reader will come away with a less than favorable appreciation of Christianity upon considering what I have to say.

Fifthly, though it will be seen that I rejected Christian theism for atheism, I am not aiming to defend atheism here. I will at times refer to it, but it is not my objective to convince my reading audience that they should be atheists. Most of the attacks I will bring will be leveled against the Christian belief system, and not always against general belief in God. I am not offering atheism to "replace" god-belief (as though that was possible), but only to show the shortcomings of one particular form of theism.

This work is my little contribution towards bringing about that great day in the still distant future where a mother and a young daughter will stand together in a museum, and the little girl will ask her mother, "Mama, did people really use to clasp their hands and pray for rain because this black book told them to?" The mother will answer, "Yes, unfortunately so, dear. There was a time when the world thought that a silly little book would solve all their problems and bring the rain too!"

---

* All Bible quotes are from the King James Version of the Bible unless otherwise noted.

CHAPTER 1
The Long Journey Begins

My Early Years and Conversion to Christianity

"Where it is a duty to worship the sun it is pretty sure to be a crime to examine the laws of heat."
- *John Morley*

"The high of righteousness is the same as the high of cocaine."
- *Dr. John Bradshaw*

My Early Years and Conversion to Christianity

I was raised in a Christian home, and like most American children, grew up hearing the jolly old tales of Christianity. Our family was very traditional with the casual observance of Christmas and Easter, and the typical Sunday morning, churchgoing life. Both I and my brother and sister were privileged to have two loving parents who cared enough to give us the best upbringing they could. Dad was an accountant for a well-known South Texas cement company and mom was an elementary school teacher. Occasionally, dad would break open the Bible and we would hear a mini-sermon or two at home if we missed services. I suppose mom and dad would be classified as mild Christian fundamentalists.

During my early years, we "church-hopped" between the Baptist Church, a few charismatic denominational churches, and the Church of Christ (the church I would later be converted into and preach for). Like many young children, the gravity of religious convictions did not become evident to me until I turned eighteen. As a child, I guess I was a decent kid, getting my share of regularly administered belt whippings and chastisements for those intermittent bouts of youthful rebellion, but overall, I was just another run-of-the-mill adolescent.

I seldom applied myself at schoolwork. When I did, I found that I was quite capable of doing it, but I was never a "book worm," as far as classroom subjects were concerned. Anything a teaching authority had to force upon me was just not worth my time. If I had it to do over again, I would go back and really work at being an academic success, but back then, the sewing of my wild oats was all that mattered to me. Naturally, I was undisciplined and not studious enough to care to seek out religion or matters of the divine.

My interest in philosophy didn't come until about halfway through the twelfth grade, but it wasn't until after I graduated from high school that my life really began to change. Mind you, this was not a well-developed or thought-out interest in philosophy, nor did I care to study books on the likes of Kant, Descartes, or Anselm. At this point, I was doing well just to begin taking an interest in the deep mysteries of life. I still remember the first series of post-high school books I ordered after seeing a TV infomercial. I distinctly recall sitting up in bed and studying them with childlike curiosity. The series was from Time Life Books entitled "Mysteries of the Universe." The books contained nothing but the usual bunk about secrets of the Egyptian pyramids, ESP, parallel dimensions, alien abductions, the Lost City of Atlantis, Stonehenge, and other claptrap topics that attract mystics and pseudoscience admirers from around the globe. Even a naïve young guy like myself could read them and see that at least some of the material had to be bogus, but it was still fascinating to learn about. As causality would have it, it was this interest in pseudoscience that later gave birth to my interest in Christianity—and Christianity, in turn, would prove to be the catalyst for my rejection of all supernaturalism years down the road. What an incredibly heartrending journey it has been!

Just out of high school, I had freedom with my first fulltime job and a "life on my own," or so I thought. I wasn't religiously minded up to this time and didn't really plan on becoming so. I wore long hair, heavy metal T-shirts, rough looking late-eighties/early-nineties blue jeans, and a frown on my face. Nowadays, I refer to myself back then as a loser. I could never have imagined a dedicated life in the church, much less the ministry. For a while there, I came to hate "all that church stuff." I had plans to quickly move out of my parent's house and get an apartment for myself. I was not looking forward to anything in particular. Concerning a college education, I had no plans and didn't want to rethink this decision. I just wanted to kick back and enjoy my newly discovered independence. The job I took was a utility laborer position at the local cement plant where dad worked. He got me the job and it sure paid more than those demeaning fast food jobs I was working up until then.

Shortly after this independence, I began to experience depression. It stemmed from the termination of a relationship I had going with a girl about six months earlier. Depression was not new to me. I had dealt with it before, but it seemed to be growing worse than I bargained for. The things I did for fun were eat, drink, sculpt, play chess, party with friends, philosophize, watch TV, and listen to my favorite tunes, but these things didn't really seem to satisfy me. I was hurting and longing for something, but I didn't really know what for. I was dissatisfied with myself. I, just like life, seemed to add up to nothing. I had no real purpose, no major goals, and nothing to ultimately look forward to. My social life soon dwindled to almost nothing, and at this point, I had found nothing I thought I was any good at doing for a long-term career. Those lonely and gloomy nights for the first several months passed by and I found myself living just to get through the next day. This was from June of 1993 to early January of 1994.

Being so discontented with myself, I would later rethink my decision about college. I decided I didn't look forward to heading to work at five each morning and spending the day shoveling gravel in the hot Texas sun, getting dust in my nose and ears, and coming home, having to take two-hour showers! There was also a bad taste left in my mouth from this job because of the experiences in the failed relationship I had endured. Each morning I would wake up, and immediately my depression would come on strong. Things wouldn't get any better until I went back to sleep again. I can still remember staring up at the rising sun, getting hoes, shovels, and pick axes to break up patches of clinker and concrete on the job site in the crisp morning air. All I could think about was that girl, the one who turned me away. I was hurting inside. I looked around me and everything just felt wrong. This wasn't the way to live! I was so depressed my stomach would actually burn with discontentment.

My sort of depression was not the life-stopping, I'm-going-to-kill-myself sort of depression that some face. It was the deceptively benign kind that you think is not serious until you get to a point where you can do some reflecting and then realize that you're not happy with your life. Depression is a dragging condition, a mental straightjacket. It bogs you down and thwarts your views of the world and your efforts to even accept happiness when you find it. I was looking for a change.

After more time to soak up the unfulfilling life I was living, I finally came to a point where I decided that I would open my mind to the comforts of religion to see if there was anything there for me. Since my mother was a strong Christian, I started to think that perhaps I would one day find the strength to give up my self-centered, aimless life and become a part of something I was sure was legitimate—Christianity.

Like any struggling and hurting person, I sought answers especially hard and wanted to find something to keep me going, but I didn't exactly long in spirit for a savior to set me free from sins either. In fact, the idea seemed a little weird at first. I remember staring at some pictures of Jesus mom bought at a flea market. I took notice of the flowing, long hair of a graceful, almost effeminate man staring back at me. I pictured him saying, "I love you. I died for your sins." It just didn't click with me. It didn't touch my heart like I thought it would. But I kept thinking about it, and then thought about myself and my situation in life; when I focused on Jesus, nothing happened, but when I compared the love of Jesus to the love of the girl who dumped me, something amazing happened! The day was January 15, 1994. As was the norm, I got up that morning, threw on some clothes for work and prepared a sack lunch, depressed as ever. The Weather Channel was on. I looked down to the corner of the TV screen and the forecast said, "Cloudy 35." I even remember the sweet melody being played as the local forecasts for the major cities flashed by. I still find myself humming that tune to this very day. At this point, in utter desperation and with tears in my eyes, I looked up to the ceiling and let out a desperate, inner prayer, a groping for relief from the sadness and loneliness that engulfed me. It was as though heaven was opened to me at that moment and I realized for the first time the love of Christ! It seemed like Jesus literally popped through the roof and said to me, "I am here and I care!"

Now I longed for a savior, one who would supply me with the hope I needed and show me the true forgiveness that my parents always taught me to believe in and expect. I figured a girlfriend or a friend may desert me, but never Jesus. So I began to open my mind to the spiritual concerns I refused to give a second thought about before. My mother was a long time member of the Church of Christ, and when I began attending with her, we were going together to a church in San Antonio, Texas—the Northern Oaks Church of Christ.

After several weeks of attending, I invited some of the congregation's young Christian men whom I had befriended over to my home to study the Bible. They came to teach me the Bible at my request. I was taken by their Bible knowledge because unlike so many of the youth in the churches I had visited, these guys could quickly and easily work their way through the Bible, quote from it, and refute "erroneous" teachings about it. On top of being knowledgeable, these young men were concerned more about saving my soul than pizza parties and youth retreats like the Baptists I knew from my past. They quickly earned my respect, and longing for answers as I was, I wanted to know the Lord like these guys. These same young men would later be my companions in preaching school. When they made it over to my house that night, they went over with me the points of the "plan of salvation," as they refer to it (hear the gospel, believe it, repent of sins, confess those sins, and be baptized for the forgiveness of sins). We talked for several hours, and by the end of the night, I decided I wanted to take the plunge and fully give myself to Jesus Christ. The following Sunday I was baptized into Christ on that chilly morning. It was an emotional time for me and my family and friends. I faithfully attended the Northern Oaks church until a year and a half later when I would move to Austin to go to preaching school.

My conversion to Christianity took place on February 14, 1994. I was on fire for the plain old gospel message. I began to read the Bible the day after my baptism. My mother and grandmother got together one afternoon while shopping at a mall and bought me an expensive New King James Version Open Bible Study Edition, which cost about $80.00. At first, I spent an hour a day, thirty minutes in the Old Testament and thirty minutes in the New, reading from Genesis and from Matthew. I upped this study pace to a little over three hours a day four months later. Finally, I had the whole Bible read through in about ten months. And over the next six months, again I stepped up the study level. I spent between four to six hours a day studying as hard as I could, usually well into the night, trying to understand as much as I could. I would get home from work and bury myself in the Bible and my Strong's Exhaustive Concordance. The nightlife of parties and foolish fun ended abruptly. I no longer desired to do anything but study the Bible and talk about Christ to those I ran into. Christ wasn't a part of my life, he *was* my life! Because after all, Christ died for me, so I'm going to live for him, and thus I did until preaching school began.

Let me stop here and stress just how much of a foothold my faith was for me. For the first time in my life, the gap was filled. I no longer wandered aimlessly, looking for the meaning of life because I had found it! No silly book about ESP or alien abductions offered the emotional satisfaction that Christianity gave me. I henceforth rejected all mysticism and embraced Judeo-Christianity completely. This was it! Everything made perfect sense now; God created this world of his because he wanted all men to give him the glory that was due him as the Creator. Ephesians 1:12 says that we are created to the "praise of the glory of his grace." God created man perfectly, but man chose to sin, and therefore, God cast him out of his perfect garden paradise to a now sin-cursed world to miserably spend the rest of his existence toiling in the ground. We couldn't live for the flesh that corrupted, so we must live to go to heaven to be with God. It seemed so right.

The depression was gone, gone totally. I walked with a spring in my step. I had confidence and self-esteem like I never knew before. I was "born again" as I knew I had to be to enter the kingdom of God. God seemed to go with me everywhere I went. Nothing can really duplicate that high feeling that almighty God is with you. My person was reformed, transformed by the power of God! I dropped every sin I had knowledge of. I completely crucified the "old man" with his worldly ways (Colossians 3:10). I believed in and was afraid of an eternal, fiery Hell that awaited the godless and was ever so thankful that God gave me time to see the error of my selfish and riotous way, and to be able to come to the "knowledge of the truth" (2 Peter 2:4).

I remember listening to one "hellfire and brimstone" sermon at a gospel meeting one evening, as it was being preached by a bellowing speaker at one of our sister congregations. I was so moved that I said to myself in a private prayer as I sat in that pew, "Thank you, God, for not letting me die and suffer so horribly in that place of torture called Hell! Thank you so much!" As the hymn goes, "Then I trembled at the law I'd spurned." Christianity totally changed my life and I was ever so thankful to be redeemed by the blood of Christ.

I became a determined personal evangelist. Before I was even one year old in the faith I was going from door to door, friend to friend, and acquaintance to acquaintance, looking for those sincere souls who would "receive with meekness the implanted word" (James 1:22). I took a cheap, green, Wal-Mart King James Bible (I had to have at least one Bible I could wear out and not care as much about!) and a backpack full of evangelism tracts as I went. The tracts were "What must I do to be saved?" and "Let's be honest: are all religions on the road to Heaven?", written by the late Church of Christ evangelist Bill Jackson. Then, I hit the streets with an unquenchable desire to see souls saved. I had truth and everyone around me was going to know it! My zeal went off the charts. The sky was the limit and I was going to convert everyone under it. I used the same green Wal-Mart Bible to memorize large portions of the scriptures, which I found I could do better than anyone I knew. Much of the text I memorized by merely reading. This helped immensely in missionary work.

On one occasion, only weeks after my baptism, I can remember tearing into a worldly friend of mine on the phone, trying to convert him. It was as though God himself was moving my lips, and I think I really believed he was at the time. My mouth opened up with scriptures and my mind almost seemed to envision God, Christ, and the Holy Spirit sitting next to me and nodding at my words with heavenly approval. When my friend said, "I would rather be condemned for who I am and not be saved as a Christian for who I am not." I said, "You don't want that and you know it! You want eternal life. It's worth it…" By the end of that thirty minute conversation, I think I had him halfway convicted of his sins. This was one among almost a hundred such conversations that year. In truth, I had quite a few captive audiences in my early evangelistic years. I had college professors and neighbors who had to be downright rude to get me the message that they weren't going to change their ways regardless of what I said. They just didn't want to hear it anymore! So, finally, I kicked the "dust off my feet" and moved on (Matthew 10:14). Life took on new and more positive directions like these. I was a living, breathing, scripture-quoting, evangelizing machine, and ever so proud of it.

My Christian faith really began to grow as I encountered different types of religious people. Of course, they were "lost" because they didn't believe in "the Bible only" and interpret it the way I thought they should. I ran into the usual Jehovah's Witnesses and Mormons coming to my door (though usually, I'd get to them first). They would present various unorthodox arguments and I would meet them head-on. The Church of Christ had no problems with the doctrines of other religions. To us, they were easy to overturn. It was just a matter of finding where the Bible condemned their practice and showing them "the truth of the matter," as we saw it.

Let the reader be aware that the Church of Christ differs from many other Protestant groups. We stayed with what we believed to be the biblical "pattern" and built our case around "every word of God inspired" (2 Timothy 3:16-17). We accepted the Bible alone as our guide and rejected more traditional ideas like original sin, predestination, a direct operation of the Holy Spirit on the human heart at conversion, and a few other common sectarian views. We opposed infant baptism, "once-saved, always-saved" (the impossibility of apostasy), premillenialism (a millennial kingdom of Christ to be set up on earth), and other "far out" positions. We believed Bible miracles but rejected so-called modern day miracles claimed by charismatic churches.

To me, the Church of Christ was proving to be more rational than just about any group out there I had found. This greatly appealed to me. I was never the type to believe in a "better-felt-than-told" sort of thing. I was not a bleeding-heart emotional bag who merely wanted a Sunday morning "oomph" to get through the rest of the week. Christianity was real to me. It was serious business, and hypocritical, lackadaisical Christians were going to burn for their iniquity! If they were denominational Christians, I was always so puzzled as to why the vast majority of the people to whom I preached weren't as gung-ho about their version of Christianity as I was about mine. If they didn't have a religion or faith at all, I couldn't understand how anyone could be so cow-like as to just stare around at the world without giving a single thought to life beyond the grave. I was convinced, as were the fellow members of my cult, that being truly converted to God meant that God, Christ, and the Church were everything. So I opposed, like a truly belligerent fanatic, anyone who dared blaspheme God's holy name, or who spotted his church with the blemish of fat-cat, retirement-home, easy-does-it Christianity.

You could say that the mainline Churches of Christ have always set themselves up as a society of spiritual sheriffs, keeping a watchful, condescending eye on the flock to make sure that it doesn't go "liberal." The Church of Christ put heavy emphasis on the study of "Christian Evidences," a thing I found necessary and delightful. I jumped at any chance to defend my Lord. I wanted to validate my faith more than anything. I had to. We accepted any debates we could get because they were good opportunities to "defend the Faith." To me, it seemed that we always got the better of any discussion we were in, and this convinced me more so that we had the one true understanding of God's Word, though, deep down, when we came away champions in every debate, I was a little concerned that perhaps I just didn't understand my opponent's position well enough. This prompted yet more study. It was as though I could never get to a point in my mind where I just accepted that my religion was the truth. I believed it fully, but I kept reaching out for more answers. Perhaps God had much more to teach me? I decided that if he did, and if it would be someone from another faith who would teach me something, that I would always be ready to listen. I was afraid of being closed-minded, like the people whom I debated, and some in my own church.

Evangelism was easy except when I confronted skeptics or atheists of any sort—this was a whole different can of worms! They attacked the Bible and the concept of worship altogether, much the same way you die of AIDS, not because of the disease, but because your immune system is attacked and rendered useless, so you die of a mere cold; if the concept of God, faith, the inspiration of the Bible, or the resurrection of Jesus were falsehoods, the entire Christian system would fail! I had to go and do a little digging on some of my responses, but I always loved the challenge.

At first, I almost laughed at non-believers and thought their presumptions to understand God and the mysteries of the universe were all manifestations of hotheaded arrogance and selfishness. I could not even conceive of a universe without God. I never had and I thought I never would! The idea alone sounded unthinkable to me. I had been indoctrinated with the idea that non-believers live only for themselves and promote a self-destructive philosophy. But aside from sneering at atheism, I realized deep down that it must be taken seriously because, if true, it rendered all that I believed in and held to be valid completely worthless. Atheism too had a logical appeal, and though I detested it, I could see how it could make sense.

Heading back to secular college was quite an experience for me. To my sanctified little mind, it seemed like Sodom and Gomorrah; all that evil philosophy, immodest dress, fornication, riotous partying, the diabolical teaching of evolution, it was all too much for me. Jesus just had to come back soon! I had several college professors tell me about the great age of the earth and that the Bible had contradictions in it. But I "just knew" they were "agents of Satan," trying to "destroy my faith." So I made it a habit to seek refuge in Christian apologetics. I read every Christian evidences book and historical work vindicating Christianity I could get my hands on. My first book was C.S. Lewis' *Mere Christianity*. I was never terribly impressed with Lewis, so I turned to the likes of Norman Geisler and Josh McDowell, as well as some others who were mostly well known in the Churches of Christ, like Wayne Jackson and Bert Thompson (At the time, Thompson had not yet been yanked out of the closet as the homosexual pedophile he is!)

Like many brave, bold, and gallantly faithful souls who had gone before me, I took it upon myself to become the "apostle of the infidels," much the same way Paul called himself the "apostle of the Gentiles"

(Romans 11:13). It took some digging (and a lot of debating), but ultimately, I found the Bible and Christianity justified against higher criticism. The thing that still bothered me was that I couldn't get the godless to see my points or leave their unbelief. So more praying and more study had to go into my work to secure the salvation of the world's most flaming and blasphemous heretics, the atheists! At this point, I knew I needed some more help in my fight against the damnable forces of Satan's dark infidel armies, so this is when I made the decision to go to preaching school. Midway into my college tenure, having majored in education, I decided to drop it all. Just like that, I dropped it. Secular college was far too worldly and unspiritual for my liking, so I was ready to get my support and go to seminary. But it was just before I went to preaching school that I began to notice several things that made me examine my faith a little more closely than I had done thus far.

The Faith Assaults Begin

The first major assault on my faith occurred when someone showed me the first Bible contradiction I had ever seen. There it was—black and white as could be! II Kings 8:26 said, *"Ahaziah was twenty and two years old when he began to reign."* Then there was II Chronicles 22:2 which said, *"Forty and two years old was Ahaziah when he began to reign!"* I felt like I had been kicked in the stomach! What now? The contexts of these verses were identical. The verses were talking about the same person. The Bible that I thought was inerrant contained a clear-cut contradiction! Now I had actually seen one and had not just heard about it. This made all the difference to me. If the Bible wasn't right on small matters like these, how many other places needed correction? And why hadn't more recent translations corrected the mistake? How could God have allowed an error to creep into his holy Book?

Of course, Christian evidences and James Dehoff's book "Alleged Bible Contradictions Explained" helped to solve the problem. It was a scribal error on the part of a copyist of long ago, which was perpetuated into later copies of the Bible as they were made (by flawed, human scribes). At the time, I didn't realize this wasn't a very good explanation. I was still deeply bothered by the fact that God had not preserved our Bible translations. If he intended to guide all men by his revealed word, it would only make sense to safeguard it from errors of all kinds, but I figured, at least we had the tools to find the right answers. By researching the problem, I found that Ahaziah had to be twenty-two and not forty-two years old, otherwise he would have been two years older than his father (see 2 Kings 8:17). So, though I was shocked, I was ready to move on and again preach.

To really relate to how much this broke my initial confidence in the accuracy of the scriptures, I share with you an insight from the car sales business, having worked in it for just over a year after my resignation from the ministry.

A customer comes in and is adamant about getting every penny he wants for his trade: "I ain't taking a penny less than $5,000!" I reply, with a smile and politely, of course, "I promise you, sir, we'll give you what is fair and right. Let's take a look at the old trade, shall we?" The customer and I then head out to look at the vehicle together. At this point, I am doing what is called in the car business *The Silent Walk-around* with the customer at my side. The Silent Walk-around is where I walk around the car and take notice of every little ding, dent, scrape, scratch, and discoloration I can find. I take time to visibly (and silently) notice each and every fault. Then I break the silence: "What happened here?" The owner explains the situation, usually with more than a few details. Then I move to the next little dent, pause for a moment, and ask, "What happened here?" and the process continues. Over and over, I "ding" the owner's confidence just a little, helping them realize that their car may not be worth as much as they want me to give them for it. Then I ask, "Where'd you get the body work done?" Now I don't necessarily know they've had any bodywork done, not always, but eight times out of ten, I hear the customer blurt out something like, "Glenn's Body Shop over on Fifth and Pine." Wow! Now they begin to explain to me the wreck and the circumstances behind it. "Ah hah, gotcha!" I think to myself. The end result is this; the customer's vehicle is either a little too beat-up to give top dollar for, or it has been in a wreck, taking down the value even more. Either way, when I hit the owner with those lower trade numbers I am going to offer him, he's more likely to accept! This is not illegal. It is smart business, since no business is in the habit of giving away money.

This illustrates exactly what happened to me each and every time I came across numerous Bible discrepancies, even if they were only "mere scribal errors," like the matter of Ahaziah's age. My confidence, little by little, was being "dinged." Each "ding" would force my mind to take note and keep a record of my faith struggles, no matter how momentary or insignificant the faith assault was. My mind was keeping a perfect logbook of these problems, and though I would not recognize them for quite a long time, they were there, waiting to be released from the back of my mind. De-conversion from any cult is seldom a one shot deal for anyone. It takes time, the necessary life experiences, and applied reasoning to finally build up the critical mass to break free from the orbit of faith. Each discrepancy would play a key role in my de-conversion years later.

The next major obstacle to my faith came when, in a Bible study, someone asked me if all the Africans who had never heard of Jesus Christ were headed to Hell. I had the answer. It was "yes, indeed they were." I answered unapologetically because the scriptures seemed to be replete on this point. These Africans did not possess the saving knowledge of the truth of Jesus Christ, and therefore, they were lost in sin (2 Thessalonians 1:8-9). "He that believeth not shall be damned" (Mark 16:16). That answer didn't bother me until some time later. The more I began to think about the issue, the more it bothered me. How could a God so awesomely powerful and omniscient allow Africans who had never heard of his Son to burn in a lake of fire for eternity? It doesn't seem right by any stretch of thought. How could a merciful being allow such a thing? I talked to some other close Christian friends who helped me to see that those Africans are not necessarily innocent because God doesn't see things as man does (I Samuel 16:7). God sees all accountable people as sinners because they inevitably think and do things that are far from his will (Romans 3:23).

Ultimately, I had to accept what preachers kept pushing me to accept, that I should just not spend so much time thinking of those poor unsaved souls who hadn't heard the Gospel. Instead, I should see to it that *no more* ignorant souls go to Hell! I should be thinking about how I'm preaching to them, giving them the chance to make it to Heaven. A soul is judged by God. This is his world. Those who would be damned must really deserve it. This, of course, did not do very much to alleviate the problem I was fretting over, but I didn't have a whole lot of options. I "knew" the answer now and it didn't bother me anymore (at least not for another few years).

The next major quandary came when a former Christian friend got into Darwinism. For a while, he was a member of my home congregation. That is where I met him. He was only there for a short time until he got some books on dinosaurs and fossils. He couldn't fathom the idea of a six or ten thousand year old earth (as the Bible really affirms). Needless to say, he didn't last long in the faith. I took it personally that I couldn't convert him back to the fold. I was hurt. A soul was being lost to the evils of Darwinism and nothing I was able to say was helping. But I wasn't going to go down with him, even though the thought that his position could be true bothered me. I stood strong because I knew there would be answers even if I didn't understand them all right off. My friend said the Bible taught the idea of a saucer-shaped earth when it referred to "the circle of the earth," where all land masses came together to form what the Bible writers described as a flat disk and not a spherically shaped one (Job 26:7). I disagreed. I told him this verse was saying that "the circle of the earth" was the earth itself as an elongated ellipsoid sphere like I knew it was and that it was a jewel of Bible inspiration for men to record such a detail about the earth that long ago (Now, I know my friend was right and I was wrong!) He was unreachable on any subject we talked about. I rejected his conclusions because the Bible must be true on the age of the earth because it was right on every other subject, I thought. He became an atheist and soon afterward moved away. I have never seen him since. Back to Christian evidences I retreated, this time to load both guns on how to deal with the subject of evolution.

I continued to study more apologetics materials. Among other Christian evidence mills, I got material from Apologetics Press and was able to hear various defenders of the faith speak at churches I visited and youth camps I was a part of. These pillars of "rational" faith in the Churches of Christ I looked up to and respected. I began to apply myself more than ever towards being able to defend the faith of Christ from atheism and faith-destroying evolution. I prided myself on being able to "clear up" Darwinian "misconceptions." I was singing the tune of creationism pretty well. I was ready to point out that Archaeopteryx was "just a bird," and how Pilt Down Man turned out to be a hoax. I made myself the usual apologetics kit out of the materials I came across…pictures of brontosauruses and triceratops printed on ancient cave walls, supposed human footprints fossilized in riverbeds, books on why rock dating methods (like carbon dating) fail, and loads of stories about finding tools – like hand axes, fishing rods, and sandals – in the same ancient rock with extinct fossilized trilobites! I was much more confident now in my competency to debate a learned evolutionist. In fact, I was itching to see what a geology professor would say about my creationist claims. I so badly wanted to end this back-and-forth debate between creationism and evolution. It seemed like a volleyball game where one side hit the ball over the net pretty hard, and now it was up to the other to hit it back with a vengeance and show who was the best, but it never ended this way. It always seemed to end up in a stalemate by our side using evidences that went woefully against the grain of the consensus of scientist's opinions on the issues. It was frustrating when real scientists never even recognized the "facts" we presented. Our side couldn't get any respect! I was distraught, but decided the tie should go to the defender, so I let creationism hold my convictions for a while, though I wasn't getting altogether satisfactory answers from my investigation of the matter.

The problem of evil was also presented to me. It bothered me for a couple of months, but ultimately, failed to shake my faith. The argument was strong, but still seemed a little presumptuous. I thought my little reply to the problem of evil wasn't half bad, considering the self-deluded believer I was. I would always answer it by contending that since God always allows freewill, he gave Satan freewill too, and since God foreknew that Satan would deceive his prized creation on earth, God allowed him to do so, and in the process, used Satan for God's own divine purpose; God would be pleased by those who loved him, and would bring judgment to those who refused to choose the Lord's ways over evil. This seemed to make perfect sense. God would recompense his saints for the suffering they endured on this cursed earth with eternal life in Heaven. No problem! The problem of evil didn't take God's wisdom into account, or his timing—just because God didn't rectify evil immediately didn't mean he wouldn't rectify it ever! God is smarter than me and I must accept his conclusions, the same way a child accepts his mother's instructions without necessarily knowing all that is good for him, or the way a soldier must unquestionably take orders from his superiors. This reasoning sounded so good to me at the time.

These little faith struggles created tiny bits of doubt in me, passing moments of anxiety. They would come and I would study them away. Regardless of my spiritual ups and downs, my mind could never rest. I was always wondering, hungering for truth. Each time I "won a battle for the faith," my faith would continue to grow, but in the back of my mind, I still had minute doubts, doubts I wouldn't face until years later.

CHAPTER 2
From Preaching School to the Ministry

The Beginning of the End

"There's something in every atheist, itching to believe, and something in every believer, itching to doubt."
- *Mignon McLaughlin*

"I lived in a fever, convulsing with tears and sighs that allowed me neither rest, nor peace of mind. My soul was a burden, bruised and bleeding."
- *St. Augustine*

From Preaching School to the Ministry

I and three friends from the same church began preaching school together. This heavily condensed, two-year, 216-hour seminary started in August of 1995 through July of 1997. I was privileged to attend the Southwest School of Biblical Studies in Austin, Texas, which is a fine preaching school recognized by conservative Churches of Christ. From day one, I endured the bombardment of fundamentals classes, expository preaching classes, speaking classes, preaching protocol classes, Greek and Hebrew classes, a verse-by-verse study of all the Bible books, hermeneutics (the science of interpreting the scriptures) classes, and counseling studies. My life as a minister had officially begun. I continued having in-house debates, numerous Bible studies, and seeking the knowledge I so desperately wanted and loved. My life was set! Even today, I must admit that the two long years of this "spiritual boot camp" were not in vain. They helped me to learn how to do biblical research and to dig deeper to look for answers. I had plenty of books and reading materials for quite a while afterwards. It was an immensely beneficial and thought-provoking time in my life. Where would I be today without those times? Looking back, however, preaching school showed me that the Bible needed a lot of defending. It dealt with the *how* and the *why* of Bible apologetics.

I have always been a "night person." I come alive at around nine o' clock at night and stay strong until about four or five in the morning (if I don't structure my schedule to be more productive in the day). As a new Christian, I remember going outside just to spend about ten minutes watching the stars and contemplating God's place for me in the cosmos. It was almost as though they would speak back to me God's will, saying, "You are my chosen servant to proclaim my word." Those euphoric feelings of spiritual ecstasy, the insatiable inner-longing for heavenly peace and oneness with my creator, I experienced them all. My relationship with God was not one of pure, mechanical rule-keeping, as my critics would like to think. It was one of great meditative depth. My mind ran a hundred miles an hour, constantly thinking and rethinking "spiritual connections." It was a catchphrase in my house: *"I feel a sermon coming on."*

One thing about me though, I always studied debates to try and prove myself wrong. I didn't feel right about being "right." The pursuit of truth for mankind has always proved to be a frustratingly endless quest. How could lowly me have been the one to just stumble onto truth? My parent's religion, did it just so happen to be the right one of them all? Something didn't seem right. My mind kept longing for answers, and looking back, I think this is what separated me from my fellow preachers and friends I went through seminary with. They never seemed to struggle with difficult concepts, logical problems, or doubts of any kind. Me, I always had disturbing doubts off and on throughout my Christian life. My gospel-preaching friends seemed more like drones, automatons set in motion to fulfill their particular goal of making their parents (and the church that paid large amounts of money to send them to school) proud. With me, it was different. Not that I was better or more virtuous than they, but I felt that I was more compelled to search for answers. I was compelled by love and logic to preach, to fulfill my own quest for greater enlightenment, and to save a sin-sick world from damnation. No doubt my friends preached for the same reasons, but not to the same degree as I felt I did. To me, they seemed more concerned with impressing our home church and the wise and reputable Bible men who taught at the school.

My friends were always intellectually content, too content for my liking. What I was wanting was a feeling of complete mental contentment, closure, certainty, that my beliefs could not be falsified. I wanted knowledge beyond the possibility of error where I could fold my arms and breathe a big mental sigh of relief. The problem was, I believed and feared that such surety was impossible to obtain, yet I was forced to concede that it was real based on 2 Timothy 1:12, *"For I know whom I have believed and am persuaded that he is able to keep that which I committed unto him against that day."* This kept me looking for this precious and longed for certainty, certainty I thought would characterize me in future years when I was more mature in the faith. In a way, you could say I was in a philosophical battle with myself over the nature of truth. My preaching companions appeared to have this closure I wanted, this "I know I have truth and I'm not ever going to question it again," sort of attitude, an attitude I loathed because it seemed selfish, naïve, and unreal. I was not lacking faith, nor was I facing any spiritual crisis as of yet. I just wanted closure. I had to constantly be delving deeper, growing in spiritual insight and knowledge.

I suppose, deep down, I never really felt knowledgeable enough. This is why every time I watched a debate, picked up a debate book, an infidel book, a book from a church not of our denomination, or listened to a tape of a sermon, my mind would automatically say to me, "Alright Lord, what lessons do you have in this material for me to better my life?" This was my attitude, but not that of my preaching companions. They were content to stay with Church of Christ books, Church of Christ Study materials, and complete brotherhood works. I felt, at times, like I was around those cultic Mormons we so opposed. Their minds didn't give any other conflicting view the chance to be right either. If they did feign objectiveness in discussing an issue, they would quickly take the side of the church, or usually a great preacher they respected who happened to hold this or that position on some controversy. I can remember being furious as one of these men bought a book at a church book sale of one of the most well known ministers from our denomination, the late Foy E. Wallace Jr. The cover of the work said, "Foy E. Wallace Jr., Prince of Preachers." How dare they! Jesus was the Prince of Preachers, not this guy! Brown-nosing and the constant adoration of stuck-up brotherhood figures like this made me sick to my stomach!

For a good while, I wouldn't say what I am saying about my friends now because I had convinced myself that they were truly objective and that perhaps it was me who needed to grow spiritually. Now I know better. In a non-hurtful way, I was obsessed with finding the truth and getting to the bottom of every question on my list. I don't know how many all-nighters I pulled trying to finish homework for school, but the time required was partially due to my combination of schoolwork and the mechanical scriptural issues I was debating in my own head. My life was study. It was my calling.

Upon entering preaching school, I went through a period where my views were not nearly as solidified as they would become by the second year I was there. I adopted a number of smaller theological views and changed them over night. I was seen as a hot-headed zealot of a guy, maybe even a little arrogant, who was still a bit immature spiritually and "rough around the edges," and by my own admission now, this description was fairly accurate. By my second year at seminary, I was more settled down and seasoned. I now knew where I stood on the issues (From this point until my resignation, I changed a few minor views only a couple of times or so). But my views were my views. It didn't matter who held them, who didn't, or what the consensus of the brethren was on an issue. The search for truth was what led me into the ministry, and by golly, truth would sustain me all the way through! In fact, the search for truth would be the very thing that led me out of the ministry. As stated, ministry school was a very influential time in my life. And with me as a student, it was no doubt memorable to every instructor there as well! I was almost socially inept and didn't have the most common sense out of the group. I was more interested in pondering dilemmas and solving difficult questions than socializing or going out of my way to display the best etiquette. I was a diehard perfectionist, constantly preoccupied with some new thought or dilemma, even when conversing with others.

I remember going into the school director's office one day and unloading on him some questions about the Garden of Eden: *"I have a number of questions. First, why did God allow a deceitful snake in his garden? Second, why put a tree there with some forbidden fruit on it?"* I had my own theological answers to these questions, but wanted to see what the school "big dog" had to say. At first, he would not even answer me. He acted like my coming in and asking him questions inconvenienced him. He had almost a frustrated, "Why are you bothering me, you stupid kid!" look on his face. Putting some books back on the shelves behind his desk, staring busily at the title of each book as he replaced it, he finally blurted out, in a patronizing way, *"We don't know."* Then he walked away from me. That's it? We don't know? I can remember feeling so dissatisfied with this answer coming from a man who had preached for twenty-five years. I mostly gave up trying to ask him anything after a few other attempts, but I had plenty of opportunities to watch other zealous students try. They never got so much as a handful of credible answers to difficult questions. Though ministry school prepared me for the *ins* and *outs* of a life devoted to gospel ministry, it was teaching me that the greatest of spiritual men are just men nonetheless, without any special knowledge or deep-rooted insights whatsoever. Though I learned a lot, I was disappointed in many ways. Everything began to seem purely academic and scholastic rather than an unlocking of divine secrets of heaven. There was no treasure chest of knowledge that would solve all doubt and difficulties of the world. I felt a little silly, having gone into it with larger-than-life spiritual ambitions. Now I was back down to Earth.

At school, study never ended. On top of the course work I was required to do, I kept busy with my own investigations, studying and questioning every thing I held dear and believed in. I had resolved, with what seemed to be a philosophical revelation to me, that all evidences can be called into question. No one, not even the Savior of the world, could be exempted from healthy skepticism. Jesus was not in front of me. I did not know the penmen of the New Testament. So if I wanted to teach the gospel with credibility to validate anyone's faith, I would have to maintain my faith by study, by logic, and by credible reasoning. It wasn't enough to be an ignorant but sincere shade-tree preacher who just wanted to see people saved. Before I learned apologetics, I had to go far and wide to find people ignorant enough to believe Christ's message. I now believed Christ's message must be verifiable so that all who investigate it can see its validity. This marked a turning point in my Christian evangelical life. When I began the ministry, it focused on sincerely and emotionally winning converts to Christ. Now it focused on what I had more of—Bible knowledge. "Knowledge puffeth up, but charity edifieth." (I Corinthians 8:1)

Suddenly, preaching Christianity was a whole new world that I didn't expect. Now I was able to better defend and reason my way through the gospel. This, I thought, would allow me to vindicate the religion of Jesus Christ once and for all. I pictured myself as becoming an apologetics master, sent by Jesus to eradicate his godless enemies, but it backfired. Instead of laying the foundation for faith, it laid the foundation for infidelity. In truth, and from a Christian perspective, I would have done a much better job to stay ignorant and just evangelize like I had been doing before preaching school. I was now well trained and ready for being a preacher, but my soul-winning days were numbered. Of course, whether I had gone to seminary or not, I would have eventually discovered all of the seeming discrepancies and endless, brooding controversies within the pages of holy writ—of that I am convinced. I was already on my way to infidelity before preaching school, and even faster when I went through it.

Thinking back, I can recall one memorable lecture on Christian evidences. The instructor was giving us a rundown of evidences that he felt supported the Bible as the Word of God. One of the reasons he stated that the Bible could be trusted was that the fruits of the Spirit and conversion could be seen in the changed life of the believer. Being the adversarial student that I could be, I spoke up, *"But professor, a materialist could simply argue that belief in any religion or religious figure could and does produce changes in people all the time."* The class was silent. Nobody else had any questions or anything to contribute. The class just waited for the teacher to answer. When he finally did (after a few silent moments of apparent frustration), he said, "Well, I'm not in a debate now, Joe." This made me a little angry because now, not only did he not have a good, witty reply to my "devil's advocate" mock-assertion, but he was ignoring the fact that this was a Christian evidences class! I couldn't hold back. I said, *"But brother, this is not a formal debate, but it is an informal one since you are teaching us how to give evidences to unbelievers of why the Bible is God's Word. A response is called for."* He didn't acknowledge me at all. He just kept speaking, and when he saw that I was planning on holding his feet to the fire on this issue, before another word could pop out of my mouth, he said to me, "Can I finish, Joe? Can I finish with my speech? You're really disturbing me!" I was angry now. Other students asked questions. Now it was just class as normal again. Questions were never discouraged before, and certainly not for anyone else, why now all of the sudden? I asked a simple question, one that infidels rightly ask, an objection that they are logically entitled to make. It is not as though I asked him to give a linguistic synopsis of the Septuagint off the top of his head! It took me about a half-day, but I cooled off and just let the issue drop. It's not that I disagreed with the instructor's conclusions even, just that I felt compelled to point out that the logic he was presenting was subject to attack.

By the end of ministry training, I was unanimously voted the most argumentative student enrolled in school at the time. I did not try to be disagreeable, just up front on dealing with hard questions. I was now well equipped to defend the Bible and win any argument I ended up in, but all this intense exposure to knowledge, particularly the ultimate controversy of naturalism versus supernaturalism, lit a flame in me that couldn't be extinguished. Before I became a professional minister, I was compelled to prove God's existence, but now, I was on my own little mini-crusade to make that a reality at all costs. That logbook of bothersome issues that was being kept in the back of my mind ended up being made a whole lot thicker from my experiences in preaching school. Instead of knowledge bringing peace like I thought it would, it brought just the opposite: more questions, more dilemmas, and more irreconcilable mysteries. Solomon was right; *"For in much wisdom is much grief: and he that increaseth knowledge increaseth sorrow."* (Ecclesiastes 1:18)

After preaching school, I landed my first preaching work on August 31st of 1997. On December 6th of that same year, I married my fiancée, Elise. My first preaching work came and went in the small town of Blanco, Texas where I preached for the Blanco Hills Church of Christ. We stayed at this work until March of 1998. It lasted six months until we had to move away on account of financial reasons. My second work was in Hubbard, Texas, a quaint, gossipy little town of fifteen hundred people. There, I was minister for the Hubbard Church of Christ. Now that I had "cut my teeth" at my first work, I determined to do the Lord's will with a fresh start in a new city. Suffice it to say, I learned more about people and human nature at this work than I cared to know.

These were "countrified" brethren, who didn't want any part of the city. They didn't like fancy words or philosophical explanations on why God must exist. They just wanted to hear the same sermon topics they were used to hearing, going back almost since the days of Abraham, Isaac, and Jacob! Sermon topics were always simple and unchallenging, like: "Baptism, essential to salvation," "The prodigal son," "What must I do to be saved?," "Conversions in Acts," "Why we don't use instruments of music in worship," etc. I loved and preached these topics, but not endlessly and thoughtlessly like many preachers I knew. I labored to give my sermons depth and meaning. I didn't want to focus on the same stale stuff that everyone had heard and knew already. I was interested in helping the congregation grow in thought, as well as action. I was resisted quite a bit. Change is never an easy thing, even when it is really needed, and it's certainly not an easy thing when those who need to make some corrections are as stuck in their ways as a moose in the quicksand! I faced quite a few social and spiritual obstacles here, but overall, I was happy. My wife, well, that is another story, but we managed to spend almost three years at this work.

My preaching life was pretty normal. I loved it. These first two works gave me the chance to really flex my preaching muscles. I got in the pulpit and did what I loved. My preaching dominated me. I came alive in ways that seemed hard to explain. I was empowered with the message I preached. I could get up, and without notes, just start talking, and the gospel would come out. When I preached, I felt like a newly converted Christian, that magical, intense, warm, inner-burning, that fiery compulsion that would come over me to speak, it never got old. I didn't want to preach. I had to! But what I also loved about the ministry was that I was able to manage my own time, to do the reading I loved, evangelism, and counseling. I loved pulpit work, teaching Bible classes, and guest speaking on numerous occasions for other congregations. Preaching was my life.

While at my second work, I can remember being really bothered by one thing in particular. One of our dear shut-in (house-bound) sisters in Christ was diagnosed with cancer. She was in so much pain from the worst case of arthritis you ever saw, and now cancer? A church prayer meeting was called. We had a great turn-out. What really surprised us was that the prayers seemed to work! I didn't realize it, but despite my praying in as much faith as I had, everyone seemed to be dying anyway, and now this situation came along and our prayers were answered. Hallelujah! The cancer went into remission almost overnight. One month later, she had a clean bill of health! The news went all around church, and we heralded this as a true example of what God does when his servants pray to him in unity and faith!

Our joy was short-lived, however. About six months later, our dear sister's life was claimed by the very cancer we thought we had defeated by the power of Christ. When I got the news that she passed, I was the one called upon to preach her funeral. I went into my office, sat down, and contemplated for a few minutes what had happened. I felt like a fool. I trusted in God to have actually healed this woman and now I'm called upon to preach her funeral. It wasn't the emotional attachment that hurt, it was the sense of failure. God failed me. God failed us! Any other church would have written this one up as a bono fide miracle. We humbly attributed it to the providential love and care of God, and then this is how we are rewarded! I was perplexed a little. It was an eye-opener for me.

It is not as though I didn't believe in prayer anymore, but years later, I would look back and consider this event the beginning of the next phase of doubt. Even if only a little, I had less faith in prayer now than I had before. Life and time were slowly changing who I was. The naivety of the old Joe Holman was giving way to a more clear-headed version of me.

On the subject of prayer, allow me to backtrack for a moment to several experiences from years before this time. The first is a little experience I had not long after my baptism. I entered a Laundromat one Thursday afternoon and noticed a particularly pretty girl in the same establishment. I had been praying diligently for a Christian wife. Well, now God was giving me what I was asking for, I thought. I prayed to God and said something to the effect of, *"Lord, it must not be coincidence that I am praying to you, needing a wife, and a girl is here now. So Lord, I am going to finish with my laundry here, go out to the car and I want you to bring her to me, and I will know that she is the one for me."* I repeated the same sort of prayer about six times, and finally, when the laundry was done, went out to my car, closed my eyes, and prayed again. This time I said, "Lord, let her be there when I open my eyes!" I was thinking back to the faithfulness of Abraham's servant when he was sent to fetch a wife for his son, Isaac. I wanted to make sure I was every bit as diligent in prayer as that faithful soul was. So I waited and waited some more. My heart raced and my legs shook. I believed with all of the hidden chambers of my heart that she would be standing there when my eyes opened. I opened my eyes only to find that the girl had just gotten into her red, 1994 Mitsubishi Eclipse GS and drove off as I watched! I was so disappointed and shocked. I felt so stupid. This awkward event may sound crazy, but this doesn't compare to the many stranger things you hear about people doing and believing in the name of God. Not a month has gone by since that I don't look back and laugh at such naivety.

The reason I mention this embarrassing incident is to emphasize how I noticed my faith start to slip every couple of years or so, as my prayer life had been changing. I went from believing *"God will answer my prayers,"* to *"You never know if God will or will not answer a prayer. It depends on God's will,"* to *"I haven't seen God work, so we must simply hope that God would help us when we need it most,"* to *"Surely there is no hidden force that sporadically and secretly answers prayers. Praying doesn't work."* How I changed as the years went by! People make a big to-do about "asking in faith" when praying. I know. I tried it many times and over many issues. I can now say that time made it all too clear that prayer is just another word for "wasting time." So, though I was troubled with the death of this sister in Christ, I put it behind me for the time.

I did quite a bit of family counseling at this same church. I remember one particularly sad woman with whom I prayed and worked. She and her husband were in their late sixties and well respected in the community. There couldn't have been a kinder person in the world than she. Like many other women who fight the tides of sexually oppressive Christianity, this woman was worried sick that she didn't have "the right to be married" to her current husband. True to form of a pious Christian woman, she internalized her struggle and kept it from her husband, a rich Methodist, who wouldn't care or understand. Going over her situation was not inspiring. She was one of those poor unfortunate few who had a complicated divorce/remarriage proceeding, creating doubt on whether or not she was "living in adultery." I finally decided that she wasn't. I was glad too. The act of breaking up families because of unauthorized sexual relationships between "unscriptural spouses" is a thing most dreaded among all the responsibilities of a minister. I am so glad I was never called upon to enforce this rule, which was based, in part, on our understanding of Matthew 19:3-9. Then it was a matter of principle; if God would command his people to put away their wives for sacred reasons (Ezra 10), then surely he would demand no less of us in the New Testament, who violated God's holy will for marriage. But to see these poor women in mental agony over this issue was disheartening.

Ever since preaching school, I had been trying to view the scriptural mandates of the Word of God in a more liberal way, so as to allow the continued co-habitation of a couple in that case, but I couldn't. The Bible said that John the Baptist told Herod, concerning his brother Phillip's wife whom he had taken as his own, "It is not lawful for thee to have her" (Matthew 14:4). John did not command him to say a little prayer of forgiveness and then to remain living in sin. I had no issues with this at the time, but even back then I was still disturbed at how unnatural this seemed. The Bible seemed to reinforce the idea that celibacy was more preferable to God than sexuality (Matthew 13:15; I Corinthians 7:42). Of course, the Bible made an honorable place for sex in the lives of his people, but it still vilified the natural desires behind it. Lust seemed so animalistic, so unholy. These and other sexual quandaries didn't make me doubt the Bible, but they made me ponder them more than once. I took issue with them, but I accepted them.

After two years, I felt like I was much wiser from this work than when I went in. There was good and there was bad, but we finally decided it was time to move on, mainly because of church politics and a few other "downers." So we left Hubbard and found another work. My next work was the West Side Church of Christ in Hillsboro, Texas. We loved the brethren there very much and found this work a fruitful one. It was ministry as normal, but it was during this preaching work that my doubts really began to resurface. On top of my normal preaching work, I began to study afresh the topic of evolution vs. creation (not a new topic for sure, but one that I never could deal with to my satisfaction). I don't know how many books I read over the years, both for and against evolution, must have been upwards of 200. One of those books was The Oliphant-Smith Debate, a debate between a minister of the Church of Christ, and Charles Lee Smith, President of the American Association for the Advancement of Atheism. The facts of the debate were antiquated by today's standards since it was from the year 1929, but it was the atheist, Smith, who introduced me to a term I hadn't paid much attention to in previous studies—*geographical distribution* of fossils. This explained nicely why, after a mountain pass or valley region, the fossil types that were found differed from the ones before it. That is, certain types of fossils were found in certain localized areas of the planet. This didn't fit with the idea of a global flood, where all types of fossils should be seen scattered throughout the world. This, among other uncomfortable fossil facts, led me to go to greater lengths to find evidence for Noah's global flood, evidences I wasn't finding except from very biased religious books and journals. And of course, the more I studied the so-called "evidences for a young earth," the more frustrated and unnerved I became with what I was seeing.

I soon became bothered by the fact that I had to throw out so many facts of science because they conflicted with Genesis. When I searched for creationist literature on how coal could form in 6,000 years, the next day I was having to look for someone to explain the mechanics of how light from distant stars could reach the earth from the moment of creation, instead of requiring hundreds of thousands and millions of years to get here. When someone said something that got me looking for an answer, or proposed an idea or concept that was contrary to what I believed, I would have scary little moments of doubt (I guess we all have such moments at times), but the doubts never became serious until now (the year 2000). Yet even then, my faith was not in any imminent danger of being destroyed. From this point onward, I would experience smaller, more piercing doubts that would come and go, doubts that came from thinking and rethinking issues and dilemmas of the past.

I don't know how to explain it, but looking back, I seemed to have had what could have been considered premonitions that my faith would someday fail. I always said to myself (simply in jest, of course) that if I did one day fall from grace, it would be to atheism. I later realized that I said this because those seemingly small doubts were becoming more frequent and increasing in intensity. The hammering doubts were starting to chip away at the anvil which was my faith.

CHAPTER 3
The Faith Fall-off

The End Approaches

"Life is pleasant. Death is peaceful. It's the transition that's troublesome."
- *Isaac Asimov*

"No agnostic ever burned anyone at the stake!"
- *Daniel J. Boorsten*

The Faith Fall-off

It was a hot August night in 2000 when a missionary friend came as a guest speaker to West Side about a particular missionary work our church was supporting overseas. I distinctly remember this night as though it was yesterday. Loosening the tie and collar that was pasted to my neck, taking off my blazer, I helped the speaker assemble his slide presentation equipment, and after greeting the brethren, services began. I sat down to watch the presentation of the progress we were making, preaching the gospel in India. At one point, the slide showed the Christian's enemies in India, a devout sect of cow-worshipping pagans who carried out a festival through the middle of town. The pictures were of primitive Indian cultists, beating drums, dancing, and pulling apart a bull in a bloody, bizarre ritual. It was as though time stopped for me at that moment. I listened to the words of our speaker. He said, *"It is sad that this sort of pagan worship goes on in the world, but brethren, what we must not forget is, that these souls are lost without the gospel! Otherwise, the gospel is useless if men can be saved without it and in ignorance!"* I agreed, but a tiny part of me was troubled and shaken like never before. I spent a few moments contemplating an eternity in Hell, an eternity of unsurpassed misery and torture, eternal retribution. I thought how, for so many centuries, those primitive ignoramuses were living and dying with the same false belief system. If I went overseas and got to know them, I'd see that they had families they loved, people they respected, and asked themselves the same questions that I asked about eternal matters. They just came to different conclusions. They were raised differently than I was. They loved to watch a sunset and take in the fresh air like everyone else. They appreciated the positive values of the human experience every bit as much as I did. They understood kindness and compassion, love and hate, just like me—only, the religious framework that embodied their sense of personhood was different than mine. So they were "evil," but my religion and the believers of it were "good."

In all of my proud piety, I couldn't mentally justify seeing these primitive souls in Hell when I pictured them in the same human context as myself. I mourned the loss of loved ones, and so did they. I faced family troubles, and so did they. My faith was dear and sincere to me, and so their own faith was to them. They felt a sense of awe by looking up at the stars at night and thanking their creator for the blessings of life, just like I did. But they were wrong, and because they didn't have the same belief system I was given, when they died expecting to find comfort, they were going to be shouting in pain like they couldn't begin to imagine. That this seemed unjust doesn't cut it; my mind jumped up and shouted, temporarily throwing off my beliefs; *"No, that cannot be! That is sick and hideous! I am ashamed to serve a god who would do that!"* Then I cooled down and realized I had blasphemed God in my heart by allowing my own will for the universe to transcend God's. But even as I had cooled down, I wasn't prepared to let this pass. I now knew I was struggling with this question. A part of me already knew I wasn't going to resolve this issue. I'd tried before. I now felt like an arrogant twerp, trying to see myself as having a saving message when so many of these pagans died without knowledge of the gospel already.

This was a breakthrough for me. If only for just a moment, the cobwebs cleared away in my mind of minds, and I seemed to realize how ridiculous and futile it was to try and impose one system of faith on top of another. This very thought made my stomach burn. I was now afraid, afraid that what I thought on this night I might one day fully believe! Without Jesus Christ, there is no salvation, but with Jesus as the only way to salvation, the great commission is a one-way ticket to damnation for anyone who has reached the age of accountability who doesn't know Jesus. I hated this dilemma! I'd faced it all my Christian life and it never seemed to go away. Why couldn't I beat it? Could it be that nobody had an answer for it? If so, could it be that no one has an answer for it because it is a legitimate fault in the setup of the New Testament salvation plan? If this was true, then it would mean the Bible is a flawed human invention, either that or God enjoys seeing unbelievers burn! I wasn't willing to accept this option either. I was so unsettled, so terribly shaken by this thought. I will never forget that night. But I wasn't yet ready to accept that my worldview had serious holes in it. You have to have experienced it yourself to know what it's like to have doubts creeping up on you like that.

I started to notice how bogged down I was getting in my studies. I found myself putting off preparing sermons because I was involved in trying to ease my mind. The debate book before me was on Young Earth Creationism. I had the usual help from the Christian evidences side. Thompson, Jackson, Gish, Morris, Ham, and a host of others like them had written many books on evolutionary "fallacies." For the time, I continued to cram any evidences for evolution under the rug and explained them away as either mistakes in geology or as simply the ignorance of man in the fields of science and biology. I felt that true science had to vindicate the Genesis record. If it didn't, it wasn't true science! It still had not occurred to me that if everything that science discovered had to agree completely with the Bible, then science could not be unbiased or objective at all. This was what my "Christian evidences" told me. At the same time, I rethought the problem of evil and numerous Bible contradictions. My restless mind was being taken to task to answer a thousand different issues, issues that I was compelled to resolve.

About a month later, I came home from the church building and cried for about five minutes. It was the strangest thing. I didn't think I was sad. Now agitated and confused, I glanced over at my wife and she just stared back at me as she was sitting on the living room couch. I told her I felt like something was wrong, that I was having doubts about Christianity. I remember her not taking me very seriously, so I just went on as normal. I guess it started to dawn on me how material this world was and how I had never seen a genuine miracle, angel, or anything divine. I couldn't help but question everything that seemed so easy to believe before. What evidence did I have to know assuredly that there was a loving father above the clouds who loved and looked down upon me with tender care? This sky father never talked to me. He just left me to dig for the answers myself, and when I found the answers that brought him glory, I could never determine how much he helped or didn't. It was the same old guessing game of looking around my mundane world and guessing how and what God wanted me to do. I was angry that I was doubting God's existence, and at the same time, I was angry at God for leaving me to figure it all out for myself, and for staying hidden from any real verification of his existence or his destiny for me. But I was also angry with myself for settling for this appalling lack of answers for so long.

Ever since preaching school, I was looking for closure, for answers, but finding more and more questions instead. How could I have settled for this for so long? I was resolving no doubts, I was putting to rest no great mysteries, and certainly wasn't able to stand confirmed in established facts. The questions and dilemmas never ended. I wondered if they ever would? Were there still more lessons on patience or humility that I needed to learn? If I must play God's guessing game, so be it! I just assumed God would lead me out of this maze of confusion like he had been leading me through all these years.

Underlying all of my thinking was a belief in the law of rationality (that we should draw only those conclusions that are warranted by the evidence), and rationality says what the principle of Occam's Razor said; it is more rational to reject supernatural explanations if natural, more plausible ones are available. This made more sense, but flew right in the face of revealed religion. Having faith in the supernatural based on the testimony of a book written 2,000 years ago was completely asinine from a logical standpoint. A book from a time steeped in myths and superstitions was likely a product of myth and superstition. Having faith that a man once calmed the seas and healed the sick contradicts rationality. Not having been there, how was I going to construct a rational, believable case for a man walking on water and doing miracles, and at the same time, be able to tell the myths apart from the facts? How was I to accept the Bible's account of things as true? The whole supernatural idea started to seem childish and overly optimistic. The Bible was full of over-the-top, outrageous claims, claims that if anyone made today, they'd be laughed at. With these thoughts fresh in mind, I then remember running into the bedroom, picking up a Bible, and hurriedly turning to Matthew 27:52, *"And the graves were opened; and many bodies of the saints which slept arose."* This was truly an outrageous claim! Outrageous claims demand outrageous proof, right? Surely we would have documentation for something monumental like this, if indeed it really happened in the first century. It seemed so clearly fantastic and too hard to believe. I didn't want to start viewing things from the rationalist's perspective, but I was unable to appreciate the sublime message and comforts of faith as before. As Paul would have said, I was in a "betwixt two" (Philippians 1:23).

Of course, in the end, I came to the same conclusion—that the God of the Bible was in charge of all that I see around me. I still couldn't imagine a life without God. I had intellectually nowhere else to go because without God, I might as well jump off a cliff, right?! My knowledge pool was small and theological, and nothing besides Christianity could even begin to make sense. I don't know how I managed to, but I put these doubts behind me for the time and decided to keep on doing God's work. From this point onward, my work went on moderately hindered for the next year and a half.

When the minister for the College Hill Church of Christ left, the West Side Church decided to merge with College Hill in the same city of Hillsboro, Texas. West Side and College Hill were sister congregations. West Side was small and College Hill was losing members, so the merge was a good move for both of us. Two churches of like precious faith coming together—Ah! You hear only about splits these days. It's nice to see merges. This was now my fourth preaching work, which began in November of 2001. I was loved and adored, as many ministers can very easily be. "Preacheritus," (getting too attached to the preacher) any preacher knows, can be a very real thing. Everything was relatively smooth sailing until the doubts again worsened, forcing themselves back to the forefront of my mind. This time, things weren't going to be like before. I would not be able to whip them.

My thoughts were now more seasoned than ever before. Ambition, faith, and zeal were slowly giving way to logic, realism, and life-hardened common sense. My knowledge pool had been increasing exponentially. Adding to my usual studies of theology and philosophy, I had been studying the natural sciences a great deal, and as I expanded my knowledge pool, very slowly, my thinking began to change. Gradually, I began to see things differently each passing day. This was because I had made the decision to broaden my horizons to more openly consider non-theist study materials. Knowledge should never be intentionally tainted with bias, one way or the other; we are subjected to enough of it just being human. Too often, we humans simply refuse to learn new positions because we deem the subject matter unworthy of our consideration, and that can be an intellectual travesty. My search for truth was more than just books, however. More than secular knowledge was fueling my tendency towards doubt and unbelief; it was time and maturity. The next three months at my new church proved uneventful. I struggled with doubts, but was able to put them behind me, largely because of the excitement of the new work, although it wouldn't be long until my excitement would turn into unbelief.

It was now February of 2002. I headed up to the church fellowship hall one early morning to prepare a meal for the congregation. I was not in the habit of cooking. I would leave that to the ladies team. The purpose of this meal was to demonstrate my success with the vegetarian lifestyle. At this point, those who know me well will be saying, "You, Joe? Lecture someone on diet?!" I am known for my exceptionally careless eating habits, but for over a year, I shed myself of sixty pounds and changed my eating habits. I was moved to do so because of high blood pressure and because the doctor strongly emphasized to me the necessity for a change. The doctor's prescribed blood pressure medications (three different types) all proved ineffective in helping things. But when I went vegetarian, I solved the problem myself. My blood pressure went from 150/110 to 118/68! The lifestyle change proved to be a good move for the most part. In addition to the weight I lost, I felt better and had more energy than I ever had. The congregation was so excited about this improvement in me that they wanted in on it. I made references to it in my sermons and pointed back to the fact that the long-lived, early patriarchs in the Bible were vegetarians. It wasn't until after the flood that meat was introduced into man's diet, no doubt as a supplement, since vegetation was still sparse and had been destroyed in the great flood (Genesis 9:1-6). I figured that going back to that way of eating would help us modern folks in a preservative-ridden society to cure a few ailments God's way.

About six months later, I was still somewhat healthy, but something was not right with me. I began to lose skin coloration slightly and I started to experience extreme "brain fog." I always thought brain fog was a non-condition as far as real medical problems were concerned, that it was just a relative term describing someone trying to function when exhausted. I was wrong! It eventually got worse to the point of realizing that diet had to have something to do with it. I was becoming borderline anemic, I think. This was due, not so much to getting insufficient amounts of important flesh food nutrients, but to my considerable consumption of onions, which have been found to kill vital red blood cells in the body. So out of caution, I added meat back to the diet gradually and the problem corrected itself, though I slowly gained my weight back.

Because of this problem I had with the diet, I began to study vegetarianism from the perspective of qualified nutritionists. This included studying the literature of doctors who were no fans of vegetarianism. Very reluctantly, I was forced to agree with their conclusions. Their central objection had to do, in part, with the body's absorption of Vitamin B12. B12 is almost entirely absent from the plant kingdom, and in the small instances where it is found in vegetation, it can only be absorbed in the colon (where no nutritional value can be gained). Of the little plant-based B12 traces found, unless those items of food containing them were consumed with Intrinsic Factor – a substance made and consumed in animal products and bi-products – absorption still could not take place. The doctors also objected to the diet based on insufficient amounts of iron, and the lack of various T-cells the body needed from animal flesh for optimum health. I had all but eliminated any animal products from my diet, and I was having problems, and this seemed to contradict Genesis. If God made our bodies to live on vegetation, why was I having trouble? Of the cases I studied, a good number of vegetarians showed verifiable deficiencies in B12 and other needed nutrients. Many vegetarians, among these were vegans and Janists, admitted they had to take supplements to get their full doses of necessary nutrients. Why would natural diets work with relatively few people? Had God changed our metabolisms after the flood? That wouldn't make much sense. Why would he do that?

In a crazy way, this brought my doubts in the Bible right back to forefront of my mind because the issue carried over into my study of the scriptures on the topic of carnivorous creatures. Does God want us to kill and consume lesser life forms for our necessary sustenance? Did God intend from the beginning for man and animals to prey on lower life forms? He didn't. Genesis 1:30 tells us otherwise: "And to every beast of the earth, and to every fowl of the air, and to every thing that creepeth upon the earth, wherein there is life, I have given every green herb for meat: and it was so." Genesis 6:21 mentioned Noah taking on the arc food for his family and for the animals, which had to be vegetation. It would have been impossible to keep dead, rotting meat for the duration of the flood for all those fanged predators. So I was bothered by the position I later was forced into taking, that something had happened after the flood, something brought on by God to change the make-up of animals and man. I guess mosquitoes didn't need to suck blood before the flood! And at some point, God gave certain predators canines for tearing flesh! But then I found biblical problems with this position too. The Bible seems to oppose this view. Genesis 4:2 says "Abel was a keeper of sheep." Wait a minute! Why is Abel keeping sheep if there were no predators?

Some readers might be wondering why this was so important to me. The answer is simple; if God originally set up a system of life where stronger life forms consume the weaker ones, this made him cruel all the more. Who in their right mind would knowingly make creatures to face pain and death? The same goes for God creating deadly parasites, viruses, and bacteria. The second problem with this scenario was that it implied something that created problems in the logical order of death's appearance in Genesis. That is, it created a death-before-sin problem. Death was supposedly a curse, the result after sin was committed; *"for dust thou art, and unto dust shalt thou return."* (Genesis 3:19). If death was a natural part of the world before the fall of man, even if it only concerned animals, what does this say about God's sense of humaneness towards animal life? Did God create humans to live lives of eternal bliss, but the lesser creatures to be preyed upon? The third problem this brought up was that it implied evolution. That evil, pernicious word kept popping up all over the place every time I studied any of the sciences! If evolution were true, predator-prey relationships, consumption of lower species, and death would be just what we would expect!

I can remember being troubled within myself when a doubting cousin of mine ask me why God allowed animals to die painfully in the jaws of predators. I could only answer him by saying, "God has it set up so that the animals don't feel that much pain when they die." He wasn't satisfied with this explanation, and I don't blame him! "Yeah right, Joe! You mean to tell me that when a caribou is being torn apart by a pack of leopards, and its hide is punctured by bites and claws, when the animal is wrestled to the ground by its neck and the neck snaps, that God arranged for the nerves not to feel pain?! God! That is a stupid explanation, Joe!" He was right. That was stupid. I had no good answer for his question, and neither did any believer I knew. All I could do was sweep the issue under the rug of the fall of man: *"That was an unfortunate consequence for man's sins."*

It's funny how things work out. Not even a month later, I found myself watching a documentary on the discovery channel where a young gazelle was chased down by a cheetah. I was urged by my conscience to change the channel, but I decided I was going to make myself observe God's marvelous creation. I felt bad about the fact that I wasn't in awe of God's creation anymore, but that doubting part of me relished in my disgust of it at that moment. I said to myself as that poor creature died by the jaws of the predator, "That is so unjust! How could you, God?" Then I felt bad for feeling this way and for saying so. These concerns stayed with me. I kept taking note of how contrary nature was to Christ's teachings; "Go out quickly into the streets and lanes of the city, and bring in hither the poor, and the maimed, and the halt, and the blind" (Luke 14:21). Nature's system was the exact opposite of God's (if indeed he created it). Survival of the fittest, as Darwinists referred to it, was the universal constant. God gave that cheetah the instincts to hunt down, not the faster mother zebra, but the slower, weaker one, the sickly calf who ran behind her. Sad wasn't the word; horrible was more like it. To satisfy myself with an answer, I used the "checks and balances" argument put forth by most apologists. God only allowed things to be this way to keep the species from overpopulating. I was not satisfied with this answer, but it was enough to put it out of my mind.

Until all these issues started flooding my head again, I preached my heart out and loved it wholly. I was completely content with my life as a gospel preacher. Like all other preachers, I dealt with church politics, countless benevolence cases, spats, gossipers, and cold, rigid hearts. I had been cursed at and threatened, in person and by phone, all in the name of what I believed over the years. I was almost taken to court at one point by a woman's angry husband who said I ruined his life. I was called every name in the book, from asshole to zealot, describing my burning conviction to stay within what I held to be the biblical pattern of truth. Everything was great, from the people, to the facilities of worship. I could not have asked for anything better. I kept plenty busy with church bulletin production, a Sunday morning radio program, fulltime pulpit preaching, writing newspaper articles, counseling, visitation, lectureships, and gospel meetings. My plate was full! I don't know how I did it, but I managed to press on with my work.

An Atheist in the Making

During this last ministry, I and another brother would hold a weekly service out at the local nursing home. I loved the ministry of visitation. I spent much of my time there and sought to bring relief and words of comfort, but I can also remember the horrible thoughts this produced in me. I think nursing homes are so depressing because they make us picture ourselves and our loved ones in that atmosphere when we get on in years. It hits us that there is nothing we can do to help anyone there.

The moment I would enter the door, the smell of urine and mustiness would invade my nostrils. I looked around and saw hunched-over backs, toothless, and sometimes dentureless mouths hanging open, and eyes that sadly and vacantly stared down at the floor. I saw the food-stained sweatshirts and sweatpants, the slobber towels, the confusion on their faces, the quivering hands, and the closed, tired eyes. Here were these poor, dying folks, just waiting to take their last breath.

I remember one resident there, a close friend from our church with whom I would visit each week. He lost both legs to Type I diabetes. He would be telling me how his week went, and suddenly, his face would turn beet-red and he would freeze up in terrible pain, unable to say another word for about a minute. He never could escape those terrible phantom pains. Another diabetic member of our congregation who was a resident there had to have a number of amputations. Every other couple of months or so, I would get news from the hospital that he required more surgeries to amputate further and further up the stumps he had left for legs. Soon, he had no legs left. This was especially troubling to me because my sister, Rebecca, had Type I diabetes. Many others were just like these two, either missing limbs for various reasons, or suffering with other debilitating illnesses.

A nursing home is a sad place because about half the people present don't know where or who they are. It brings a tear to one's eye to think of those who are singing the national anthem in the lobby and in the hallways, or the frustrated folks who sit in their wheelchairs and grumblingly curse like sailors at those who try to help them. I felt particularly sorry for the type with their heads falling forward who would "Amen" anything I said in the lesson, and then let out an "Oh glory!" here and there, anytime I would reference the name "Jesus Christ" in a message. I would give a ten-minute sermonette at the longest, and the brother who came with me would sing some encouraging hymns. What really bothered me was that half the people I was talking to couldn't remember anything I said long enough to let it benefit them. Some of them didn't have the ability to comprehend my words in the first place. And it is hard to offer words of comfort to someone writhing in phantom pains from amputated limbs, or from the uncomfortable measures taken to monitor and treat various diseases. Many of them needed round-the-clock care and enough pain relievers to sedate a fully-grown rhino!

Every time I went into that place, I thought about our continually growing church bulletin shut-in list. It kept getting bigger and bigger, despite our increasing congregational prayers. No one was getting any better, only worse. "This is wrong, so wrong!", I thought to myself. It was like every person I encountered in this sad place had a great big

"About to Die" sign over their heads. I couldn't help but think about that fact and about how they had me there to help them remain in denial about it. They wanted me to tell them how they were going to live forever beyond the clouds. What I wanted to do was to help them, but I couldn't. What I needed to do now was help myself.

My energy level dropped dramatically. I felt like a different person inside. I was overwhelmed suddenly. All I could focus on were the doubts I couldn't resolve and the two dominant things I was seeing in my world—death and misery. I was depressed and tired. I felt insane at times. I wanted to be the old me. I wished I could have been again.

I recall going to the church building one Friday morning to finish up the coming Sunday's church bulletin. My dear friend and church secretary, Rebah, had just gone over the bulletin article for that week and made some minor corrections. As usual, she would hand the corrected copy back to me for some last minute changes. She found the door to my office closed that morning. She knocked, and when she came in, she saw the frown on my face and one hand supporting the weight of my head against the desk. She just laid the bulletin on my desk and left the room. She was one of the first to start seeing in me that something was wrong. What I was thinking about was an issue that troubled me, off and on, for a number of years by then. It was the issue of divine providence. I thought back to a cold morning in February of 1999, when I found myself watching the news before heading up to the church office.

The news had a feature about a massive accident on a freeway near downtown Dallas, Texas. It was about an incredible pile-up of fourteen cars, twelve deaths. In the two cars that didn't house fatalities, there was a husband in one car and a wife in the other. Their cars were demolished, but aside from minor bruises and cuts, they were alright. As I suspected they would, they got on TV and thanked God for their deliverance, saying something to the effect of, "I just want to thank God my Savior for looking out for us." I still remember the feeling to this day; as I was watching, it hit me like a slippery fish, that if God spared the two, providentially delivering them from harm's way, then he providentially sentenced to death the twelve, by leaving them to bite the dust in their soon-to-be-demolished automobiles. It occurred to me back then, if only for a few moments, that as a minister, I seemed to be a master of the art of ignoring unpleasant circumstances, but by now (thinking back on the event) I was almost sure of it! I would praise God for the good that happened, but ignore the bad things by mentally sweeping them under the rug of my mind, by ignoring what I didn't want to believe. I was starting to realize that I was not being fair with the evidence like I thought I was. For so long, I refused to see what I didn't find agreeable to my faith. This took some humility to accept. I always prided myself on being just and unbiased, and now I found out that I could be just as unreasonable as anyone else when it comes to accepting something that goes against the grain of their beliefs. I could be just as irrational as some of the brainless, conviction-less church members I looked down on. Of course, I still hadn't decided patently that I was wrong altogether to say that there was a purpose behind their suffering—only that it was rational to consider that maybe there might not be.

To this day, I remember clearly that morning, sitting at my walnut wood desk at the church office, contemplating the gravity of this observation; I had always believed and taught that though man doesn't understand everything, suffering has a purpose in that it builds spiritual character and teaches us lessons about life. But the way God had this world set up, so many people weren't learning the lessons they should have from pain. The pressures of life may very well take more people away from God than to him. People go insane, have nervous breakdowns, become drug addicts and alcoholics, not to mention, commit suicide and become atheists from the horrors that plague humanity. It made no sense for God to arrange life this way. Why hide such important details of his divine plan, especially when the nature of his world causes people like me to be led astray, thinking that perhaps there is not a God! Whoops! I said it! Am I really at the point of being an agnostic, of saying I don't know if there is a god? I thought not, but for the first time, I was able to say out loud what I had been thinking for a while: *"If there is a god, he sure has made this world so that people like me can't know for sure!"* The development of these doubts was subtle and illusive. The doubts would creep up on me, noticeably bother me, then I would end up crossing a new threshold by mentally accepting that I was slipping in faith. I would react by resolving to have patience and to pray harder, and to trust God to get me through it. But every time this happened, I was noticing bigger chunks of my faith being whittled away.

You would think a doubter would find comfort going back to the "good book" for some serious reading and reflection. But this only made things more difficult. When I would read the Bible, I found that most of my time was spent dealing with false teachings about the Bible. The book was steeped in so much confusion and controversy that it was hard to stay focused, much less actually resolve anything. It was either harmonizing alleged Bible contradictions or answering moral questions as to why God allowed the killing of women and children in the Old Testament. I was tired of "patching up" the Bible. I was growing tired of the Bible, period. Indeed, it seemed to be the source of my discomfort.

This frustration I was having started to change my attitude. I was beginning to be sickened by everyone around me giving God the credit every time a paralysis victim got a little more feeling back in one arm, or every time a chronic gout sufferer showed a little improvement. I had performed at least 18 funerals by then. Though I wanted so badly to believe, I saw no hand of God, and I was tired of making excuses for why he fails to make good on his promises to care for us. All the apologists I had ever known were grandmasters at making excuses for why God doesn't intervene positively and undeniably in human affairs. Come to think of it, that's what I had been doing! I was one of them.

Things kept getting worse. My preaching work was starting to show serious signs of sloppiness and hurt. People could see that something was wrong. I stepped into that pulpit every Sunday and gave my weekly motivational speeches and forgot about my doubts for the time, but they always came back. I could no longer heartily strive to excel in my ministry like I had before. I had no patience with anyone. I cut down on the amount of time I spent in visitation. I took frequent two and three day vacations and spent less time preparing sermons. I had such waning confidence in it that all I could do was just keep trying to see my way through this "temptation." I kept waiting for it to end. For a while there, I really thought God was teaching me a lesson on how to minister to others who went through periods of doubt like I did. Until now, I really believed I would make it out with my faith intact and be able to help others defeat doubt. But I wasn't going to get my faith back. A big part of me was almost resigned to finally accepting that my God had bailed on me! I couldn't let that happen, so I decided to reach out to other ministers for help.

I went to their houses, swore them to secrecy, and unloaded on them my issues. I thought about trying this a couple of times before but decided I wasn't ready to share my hurt. Being as desperate as I now was, I thought it was time to give it a try. My soul was worth that much. As the preacher, there were few I could go to or confide in. It's kind of hard for one who has to be ready with the answers and be a spiritual source of strength for everyone else to humble himself and admit that he needs help. I guess it's a small source of pride. But at this point, I knew I needed help and direction in my life. I knew I could no longer handle my problems by myself.

The ministers I went to for help were abysmal disappointments. They didn't understand and actually attacked me viciously for asking them demanding questions they only *thought* they had answers to. I made it clear going in that the arguments I would be making were not yet my views, but that I was struggling with them and needed help to refute them. I wanted to stay on the Lord's side. I guess that didn't matter to them. I never will forget their smug demeanors, the looks on their faces like I had just threatened to kidnap their children. They became incensed that I would ask such spiritually below-the-belt "atheist" questions. Listening to them reply to my "devil's advocate" arguments reminded me of the way I would use typical theistic arguments. I knew the jargon of religious apologists. I had heard it before, and by now, those words lost their power for me. Our discussions turned into heated debates and sometimes on into character attacks. I found very little understanding and no sympathy. The answers they gave were impotent and evasive. I found not one compelling answer for the now incredibly staggering list of complex issues that needed resolution. Theists had no answers. It became quickly evident after only talking with a few preachers who were supposedly well versed in secularism that they offered me nothing. The people I went to for comfort ended up chiding me for being in a situation I wished I wasn't in. I almost cried in front of one of them. My face was red with shock, and inside, I was so jolted that I could hardly think of words to respond to the personal jabs I received. I was hurt and it didn't take long to realize that I was on my own in this search. And who was I kidding? I seemed to know going in that these attempts would be futile.

I took any down time I had and investigated other world religions more clearly than I had in the past. This was primarily to get my mind off of studying my own religion so much. To sum up the matter, not one of them struck me as divine and all of them seemed at least a little more credible than the religion I promoted. No one of them had any of the big answers to the world's problems, and no one of them could explain human suffering. Looking into psychic phenomenon was a joke. They were like televangelists. I discovered only deception, chicanery, and manipulation in their ranks, but at my lowest point, I did give spiritualism a try. I felt so stupid for it, but I was at rock bottom and was compelled to try it out of sheer desperation.

My mother had given my wife a spirit guidebook to read. I don't know why my wife was interested in that topic when she never cared to pursue it, but it wound up in my hands anyway. I read it over as it gave specific instructions on how to find my spirit guide. I tried, step by step, and on top of feeling like a total moron afterwards, I got nothing in return! I felt like king Saul who was cut off from God. It's amazing the depths to which a soul can sink! Now I felt faithless, depressed, and sinful for dabbling in witchcraft, but in the spiritual condition I was in, not offending a spirit was not top priority on my list. I just wanted answers. I was not sold on any religion.

I went through a period where I considered more liberal versions of Christianity, and also Judaism (which I found fascinating), but this period was brief for the simple fact that if I was ever to accept any version of Christianity again, or Orthodox Judaism, I would have to settle for watered down versions of these, and that I couldn't live with. If I were ever to serve the Abrahamic God in any form, it would still demand belief in the outrageous. Who is Jesus Christ stripped of his deity anyway? What use is there in consulting the Bible as strictly a book on good advice when so many better, more up-to-date works were available, ones that didn't teach slavery and ethnic cleansing? A watered down version of Christianity is a useless version of Christianity. I was not about to spend the effort to chop up the Bible further to determine which parts were salvageable and which were not. I promptly gave up on this endeavor.

While I was not yet an atheist, I was at a stage where I could at least be honest enough with myself to admit what didn't work for me as justifications for Christianity. I was able to admit that the evidences for Christianity I was given were weak at best, if not altogether erroneous. None of the basic philosophical arguments for God (the cosmological, teleological, ontological, axiological arguments, etc.) proved a thing, and an investigation of philosophy led me straight away from a life of faith. I had been taught the words of Francis Bacon, "A shallow understanding of philosophy leads one away from God, but a deeper understanding leads one back to him." I can remember thinking, "What a lie!"

I came to see that all those shelves of creationist books spoke for not so much as a microscopic part of the scientific community, and that even my preaching brethren with actual degrees in the natural sciences rejected fully the scientific consensus of the real experts' opinions on evolution and cosmology. I had been listening to dishonest crackpots who knew very little to nothing about what evolution really taught, and yet they trashed it and taught nonsense to support the worldview of an archaic book. I was starting to see a bigger world out there than my limited Christian worldview would allow for, and I was starting to see that I needed to go back and relearn what little I was taught about science, knowing that the sources I trusted before were no good now. In fact, I was altogether shocked at how much blatant dishonesty there was in the "Creation Science" movement, both in and out of my denomination.

As time went on, I became bitter, very bitter. I realized I had been lied to. The earth was not six thousand years old (a correct and honest understanding of Genesis does not permit a figurative interpretation of the days of creation). There was no water canopy that surrounded the earth at creation (allegedly to protect the earth from ultraviolet radiation from the sun to prevent aging) as I had been taught (Genesis 1:6-8). There were no "alternative" ways to make oil, coal, and diamonds in only a few thousand years, though my church felt compelled to write whole series' of books on explaining away the evolutionary understanding of how these natural substances were really formed. In an attempt to bolster the credibility of the Noahic flood account, I had been told that many flood myths of cultures around the world existed. This was true, but what I was *not* told was that a huge portion of those myths were not stories of universal floods, but local floods—natural exaggerations from floods in history, some of which came about as fall off from our most recent ice age. Exaggerations like this are to be expected, as myths have always developed about natural disasters, and this shouldn't be surprising since we live on a mostly water-covered planet.

I also learned that many of these flood sagas had virtually nothing in common with each other; for instance, the Pygmy version of the myth describes a flood as an act of a God creating humanity in water, nothing to do with judgment at all. Other accounts, like that of the Hopi Indians, have an impending flood averted. The Hebrew's take on the flood was not unique and not original. Many flood stories predate theirs—the Babylonian account of Enuma Elish, for instance. The Egyptians and the Chinese have detailed and reliable records going back a long way, verifying that no worldwide flood occurred some 5,000 years ago or roundabouts. So, what I once thought supported the Genesis record actually robbed it of credibility. Add to this also that the science behind the flood didn't add up. Modern geology utterly rejected the worldwide flood hypothesis.

If our planet contained enough water to cover the top of Mt. Everest, this would raise our atmospheric pressure to a thousand times what it is, and there would be no place for all this water to recede in such quantities (water in the poles and under the earth would still not provide enough storage). Different races did not exist because Noah had three sons that emerged from an ark and repopulated the world (Genesis 9-11). A rainbow was not the product of the finger of God drawing in the sky after a flood or rain (Genesis 9:12-13). Languages did not originate from a mysterious separation of peoples while building a tower to heaven (Genesis 11:1-9). The pyramids of different cultures around the world were not built in similar shapes because their ancestors came from some tower called Babel. They were built as pyramids simply because they had no rebar or similar technology that would allow them to build straight upward to support their own weight when multiple stories were added to a structure. I had been misinformed about the second law of thermodynamics. The second law did not prevent or hinder evolution or an eternal universe at all. I had been misinformed about DNA and the facts of taxonomy, mutations, and genetic variants in species.

For the first time since my conversion, I was able to be unintimidated by the findings of science. Rather, I jumped at the chance to learn. My knowledge pool was filling, and my worldview that was kept so small before, so full of intolerance and scientific illiteracy, was growing at a dramatic rate—and with this knowledge came peace like the Bible only claimed to give. A small part of me still wanted the Bible to be right, but now that my love for science and truth had been ignited, and now that I decided I would accept what I found to be true, regardless of whether I liked it or not, the love for truth was winning out. Too, I was realizing that morality, which I thought was delegated by a book, had nothing to do with religion. Once again, I looked around and saw a bigger, more natural world around me, a world that made more sense, but I was not free from religious indoctrination yet.

At nights, I would sometimes try and get relief from the doubts by just going outside and taking in all the majesty of the stars of the heavens, but this didn't work for me anymore. Astronomy was one of my biggest evidences against the existence of God. To me, the heavens wreaked of chaos; bags of rock and gases, worthless planets, swirling aimlessly in huge, cold vacuums of nothingness—hardly signs of a creator. And for so long, I tried hard to see uniqueness in planet earth, but I couldn't. It was just one of nine different spheres in our solar system. Earth had to share its glory with eight other spheres, dead planets, twirling around the sun. Our solar system was not unique either, nor our star, nor yet our position in the cosmos. The universe was so much bigger than I had ever imagined. We are not even a grain of sand or a speck of dust in this demilitarized zone called the Milky Way.

Up till now, I had been willing to accept that a snake deceived a woman and sin entered into the world, causing disaster and evil. But there were so many talking animals in the world of mythology, and my Bible's talking snake stood right there with all of them! Why were animals condemned to suffer the same fate of death as humans, even though they weren't apart of our "curse"? Why were there craters on the moon? Why did certain moons of Jupiter and Saturn show signs of the same celestial buckshot? These observations didn't mesh with the idea that this universe was created by the hand of a deity who called it "very good" (Genesis 1:31). Instead, my universe seemed to be carved out from the raw, by the blind forces of nature.

God's living room just kept getting smaller, beginning with Greek philosophers, like Democritus, who believed in an atomic makeup of all material substances, and later, Copernicus, Galileo, and Newton, with their banishment of geocentrism, right down to our modern age. It was the church that destroyed the great library of Alexandria and stifled intellectual and technological progress for centuries. The gluttonous church thrived while science and learning suffered for over fifteen hundred years.

Evolution explained every facet of the world I was able to observe with my own two eyes. Why do we have hair on our bodies? Why do we have wisdom teeth and appendixes? Why do we get goose bumps when we are cold or scared? Why does our species have chronic problems with flat feet and herniated disks? Why are some snakes born with useless walking appendages? Why can certain birds not fly? Why does human DNA resemble our chimpanzee cousins to almost 98 percent? Only one answer stood out: As Charles Darwin said, *"I can entertain no doubt, after the most deliberate study and dispassionate judgment of which I am capable, that the view which most naturalists entertain, and which I formerly entertained – namely, that each species has been independently created – is erroneous."* (The Origin of Species, p. 68)

Of course, these realizations were taking a mental toll on me. It scared me to admit that I was beginning to believe them. Every time I would say them out loud, I was even more afraid. I was slowly but surely having to accept that my religion was losing out to a world of reason. I was compelled to acknowledge that by now my faith in God had taken a back seat to a newly found love of philosophical naturalism. In my heart of hearts though, I still hadn't accepted it.

From this point onward, I felt like I partially understood what those mental victims of war go through when they've been on the battlefield and seen their friends blown to bits right in front of their eyes. They come home with a well-deserved hero's welcome, but it doesn't matter, because they come home with spirit damage and as infidels. In a different way, I had spirit damage too. I was hurting from doubt and could no longer deny it. I could only watch as my theological worldview was coming unraveled at the seams.

As the weeks and months went by, I found it more and more difficult to even think about ideas like Heaven or Hell. They seemed like intelligence-insulting concepts dreamt up by a suffering humanity. It made so much sense. Obviously, humans can visualize a perfect world. Since we can't live in one, we want one "beyond the clouds." This seemed like such a cartoon, a pipedream, a comforting illusion in a world of agony. Everywhere around me, people wanted "eternal life with God." How selfish it seemed and how ridiculous! Just like the guy in the desert who sees a fountain when he's about to die of thirst, so this afterlife seemed more and more the formidable illusion. It made so much sense for everyone to just pass out of existence, to become part of the dead, cold matter again. This simplified everything. As a minister, I was majoring in minors, so to speak. I was trying to obtain a pot of gold at the end of a rainbow, but I couldn't find it after all these years of searching. All that became apparent to me now was the insignificance of man and the intriguing horizons of science.

Now Hell was a different matter. I couldn't bear to think about it. It was too terrible. Hell is what really makes an infidel out of a believer. God actually went through the trouble of creating a place of pain for unbelievers. I would try and imagine this black and smoldering place of unbearable and eternal pain from fires that never die, where souls cry out with endless desperate groans and never enjoy a single moment of peace. It couldn't be real. The more I thought about it, the harder it was to even imagine that a being who calls himself loving could invent such a place. I suppose it was only the terrifying fear of Hell that boosted me up for one last-ditch effort to reclaim my faith. I began to pray harder than I had ever prayed. Only, it really wasn't praying anymore, more like psychedelic groaning, begging in crazed ramblings for God to save me from hellacious wrath. I remained desperate to get my faith back. A greatly cherished faith is not easily let go, even if you are convinced it is untrue.

This was the hardest struggle I ever faced, no less than a divorce or a death in the family—and it would get worse before it got better. I didn't feel like me anymore. I was a fish out of water, or more accurately, a fish suffocating in a puddle of slushy mud. I felt like a stranger to myself, insignificant, like graffiti on an outhouse wall. On several occasions, in the privacy of my bedroom or office, I remember commanding the Devil to get behind me and to take his doubts with him. Once I found myself raising my hands toward the ceiling and praying in tears for God to make things like they were. It was not going to happen. The God I knew and loved now seemed so far away and inscrutable. The very concept was out of my grasp. That "high" in worship was no longer there. I felt like I was headed right for the place I preached so hard for everyone else to avoid—Gehenna! It was like I could see the face of Jesus frowning at me in disgust. I was a "sinner" again. This was a nightmarish ordeal.

CHAPTER 4
Faking Faith

The Minister Turns Atheist

"You're lost. We're all lost. The world is lost!"
- *Keith Young*

"All that we see or seem is but a dream within a dream."
- *Edgar Allen Poe*

Faking Faith

I now had an atheist and a Christian living together inside me, and they both had to get used to each other. I made them get along. One was much stronger than the other. The atheist Joe Holman won the fight, but the Christian was not yet dead. He was on life support, the life support system being my surrounding Christian influences and concerns. I was still a preacher. I had to be there for everyone, and in order to give so much of yourself to a cause you don't believe in, you must convince yourself that you do believe it for the time. So Christian Joe Holman still served a purpose. For those short times when I convinced myself that none of this was happening, I would get in the pulpit and preach my heart out. The religious man I was so accustomed to living as would come off life support and begin talking. But this was always short-lived, an elaborate form of denial. To get through it, I had to get lost in the feel of the moment to get up in that pulpit and preach what I didn't believe.

Before he went back on life support, Christian Joe did some thinking. I kept imagining the drama that went on as Satan was before God, telling him I would fail the test, but that God was telling Satan that I would pass it, just like Job's triumphant journey into greater faith. I had to stay faithful! Then Christian Joe went back on life support! Atheist Joe resumed control.

The ship of apostasy may have sailed, but the maddening depression this created in me was not finished doing its damage. I prayed and cried and stayed up late into the nights, thinking and rethinking the dilemmas, looking for those magic resolutions that would shed light on my problems—needless to say, they never came! You get so sick of the issues you are trying to resolve because you've tried so many times before with no success, that you start to get a headache just attempting to think about them. In such a painful dilemma, you keep waiting for the right tract, book, email, suggestion, or conversation from a friend to come along and "set you straight," but it never happens.

What had happened? I had no evidence or experience with this God at all, yet all these years I trusted and prayed to him, and this seemed to justify my worldview. What went wrong? Did I sin? If I did, I didn't know about it. I never cheated on my wife, though I had opportunities. I never so much as used a curse word as a believer, and yet what seemed like a punishment was upon me. Did I not pray sincerely enough? Did I need to learn patience? Was my God going to burn me for doubting when I couldn't help it and while I still wanted to continue with him in full faith?

Come to think of it, I couldn't even define this God I served. The term was unintelligible. I could tell you traits my God had (omnipotence, omniscience, omnipresence, and omnibenevolence), and what God wasn't (a man, a liar, Numbers 23:19, Titus 1:2). I could even tell you that God was a "perfect Spirit" (John 4:24). But again, I had no experience with a "Spirit" entity. What was that? Was it matter? No, it can't be matter because matter is a thing of the temporal universe, and God was eternal—outside and above the universe. Therefore, whatever God was, he was unknowable because he was outside of the universe, but now my speech was again rendered unintelligible. Since I couldn't give the term "God" any real meaning, I was projecting into it what I thought God was—just a really power version of myself! So, I was forced to retreat back into the safe-haven of illusive theistic jargon by saying, *"God is above our understanding. God is unknowable. We would have to be God to understand him."* Now I was right back where I started—with no answers.

And if you think defining God is hard, imagine trying to define a Trinitarian God (Matthew 28:19). As a minister, I would explain the trinity as *water, steam, and ice*—three components making up one substance. This doesn't apply very well to individuals, does it? Now I had three uncreated, perfect, and infinite beings existing forever! This was an even less intelligible idea. I was in the business of answering life's difficult questions and showing how God's book had the answers, but I didn't believe these answers myself. I had gone from zealous evangelist to burnt-out preacher in eight years. My relationship with the Lord was like a marriage on the rocks. I had to finally admit that this was so. When all was said and done, I was an atheist.

The few close family and friends who managed to listen to my problems long enough tried to help, though they really couldn't offer me anything. The only good advice they gave me was about "over-thinking things." This was a valid warning, and one I took seriously, but I feared the flipside was true; perhaps "under-thinking" and not objectively thinking enough was the problem. Perhaps that's why they were still believers.

All preaching aspects of my work became unbearably difficult. I could barely preach. I had long since quit evangelizing. I was doing as little as I could to get by in my work. One thing I decided I wouldn't do was get into marriage counseling. As frayed as my nerves were, I'm sure glad I didn't have any counseling to do at the time. I know for sure I would have told a divorced/remarried couple "living in sin" to take each other out for dinner, have a pizza and a beer, and forget about the whole damn "who has the right to get remarried?" issue! Many of my congregants, preaching friends, and colleagues could now see that something was definitely wrong.

I was tired of the useless bickering and fighting over issues that could never be solved. I was sick of the minutia of trying to draw theological lines in the sand and proclaim objective truth that I myself couldn't establish. I was tired of being the soul guru, the village sage, the witch doctor. I was tired of trying to answer questions I had studied probably a thousand times before and was no closer to having any authoritative answers to beyond the boundaries of my church's denomination. Whether I submitted to the most fanatical of beliefs or the most liberal made no difference. Life was all the same regardless. I was through with feigned religious piety and that ever-so-illusive quest for God's right hand of fellowship. You could hear the frustration in my voice. I had a lot of people worried. My new views began to slowly come out in casual conversations with close friends and brethren. Their expressions of shock grew; *"What's the matter with you, Joe?", "I am really worried about you, Joe", "If that's really what you believe, then I fear for you!", "You're starting to sound like an atheist, Joe!"* It was time for me to get as far away from church as possible.

This caused trouble on both sides of our families. Dad never really cared too much for religious debate and controversy. He was a little bothered by my faith collapse, but not like mom was. Mom was as charismatic and bubbly as could be, dominated with emotions. Since as early as I could remember, my mother and I would argue ourselves hoarse. If you heard us, you'd swear we hate each other, but we love each other dearly. Mom had a hard time with this. After all, her firstborn son, arrayed in the glories of the ministry, was now a closeted unbeliever. That took some serious getting use to. My rightwing, Rush Limbaugh-supporting parents-in-law dropped singing my praises almost the very moment the news of my wavering faith made the rounds through the family.

And the dregs of faking faith didn't end there. On one disturbing occasion, a friend of mine casually asked me about human suffering. He was a doubting Baptist friend who knew I was a minister and came by to do repairs on my house. He would ask me questions, legitimate questions along the lines of the ones that were costing me my faith; "If you can explain why children are harmed everyday in this country, you will be the first minister who could," he said to me. I was heartbroken in a way. I had to defend my public theology and make excuses for why "the big man upstairs" wouldn't show himself in the face of children murdered and the like. To keep from being outed as an atheist, I spun my web of theism. The really sad part was, he was a little impressed with my explanation! I so badly wanted to tell him how I really felt and that I was struggling with the same doubts he was. But I had to "be strong" for the congregation. I couldn't let it get out yet that I was an atheist.

To me, it became painfully obvious just who we were converting to the church. During this stage in my loss of faith, I was called upon to baptize some sincere souls who came forward to "be saved." I could barely go through with it. The congregation was rejoicing, but I was almost crying. I studied the cults before. I knew how they preyed upon people who were going through hard times. We were taking advantage of these simple souls. Conversion candidates are not particularly stable during conversion. They have probably gone through a bad relationship, a divorce, or some emotional ordeal that prompted them to start vulnerably looking for answers to life's lofty questions (just as it happened to me). Christianity is so dominating in American culture as Islam is overseas. It was there waiting when people fell from their highest point of mental well-being to their most vulnerable.

And then there was family. The family religion is sought in times of need. Very often, folks don't get involved with religions they haven't been brought up to trust. And what bothered me even more was that we didn't appeal to the educated and levelheaded, only to the uneducated and the emotionally weak, the indoctrinated, or the unstable soul who was searching for hope. It is incredible how many would never have otherwise been converted to a belief system if a number of mental factors remained in place. Cults all work the same way, playing on the same unsuspecting human weaknesses. With no exceptions I can say that everyone over the years with whom I studied the Bible, hoping to convert, knew nothing about Bible contradictions, and nothing about the mythical nature of Jesus and his similarities to older myths of pagan gods in ancient, dead religions. They knew nothing of evolution, or of the horrible atrocities contained in the pages of the Old Testament. My religion seemed no different than anyone else's, being charming and appealing to the unsuspecting bystander who wants to find heavenly rest some day. I was a gold brick salesman, a con man of the highest order—respected, loved, and trusted by the local community.

I had spoken to my wife, but she could not relate to my troubles. In time, this caused great difficulties in the marriage. Ultimately, it would destroy it. I would spend enormous amounts of time in my study and this bothered her, laying even more disappointment at my feet. Not only was I faltering before my Lord, but I was hurting my wife as well. That was something I never wanted to do.

The Darkness Falls

As stated earlier, things would get worse before they got better. Now was that time. The zenith of the struggle had emerged. The horribly unsettling fears of Hell, death, loneliness, and an unparalleled feeling of worthlessness climaxed. I remember the long nights, losing sleep, sitting up in bed, then getting out of bed and standing up, rocking back and forth, talking to myself. I remember the restless nights, twisting and turning, waking up just to confirm I was still alive. The worst thing was the immense isolation, that feeling of being alone in a purely physical universe. I was cut off from the world I had come to identify with. In a cold sweat, the weight of the whole world crashed down upon my shoulders. I lost my place in the cosmos. My identity was gone. Such a terrible feeling, so unsettling. I was nameless. I was in the twilight zone. I always hated that damn show. I hated it because in every episode, the rules were different. The laws of reality did not operate. There was no consistency, no truth. Nothing seemed real and everything everywhere was a blur of the unexpected. Nights were the hardest times for me because when my wife went to sleep (and she always did before me), I would look over at her and just cry. I would stare around the room and try to take it all in, but I couldn't. The silence of those nights was truly deafening.

The fear of dying was terrible. Not only was my soul at risk, but if atheism proved true, an eternity of sleep was frightening to me. I would never exist again. It took serious time to come to terms with this. Every heavenly consolation I ever had was shattered, like an apartment window in the Bronx. The joys I knew in life were now all I had left. My life was reduced to utter futility. To live well was great, but to die was even better—anything to get me out of this nightmare. With nothing more to look forward to in the great beyond, I could only look to the here and now. Life never seemed so bland. I was so small and the universe so big. It was cold and careless, pitifully indifferent. I had to take deep breaths to get a sense of what was around me. How many other worlds had come and gone in universes of long ago? How many planets might have existed with intelligent life on them with beings like me asking the same questions? Their memories were forgotten like mine would be in the distant ages to come.

The merciless dread of Hell was unmatchable. I was now the child of Lucifer I could never have imagined I would become. I was a faithless, nauseating stench to my on-looking God. My place was in the Lake of Fire, the abode of the damned. It was as though God had already said to me, *"Depart from me, ye cursed into the everlasting fire prepared for the Devil and his angels!"* (Matthew 25:41). I could see the world ending, and Joe Holman, the once proud and pure-hearted "good soldier" of the cross, standing on his left hand with all the goats, preparing for an existence of torture. A googol eons would pass by and not one second of eternity would have elapsed without the abiding agony of Gehenna! De-conversion is both mental and psychological; first, it is mental, and then it is psychological. Psychologically de-converting is the hard part; in order to do so, you must prepare yourself for damnation. In order to get past the fear of damnation, you must learn to accept it!

The Morning Sun Vanquishes The Horrible Night

Although it seemed like it never would, the fever from my painful paradigm shift broke at last. By early 2003, the long and dark night of madness finally gave way to the light of a morning of sanity. The intense pain and disappointment of losing my faith was replaced by the acceptance that what had happened had to happen. And at last, I could perspective-ize the chaos; so my beliefs turned out not to be true, so what? So the religion I was raised to love was false, so what? Could it not have been worse? In a world filled to the brim with devastating problems, was this really that bad? At least I have my sanity and my faculties of reason, and this turned out to be the opening of a new door for me. My destiny was now a blank chalk board. I could write on it my own distinct legacy. I could steer my life in whatever direction I saw fit. This took some getting use to. At first, I didn't know what to do with myself, but the feeling of out-of-place-ness gave way to opportunity. I realized I could make life what I wanted it to be.

It wasn't long until I made contact with other former ministers who identified themselves as atheists, telling them of my experiences. They stood openly for what I still felt awkward saying out loud—that I was an atheist. But it would be only another three months when, sitting at a local hamburger joint with a cousin, talking about this long journey, that I was moved to say out loud: "Hey everybody! I'm a goddamned atheist!" Sure, I got a couple of weird stares and a chuckle from the people one table over, but it was worth it! There was no fear of damnation anymore. Having ridded myself of the last vestiges of enslaving piety, I was ready to live life again. I should also add that this was the first time I had a beer since 1993—and without fear of eternal damnation too! It was worth a picture!

Another month came and went and my wife began to take notice of the new faithless Joe. She was so troubled by this that it accelerated the dissolving of our marriage. Arguments became more heated and the already love/hate nature of our relationship grew even worse. After prolonged prodding and hounding, I gave in to her petitions to see a doctor. I was willing to go through with it *only* to save our marriage.

She was convinced I was chemically depressed and needed medication. I knew I didn't need any and didn't need to talk to some shrink. Only after much hesitation did I agree to accommodate her on this. When we finally got in to see a counselor, I laid out to him my situation. He listened as my wife and I recounted in the space of an hour and a half all that led up to this point. He gave us his opinion on the matter. I was not surprised at his words, but for my wife's sake, I was glad she could hear them: *"No. You're not clinically depressed. You are as normal and mentally healthy as any guy I've ever talked to. You don't need medication."* Vindication! My wife was wrong! I was not depressed. I knew it and now she knew it. At this point, the ball was in her court to accept that what had happened to me was for legitimate reasons and not the result of some chemical imbalance. I could accept all that had happened to me by now, but she could not. This was the beginning of the end of our marriage.

Day by day, I was still growing away from the religious components that for so long had held my mind captive from the liberty and fresh air of living and thinking for myself. I learned to accept just how little control I had in life. I learned to live each day and make the best of it because life is precious – not because it is eternal, but because it is temporal – and this increased its value. Heavenly idealism is wrong and deceiving. My efforts should not be on some illusive life above the clouds, but on the life I'm living now.

De-conversion is tough because the healing process doesn't kick into high gear until one is able to admit to one's self that *your beliefs choose you, and not the other way around!* One might feel accountable to a higher power, but one is always accountable to one's own mind. To follow a doctrine or a philosophy that seeks to suppress or deny any part of a working of rationality is to commit a crime against the spirit of reason. The healthy mind lets reason take center stage. The healthy mind cannot allow for belief in a deity that condemns because of disbelief. Time got me ready for Hell, but better than that, it showed me that there was no ghost mad at me, waiting around the corner to cause some terrible thing to happen. There is indeed a Hell, but it exists only in the chasms of the fearful mind.

Since my de-conversion, I could look at people differently. I could look at an individual and see their good and bad qualities without having to resort to thinking of how sad it will be to see them suffering in a pit of flames. Natural phenomenon explained away the mysterious and the supernatural. The world was moving on with progress in every field, yet I had been holding onto an archaic book that did more to hold back progress than any other. The Bible was the very source of my pains all along. It claimed to offer peace and hope, but it created every problem it supposedly solved. It grew less and less appealing the more flaws I found in it. It was now all too obvious that the world's problems, like violence, discrimination, and intolerance (to name just a few) were largely created by the very book that was fronted as a solution to them.

There was so much more to life than I realized. There was virtue, peace, intellectual honesty, joy, laughter, pleasures, dignity, reminiscing, challenges, and the ceasing of my plaguing doubts. But best of all, there was love, that force that exists, permeating all rationally healthy beings. So many of the horrors of life are lessoned by love, and the best part of it all for me was that love was a natural thing, not a divine thing. My daily driving force was appreciation of my own little part in this endless cycle of life and whatever purpose I chose to make for myself. My functional tool was reason. I could direct my own destiny based on my view of the world's problems and the solutions to them as I perceived them. My problem-solving team was science. Through education and investigation, any problem could be tackled, so fear is rendered moot.

Happiness for Joe Holman finally returned, though not like I expected. In fact, I believe I never was as happy as when I could find my true self amidst all this confusion and pain. I think part of the victory of becoming a freethinker is finding that nothing really changed when you de-converted. You still have your same old idiosyncrasies and quirks, you just changed your view of your destiny and estimation of self-worth from being worth your weight in gold "beyond the clouds," to actually claiming your value here. You once hoped to be great in the eyes of heavenly onlookers, but now can make yourself highly valued by serving yourself, your society, and your species.

The Finality

I never quit getting asked what it was that finally closed my door of faith forever. If I had to pick a *"nail in the coffin"* moment that ended my theological journey, I don't think I would be able to. De-conversion takes time and a lot of thinking and rethinking. I do not expect that everyone can be an atheist. I am convinced that it will not happen for a good many people because religion is a psychological thing, and many people just aren't ready to make the leap to a purely material world, but as it was for me, so it will be the right move for a good many religious thinkers who find no stopping place short of rejecting theism. By September of 2003, I decided I had been an undercover atheist for long enough. I was ready and willing to "come out" of that other closet. September 28, 2003 was the date of my resignation. I have never regretted that decision for even a moment.

Looking back now, I can remember sitting on the couch shortly before my resignation and recalling the end of a movie I saw years earlier, the 1991 movie Drop Dead Fred. It's a silly little flick that focuses on a troubled girl with an imaginary friend who stays with her until this friend feels she has grown up enough to be on her own. I can remember the emotion that ran through me as I applied it to my situation. Drop Dead Fred says to her towards the end of the movie, "I've got to leave you now. You don't need me anymore." After that, the girl went on about her life as a normal girl, and Fred became some other little girl's imaginary friend. For me, it was exactly as though my God, my imaginary friend who was a stepping stone to help me develop confidence and to reach out towards maturity in life, suddenly said to me, *"I've got to leave you now. You don't need me anymore."* It was inevitable. I "grew up" in my mind. My imaginary friend was gone. Santa Claus was dead. There was no ghost in the machine. Pinocchio's strings had been cut. Cinderella's magic carriage ran out of gas. My little green dragon I clutched so tightly in my arms as a small child at bedtime was useless now.

My journey through Christianity and into atheistic freethought was a journey of finding myself, and now I can say with great confidence that I have. I am one small link in a long chain, and all I can do is my little part to make my fellow links feel that much happier and that much more loved. The standards of peace and happiness I sought as I believer, I found as an atheist—who would have thought? I was never a "sinner" and didn't need a savior. What I needed was truth and the liberty of enlightenment. I found that life is not about Joe Holman, planet earth, or my wants and desires, nor yet those of my family. Life is about change: blind but awesome, disappointing but surprising, change. Life is about being born, growing, and dying for no purpose at all except for the one we make for ourselves.

For me, life is not the main event anymore. I am no longer afraid of death. There is no reason to fear what must come. When my time on earth is spent, I will enjoy my eternal sleep, the only place where genuine, lasting tranquility can be obtained. In an eternal universe, who knows how unthinkably long it will be before another galaxy sprouts up somewhere, and another planet is formed, where another innocent, naive, and zealous Joe Holman comes around again, asking the same questions and learning the same lessons?

CHAPTER 5
The Chips Fall

Reactions to My De-conversion

"The religious persecution of the ages has been carried on under what was claimed to be the command of god. I distrust those people who know so well what god wants them to do, because I notice it always coincides with their own desire."
- Susan B. Anthony

"Nothing is more logical than persecution. Religious tolerance is a kind of infidelity."
- Ambrose Bierce

It was July of 2003, two months before I would resign. I spent several evenings and mornings at my word processor, typing up a heartfelt letter of resignation. I knew the way in which I handled the resignation had to be well thought out. This decision would change my life in the biggest way, and it would affect every valued relationship I had with family, friends, and with former congregants. The ripples would shoot out into the furthest reaches of the brotherhood and would come right back at me. I wrote articles for brotherhood publications and was contacted by readers from literally across the world, and so it would be no surprise when a story about an apostate minister leaving the fold attracted much more attention. I had to go about resigning the right way. I couldn't afford to mess up.

In fairness to my church friends, I wanted to tell them the truth about why I was resigning, and they deserved to know. My departure would conjure up questions, innuendoes, gossip, and suspicion. I had to craft a letter of resignation that would deal with these whispers and would quell the unrest. I sat at that word processor, trying to best express the reasons for my departure.

The following long-winded and argumentative letter was composed. You can just hear the "preachyness" of it. I came a hair's breadth away from sending it, but never did. It was too abrasive and adversarial to send. I include it here, unedited, merely to give my readers a look into what was going on inside my head at the time...

9-28-03

Dear believers in Jesus Christ,

I am writing those of you who have known me and worked closely with me during my nine years as a Gospel preacher and Christian. I believe my friends deserve to know about my new worldview before it goes through the grapevine.

As of Sept. 28, 2003, I have resigned as pulpit minister for College Hill Church of Christ. At first, I did not want to do this and I never thought I would have to, but I must because I am no longer a believer in Christ, the Bible, or theism. This may come as the biggest shock of your lives, and I can only say it has been 10 times more of a shock for me to go through this change. From conversion onward I experienced occasional doubts about religion, but my Bible faith and outlook vindicated any other possibility for a different worldview. Not any more. I must be honest with myself. I cannot believe the things I once believed and I am now even surprised I ever believed them at all.

Someone said, "You don't choose your beliefs, your beliefs choose you." How true I have found this to be. I used to say as a non-Christian that I never would have even thought about becoming a preacher. But as a preacher I said I never would have thought I would become an atheist. Just over four years ago, I used to believe that the very idea of atheism was an absurd, prideful, vain, and materialistic concept that enslaved carnally minded, selfish people who want to reject all that is good and proper. Now I know differently.

The biggest question you are going to have is why. There is scarcely enough space in fifty pages to adequately answer that, but here, I will try and summarize it all; I found Christianity to be an erroneous, arrogant, unnatural, intellectually dishonest, divisive, confusing, and contradictory religion. Like all religions, Christianity's God is made in the image of man and not the other way around like many are led to believe. Religion is an attempt to try and explain the mysteries of our world and to give intelligent man a reason to keep on laboring and toiling under this sun. But you cannot explain a mystery with a mystery. Like all religions, Christianity has succeeded in giving society a meaning for life. But also like all other religions, it has failed to come through as legitimate. Theology does not adequately explain the suffering of the innocent, natural (evolutionary) selection, or morality. This is why I came, over time and with a lot of tears, to see how fruitless it all was. To this day, the more I study, the more I find it hard to believe how charmed I was with Christianity at my conversion and how I needed something to believe in at the time. Religion evolved to help learning minds work in concert with each other. It helped to organize primitive man into a cohesive framework and purposeful unit of action—a society. But today we live in a drastically different world than long ago. Today man is different. He is a thinker, and education and self-confidence need no longer be found by belief in sky spirits that once motivated ancient societies lacking enough knowledge to explain the world around them. The more I began to study Christianity and answer the questions within the system, the more questions were raised instead of answered. I soon realized that there were no answers to be found.

Please understand. I am not mad at anyone, not even the myth I once believed to be a god. I am not trying to seem arrogant, intellectual, or in any way prideful. If anything, I would have been prideful to stay in the pompous preacher position I was in and keep on trying to believe that I am changing the world and that the all-powerful creator of the universe depends on lowly me to get things done. That is arrogance of the highest order. And I am not going off half-cocked not having carefully thought out the position I have taken. I have resisted and suppressed the things I am revealing as long as I could. I have had faith and told myself "these doubts will surely subside after a while and in the mean time I am going to preach on." And it worked for a while, but I can't believe something if I can't believe it. I have had about four years to really think and rethink my stand. Again, my beliefs chose me. I was totally happy and fulfilled with my life as a Christian and preacher. I had no desire to change at all, but I was forced to do so by myself.

I studied out of Christianity. To me, atheism was the only stopping place short of intellectual dishonesty and denial. Bottom line is, I did not lose faith, I simply found something (reason) that replaced it and goes far beyond faith's limited scope. The more I studied Christianity, the more it (and theology for that matter) didn't make sense. I spent countless nights in prayers and tears waiting for this storm in my mind to subside. My faith gave way to knowledge. For so long, I studied theology, and the defenses put up by theists never appeared so weak and untenable as they do now. Using belief in God to explain this universe is another desperate attempt on man's part to build human significance.

Unless a believer has been through what I have gone through they cannot possibly understand how painful it has been. It was like developing a terminal but rare disease and having to search far and near to find people who can relate to what I was going through. You cannot know the pain of finding that your worldview has fallen to the ground. For so long, I could not begin to see any purpose to life without God. It was once very hard to cope with many aspects of my change, but finally I saw the light at the end of the tunnel. There is so much more to learn than the Christian worldview allows for.
Why specifically did I defect?

- I cannot believe that the incredible massive numbers of people ignorant of Christianity are frying in a place called Hell. No divine "higher being" would have it so. It is a childish, vindictive, and most hideous concept.

- I cannot believe that a lovingly divine and all powerful creator would allow the most evil spirit to take the body of a snake and deceive the whole world resulting in the ultimate loss of countless souls, when by stopping that serpent before the fall, and thus, eliminating evil, God would have received more glory from more souls that would have served Him.

- I cannot believe a holy God could stand by while innocent men, women, and children are murdered, raped, molested, tortured, and cursed with every disease we know of so far (as we see and hear about every day in our world) and not be guilty himself of failing to stop it all.

- I cannot believe a God who once worked miraculously and now (conveniently) no longer works that way, despite the fact that teachers of the Bible could still use the alleged gift of tongues to teach other nations, and many people would believe and be saved. Too, many more people would be saved if they could have their diseases healed.

- I cannot believe that an all-powerful God who wanted us to know and preach his will would leave us with a book containing scribal errors, contradictions, and highly questionable religious content like (Numbers 31:15-18).

- And, lastly, I cannot believe in a virgin born Son of God who had many counterparts long before the Christian era. Jesus was only a *remake of former concepts of virgin born savior-gods. A wicked leader tried to kill them at their births, a chorus of angels sang at their births, and they were usually born on December 25th. They turned water to wine, cast out demons, did miracles and were killed for a people or, in some way, atoned for the sins of their believers. These similarities are not coincidental, but evidence that Jesus is reborn mythology, created by Hellenized Jews, who, under the tyranny of Roman oppression, enduring the absence of the long-awaited Jewish messiah, decided to erect a modernized, more heathenish messiah in their own time, who would offer the longed-for assurances of their people. These are just a few of the things I can no longer believe.*

Yes, I am the same old Joe you always knew who seeks truth but has a plentitude of idiosyncrasies, strengths, and weaknesses. And yes, I hold just about the same and even better moral views as before, only now I see their true source. And yes, I do believe in objective morality. And yes, I can bind that morality on others and allow secular humanism to be the true foundation for morality that it is. No, I am not evil, I have not made a pact with the devil, nor do I seek to destroy humanity or any silly thing like that. Despite what you have been conditioned to think about infidels, I am not hateful. I have the same good conditioning my mother and father raised me with, and you would too. If you lost faith in your religion tomorrow, you would still be conditioned the same way you are to do what you find is right. Yes, I am still your friend and will continue to be so. I love and respect all your decisions to be who you are. I do not expect, nor will I seek to force anyone to see things as I see them.

A few of you reading this letter will be downright angry with me, but that's OK. I don't really expect you to understand. Don't feel sorry for me. Just accept that something has happened in my life that you do not understand. I know there are a number of readers who will be talking about me and how I am going to "burn in Hell!" That's fine if you feel that way. I once would have thought the same thing about my condition now.

I know the same warped theological arguments and so-called Christian evidences and "Creation Science" (if it can be called that) which is just as much nonsense as the mythology it is built upon. I have read, taken, and taught enough Christian evidences materials to fill a decent sized bookshelf. I am not saying I will not open my mind still. I will. I will always seek truth the way I have. It is in my nature. But I do not need threats of damnation and Bible fundamental reminders or Bible verses about God's existence. Others have said to me and are saying "Joe, you are experiencing Satan's temptations." I believed that too once until I saw how clever a superstitious religious ploy it was. I was once afraid of a man in red with horns and a tail and the flames of his awful Hell, and that was one of the things that made this switch so difficult.

And please, preachers, before you go writing me up and dismantling this article piece by piece trying to obliterate what I have said, talk to me first. I plan to write a book containing the exhaustive layout of my experiences and the full reasons for my conclusions. I dare say that many more Christians suffer from the same doubts but they force them down like I once did. Frankly, I am amazed that more preachers do not quit preaching. They know better. That's right. I dare say that modern, intelligent Gospel preachers have seen Bible contradictions, atrocities, and other embarrassing material in their book but they refuse to accept it. I believe preachers are guilty of the very deceptions they preach against. They ought to know better, and if I'm right, they do, but will not let it out.

I am now a freethinker, an atheist. I have nothing that I see as convincing proof of the existence of a god. I now spend my days learning, loving, laughing, and being happy as much as is possible. To me, this is the only way to live.

*My advice to all is that they continue to seek truth, but do so honestly and give both sides the chance to be right. Promote the things you find to be valid, good, and true. No matter where we fall (in theism or atheism) and whether we like it or not, we are all seeking to find happiness and meaning in life. Seek truth using reason—it is the only universal force **we both know** exists.*

Sincerely,
Joseph E. Holman

Taking note of the glaringly adversarial tone of the letter, I decided not to send it. But what was I to do? I had already decided that my congregants deserved to know the truth. I was always one to "tell it like it is." My entire preaching career was about standing strong for what I believed, but things were so much different now. My brethren wouldn't want to hear my new views, and all I would get from the move would be division-causing resistance.

Just reading over this letter caused me to reflect back on the career I was leaving behind, and when I did, I was ashamed of what I saw—an argumentative, intolerant, fundamentalist man who tried to change the world in a vain little crusade, thinking he and his religion held a monopoly on the only way to get to the heavenly goods. And here I was, about ready to make the same mistake of trying to "convert" everyone to atheism—at least that's the way giving the reasons for my defection in this letter would be taken. I didn't want to be seen as an intolerant idealist anymore. I spent years trying to get people to agree with me. No more. I just wanted to live my life and enjoy what remained of it. It took me three minutes to craft the following resignation…

Dear brethren,

Due to some personal issues and trials in my life right now, I have decided to resign as pulpit minister for College Hill Church of Christ. These issues are beyond the scope of discussion and are better kept to myself. I enjoyed my time here and love every one of you. I wish you the best.

Sincerely,
Joe Holman

This letter was read from the pulpit by a prominent man of the church, a close friend of mine, who had been a faithful, listening ear during my time of trial. He and his wife were in the know and sympathetic to my turbulent situation. They were expecting me to beat my doubts, but when I told them I would be resigning, they were deeply saddened. Only they and a small handful of Christian friends I let know about my haranguing doubts because they were the only faithful friends I felt I had. We decided the church didn't need to know because it would just cause trouble. Despite all the pain, these individuals stuck by me. They proved to be real friends.

Before I knew it, the night of my resignation came. As it happened, I stayed home for both services that night due to a lingering case of bronchitis, and it was for this reason I had my friend inform the congregation of my decision to leave. The time was at hand. I would finally be able to quit living the lie I was living. Even with the threat of discord and fallout looming, it was still relieving to know it was all about to be over. Finally, I remember looking at the clock. It was 7:17 PM. Services had just ended. I knew the calls would soon start coming.

Pretty soon the first of the calls came: *"Joe, whatever problem this is, the Lord will help you with it. Don't quit preaching because you're too good a preacher."* That was easy enough! Many more calls followed suit. There were some perplexed people and some tears shed, but all seemed well. A few tense calls came, but none like what was to come.

At the end of two weeks, word got around to a preacher friend of mine whom I had been close to years earlier. Being shocked that I had resigned, he was wondering why. He could sense I had been troubled, but didn't know the reasons behind it. He came to my house and let me know that he would settle for no other answer than what I was really struggling with. I repeatedly asked him to understand and be patient with me as my experiences had been painful, and that it was a personal thing. "You're not going to believe this," I said. "You'll wish you hadn't asked." He persisted and agreed that whatever it was, he could handle it. I knew he couldn't, and sure enough, he didn't. I told him, "Alright, the truth is, I am an atheist." He turned red after several prolonged moments of speechlessness. You could see his mental hard drive fighting, searching for some responses, and when he had no good ones, he went on autopilot. The first words out of his mouth were, *"You have no morality, Joe!"* said in the tone of voice a third grade teacher uses to addresses disobedient students from across the classroom. Now, regretting having said anything, I just listened to him, thinking to myself, "Damnit, I knew he couldn't handle it!" His face turned bright red, and he shot off a second response: *"Will you have sex with your dog now, Joe! Huh? Will you? You have no morality, Joe! You have no morals and no hope! You have no hope, Joe, no hope!"* I should have been offended, but more than anything, I was moved to laugh at the heated string of absurdities I was hearing. Neither the intensity of his five-minute tirade, nor the bizarre statements he made were surprising.

This "friend" was a firebrand "supersaint," surpassing even the likes of my own former level of Christian bigotry. He was the sort of preacher everyone was intimidated by, the type that always seemed to have more concern for church dogma than the people that make it up. Never were these words of Jesus more fitting than towards this Christian…

> Woe unto you, scribes and Pharisees, hypocrites! for ye compass sea and land to make one proselyte, and when he is made, ye make him twofold more the child of hell than yourselves. (Matthew 23:15)

This radical individual was indeed a "twofold more the child of Hell" to which Jesus in principle referred. Like I had been, he was an indoctrinated bigot from a long line of bigots, intolerant fools who studied only the Bible and thought they had a sound grasp of reality. The resistance he put up was far worse than what I put up with from other bigoted preachers I confided in. The conversation went from a dialogue to a monologue very quickly. He made not the slightest effort to hear me out, but accused me of being a thief, a liar, a communist sympathizer, and a godless wretch.

I thought this guy was a friend for years. We spoke at each other's churches. We helped each other move. We went out with our families for meals and special occasions. My wife and I stood by and watched them teach their two-year-old child the names of well known Church of Christ preachers instead of Big Bird and Oscar the Grouch. We sat on their couch and listened as this friend's wife pulled out stacks of G-rated movies and proudly declared that nothing of a PG rating or above could be found in their house—they were far too holy for that! Angrily leaving my house, this man would be the one to expose me to the members of my former church. He wasted no time in his efforts, even after I informed this fanatic friend that I had confided my doubts in several men of the church and they chose to keep it quiet since it would only cause schism. None of this mattered to him.

I later learned that this former friend lambasted me from his pulpit and started a phone war with my old congregants, and from there, news spread like the plague all throughout the brotherhood. By the end of that day, my wife and I were getting calls from members of the church, asking if the things he said were true. We explained to them that they essentially were, but had best not be discussed. Those few who managed to remain my friends accepted this with a simple, "We'll be praying for you, Joe."

Suddenly, it seemed, I was getting calls from brethren I hadn't heard from in years, asking me questions, telling me they would be praying for me, and reaming me out. It quickly got around which members were my friends and which were not. The network of criticism expanded. Through the grapevine came all sorts of hurtful names.

While this was happening, another preacher I had confided in before I defected got wind of my resignation. This well-known and well-respected preacher decided that he too should reveal what he knew of my secret struggle with infidelity. He told the world that I came to him with doubts about the existence of God some time before, but that I had now "completely forsaken the gospel of Jesus Christ." A concerned friend called me and told me exactly what was said. I can only imagine that he justified breaking confidence by just assuming I had resigned for openly atheistic reasons, since that was what was rumored. I was the new apostate story around the brotherhood. Everyone seemed to be talking about it.

So in the end, my efforts to resign from the ministry quietly were thwarted by the loudmouthed ministers I trusted to keep my confidence. All I wanted to do was walk away from my old life discreetly. I didn't want to stir up trouble and debates along the way. I was tired of the controversy, tired of the fighting, but I was having to keep explaining myself in a flurry of phone calls and emails. As a part of me suspected might happen, an easy out would be tough to pull off, and as it turned out, I just didn't get that lucky!

Among the condescending and confused calls were compassionate voices, a couple of them from brethren claiming to understand what it was like to fight doubts. While I was assured that they understood, they showed me that they did not understand at all. I found myself explaining away rumors and misconceptions about my views. I had to dodge a few shouting matches over the phone, and after taking the time to defend my beliefs over and over, it became too tiring.

Reactions to my change were quite varied. I got a wide range of calls and visits, from the inquisitive and emotional, to the kind and angry. I was told by some to, "hold on," telling me that God had great plans for me. Others, upon hearing about me, denied everything; "Joe Holman? No! He's too sound a man of God to fall into that belief." Then, when they called me and got it "straight from the horse's mouth," they were speechless. It is nice that I kept some good friends when I walked away from the ministry. I still get a few cards from them once in a while. And I particularly enjoyed one response from a preacher friend when I informed him of my situation: *"Aw, Joe, if you weren't so far away, I'd give you a hug."* Now that's friendship!

Among the many negative sentiments I received were the usual misconceptions on why I left the fold; *"You were never really converted." "You were pushed into preaching too soon." "You just had too strict a church and their interpretation ruined you to real moderate Christianity." "You were just frustrated by the brethren." "You are just going through a phase, a sort of midlife crisis." "You just needed more vacations." "You needed medication because you were depressed."* But when I defended my decision to leave, discovering that my decision to defect was an informed one, I quickly became viewed as the flaming heretic without hope of saving. At least several preachers and long-time church friends forbade me to contact them ever again, and most of them haven't reached out to me since. The memorable comments were there...

> *"You are deceived by Satan, Joe." "Now you've thrown the baby out with the bath water." "Joe is not letting God be God. He's got to let God do it his way." "How could you do this to your wife?" "I am going to keep praying that you be delivered from the snare of the wicked one." "I feel sorry for you. We will be praying for you." "You are irrational. I've never met someone as irrational as you and with such poor reasoning skills." "Joe, I love you too much to see you just throw your life away for a worthless belief." "You don't really believe that. You're just trying to get attention." "You are lost!" "Joe thinks he knows it all. That's his problem."*

Then there were the idiotic questions and bamboozling statements I got, which I'm glad I made a point to write down...

> *"Do you worship the devil now?" "Will you beat me and take my wallet now that you're an atheist, Joe?" "Will you become a Muslim now, Joe, and start bombing buses full of children?" "You are so sick*

in the head to believe that." "You might as well piss on kids and kill yourself!" "I'm afraid to get you too angry with me, Joe, because I want to be able to have kids." "Joe, I know you don't believe now, but when you get shipped off to Hell with the demons attacking you, just call out the name of Jesus and you will be delivered." "Do you use black magic?"

If all this social turmoil was not enough, I had become the object of pity in my highly religious community of ten thousand. Just about everyone was religious and everyone knew of my infidelity. When Elise invited church friends over to the house, I could see the pity in their eyes when they saw me, the "I'm sorry you're going through a stage where you're mad at God, Joe." sort of look. I finally made it a habit to be out of the house when her friends would come over most of the time.

My wife resumed her church life as normal, and it was tough as she drove off to church the following Sunday without me. A tear came to my eye, but because of the pain this caused me, I decided I would not be going back into a church building again.

It was shocking to experience. It almost seemed like I was being interrogated by the police as a murder suspect, but this was only the persecution from outside of the family. Inside the family was even worse. The attitudes of everyone I knew changed around me. The family had an immensely difficult time excepting that I really believed what I was saying. My new worldview seemed more like a phase of depression to them than it did a reformation of thinking. Only time would allow for readjustment. It took some wisdom to maneuver myself out of the way of arguments to keep from ruining a Thanksgiving or Christmas dinner. Heated arguments with my parents and parents-in-law did their damage. We seemed to be growing further and further apart. As my marriage crumbled, relationships with the family gradually deteriorated. No one understood my situation. No matter how I tried to explain it, no matter how many illustrations I gave, I failed to get through to anyone. The exclamatory statements, the gasps of unbelief, the crying and shouting matches, the cursing and yelling ourselves hoarse took its toll. I became the subject of countless prayer groups and the focus of gossip and spiteful conversations that trickled back to me. It was especially frustrating to have no opportunity to defend myself and put my position in an intelligent light. I got used to the unfair and hurtful accusations hurled my way. Arguing in times like these is seldom fruitful.

There were some who did show interest in the reasons behind my rejection of the faith. Of the few good minds that did sit down with me and were willing to broaden their horizons, their willingness to learn was soon quenched; "I see what you're saying, Joe, and that may be true, but I'm not leaving the church." "You are smarter than me, and I can't defend our beliefs that well, but maybe someone else can." "I don't know what to say to that." I didn't expect anyone to de-convert, and I certainly didn't want any followers. All I wanted was the respect as someone who follows his convictions wherever they lead. Even when intellect seemed to create doubts about the faith, the doubts for them were snuffed out by community influence. The pulling of the Christian community drew them right back into it and away from a consideration of the legitimacy of the belief system.

The shunning, the isolation my position put me in, though not surprising, took some getting used to. I will never forget one occasion when my parents brought up the finding of the alleged Ossuary of Joseph, the brother of Jesus, found in October of 2002 and initially hailed by the media and the entire pro-Christian world as authentic. I pointed out nicely that the inscription on the box, "Joseph, the brother of Jesus," was a forgery. I was told, "You don't have credibility with us anymore. We don't trust you." It was a simple matter; over two years later, they were still uninformed that the find was declared a fake in the news, but they wouldn't accept this. After repeated attempts to point out that the Christian world itself would tell them just what I was telling them, they still refused to listen; "Talk all you want, but we're not listening to you." This was extremely hurtful. The exchange that followed was not one of my calmest and most pleasant ones, but I got my revenge! Some time later, I found the headline and showed it to them, that the owner of the box, Oded Golan, and three other prominent con men were arrested by the authorities in Israel in December of 2004 for this and other frauds perpetrated on the public. With the accompaniment of a few colorful expletives, I dropped the paper in front of them and walked away. They remained speechless for a few moments and then acted like they were blameless.

Fighting the bitterness and anger that comes from such turmoil was difficult, but not when the effort was prodded along by a sense of understanding. It was not about me accepting them, it was about them accepting me. Understanding that made the time go by much faster. Eventually, it happened, though for a very short while, my parents and I were not on speaking terms. For all practical purposes, my de-conversion marked the beginning of a new identity for Joe Holman. I had to make a fresh start. It was as though I was walking backwards along a dirt road to the tune of pretty piano music, with a backpack over one shoulder, thumbing for a ride.

Reflecting back on the long and painful journey, the worst thing about de-conversion was the loneliness of the process, the mental and social isolation. If it must be gone through, best it be with a spouse, or failing that, a close friend. I had one close cousin who was there for me when no one else was. Just someone to talk to is better than no one, but it cannot be forgotten that the road to de-conversion is not a paved highway, just a bumpy, dirt road, a road seldom traveled. It is a lonely and thankless path, and if it is to be walked, it must be done for the sake of the journey itself, and not to arrive at a glamorous destination, because the destination on the path to de-conversion leads you nowhere but right back to yourself.

Though a thousand likeminded souls stand with you, ultimately, the journey down the road to de-conversion is one the individual must face alone. The bleakness of the grim path is the freethinker's Gethsemane, and sorrowful though it may be, the finish line will be crossed. I sacrificed everything for what I considered to be truth. A well-paying job, my marriage, my relationship with family, and my reputation were sent down the river, but never a once did I question whether or not I did the right thing. As my old debate coach, Jerry Moffitt, used to tell me, "When someone wants the truth bad enough, you won't be able to beat them away from it with a stick."

Chapter 6
Against Inspiration - I

Hints of the non-inspiration of the Bible

"What the people want to hear is the truth."
-   *Winston Churchill*

"We have learned to speak the truth out of our hearts, with words that are soaked in our feelings. All other words are like empty bottles floating in the ocean."
-   *Gerry Spence*

The Critical Eye

In this chapter, we will do more than discuss reasons why the Bible cannot be the product of divinity. We will find that the Bible was never intended to serve as a complete guidebook for the church. We will highlight what has long been neglected in attacks on Christianity—the fact that the Bible as we know it was never meant to be compiled into one book or to serve as an all-encompassing "instruction manual" for a religion. We will be looking at very basic textual criticism, the issue of the canonization of the New Testament scriptures, and the subject of biblical inspiration. Starting with the last two items first, it is a necessary first step towards understanding Bible inspiration to understand the common man's view of it.

Bibliolatry

Take a survey in your local neighborhood. Ask the average person, "Who wrote the Bible?" and chances are, the answer you get will be that "God did." The general public's opinion of the Bible is that it is an "owner's manual" of the human body and of creation. It is the instruction booklet on how to live, a universal roadmap to heaven. God crafted every word of it and put it together into one big book to serve as a complete revelation to mankind. This distorted thinking is sometimes called bibliolatry because it amounts to a type of book worship, a false adoration and exaltation of holy scripture.

What is Meant By "Inspiration"?

When the Bible is referred to as being "inspired," poetic inspiration or genius inspiration is not what is being discussed. Even the concept of thought inspiration – the belief that the Bible contains the principles of God using the human written text as a vessel for the general thoughts or plans of the almighty – is not in focus either.

What is being discussed is the concept of verbal plenary inspiration—the belief in "every word of God inspired." In this view, God actually spoke the words of scripture. Human intelligence did not create these words, nor did Shakespearian prowess. It is not just the thoughts and principles of God that are recorded for us, but the very words from his mouth. These words began being given to us in the days of Moses and ended when the last New Testament apostle or prophet died, closing the sacred canon of scripture.

The True Nature of Verbal Plenary Inspiration

The apostle Peter explains for us biblical inspiration...

> 20. Knowing this first, that no prophecy of the scripture is of any private interpretation. 21. For the prophecy came not in old time by the will of man: but holy men of God spake as they were moved by the Holy Ghost. (2 Peter 1:20-21)

Says Peter, the scriptures, as they were passed on to us by the prophets, were not subjected to the messenger's private interpretation of the things they received. The prophets did not try to interpret what they were hearing or seeing. God was giving them verbatim what was to be written down and spoken. So God did not show a prophet an image of a sick animal and leave that prophet to interpret it to be a plague, but spoke directly, "And this shall be the plague wherewith the LORD will smite all the people that have fought against Jerusalem; Their flesh shall consume away while they stand upon their feet, and their eyes shall consume away in their holes, and their tongue shall consume away in their mouth." (Zechariah 14:12)

Peter is seeking to convince his audience of the truth of Christianity by reassuring his readers that he was an eyewitness of God's resurrecting power in Jesus, but Peter doesn't stop there. He seeks to convince his audience by deferring to a "more sure word of prophecy; whereunto ye do well that ye take heed." (2 Peter 1:19) We needn't worry about the accuracy of the prophets who spoke of Jesus, says he, because there were no vague elements involved in the transmission of the message of the prophets which the Christian church believed spoke of Jesus. Every word that came down to man was from God. So when we attack the Bible in demonstration of the fact that it cannot be a work of divine inspiration, we are attacking the concept of verbal plenary inspiration. The purpose of this chapter is to demonstrate that belief in this concept is false and unwarranted.

Relying on Human Reasoning

In almost all of the Old Testament – but in very few places in the New Testament – we are told when God is speaking to man. In the Old Testament, "thus saith the Lord" preceded a command or a declaration from the almighty, but in the New Testament, very seldom is this ever seen, leaving us to wonder which passages are anything more than letters to individuals. Notice the reason Luke gives when he tells us why he wrote the gospel bearing his name...

1. Forasmuch as many have taken in hand to set forth in order a declaration of those things which are most surely believed among us, 2. Even as they delivered them unto us, which from the beginning were eyewitnesses, and ministers of the word; 3. It seemed good to me also, having had perfect understanding of all things from the very first, to write unto thee in order, most excellent Theophilus, 4. That thou mightest know the certainty of those things, wherein thou hast been instructed. (Luke 1:1-4)

Why did Luke write his gospel? For the purpose of informing a man named Theophilus because Luke possessed "perfect understanding of all things" related to the Christian message, but he relied on his own understanding. There is no mention of his being led by God to record specific words, no mention of the Holy Spirit, and no mention of being "inspired." Luke was just one more person who wrote to others to pass on his individual beliefs. We have no reason to give any of his words more credit than this.

Our Bibles are composed in part of 21 letters by the apostle Paul, and though Paul repeatedly claims to be speaking the words of God, his writing does not reflect this. On the contrary, he wrote letters addressed to individuals and churches, and these letters are full of human nuances that, had a deity been inspiring him to write, would not have been included, like forgetfulness, "And I baptized also the household of Stephanas: besides, I know not whether I baptized any other." (1 Corinthians 1:16) Furthermore, Paul uses details too personal to be apart of a letter that was to be used as a universal canon of law for the church, "The cloke that I left at Troas with Carpus, when thou comest, bring with thee, and the books, but especially the parchments." (2 Timothy 4:13) The entire book of Philemon is a short letter by the apostle Paul to his friend Philemon. Paul crossed paths with a runaway slave of Philemon's (Onesimus) and converted him to Christianity. Paul encourages Philemon to accept Onesimus back with open arms and forgiveness. That a book like this would be included in the Christian canon of scripture to be a universally accepted creed book for the religion is unthinkable. Had the letters of the New Testament we possess been intended as a canon or creed book for the church throughout the ages, it would have been constructed like the five books of Moses or the writings of the prophets—with universal intent and purpose shown throughout. But the Bible we have is merely a compilation of independently circulating letters, and in no book is a list to inform us of which books are to be included as part of a canon.

Canonization

If indeed the Bible was somehow designed as a guidebook, we are then left to wonder how canonicity could be determined with certainty. The Bible itself doesn't tell us which books belong in the Bible. So tradition is all the believer has to go on to determine this.

If we look for self-authenticating works by New Testament apostles and prophets, we only find a few, and these stand on their own. They offer us nothing but justification for their own presence in a so-called New Testament canon of scripture. In I Thessalonians 5:27, Paul commands the reading of his epistle: "I charge you by the Lord that this epistle be read unto all the holy brethren." But this only gives the canonical stamp of approval on this work, not other New Testament books. The gospel of John would be another work that would make the list of canonical books (John 20:30-31), but beyond these, we have no biblical authority from the Bible to determine what constitutes "the Bible." In the case of Hebrews, we have no idea who the author was, and many books – like 2 Peter and Revelation – were almost universally rejected from the canon of Bible books we now have. The canon of scripture as we know it today was not fully decided upon until the Council of Carthage in 397 C.E. (common era).

We have plenty of the writings of Barnabas, Clement of Rome, Clement of Alexandria, Tertullian, Polycarp, and Ignatius of Antioch, whose writings were once thought to be inspired and almost made it into the sacred canon of Christian scripture. We very easily could have had a different set of "inspired" Bible books handed down to us. Whichever way the winds of orthodoxy and tradition were blowing in the first four centuries of the church determined which books went into the official canon of scripture and which books were rejected.

Uninspired Statements

In a few places in holy writ, we have statements from Paul that he admits lack inspiration. In I Corinthians 7:6, we have Paul using space in the holy scriptures to share some of his own personal advice with the Corinthian brethren; "But I speak this by permission, and not of commandment." He then proceeds to recommend celibacy as a superior lifestyle to marriage. Paul does this more than once; "But to the rest speak I, not the Lord." (1 Corinthians 7:12) These portions of the scriptures are not inspired texts, but the opinions of one man—mere historical opinions at best. This destroys the prevalent idea that cover-to-cover everything written in the Bible is the work of God. Paul was not writing a law for a religion, he was corresponding with one particular church, as he was in all of his writings. This fact further erodes the idea of an "inspired" Bible.

Lost Bible Books

Now we come to a most damning issue for the church—the matter of lost Bible books. Those who believe that the Bible as we know it was providentially preserved by God and handed down to us today must confront this problem.

As before, we begin with Paul's writings, the Corinthian letters being a prime example. Had the Corinthian letters been intended to be relied upon as inspired works for all the world to read through the centuries, they would have been preserved, but only two of them came into our possession. One letter of Paul to the Corinthians was lost (2 Corinthians 2:3, 4, 9; 7:8). This letter was not First Corinthians, but another letter dealing with Paul's authority being challenged at Corinth, and certainly it would not have been had God been preserving Paul's words for the Bible. If two letters to a specific church from Paul contained sacred truths for the world, then why not the third?

Why is God using personal letters to individual churches to universally address the entire body of Christ on earth? Would it be fitting for someone to prepare an instruction manual for a company by compiling a series of replies from selected email correspondences, or would it be more appropriate to craft from scratch a more exhaustive and comprehensive work designed specifically for that purpose?

The Bible makes reference to many other "inspired" books that have long since been lost in time. The Book of the Wars of the Lord is one such book…

> Wherefore it is said in the book of the wars of the LORD, What he did in the Red sea, and in the brooks of Arnon, (Numbers 21:14)

The Book of the Wars of the Lord is not just a passing reference like the one used by Paul, who quoted a heathen poet as a motivating technique in a sermon (Acts 17:28) or Peter, who used the Greek word "Tartarus" as a reference to the well-known Greek mythological version of Hell (2 Peter 2:4), comparing it to his own Christian concept of Hell. The Book of the Wars of the Lord was a record containing details of God's works in and around the Red Sea—details not found in canonized scripture. This poses a serious problem for believers. The average Bible student will recall the frequent instances where the writers of the Kings and Chronicles refer back to each other for details…

> Now the rest of the acts of Rehoboam, and all that he did, are they not written in the book of the chronicles of the kings of Judah? (I Kings 14:29)

> Now the rest of the acts of Amaziah, first and last, behold, are they not written in the book of the kings of Judah and Israel? (2 Chronicles 25:26)

What might you guess is the purpose of these verses? Like the citing of a source in a modern book, it is a way for the reader to reference more information on the subjects they address. Naturally, if these books contain valuable information to the reader, and if indeed they are products of divine inspiration, we should have them. In this case, we do; the books of Kings and Chronicles are included in the sacred text, but in other cases, this is not so. In addition to The Book of the Wars of the Lord, here are some other books referenced in the Bible as being prophetic in nature, but which have not been preserved for us...

> And the sun stood still, and the moon stayed, until the people had avenged themselves upon their enemies. Is not this written in the **book of Jasher?** So the sun stood still in the midst of heaven, and hasted not to go down about a whole day. (Joshua 10:13)

> Now the acts of David the king, first and last, behold, they are written in the **book of Samuel the seer**, and in the book of Nathan the prophet, and in the **book of Gad the seer**. (I Chronicles 29:29)

> Now the rest of the acts of Solomon, first and last, are they not written in the **book of Nathan the prophet,** and in **the prophecy of Ahijah the Shilonite,** and in **the visions of Iddo** the seer against Jeroboam the son of Nebat? (2 Chronicles 9:29)

If these texts are truly works of God, and if they are relevant enough to be referenced in the word of God, why do we not have them? That God would make reference to these works and then not make them available to us is another strike against the concept of an inspired Bible.

Pseudopigraphical Quotes

In quite a few places, we see little errors, small discrepancies that only a skeptical mind would hone in on. Then there is another type of discrepancy, those fewer places where a Bible writer makes a big blunder that there is no talking down. A pseudopigraphical work is a written work whose author fraudulently attributed it to an author of the past. On this occasion, we have Jude to thank for a colossal mistake...

> And Enoch also, the seventh from Adam, prophesied of these, saying, Behold, the Lord cometh with ten thousands of his saints. (Jude 1:14)

The quote Jude makes is from a pseudopigraphical book, the so-called "Book of Enoch." If Jude were a spokesman of God, he would have known that Enoch did not write this book. The book claiming to be from the patriarchal prophet is a fake dating just before the first century of the Common Era that has been known to be counterfeit for the longest time. The quote is...

> And behold! He comes with ten thousand Holy Ones, to execute judgement upon them, and to destroy the impious, and to contend with all flesh, concerning everything that the sinners and the impious have done and wrought against Him. (I Enoch 1:9)

The Book of Enoch is a recognized fake, both by secular and religious scholars. Books in this category are kept around as ancient folklore only, and not as trusted history or divine testimony. What does it say of Jude that he would mention such a book as having authority from God? What are we to think of a "prophet" of God who considers a fraudulent work the testimony of his God?

Plagiarism and Redundancies

The Bible is imperfect in yet another way; it contains minute instances of plagiarism. The accounts in the Kings and the Chronicles are the offending parties here. Being almost word-for-word plagiarized, we have here a redundancy...

> 2 Kings 22:11-20

> 11. And it came to pass, when the king had heard the words of the book of the law, that he rent his clothes. 12. And the king commanded Hilkiah the priest, and Ahikam the son of Shaphan, and Achbor the son of Michaiah, and Shaphan the scribe, and Asahiah a servant of the king's, saying, 13. Go ye, enquire of the LORD for me, and for the people, and for all Judah, concerning the words of this book that is found: for great is the wrath of the LORD that is kindled against us, because our fathers have not hearkened unto the words of this book, to do according unto all that which is written concerning us. 14. So Hilkiah the priest, and Ahikam, and Achbor, and Shaphan, and Asahiah, went unto Huldah the prophetess, the wife of Shallum the son of Tikvah, the son of Harhas, keeper of the wardrobe; (now she dwelt in Jerusalem in the college;) and they communed with her. 15. And she said unto them, Thus saith the LORD God of Israel, Tell the

man that sent you to me, 16. Thus saith the LORD, Behold, I will bring evil upon this place, and upon the inhabitants thereof, even all the words of the book which the king of Judah hath read: 17. Because they have forsaken me, and have burned incense unto other Gods, that they might provoke me to anger with all the works of their hands; therefore my wrath shall be kindled against this place, and shall not be quenched. 18. But to the king of Judah which sent you to enquire of the LORD, thus shall ye say to him, Thus saith the LORD God of Israel, As touching the words which thou hast heard; 19. Because thine heart was tender, and thou hast humbled thyself before the LORD, when thou heardest what I spake against this place, and against the inhabitants thereof, that they should become a desolation and a curse, and hast rent thy clothes, and wept before me; I also have heard thee, saith the LORD. 20. Behold therefore, I will gather thee unto thy fathers, and thou shalt be gathered into thy grave in peace; and thine eyes shall not see all the evil which I will bring upon this place. And they brought the king word again.

2 Chronicles 34:19-28

19. And it came to pass, when the king had heard the words of the law, that he rent his clothes. 20. And the king commanded Hilkiah, and Ahikam the son of Shaphan, and Abdon the son of Micah, and Shaphan the scribe, and Asaiah a servant of the king's, saying, 21. Go, enquire of the LORD for me, and for them that are left in Israel and in Judah, concerning the words of the book that is found: for great is the wrath of the LORD that is poured out upon us, because our fathers have not kept the word of the LORD, to do after all that is written in this book. 22. And Hilkiah, and they that the king had appointed, went to Huldah the prophetess, the wife of Shallum the son of Tikvath, the son of Hasrah, keeper of the wardrobe; (now she dwelt in Jerusalem in the college:) and they spake to her to that effect. 23. And she answered them, Thus saith the LORD God of Israel, Tell ye the man that sent you to me, 24. Thus saith the LORD, Behold, I will bring evil upon this place, and upon the inhabitants thereof, even all the curses that are written in the book which they have read before the king of Judah: 25. Because they have forsaken me, and have burned incense unto other Gods, that they might provoke me to anger with all the works of their hands; therefore my wrath shall be poured out upon this place, and shall not be quenched. 26. And as for the king of Judah, who sent you to enquire of the LORD, so shall ye say unto him, Thus saith the LORD God of Israel concerning the words which thou hast heard; 27. Because thine heart was tender, and thou didst humble thyself before God, when thou heardest his words against this place, and against the inhabitants thereof, and humbledst thyself before me, and didst rend thy clothes, and weep before me; I have even heard thee also, saith the LORD. 28. Behold, I will gather thee to thy fathers, and thou shalt be

gathered to thy grave in peace, neither shall thine eyes see all the evil that I will bring upon this place, and upon the inhabitants of the same. So they brought the king word again.

Another example is found in 2 Kings 19 and Isaiah 37. Good historians have no need to plagiarize, even when drawing their information from the same source. And what purpose could the Holy Spirit have had in repeating words already present in one place in the scriptures? Perhaps emphasis? Moral imperatives are repeated for emphasis, and yet the books of the Kings and Chronicles do not contain moral imperatives, but historical information. So the question of why we would find redundancies in God's book remains unanswered.

Ruined by Myth

Throughout the years, I've had the pleasure of meeting people I considered to be fine individuals. Then they exhibited some whacky trait that made me think twice about my earlier estimation. I've had otherwise excellent people I met who professed belief in some unforgivably whacky notion. One that hit a little too close to home was my own grandmother on my father's side. There we were at a family get-together, chatting about dear old dad when grandma shared her conviction that pop's teeth were as bad as they were because when she was pregnant with him, she once stared too long at a man with rotten teeth. I asked her to repeat the statement, thinking perhaps I misunderstood her, but I hadn't. The Bible and she had something in common; they both defended the superstitious idea of prenatal influence—a discredited idea any zoologist will quickly toss into the can...

> And Jacob took him rods of green poplar, and of the hazel and chesnut tree; and pilled white strakes in them, and made the white appear which was in the rods. 38. And he set the rods which he had pilled before the flocks in the gutters in the watering troughs when the flocks came to drink, that they should conceive when they came to drink. 39. And the flocks conceived before the rods, and brought forth cattle ringstreaked, speckled, and spotted. (Genesis 30:37-39)

In order to get his rightful wages from Laban, Jacob decided to ask that his pay be of whatever striped, brown, or spotted animals he could breed for himself. He put striped rods in front of the all white animals at his disposal, and as they came to the watering trough and saw the rods, they mated and conceived spotted, streaked, and striped offspring! The belief that visual stimulation affects offspring was a common belief in Bible days—and as I found out for myself, still is today in some parts.

In 2002, I sat down in my church office with a Christian man who astonished me by admitting he believed in the South American superstition that if a pregnant woman handles snakeskin, the baby will be born with snake qualities (usually a forked tongue)! Backwards ideas like these seem to be popping up everywhere.

False Prophecies

Ezekiel 29:8-11: Egypt Will Be Desolate 40 Years

> 8. Therefore thus saith the Lord GOD; Behold, I will bring a sword upon thee, and cut off man and beast out of thee. 9. And the land of Egypt shall be desolate and waste; and they shall know that I am the LORD: because he hath said, The river is mine, and I have made it. 10. Behold, therefore I am against thee, and against thy rivers, and I will make the land of Egypt utterly waste and desolate, from the tower of Syene even unto the border of Ethiopia. 11. No foot of man shall pass through it, nor foot of beast shall pass through it, neither shall it be inhabited forty years.

Never was the land of Egypt uninhabited. The prophecy has never been fulfilled in any sense, and part of God's purpose in cutting off Egypt was for Israel's sake (vs. 16)...

> And it shall be no more the confidence of the house of Israel, which bringeth their iniquity to remembrance, when they shall look after them: but they shall know that I am the Lord GOD.

This means that this prophecy cannot be fulfilled at any future date—because certainly today, Israel no longer has confidence in Egypt as the nation did back when this pronouncement was made.

Jeremiah 34:4-5: The Death of Zedekiah

As it was for Josiah, it was predicted for Zedekiah that he die in peace...

> 4. Yet hear the word of the LORD, O Zedekiah king of Judah; Thus saith the LORD of thee, Thou shalt not die by the sword: 5. But thou shalt die in peace: and with the burnings of thy fathers, the former kings which were before thee, so shall they burn odours for thee; and they will lament thee, saying, Ah lord! for I have pronounced the word, saith the LORD. (Jeremiah 34:4-5)

Did this happen? Certainly it didn't...

10. And the king of Babylon slew the sons of Zedekiah before his eyes: he slew also all the princes of Judah in Riblah. 11. Then he put out the eyes of Zedekiah; and the king of Babylon bound him in chains, and carried him to Babylon, and put him in prison till the day of his death. (Jeremiah 52:10-11)

If he was in chains in a prison until the day of his death, then he definitely didn't die in peace. He died in the confines of captivity, in the cruel hands of his enemies, who murdered his sons and his fellow rulers before his eyes, and then blinded him. If this is a peaceful death, then I don't know what a violent one is!

Hit-or-miss Thinking

The account of Israel's massacre of Benjamin is found in Judges chapters 19 and 20, and it is one of the most bizarre and bloody episodes in the scriptures. Of significance to us here is the fact that it reflects hit-or-miss thinking—the trial and error thinking that was and is so prevalent in the religious mindset when dealing with the subject of unanswered prayer.

Chapter 19 sets the stage for the event; an unnamed Levite has a concubine who plays the harlot on him, and thereafter returns to her father's house. He reunites with her, and after staying a few days, they leave together and soon end up staying in Gibeah, a Benjamite territory. This cruel man sees fit to give his concubine over to being raped, murdered, and dismembered by "sons of Belial" (a common Hebrew description of degenerates). She dies and the man decides to graphically let all the tribes of Israel know just what type of people did this.

The children of Israel are angered incomprehensibly when cut up body parts of the concubine arrive in their camps. When they catch up with the man who sent them, he explains to them how she died, and the armies of Israel vow, "We will not any of us go to his tent," until Benjamin was rewarded for "all the folly that they have wrought in Israel" (Judges 20:8,10). Upon confronting the Benjamites, "the children of Benjamin would not hearken to the voice of their brethren, the children of Israel" (vs. 13). War is upon them now. It is an unfair battle; all the tribes of Israel's soldiers (700,000), take on the Benjamite's most valiant men (26,000). This should not be a challenge at all, but let's just say this battle is not the Israelite's shining moment of glory.

The people of Israel did what any good god-believers would do; they inquired of their deity what the best move would be. God gives them the go-ahead for war: "Judah shall go up first" (vs. 18). The result: 22,000 Israelites slain (vs. 21). They lose. They rally around and build up their spirits and ask God once again for advice: "Shall I go up again to battle against the children of Benjamin my brother?" "Go up against him," God instructs (vs. 23). The second day of battle is almost as bad as the first with a loss of 18,000 men (vs. 25). Judah lost a lot, a total of 43,000 men! But, in the spirit of strong faith in their deity, the Israelites asked council of God yet again, but this time, God decided he would be good enough to do what he could have done the first time—give them the victory: "Go up, for tomorrow I will deliver them into your hand" (vs. 28). After going through the trouble of setting a trap, a close battle ensues (vs. 34). Israel finally wins, but the sum total of losses for the side of Benjamin are 25,000 men (vs. 46). This was not a victory; it was a travesty. Benjamin lost less men than the rest of the Israelites!

For so long, I wondered why any scribe would dream of putting a story like this into their holy book. Hyde nor hair, it just didn't make sense. I kept asking myself why God sent Israel to battle only to lose when he could have given them the battle on the first try. Then it hit me: this was the mindset of those who wrote the Old Testament. It was no big deal to them if it would have taken God one or a hundred battles to come through for them and finally win. That would simply have been "God's will."

It occurred to me that Judges was written well after the events allegedly occurred. The scribes who recorded the results of this battle were perhaps just honest enough to record the results of the battle correctly, and yet theologically-minded enough to color their record of the events as though God intended from the start to have the tribes whip Benjamin in three battles. The text was worded as though God commanded, "Judah shall go up first," "Go up against him," "Go up, for tomorrow I will deliver them into thine hand." Painful losses in attempts to win were chalked up to God's will. This is the way religious people paint their history to exalt their deity or to politically/spiritually motivate their people. And there are other examples of this clumsy honesty.

From Judges 1:19 we learn that God was powerful enough to give his people victory over their enemies on the mountains, and yet *not* powerful enough to give them the victory over certain enemies in the valley who had a simple militaristic advantage...

> And the LORD was with Judah; and he drave out the inhabitants of the mountain; but could not drive out the inhabitants of the valley, because they had chariots of iron. (Judges 1:19)

The severely contorted mindset required of any scribe to make such a stupid statement is as amazing as the Grand Canyon itself! Imagine—the creator of the stars and planets was outdone by a few small chariots made of the iron ore that he himself created! Is there a Christian alive who would not poke fun at this verse if it were found in any other holy book?

Conclusion

This very small sample of biblical problems is all that is necessary to make us begin to question the integrity of what is considered an "inspired" Bible. In the following chapters, we will be considering other evidences of the non-inspirational nature of holy scripture.

CHAPTER 7
Against Inspiration - II

On the Nature of Biblical Contradictions

"Bible verses, like turtlenecks, go in and out of style."
- *Hanna Rosin*

"The voice of the Lord breaketh the cedars of Lebanon. He maketh them also to skip like a calf."
- *Psalm 29:5-6*

On The Nature of Contradictions

The reader should proceed with caution from this point onward, as we will be covering some very shifting ground. For as long as the Bible has been attacked by her astute critics, she has been ardently defended by inerrantists who maintain with solidarity that the Bible is the most accurate spiritual treatise ever written. Having hailed from the fundamentalist's camp, I speak from personal experience when I say that the hardest of all efforts for the skeptic is to get the believer to admit to a contradiction in their holy book when one is found. If not impossible, the task proves intensely difficult, and this shouldn't surprise us due to the fact that we are dealing with deeply cherished personal beliefs. We should expect the highest levels of resistance.

Strictly speaking, a contradiction should be easy to demonstrate. If, when reading an instruction manual on how to assemble a bookcase, I find two irreconcilable statements on where to place piece "J" on a structure, I have a fairly obvious contradiction. After reading it over, after getting several more mechanically inclined people than I to have a go at interpreting it, I at last resign to the fact that the problem of reconciling the two conflicting directions lies not with me, but with the instructions themselves. If I want further clarification, I can call the help number on the box, and if they will admit the contradiction when it is pointed out, then beyond any shadow of a credible doubt, a contradiction exists.

But unlike the kind person on the other end of the help line with regard to a simple matter like the assembling of a bookcase, inerrantist believers will not admit anything. In their eyes, the Bible is infallible. It cannot be otherwise. They have too much of themselves invested in it to readily admit its fallaciousness. So we unbelievers are facing not one, but two problems; the first is exhausting all possibilities in efforts to reasonably demonstrate the contradiction between two or more opposing passages of scripture. The second is getting the believer to admit it when they see it, and therein lies the more difficult of the two. We're not dealing with the assembly of some dead bookcase. We're dealing with time-honored beliefs, beliefs that won't easily be sacrificed.

Before I begin with the mechanics of contradictions, I must first explain why the justifications preachers and apologists use to explain away contradictions are taken to dishonest extremes. Utilizing the principles inerrantists use to keep the Bible from contradicting itself, there is not one holy book in the world wherein I can find a contradiction. The way apologists reason, contradictions are impossible to find.

When I was a preacher, I came to find myself playing games in scriptural debates. Early on, when someone approached me, trying to demonstrate a contradiction between two passages, I was anxious, even a little nervous to see the matter resolved with integrity. I prayed about it and studied it. I gave of myself to see that problem solved. But as the years progressed, this fervor was lost as I came to be satisfied with whatever Christian answer to a problem I could find. We had an answer for everything, and if an answer was available, if a reply could be made of *some* kind against an infidel's accusation, that was good enough, right? The trouble was, every Bible discrepancy dispute I ever had ended up with both parties leaving unconvinced of the other's position. It was no longer a search for truth, just a chess game where you have to make the right moves to counter a series of attacks. I was playing a game, not searching for truth anymore. Realizing that was a turning point.

As the years passed, I became suspicious, suspicious because as believers, my side had the most to lose in admitting a contradiction. But, of course, we never found one—at least not one we would admit to, and that was the problem. If a believer doesn't want a contradiction to exist, it won't!

As stated, the reasoning of apologists is failsafe. Let's take a random, non-religious example...

> At 4 pm each day, 12-year-old Mary S. Gaigos of Plymouth Rock, Michigan, loves to play with a large, red ball.

And...

> At 4 pm each day, 12-year-old Mary S. Gaigos of Plymouth Rock, Michigan, hates to play with a large, red ball.

Provided we can verify there aren't two Marys in this town, based on the wording of the sentences alone, I am ready to call this a contradiction. Most would say so. But if I'm an apologist, and I happen to have a vested emotional interest in not allowing these statements to collide, you can bet your bottom dollar they won't. For instance, if we want to tear this apart, we could be talking about two different balls Mary played with, one she loved and one she hated, but had to play with in a specialized therapy session. Little Mary could have loved one ball at one point in her twelfth year of life and grew to hate it at a later point. Then we could attack the wording of the sentence itself; the word "love" was perhaps mistranslated from another language and really meant something else, or we could say that one sentence is in another context and has a figurative or allegorical meaning. We could say one sentence is a code used by an army to throw off enemy intelligence forces in a time of war. We could say that one Mary was a fictional character from another story, and if we spent the rest of this chapter nailing down every conceivable detail in efforts to prove the statements contradictory, I could still opt for increasingly far-flung explanations rather than admit defeat. I can squirm and wiggle till I'm free, no matter the absurdities I leave in my wake. The contradiction will not be there if I don't want it to be, and by shifting details and looking for subtle loopholes, I have the sky as my limit in the number of ways at my disposal to pick and choose the easiest way out. This is how Christians are in their handling of Bible discrepancies.

In *Alleged Bible Contradictions Explained*, Church of Christ apologist James Dehoff says the appearance of biblical discrepancies are due to...

> *the nature of language; the nature of the mind; the nature of truths revealed; the nature of God; the corruption (or darkened, sinful hearts) of mankind; misinterpretations of the meanings of scriptures; differences of authorship; differences in the dates of passages; differences of objects in view; different principles and methods of arrangement; different modes of computation; man's misapprehension of the facts of history; man's ignorance; the Oriental custom of applying a plurality of names to the same person or object; the peculiarities of the Oriental idiom; use of the same word with different and sometimes opposite meanings; errors (scribal) in the manuscripts; the imagination of the critic.* (p. 26-41)

Now this is quite a comprehensive list! Whatever contradiction I or another infidel could cite would be explained under one of these headings, and it may indeed be that the answer to a given contradiction is available. It is possible for a contradiction to be apparent only and resolvable with some research. I myself will sometimes disagree with my freethinking friends on which passages are truly irreconcilable contradictions and which are not. But now the oil is applied to an already slippery slope; we can take any one of these categories for resolving contradictions and stretch them to fit any dilemma we want; we can explain discrepancies as originating from "the nature of the mind," "the nature of truths revealed," or "the corruption of mankind." These are catchall categories that are too big to serve a purpose. I could say, for instance, that the reason skeptics see contradictions in the Bible is because their hearts are too evil to reason correctly on a subject and that their minds are being controlled by demonic forces, or I can say that a certain subject is too theologically deep for man and that we shouldn't hold it up as a contradiction because "we don't have all the answers yet," or because without a certain esoteric religious experience, a passage can't be understood. The possibilities are endless. The point being: just because I can resolve two conflicting passages of scripture doesn't mean I should! If the believer is honest, he must be cautious not to take whatever options he has to smooth out a contradiction and force an answer to a problem to fit. Apologists are masters at doing this.

When the dust from the skirmish has settled, the only factor that determines the validity of a contradiction is self-honesty. My own discovery of biblical errors came about after years of studying and re-studying certain problematic passages of scripture, problems I thought I'd resolved, but came to see that I hadn't. After I got over thinking well of myself for coming up with answers to each one, I came to see how dishonest my answers were. In time, I was able to cut away from my inerrancy assumptions and look at the problems I had been pompously glossing over, now affording them a fresh investigation. This led to my eventual realization that these contradictions could not be resolved in an honest and legitimate fashion.

The contradictions I have selected below are, to me, some of the most clear-cut and easy to prove I could find, but as we have discussed, just because I can demonstrate their problematic nature does not mean that I will successfully demonstrate this *to every reader*. The issue at heart in discussing Bible contradictions is not whether a reply can be offered, but which reply is the most logical and most likely true. And so we begin.

I. Factual Contradictions

How Old Was Jehoiachin When He Began to Reign?
- 8 or 18 years old? -

> 2 Kings 24:8. "Jehoiachin was eighteen years old when he began to reign, and he reigned in Jerusalem three months. And his mother's name was Nehushta, the daughter of Elnathan of Jerusalem."

> Vs.

> 2 Chronicles 36:9. "Jehoiachin was eight years old when he began to reign, and he reigned three months and ten days in Jerusalem: and he did that which was evil in the sight of the Lord."

Contradictions of this nature are called scribal errors. They can almost never be traced back to their original source, and though they are not huge parts of the skeptic's arsenal against Biblicists, they nonetheless do demolish the belief that the Bible is God's word, handed down to man in a perfectly translated state. The Bible is littered with errors like the above; dates, ages, numbers, sentences, paragraphs, and fine details are omitted or conflict throughout. In a few cases in the New Testament, entire Bible passages are omitted from the earliest manuscripts—like Mark 16:9-20, John 7:53-8:11, Acts 8:37, and I John 5:7. These passages are in our Bibles, but were later additions to the text. None of these were written by a prophet or apostle.

Even modern translations are often found to still have them uncorrected. The original autographs of these texts no longer exist, making it impossible to go back to the source to determine whether or not the contradiction was originally with the "inspired" man's work or was introduced at a later time. However, we needn't concern ourselves with the task. The text of the Bible we have today is flawed and riddled with errors. God did not preserve his word for us, because the only way to do that would have been to translate accurately every copy of the original inspired word. What good do inspired autographs of the apostles and prophets do for us if they are not transmitted to us in the same perfect condition?

How Many Valiant Men Drew the Sword?
- 800,000 or 1,100,000 men? -

> 2 Samuel 24:9. "And Joab gave up the sum of the number of the people unto the king: and there were in Israel eight hundred thousand valiant men that drew the sword; and the men of Judah were five hundred thousand men."
>
> Vs.
>
> 1 Chronicles 21:5. "And Joab gave the sum of the number of the people unto David. And all they of Israel were a thousand thousand and an hundred thousand men that drew sword: and Judah was four hundred threescore and ten thousand men that drew sword."

The typical explanation for these verses is that the author of 1 Chronicles is just rounding off the number of soldiers. Using a little common sense, this is seen to be false; 800,000 is not rounded off to 1,100,000, but to 1,000,000. Why would an inspired writer round off 300,000 soldiers, anyway?

Did Asa Leave the High Places Intact or Remove Them?

I Kings 15:14. "But the high places were not removed: nevertheless Asa's heart was perfect with the Lord all his days."

Vs.

2 Chronicles 14:3. "For he took away the altars of the strange gods, and the high places, and brake down the images, and cut down the groves."

The high places were sanctuaries or places of pagan worship in the sides of hills and on mountaintops. To preserve secrecy, the people would flock to the high places to honor their respective pagan deities away from the public condemnation of Judaic monotheists. Here, we have one passage telling us Asa removed the high places and another telling us the opposite.

What do defenders of inerrancy give us in response to this? The justification is that II Chronicles 15:17 explains that these high places were not removed *in Israel only,* "But the high places were not taken away out of Israel." This is nothing more than a temporary "escape hatch." It is a totally unjustified "out" to take advantage of for the simple reason that Baasha ruled Israelite territory, not Asa—though Asa conquered and spiritually restored a few small cities of the Israelites (2 Chronicles 15:8). No one would have expected the high places to be removed by Asa in Israel. Asa was a king of Judah. The writer(s) of Chronicles merely inserted "out of Israel" (II Chronicles 15:17) to ease the discrepancy between the accounts of the books of Kings and Chronicles.

Think I'm making that up out of thin air? Notice how the writer of Kings has an obviously different take on another morally questionable king, Asa's son, Jehoshaphat. According to the Kings writer, Jehoshaphat, son of Asa, was a decently righteous king…

> I Kings 22:43, "In everything he walked in the ways of his father Asa and did not stray from them; he did what was right in the eyes of the LORD. **The high places, however, were not removed**, and the people continued to offer sacrifices and burn incense there."

But we have yet another contradiction, because according to the Chronicles writer, Jehoshaphat was virtually flawless…

> II Chronicles 17:6, "And his heart was lifted up in the ways of the LORD: **moreover he took away the high places and groves out of Judah.**

Strange similarity here! Again, we have a contradiction, the same contradiction concerning Jehoshaphat as with Asa—only this time without a convenient "escape hatch" for Biblicists to take advantage of. The writers of Kings and Chronicles had two different viewpoints on these two kings, which settles for us the question of the contradiction regarding Asa.

Did Jesus Command the Twelve to Take Staves or No Staves as They Preached?

> Mark 6:7-8. "And he called unto him the twelve, and began to send them forth by two and two; and gave them power over unclean spirits; And commanded them that they should take nothing for their journey, save a staff only; no scrip, no bread, no money in their purse."

> Matthew 10:7-10. "And as ye go, preach, saying, The kingdom of heaven is at hand. Heal the sick, cleanse the lepers, raise the dead, cast out devils: freely ye have received, freely give. Provide neither gold, nor silver, nor brass in your purses, Nor scrip for your journey, neither two coats, neither shoes, nor yet staves: for the workman is worthy of his meat."

> Vs.

> Luke 9:3. "He told them: "Take nothing for the journey–no staff, no bag, no bread, no money, no extra tunic." (NIV)

To be clear, Luke's words are actually more damning to Mark's than Matthew's, as the Greek of Luke 9:3 has Luke saying, "Do not take a staff" (singular). A casual reading of other translations bears this out...

> "And He said to them, Take nothing for [your] journey, neither a staff, nor a bag, nor bread, nor money; and do not [even] have two tunics apiece." (NASB)

> "And he said to them, Take nothing for your journey, no staff, nor bag, nor bread, nor money; and do not have two tunics." (RSV)

And many other translations back this up, leaving no doubt of there being a contradiction here. Mark has Jesus commanding to take a staff only. Luke clearly says not to! The minuscule nature of this contradiction does not render it useless, though I constantly get flack from Christians for mentioning it. Matthew (written later than Mark) has Jesus giving a point of instruction that is opposite of what Mark says Jesus said. The claim sometimes used by Christian apologists that

Matthew is commanding each person not to take more than one of each item is false except in the case of two coats.

Is it necessary for Jesus to tell the apostles that they should only carry one staff a piece? This would be a very silly lesson—it seems bizarre to imagine someone troubling themselves to carry two staves at any one time! Why would they take more than they need? The same problem shines out when we consider how "shoes" are listed here as well. Is Jesus telling his disciples not to take an extra pair of shoes (sandals), like today we have one pair of Adidas sneakers and another of Reeboks, and maybe a pair of cowboy boots? Certainly, he wasn't.

This was a time when not everyone had sandals. In many places, it was against the law for slaves to wear shoes. The disciples may or may not have all had shoes, so it seems Jesus was telling his disciples that they should not aim to take anything with them that they didn't already have. "The workman is worthy of his meat," the text says, meaning whatever they needed would be provided by whatever household received them. But why did Jesus instruct them to take a staff only in Mark? And why does Luke's account specifically mention for it not to be taken? The meaning of these verses is clear, but as it stands, the language creates a contradiction in Jesus' instructions, which makes us wonder if he really said these things at all.

In What City Did Josiah Die?

> 2 Chronicles 35:24. "His servants therefore took him out of that chariot, and put him in the second chariot that he had; and they brought him to Jerusalem, and he died, and was buried in one of the sepulchres of his fathers. And all Judah and Jerusalem mourned for Josiah."

Vs.

> 2 Kings 23:29-30. "In his days Pharaohnechoh king of Egypt went up against the king of Assyria to the river Euphrates: and king Josiah went against him; and he slew him at Megiddo, when he had seen him. And his servants carried him in a chariot dead from Megiddo, and brought him to Jerusalem, and buried him in his own sepulchre. And the people of the land took Jehoahaz the son of Josiah, and anointed him, and made him king in his father's stead."

There is a difference in dying at Jerusalem and dying at Megiddo, and if the only verses on this matter stated that Josiah died in Megiddo (or vice versa), we would be more than justified in assuming that he did, but instead, we have two conflicting texts. It will be argued that the more detailed account is that of 2 Kings, and that Josiah actually died at Jerusalem as stated in Chronicles, but the text refutes this; Pharaoh Nechoh slew him in Megiddo "when he had seen him" and he was carried in a chariot "dead from Megiddo." But "they brought him to Jerusalem and he died," the text in 2 Chronicles says, leaving no wiggle room for a justification.

These verses contain two contradictions. The second is whose sepulchre he died in, "one of the sepulchres of his fathers," or "his own sepulchre." The Bible contradicts itself twice here.

Who Provoked David to Number Israel and Judah?

> 2 Samuel 24:1. "And again the anger of the Lord was kindled against Israel, and he moved David against them to say, Go, number Israel and Judah."

> Vs.

> 1 Chronicles 21:1. "And Satan stood up against Israel, and provoked David to number Israel."

Who moved David against Israel? Well, it depends on which account you believe. "He" (God) moved David, and not Satan according to 2 Samuel 24:1, but "Satan stood up" and "provoked David," according to I Chronicles 21:1. Apologists cannot claim that God just "allowed" Satan to move David to provoke Israel. The texts are clear on the agency of the actions taken.

Was the Robe Christ Wore Before His Crucifixion Scarlet or Purple?

> Matthew 27:28. "And they stripped him, and put on him a scarlet robe."

> Vs.

> John 19:5. "Then came Jesus forth, wearing the crown of thorns, and the purple robe. And Pilate saith unto them, Behold the man!"

Scarlet: not the same as purple. Purple: not the same as scarlet. There are those who are happy to say that two garments are being discussed here. This is not a very defensible position. I can see someone saying that these two coats were the same, that Matthew, Mark, and John were different people who described things uniquely, but this does not reflect "inspired" writing. It reflects flawed, human testimony, and as we see here, serves as a point of discrepancy.

The gospel accounts in question were written by different authors, thus, increasing the likelihood that a slightly off detail was a genuine mistake. And then you must ask, would they put two different robes on a man about to be delivered up to die? That explanation just doesn't seem to jive to me, and the closeness in appearance between scarlet and purple also imply one robe. So when Matthew says, "They stripped him and put a scarlet robe on him." (Matt 27:28), and when Mark says, "They put a purple robe on him, then twisted together a crown of thorns and set it on him." (Mark 15:17), the fact that they each referred to one robe means that they were talking about one and the same item.

Did the Centurion or the Centurion's Servant Speak to Christ?

> Matthew 8:5-8. "5. And when Jesus was entered into Capernaum, there came unto him a centurion, beseeching him, 6. And saying, Lord, my servant lieth at home sick of the palsy, grievously tormented. 7. And Jesus saith unto him, I will come and heal him. 8. The centurion answered and said, Lord, I am not worthy that thou shouldest come under my roof: but speak the word only, and my servant shall be healed.

Vs.

> Luke 7:6-7. "6. Then Jesus went with them. And when he was now not far from the house, the centurion sent friends to him, saying unto him, Lord, trouble not thyself: for I am not worthy that thou shouldest enter under my roof: 7. Wherefore neither thought I myself worthy to come unto thee: but say in a word, and my servant shall be healed."

The place was the same (Matthew 8:5; Luke 7:2). Both texts are speaking of the same event, but the two accounts differ significantly, and agency is not the issue here, but accountability. It is possible for someone to go shopping through someone else. I can send someone to the store on my behalf, and it can be said that *I* bought a product that *they* bought for me, but this is not always possible. It cannot be said that I "came to the checkout counter" through agency, and that is the circumstance as presented by Matthew: "there came unto him a centurion, beseeching him." The language represents the event to be the centurion in person, whereas Luke's account speaks of him sending elders of the Jews to meet Jesus (Luke 7:3), and then more friends to speak on his behalf (Luke 7:6). These details are incompatible with Matthew's account.

In so many details of the gospel accounts, we find insurmountable differences between the stories told by each author. We have one as opposed to two demoniacs (Mark 5:9; Matthew 8:28), one angel at the tomb of Jesus instead of two (Matthew 28:1-7; Luke 24:4), and many other such differences. In every case, it is as though each gospel writer had no idea another would be chronicling the same events.

Was John the Baptizer the Elijah to Come?

> John 1:21. "And they asked him, What then? Art thou Elias? And he saith, I am not. Art thou that prophet? And he answered, No."

> Vs.

> John 17:12. "But I say unto you, That Elias is come already, and they knew him not, but have done unto him whatsoever they listed. Likewise shall also the Son of man suffer of them."

Predicted in Malachi 4:5-6 was the coming of The Elijah, a great prophet who was to come in the spirit and power of the original Elijah the Tishbite from the days of Ahab (I Kings 17:1). He would lead a great revival to prepare the world for the Jewish end times. John the baptizer does not fit this prophecy as alleged. The scope of his work was far too limited. The real Elijah would keep God's judgment from smiting the earth with a curse, implying his work had to be on a global scale, but John's work certainly wasn't.

The writer of John represented the matter truthfully. When asked if he was the Elijah to come, the baptizer replied "no," and yet Jesus himself identified him as that prophet. It would have been nice if the left hand knew what the right hand was doing.

How Did Judas Die?

> Matthew 27:5. "And he cast down the pieces of silver in the temple, and departed, and went and hanged himself."

> Vs.

> Acts 1:18. "Now this man purchased a field with the reward of iniquity; and falling headlong, he burst asunder in the midst, and all his bowels gushed out."

The justification for this contradiction is as humorous as it is unbelievable. We have to try and envision this situation as it is seen in the eyes of biblicists; Judas betrays Christ, and in overwhelming shame, throws the blood money down on the temple floor and runs out to the field the Jews would later purchase with the returned money (Matthew 27:3-8). On this field, Judas finds a tree and hangs himself, and as his body decomposes, and the rope suspending him comes lose or the branch breaks, he falls headlong, hitting the ground so hard that his innards burst out.

The phrase "straining to do some explaining" certainly applies here! The two verses were written by two different authors, and neither appears to be aware of what the other one had to say. Matthew says Judas hung himself, and Luke in Acts implies Judas was just walking around the field and suffered a fatal fall. Apologists try to harmonize this by saying Judas hung himself *and* suffered what would have been a fatal fall had he been alive! But the odds of Judas hanging himself and *then* "falling headlong" and becoming earth-splatter are amazingly small. If he hung himself and the rope broke, he would have had to have fallen a great distance for the body to re-position itself in mid-air so that the head hit the ground first. This is ridiculous, so we won't spend anymore time on it.

Did Mary Witness the Resurrection?

> Matthew 28:1-6. "1. In the end of the sabbath, as it began to dawn toward the first day of the week, came Mary Magdalene and the other Mary to see the sepulchre. 2. And, behold, there was a great earthquake: for the angel of the Lord descended from heaven, and came and rolled back the stone from the door, and sat upon it. 3. His countenance was like lightning, and his raiment white as snow: 4. And for fear of him the keepers did shake, and became as dead men. 5. And the angel answered and said unto the women, Fear not ye: for I know that ye seek Jesus, which was crucified. 6. He is not here: for he is risen, as he said. Come, see the place where the Lord lay."

Vs.

> John 20:2. "Then she runneth, and cometh to Simon Peter, and to the other disciple, whom Jesus loved, and saith unto them, They have taken away the LORD out of the sepulchre, and we know not where they have laid him."

Mary didn't know where Jesus was? That's awfully strange because according to Matthew, Mary went to the tomb and met an angel who announced Jesus' resurrection. How could she have run back to Peter and told he and John that she was unaware of what had happened to their Lord? Attempts to reconcile the gospel passion narratives have been endless, ranging from multiple trips to the tomb, to one of the trips occurring in a vision, but none of these attempts have come anywhere close to getting the accounts to speak in one voice.

If, as the apologists say, Matthew, Mark, and Luke's versions of the events is of a return trip to the tomb for Mary and the women, why would the angel say, "He is not here; he is risen; come and see the place where the Lord lay"? The angel should know that they had already been there. And why do other gospel accounts (Mark 16:1: Luke 24:1) have the women bringing the spices to anoint the body of Jesus? If John's gospel was the women's initial trip to the tomb, and they knew the body of Jesus was missing, why bring the spices?

Was Paul Guided by Inspiration as He Stood Before Ananias?

> Matthew 10:18-20. "18. And ye shall be brought before governors and kings for my sake, for a testimony against them and the Gentiles. 19. But when they deliver you up, take no thought how or what ye shall speak: for it shall be given you in that same hour what ye shall speak. 20. For it is not ye that speak, but the Spirit of your Father which speaketh in you."

> Vs.

> Acts 23:1-5. "1. And Paul, earnestly beholding the council, said, Men and brethren, I have lived in all good conscience before God until this day. 2. And the high priest Ananias commanded them that stood by him to smite him on the mouth. 3. Then said Paul unto him, God shall smite thee, thou whited wall: for sittest thou to judge me after the law, and commandest me to be smitten contrary to the law? 4. And they that stood by said, Revilest thou God's high priest? 5. Then said Paul, I wist (knew) not, brethren, that he was the high priest: for it is written, Thou shalt not speak evil of the ruler of thy people."

Here, we have the awkward situation where the apostle Paul admits he was wrong in speaking against the high priest. The Holy Spirit certainly did not come through for Paul here! He was not guided by God on what to say to Ananias. Had the Holy Spirit been divinely inspiring Paul's words as Jesus promised he would, Paul would not have made such a careless mistake. The apostle is before a ruler and has every opportunity to establish the word of God before his hearers. Yet, out of unguided human ignorance, he ruins the opportunity. If only Paul had been told by the Holy Spirit that he was facing a high priest, there would have been no problem here. What happened to the promise of being given the right words to say before rulers?

Commenting on Paul's little slip-up, J.W. McGarvey observes in his *New Testament Commentary on Acts of the Apostles*, p. 223-224...

> When told, however, that it was the high priest whom he had denounced, Paul at once admitted, not that the rebuke was unjust, but that it would have been improper to so address this dignitary, had he known who he was. And here is a proper distinction. A rebuke which is perfectly just and right in itself may be improper on account of the official relations of the person addressed. Had Paul known that Ananias was the high priest, and had he been left to himself without the guidance of the Holy Spirit promised for such occasions (Matt. X. 17-20), he would have withheld the rebuke; and the world would have been the loser; for rebukes like this help to strengthen the moral sense of men.

McGarvey was aware of the discrepancy here, but because of his skewed religious thinking, he got it backwards. It was not because of Paul's having divine guidance that screwed him up, but *not* having it. Like a sore thumb, this contradiction is hard to miss. It shows us that God did not do what he said he would do with those who spoke his word. This contradiction is a good example of just how the Bible writers let things slip into the text that they didn't realize could be so damning. This problem is a contradiction of a hallmark principle of apostleship—divine guidance!

A Mule...or Two?

> Matthew 21:2. "Saying unto them, Go into the village over against you, and straightway ye shall find an ass tied, and a colt with her: loose them, and bring them unto me."

> Vs.

> John 12:14. "And Jesus, when he had found a young ass, sat thereon; as it is written."

This is by far and away the most embarrassing contradiction in all of the Bible. The absurdity of it is inexcusable. One passage mentions two colts and the other gospel accounts (along with John) mention one, as they should (Mark 11:4; Luke 19:30). The quotation comes from Zechariah 9:9. The reason for this incongruence is Matthew's lack of knowledge of Hebrew parallelisms. A parallelism is the use of identical or similar syntactic constructions in certain clauses or phrases. Hebrew parallelisms are found throughout the Old Testament, but they are in place merely for rhythm and flow, and usually do not add anything to the meaning of a sentence. Zechariah 9:9 states...

> Rejoice greatly, O daughter of Zion; shout, O daughter of Jerusalem: behold, thy King cometh unto thee: he is just, and having salvation; lowly, and **riding upon an ass, and upon a colt the foal of an ass.**

Matthew mistakenly thought this to be referring to two animals, but even the average churchgoer might not make this mistake. When Solomon wrote, "These six things doth the LORD hate: yea, seven are an abomination unto him." (Proverbs 6:16), he used a parallelism. He did not mean six plus seven, just seven. When Joshua 13:24 declared, "And Moses gave inheritance unto the tribe of Gad, even unto the children of Gad according to their families.", this did not mean the tribe of Gad and the children of Gad are two different things. He is speaking of the same thing. These scriptures are Hebrew parallelisms, a thing clueless Matthew had no idea about, and as a result, an embarrassing error stands immortalized in scripture.

II. Chronological Contradictions

Coming or Going to Jericho?

> Luke 18:35, "And it came to pass, that as he was come nigh unto Jericho, a certain blind man sat by the way side begging."

> Vs.

> Mark 10:46, "And they came to Jericho: and as he went out of Jericho with his disciples and a great number of people, blind Bartimaeus, the son of Timaeus, sat by the highway side begging."

The context of the text in Luke makes it clear that the "blind man" was Bartimaeus mentioned in Mark. In one text, Jesus is coming out of Jericho, and in the other, he is approaching Jericho. Apologists think they are on safe ground saying that Jesus was leaving the old Jericho (the ruins from the time the city was conquered back in the days of Joshua), and entering the newer, populated Jericho. Only, we have to ask why, with the similarity that both texts exhibit in content, one text would be describing the ruins where few (if any) people would care to go?

In What Order was Christ Tempted?

> Matthew 4:5-11. "5. Then the devil taketh him up into the holy city, and setteth him on a pinnacle of the temple, 6. And saith unto him, If thou be the Son of God, cast thyself down: for it is written, He shall

give his angels charge concerning thee: and in their hands they shall bear thee up, lest at any time thou dash thy foot against a stone. 7. Jesus said unto him, It is written again, Thou shalt not tempt the Lord thy God. 8. Again, the devil taketh him up into an exceeding high mountain, and sheweth him all the kingdoms of the world, and the glory of them; 9. And saith unto him, All these things will I give thee, if thou wilt fall down and worship me. 10. Then saith Jesus unto him, Get thee hence, Satan: for it is written, Thou shalt worship the Lord thy God, and him only shalt thou serve. 11. Then the devil leaveth him, and, behold, angels came and ministered unto him."

Vs.

Luke 4:5-13. "5. And the devil, taking him up into an high mountain, shewed unto him all the kingdoms of the world in a moment of time. 6. And the devil said unto him, All this power will I give thee, and the glory of them: for that is delivered unto me; and to whomsoever I will I give it. 7. If thou therefore wilt worship me, all shall be thine. 8. And Jesus answered and said unto him, Get thee behind me, Satan: for it is written, Thou shalt worship the Lord thy God, and him only shalt thou serve. 9. And he brought him to Jerusalem, and set him on a pinnacle of the temple, and said unto him, If thou be the Son of God, cast thyself down from hence: 10. For it is written, He shall give his angels charge over thee, to keep thee: 11. And in their hands they shall bear thee up, lest at any time thou dash thy foot against a stone. 12. And Jesus answering said unto him, It is said, Thou shalt not tempt the Lord thy God. 13. And when the devil had ended all the temptation, he departed from him for a season."

If chronology in the gospels means anything, we must make an objection here. In Matthew, the second temptation is the taking of Jesus and setting him on a pinnacle of the temple, but Luke places this event last and the taking up of Jesus onto a high mountain, just after his refusal to turn stone into bread. In narratives, it shows a lack of credibility to mix up details between accounts. Even in those cases when the gospel writers don't exactly contradict each other, they create contradictions by presenting twisted testimonies that would easily be torn apart on cross examination in a court of law.

The same problem was presented with the cleansing of the temple. John places this event at the beginning of Jesus' ministry (John 2:11-16) while Matthew, Mark, and Luke have it towards the end (Matthew 21:12-13; Mark 11:15; Luke 19:29, 45-46). These important details cannot be swept aside.

When Was the Body of Jesus Prepared for Burial?

> Mark 16:1. "And when the sabbath was past, Mary Magdalene, and Mary the mother of James, and Salome, had bought sweet spices, that they might come and anoint him."
>
> Luke 23:54-56; 24:1. "54. And that day was the preparation, and the sabbath drew on. 55. And the women also, which came with him from Galilee, followed after, and beheld the sepulchre, and how his body was laid. 56. And they returned, and prepared spices and ointments; and rested the sabbath day according to the commandment...1. Now upon the first day of the week, very early in the morning, they came unto the sepulchre, bringing the spices which they had prepared, and certain others with them."

Vs.

> John 19:40-42. "40. Then took they the body of Jesus, and wound it in linen clothes with the spices, as the manner of the Jews is to bury. 41. Now in the place where he was crucified there was a garden; and in the garden a new sepulchre, wherein was never man yet laid. 42. There laid they Jesus therefore because of the Jews' preparation day; for the sepulchre was nigh at hand."

According to Mark and Luke (Matthew is silent on the spices), the women brought the customary spices with which to bury the body of Jesus, but according to John, the spices were already applied to the body before the Sabbath day.

When did Jesus Make Known his Crucifixion?

> Matt 10:38. "And he that taketh not his cross, and followeth after me, is not worthy of me."

Vs.

> Matthew 16:21,24. "21. From that time forth began Jesus to shew unto his disciples, how that he must go unto Jerusalem, and suffer many things of the elders and chief priests and scribes, and be killed, and be raised again the third day...24. Then said Jesus unto his disciples, If any man will come after me, let him deny himself, and take up his cross, and follow me."

In chapter ten, Jesus was addressing a multitude and spoke of taking up his cross and following him, inspiring the people to obedience. Then, in chapter sixteen (much later in Jesus' ministry), Matthew declares that Jesus began telling his disciples of his fate to die on the cross and be raised again on the third day. The only problem is, in Matthew 10, *no one would have understood what Jesus was saying when he spoke of taking up his cross!* The audience would have had no reference point to understand his speech because his impending crucifixion was not yet made public. How were they to make sense of what was said? Notice Matthew 10:38 is to be considered a quote from Jesus, and not just Matthew's own description of his message. This is an indication that Jesus didn't really make such a statement and that Matthew had Jesus "letting the cat out of the bag" too soon. This, of course, tells us that Matthew is not speaking the truth.

III. Principle Contradictions

To Swear or Not to Swear

> Matthew 5:34-37. "33. Again, ye have heard that it hath been said by them of old time, Thou shalt not forswear thyself, but shalt perform unto the Lord thine oaths: 34. But I say unto you, Swear not at all; neither by heaven; for it is God's throne: 35. Nor by the earth; for it is his footstool: neither by Jerusalem; for it is the city of the great King. 36. Neither shalt thou swear by thy head, because thou canst not make one hair white or black. 37. But let your communication be, Yea, yea; Nay, nay: for whatsoever is more than these cometh of evil. "swear not at all"
>
> James 5:12. "But above all things, my brethren, swear not, neither by heaven, neither by the earth, neither by any other oath: but let your yea be yea; and your nay, nay; lest ye fall into condemnation."
> Vs.
>
> Hebrews 6:13. "For when God made promise to Abraham, because he could swear by no greater, he sware by himself,
>
> Revelation 10:5-6. "5. And the angel which I saw stand upon the sea and upon the earth lifted up his hand to heaven, 6. And sware by him that liveth for ever and ever, who created heaven, and the things that therein are, and the earth, and the things that therein are, and the sea, and the things which are therein, that there should be time no longer."

The really funny thing about this is not that God said not to swear and then directly contradicted himself, but that God would bother to swear. When someone swears, it is done in circumstances where he or she must answer to higher powers, but since there is no higher power than God, it seems a little strange for God to find the need to swear to lesser beings, especially when he gave us his word on the matter; "Let yeah be yeah and no be no, for whatsoever is more than these cometh of evil." When someone swears, they are professing with rigor that the words in their oath are more important than other words they use. For God or a heavenly messenger to swear is to principally contradict Jesus' and James' words because swearing entails some words being of greater truth than others.

God's Esteem of the Handicapped

> Luke 14:21-23. "21. So that servant came, and shewed his lord these things. Then the master of the house being angry said to his servant, Go out quickly into the streets and lanes of the city, and bring in hither the poor, and the maimed, and the halt, and the blind. 22. And the servant said, Lord, it is done as thou hast commanded, and yet there is room. 23. And the lord said unto the servant, Go out into the highways and hedges, and compel them to come in, that my house may be filled."

> Vs.

> Leviticus 21:17-21. "17. Speak unto Aaron, saying, Whosoever he be of thy seed in their generations that hath any blemish, let him not approach to offer the bread of his God. 18. For whatsoever man he be that hath a blemish, he shall not approach: a blind man, or a lame, or he that hath a flat nose, or any thing superfluous, 19. Or a man that is brokenfooted, or brokenhanded, 20. Or crookbackt, or a dwarf, or that hath a blemish in his eye, or be scurvy, or scabbed, or hath his stones broken; 21. No man that hath a blemish of the seed of Aaron the priest shall come nigh to offer the offerings of the LORD made by fire: he hath a blemish; he shall not come nigh to offer the bread of his God."

Here, we have none other than a principle change in God's esteem of the unfortunate "blemished" ones in his presence between the Old and New Testaments. Why the change in outlook on the part of the almighty in the New Testament?

If the text in Leviticus had read something to the affect of, "Speak unto Aaron, saying, 'Welcome the blemished and the blind and the lame...because I am a God who regards the lowly,'" Christians would be holding this up as proof-positive that Jesus and Jehovah are the same God. It would be quoted and regularly used to bolster the claim of the Bible's unity, much like believers try to use so-called Old Testament "prophecies" and apply them to Christ. But no passage in the Old Testament affirms such, so this text in Leviticus is given a lower ranking with believers today as a mere Old Testament regulation, teaching how "holy" God is to command the blemished to keep away from Him.

God was too holy, but now Jesus has a different attitude. He welcomes all, he heals the sick, and adopts such an openly humanitarian position. If such a historical figure existed, no wonder the Jews rejected him! The God of the Jews was a heartless God – one that did not take kindly to imperfections – even though (sadly) God himself created them that way...

> Who hath made man's mouth? or who maketh the dumb, or deaf, or the seeing, or the blind? have not I the LORD? (Exodus 4:11)

If it is, as theists say, and God is teaching holiness in the Leviticus passage, why did Jehovah have to include the handicapped? Could he not have maintained his holiness and pure prowess by simply commanding pure sacrifices, dietary laws, and otherwise strict prohibitions while still having a special place for the "blemished," as Jesus would later do in the New Testament? If the Bible is one unified work, guided and written by one unified God, I would think so. And if all men are condemned under the law and "not good enough" for God, then why did Jehovah need to go that extra step by forbidding those with blemishes from making offerings before him? There was simply no need for this...unless, of course, the God of Judaism purposely considered the blemished a stain on his white carpet. So it is safe to conclude that the God of the Old Covenant felt very differently about the blemished than does the one of the New. God wanted only the finest to go before him, and he is telling us in Leviticus that he considers people with blemishes unworthy of this role. The God of the New Testament made no such distinction, but welcomes all. I thought God didn't change?

Should We Put Away our Swords or Go and Buy One More?

> Matthew 26:52. "Then said Jesus unto him, Put up again thy sword into his place: for all they that take the sword shall perish with the sword."

> Vs.

> Luke 22:36. "Then said he unto them, But now, he that hath a purse, let him take it, and likewise his scrip: and he that hath no sword, let him sell his garment, and buy one."

Peter gets ready to defend Jesus. He takes out his sword and slashes off the ear of the high priest's servant. Jesus says no. Why does Jesus tell Peter no? Obviously, Jesus wants Peter to understand that the salvation of all the world is at stake, and that the act of his death on the cross must commence, and so logically, Jesus instructs Peter to put away his sword. Then he tells Peter that those who live by the sword will die by the sword. No problems here. In Luke's account, however, he seems to be changing his tune a little.

Why would Jesus command his apostles to buy swords? I thought those who live by the sword will die by the sword? Is Jesus telling the disciples to buy swords to defend against wild animals when fleeing from Jerusalem in the great siege of C.E. 70? Maybe Jesus is teaching militia action, like the radical anti-government groups of today suggest, or maybe Jesus is telling the church to resist persecution by the sword? Maybe Jesus is secretly teaching lessons on self-defense and gun control for when these issues would pop up in later centuries? I have heard all of these positions espoused by Christians over the years.

All of these fanciful and silly explanations fail; the idea of Jesus telling his disciples to get weapons to fend off wild animals is silly. That Jesus is teaching action against government is self-refuting. Jesus had every opportunity to rebel against his government, but he never did, nor do we have record of such incidents anywhere in religious traditional stories, much less secular history. Finally, if Jesus was teaching his believers self-defense, then we have another problem. Jesus could have defended himself when being attacked by his persecutors and never did. Instead, he chose to run away from those who tried to stone him (John 10:39). The disciples or church fathers never made note of such lessons, and the Bible denies this position. James 4:6 says, "Ye have condemned and killed the just; *and he doth not resist you.*" James says the Christian man does not resist violence with violence. (John 18:36) So we are left to conclude that Jesus taught passivism and diligently lived it according to one gospel, but contradicted this message in another.

No Graven Images of any Kind or No Graven Images Except Cherubims?

> Exodus 20:4. "Thou shalt not make unto thee any graven image, or any likeness of any thing that is in heaven above, or that is in the earth beneath, or that is in the water under the earth:"
> Vs.
>
> Exodus 25:18. "And thou shalt make two cherubims of gold, of beaten work shalt thou make them, in the two ends of the mercy seat."

Anyone who understands how monumental the stumblingblock of idolatry was for ancient Israel will see the seriousness of the diametrically opposing command from Exodus 25 to build carvings of worshipping angels (called Cherubims). The Israelites were instructed specifically not to build anything of a religious nature that resembled any item. This included icons, symbols, and any material creations whatsoever of spiritual significance. The most novice Bible student need only read through the Old Testament to observe on every other page instances when the Israelites fell into and out of idolatrous stints. With a people so easily led into repeated betrayals of God, how could they have been commanded to build two images of angels without violating this commandment?

If you find my criticism here unjust, consider the grievous error God caused in a similar circumstance. Moses was commanded by God to create an image in the form of a brass serpent. In Numbers 21:1-9, we learn that because of their constant bickering and murmuring, God struck the Israelites with biting "fiery serpents," and when the people turned back to God and wanted to live, the brazen serpent, if looked upon, would give life to the dying. Jesus used this idol as a comparison of himself (John 3:14). But God should have healed them some other way, because this caused immense trouble. In 2 Kings 18:4, we learn that righteous Hezekiah destroyed the brazen serpent Moses made because the people began to worship it. One would think that an all-wise creator would have had the foresight not to allow his people to be led into idolatry by his own commandments and ways of deliverance.

Do the Sins of the Father Pass to the Son?

> Exodus 20:5. "Thou shalt not bow down thyself to them, nor serve them: for I the LORD thy God am a jealous God, visiting the iniquity of the fathers upon the children unto the third and fourth generation of them that hate me;"

> Exodus 17:14-16. "14. And the LORD said unto Moses, Write this for a memorial in a book, and rehearse it in the ears of Joshua: for I will utterly put out the remembrance of Amalek from under heaven. 15. And Moses built an altar, and called the name of it Jehovahnissi: 16. For he said, Because the LORD hath sworn that the LORD will have war with Amalek from generation to generation."

> Vs.

> Deuteronomy 24:16. "The fathers shall not be put to death for the children, neither shall the children be put to death for the fathers: every man shall be put to death for his own sin."

> Ezekiel 18:20. "The soul that sinneth, it shall die. The son shall not bear the iniquity of the father, neither shall the father bear the iniquity

of the son: the righteousness of the righteous shall be upon him, and the wickedness of the wicked shall be upon him."

Colossians 3:25. "But he that doeth wrong shall receive for the wrong which he hath done: and there is no respect of persons."

There is not a bigger contradiction anywhere in scripture than right here. On the one hand, we get the biblical picture of a just deity, a deity who renders to every man as he or she deserves, but on the other, we behold a wroth and vengeful being, an entity that can become so angry that he punishes your descendants for your sins unto the third and fourth generations. On their departure from the land of Egypt, the Amalekites attack Israel. God gets so mad about it that he swears with an oath that a state of war between the Israelites and the Amalekites would be unending until Amalek is no more.

To think that your life may be calamitous because of a sin your grandfather committed is manifestly not right. To support waging war with a people because of sins of previous generations is atrocious. Only a fiend holds individuals or nations accountable for wrongs they aren't personally responsible for. When people do this today, this is called a hate crime. To punish someone for what someone else did or what someone's race did is a moral travesty. The concept of original sin is one such travesty, an application of this treacherous principle. You and I supposedly face death because long ago the first parents of our race made God mad, and he's going to punish not just them, but you and everyone else in the world for it. Tribal war-gods have always operated this way, and even today, we have armies of citizens from every country in the world who will defend to the death a book that teaches these principles.

How do believers reply to this? By splitting up the *consequences of sin* and the *guilt of sin*. God might punish "to the third and fourth generation" a woman who drinks alcohol by sending her to Hell (the guilt of sin), and he might punish her child with fetal alcohol syndrome (the consequences of her sin without the guilt). Preachers will give similar examples, but they are all for naught and are meaningless. Any "consequences of sin" always emanate as natural results of physical abuses or disasters, and as such, it is needless to attribute them to a deity. This distinction then is merely a wordplay on the part of theists. Either God unleashes judgment on a person or a nation, or he doesn't; if he does, he holds them guilty, and if not, they are blameless.

In the case of Amalek, the judgment was direct, and all the children of Amalek were targeted for extinction. In Genesis 9:25, when Noah awoke from a night of lying naked and drunken on the floor of his tent, having been disrespectfully stared upon by Ham, he put a curse not on Ham directly, but on his grandson, Canaan (Genesis 10:6). It is little wonder that white supremacist groups – and before them – devout Christian slave owners for hundreds of years have used these verses in support of slavery. Going around talking about curses today will make some people want to lock you up. However, the God of the Bible not only spoke about curses, but was a big proponent of using them in a wide range of situations—including punishing adulterous women by causing their thighs to rot and their bellies to swell (Numbers 5:1-27).

Before we leave these verses, we must address another problem for Christians that these verses bring up; that problem is the crucifixion of Jesus. The concept of a "perfect sacrifice," a human sacrifice to forgive the sins of all mankind, is a belief not found anywhere in the Old Testament scriptures. Ezekiel 18:20 and Deuteronomy 24:16 do not allow for one person to bear the sins of others. A sin-bearing savior only accents this contradiction further.

The idea that "without shedding of blood is no remission" (Hebrews 9:22) is false and a manipulation of Leviticus 17:11; "for the life of the flesh is in the blood: and I have given it to you upon the altar to make an atonement for your souls: for it is the blood that maketh an atonement for the soul." Leviticus 17 was intended to instruct God's people not to eat blood. In so doing, we are told the purpose for blood; it is to make atonement, not for anything else, but this is not to say that *only* blood makes atonement. Under Jewish law, a sacrifice was just one way to atone for unintentional sins (Leviticus 4; 16). David was forgiven of his sins in the Bathsheba affair without a sacrifice…

> And David said unto Nathan, I have sinned against the LORD. And Nathan said unto David, The LORD also hath put away thy sin; thou shalt not die. (2 Samuel 12:13)

The prophets spoke of those times when the Jewish people would be without a sacrifice (Hosea 3:3-4), and what would they offer to God during these times?

> Take with you words, and turn to the LORD: say unto him, Take away all iniquity, and receive us graciously: so will we render the calves of our lips. (Hosea 14:2)

In place of calves sacrificed on the alter, the "calves" of the lips (praise) would be given to God. Forgiveness of sins could be achieved without bloodshed. It will surprise many to learn that of all the sacrifices in Exodus and Leviticus, only a few are for sin. A sacrifice was to be done out of closeness to God (Psalm 66:15-16), which is why the prophets often renounced oblations (I Samuel 15:22; Psalm 40:6; 51:17). A sacrifice was to follow an unintentional sin. A sacrifice meant nothing when rebellion was involved. In that case, repentance was the atoning grace (Ezekiel 18:21-23). When a sacrifice was carried out for sins, the message was to be considered one of love; the animal was killed out of God's mercy for the human, but this was never to be associated with the pagan idea of vicarious atonement.

In upcoming chapters, we will see more graphically the incompatible natures between the Old and New Testaments. In this chapter, we have seen only a handful of discrepancies from the Bible, and with these alone, we have seen glaring glitches that men have spent centuries trying to resolve to no avail. But I have no doubt that this ongoing denial of what should be obvious will abide still.

Chapter 8
Against Inspiration – III

The Morality of the God of the Bible

"How blessed is harmlessness towards all, and self-restraint towards living things."
- *Buddha*

"I love this God fellow. He's so deliciously evil."
- *Stewie Griffin*

What we find when considering the morality of the God of the Bible is that his character is indistinguishable from the character of contemporary gods of the time, and this invariably factors into our estimation of his worthiness of worship and Godhood. As with humans, we judge the gods based on their conduct.

Comparing the Gods

A great number of things have always stood out when comparing the gods of antiquity; they are vicious and cruel, demanding bloody sacrifices and inhumane punishments for the littlest offenses; they are all pro-segregation in the national sense; that is, they exalt the ways of their own customs and laws and are always at odds with other gods and their tribes and lands; they are all unwavering in their conviction that their own elect will triumph over all others. Some shades are darker than others, but the sketches are pretty much the same.

How Far We've Come

Progress has been made. As a people, we have abolished slavery in all but a few small portions of the world. We have brought to a slow drift male and female forms of genital mutilation. We have risen to promote the rights of women, and we have more recently come to understand and fight for civil rights and personhood across the racial board. We have thrown away theocracies and fascist faith-based regimes for democracies. We have tossed out the drivel from the hungry mouths of greedy religious men and their terrorizing tribunals. We awake each day to enjoy lives of relative tranquility and intellectual freedom with fewer restraints from our pious past.

Progress has been made, but progress is still to be made. We are fighting the tides of the spiritual opposition, of those who seek to bring mankind back to the adoration of a book that would have us follow bronze age ethics in service to a being who, like contemporary gods and goddesses of the time, were always fighting, fighting and killing, and demanding that everyone else do the same.

Many are unaware that these highly disturbing passages are in their Bibles. They can quote John 3:16 and perhaps Matthew 16:18, but not the verses we are about to study. It is reasonable to conclude that any deity who inspired the writing and recording of such events is a deity nobody needs.

The Merciless Slaughter of the Midianites

> Num. 31:15-18. "15. And Moses said unto them, Have ye saved all the women alive? 16. Behold, these caused the children of Israel, through the counsel of Balaam, to commit trespass against the Lord in the matter of Peor, and there was a plague among the congregation of the Lord. 17. Now therefore kill every male among the little ones, and kill every woman that hath known man by lying with him. 18. But all the women children, that have not known a man by lying with him, keep alive for yourselves."

The tragedy of having this staring back at us from the pages of the Bible is unspeakable for two reasons; first, the vile nature of the words you have just read and the atrocity of this act speaks for itself; and secondly, the writer of Numbers had no sense of moral outrage that many of us feel when we read it. This was just everyday life in a primitive society. It was no different from seeing the police arrest a shoplifter at the mall. It wasn't big news. But it is certainly big news today. Why? Because the moral climate of the world has changed drastically. Much of what was acceptable in the year 1707 is not acceptable in the year 2007, and much more so four thousand years back. Times have changed. Morality has changed, and defenders of the inspiration of the Bible find themselves hard-pressed to give a rational answer for why their "loving God" condoned such horrific behavior.

Justifications for this conduct have ranged from absurd to insulting, as we shall see below (points a-d). I wrote a series of articles on this very topic as a minister entitled "God's Morality and the Case of the Midianites," in which I attempted to answer infidel objections on the issue. I quote from part two of that article series, summing up these so-called justifications...

> *God gave life and can take it for whatever reason...The Midianites were sinners and God had to stop them from their continual sinning against him because Jehovah was righteous, and because he didn't want their young ones to grow up and become accountable to sin and go to hell, so in killing them, he was having mercy on their souls...By ordering the execution of the children through Moses, God was ensuring no revenge killings against his people in later years.*

(a) "God gave life and can take it for whatever reason": This is a nice dodge of the moral issue at hand. The fact that God can take life and bring the drama of death to an individual or group does not mean he needed to. Options other than execution were at his disposal. For God to "pull rank" and justify his butchering merely because he can is still ruthless and unjustifiable.

All throughout the conquests of the promised land, the Israelites were called upon to have no mercy on the pagans they would uproot along the road to the new home...

> And when the LORD thy God shall deliver them before thee; thou shalt smite them, and utterly destroy them; thou shalt make no covenant with them, nor shew mercy unto them. (Deuteronomy 7:2)

It would have been much more humane for an omnipotent God to providentially remove the pagans from the land and relocate them. A mass migration of God's enemies to a far away land would be a small thing to an almighty being, and yet true to form, Yahweh took the more bloody path.

(b) "The Midianites were sinners and God had to stop them from their continual sinning against him because Jehovah was righteous.": This explanation doesn't go far enough. The Midianites were only one pagan people who lived in that area; why not massacre all sinful peoples? But God only commanded the massacre of those nations that stood in the way of Israel. If God was mad about "sin" being in the lives of unbelievers, this anger wouldn't have been limited to only the Midianites. And the context of Numbers chapter eighteen tells us why God commanded this bloodshed—because the people of Midian had caused Israel to sin (Numbers 31:3). This battle was not about sin or the "cleansing" of unrighteousness, but about a spiritual vendetta, about payback!

It is true that Midian, like many contemporary pagan religions, practiced child sacrifices and bloody, sadistic rituals, but these were extremely common in the old Gentile world (and very often, in the Israelite world as well. See Genesis 22; Judges 11:29-40; Exodus 22:29-30; Numbers 31:40). Though despicable by modern standards, the non-Jewish societies of the time had their own means of preserving order—much the same way priestly tribal clans known for their brutality still exist in our time.

(c) "God didn't want their young ones to grow up and become accountable to sin and go to Hell.": According to Christians, the adults were already grown and thus already corrupted by a mature knowledge of sin, but the young ones were still impressionable and "innocent" without a knowledge of sin. So God wanted to get rid of the evildoers but save young souls to give them a chance at life. If this was the case, why were only the young girls spared and not the boys? The reason is simple; the virgin women offered the pillaging soldiers something the men couldn't!

(d) *"By ordering the execution of the children through Moses, God was ensuring no revenge killings against his people in later years."*: If this was true, then Moses should have ordered the girls executed too. What was to ensure that they would not remember the murder of their parents and conceive of a way to settle the score in future years? Remember, it was women alone who caused Solomon to sin by building idol temples to false gods, and this undoing was ultimately responsible for ripping God's united kingdom in half (I Kings 11:1-43). If it was the safety and wellbeing of Israel they were after, no one should have been spared, as was intended in the Amalekite slaughter...

> Now go and smite Amalek, and utterly destroy all that they have, and spare them not; but slay both man and woman, infant and suckling, ox and sheep, camel and ass. (I Samuel 15:3)

I look back and shudder at my attempts to justify such heinous and barbaric conduct. The motivation for the killing, the mindset behind it is clear, but perhaps this is not enough to enable us to understand the horror of this occasion; twelve thousand Israelites lead a bloody tirade, killing many. By this time, the Israelites were not new to the taking of lives. The bloodshed gets old, and the techniques of execution become sloppier with every new kill. Every time a rusty, Bronze Age sword is thrust – like the puncturing of a butter knife through a ripe tomato – into a pregnant woman's womb, or the unscarred abdomen of a kindergarten-aged child, the pain is greater, the death is slower. Teeth can be seen, chattering jaws, mouths wide open with screams. The grabbing of stomachs, rolling around on a sandy earth, the blood is quickly absorbed into the sand, but it takes hours to die. Families covered in red, huddled around each other, screams quieting, voices calling out for help begin to fade. Soon, all is silent.

Slavery and Cruelty

> Exodus 21:20-21. "20. And if a man smite his servant, or his maid, with a rod, and he die under his hand; he shall be surely punished. 21. Notwithstanding, if he continue a day or two, he shall not be punished: for he is his money."

"He is his money." Those are the words from this text that really stick in my head, but the NIV might be a little clearer here...

> 20. If a man beats his male or female slave with a rod and the slave dies as a direct result, he must be punished, 21. but he is not to be

punished if the slave gets up after a day or two, since the slave is his property.

We are told by believers that the Bible stands opposed to slavery, that God merely regulated it when it was a vital part of the world's economy, that is was just indentured servitude, a type of willful employment on the part of the slave. These claims are all laid to rest with this one verse. Not only is slavery advocated and approved of here by the almighty, but not a single negative word against cruelty of a human being is uttered. In fact, according to these verses, a slave is not a human being, for "he is his money."

Vindictive and Vulgar

> Numbers 25:3-4. "3. And Israel joined himself unto Baalpeor: and the anger of the Lord was kindled against Israel. 4. And the Lord said unto Moses, Take all the heads of the people, and hang them up before the Lord against the sun, that the fierce anger of the Lord may be turned away from Israel."

From this we get the impression that the Lord had to actually *see* the hanging, decapitated heads so that his anger could be appeased, just like the rest of the tribal war-gods of the time. Vile doesn't quite describe this; depravedly boorish is more like it.

Unrelenting Barbarism

> And David commanded his young men, and they slew them, and cut off their hands and their feet, and hanged them up over the pool in Hebron. But they took the head of Ishbosheth, and buried it in the sepulchre of Abner in Hebron. (2 Samuel 4:12)

Can you imagine seeing a sight like this in your neighborhood? Can you picture coming out to sit by the pool of Hebron, only to find two handless and footless, bled-out bodies hanging above it? The horror, the grotesque sickness of this scene is something to contend with.

> Wherefore David arose and went, he and his men, and slew of the Philistines two hundred men; and David brought their foreskins, and they gave them in full tale to the king, that he might be the king's son in law. And Saul gave him Michal his daughter to wife. (I Samuel 18:27)

The mutilating practice of circumcision has caused it's share of debate among medical professionals, but this sick obsession with taking the foreskins of enemies has to be unhealthy in and of itself.

Child Abuse

> 23. And he went up from thence unto Bethel: and as he was going up by the way, there came forth little children out of the city, and mocked him, and said unto him, Go up, thou bald head; go up, thou bald head. 24. And he turned back, and looked on them, and cursed them in the name of the Lord. And there came forth two she bears out of the wood, and tare forty and two children of them. (2 Kings 2:23-24)

God's ego was so bruised that he decided to kill children to preserve the honor of his prophet. The word translated "children" is "yeled," a Hebrew word used 75 times in the Hebrew Bible to denote babies or young children. The same word is used of baby Ishmael (Genesis 21:8-16) and baby Moses (Exodus 2:3), and a pregnant woman's child (Exodus 21:2). Efforts are made by apologists to make the word for "children" to mean "young men," teenagers—as though this somehow lessens the horrible nature of the verses. But what would young men find funny about a bald man to the extent that they mock him publicly? This is something small children would do, and thus, it shows the ferocious nature of the God of the Bible to unleash his fury over such an ego-driven reason.

While it is true that the word used here can refer to teenagers, as well as small children, note that two bears tore these children to bits. Two bears might well tear apart 42 young children, but 42 teenagers would be a different matter. 42 young men who grew up hunting and living in the wild as people did back then would not be overcome by a mere two bears. Elsewhere in the scriptures, God shows that he is not beyond commanding the ravaging of children (Genesis 22:2; Numbers 31:15-18; I Samuel 15:3; Isaiah 13:16), so why is it so hard to believe that in 2 Kings God sent two she-bears to kill young children?

Torture

> And he brought forth the people that were therein, and put them under saws, and under harrows of iron, and under axes of iron, and made them pass through the brickkiln: and thus did he unto all the cities of the children of Ammon. So David and all the people returned unto Jerusalem. (2 Samuel 12:31)

> And he brought out the people that were in it, and cut them with saws, and with harrows of iron, and with axes. Even so dealt David with all the cities of the children of Ammon. And David and all the people returned to Jerusalem. (I Chronicles 20:3)

If the verse from Samuel wasn't clear enough, the Chronicles passage clarifies for us that this was not forced labor, but torture. If ever there was a barbaric individual, it was king David. Saul made an earlier effort to eradicate the Ammonites (I Samuel 11:11). David made sure he finished the job. The children of Ammon did not return with David to Jerusalem.

Animal Cruelty

> And David took from him a thousand chariots, and seven hundred horsemen, and twenty thousand footmen: and David houghed [humstrung] all the chariot horses, but reserved of them for an hundred chariots. (2 Samuel 8:4)

As righteous as David was said to be, it's no wonder that even God found his hands too bloody to build his house (I Chronicles 22:8), and decreed that Solomon was to be the one to build the temple instead. The irony is that the God of the Bible himself was the one to command the mass killings of others, and was guilty of shedding a million times as much blood by taking an innumerable quantity of lives up to that time. But true to his reputation, Solomon was wise and even humane when it came to animals...

> A righteous man regardeth the life of his beast: but the tender mercies of the wicked are cruel. (Proverbs 12:10)

Apparently, David did not share this conviction, but instead of releasing the remainder of the horses, he had them hamstrung (cut the sinew in the back legs virtually incapacitating them of movement). God warned against Israel having too many horses...

> But he shall not multiply horses to himself, nor cause the people to return to Egypt, to the end that he should multiply horses: forasmuch as the LORD hath said unto you, Ye shall henceforth return no more that way. (Deuteronomy 17:16)

Why the Israelites could not have released these animals into the wild or sold them to neighboring nations or traveling merchants we are not told. But the cruelty of this act is unjustifiable and a terrible waste.

Merciless

> And the other ten thousand left alive did the children of Judah carry away captive, and brought them unto the top of the rock, and cast them down from the top of the rock, that they were all broken in pieces. (2 Chronicles 25:12)

The terror in their eyes, the desperate wrestling, begging for their lives, offering to be slaves, saying anything to escape certain death, only to be forced to the edge, and then over it to a traumatizing death on the rocks below. Such horror, and yet this is recorded like any other story in the Bible.

Terrorism

> So the LORD sent a pestilence upon Israel from the morning even to the time appointed: and there died of the people from Dan even to Beersheba seventy thousand men. (2 Samuel 24:15)

God sends a plague, and this plague kills seventy thousand men. Why does God send this plague? Because one man (David) sinned (2 Samuel 24:9-10). Instead of requiring David to pay the penalty for himself, God chose another route. Like a hostage-taker from Beirut, God turned the gun on all his people and made them pay the price.

Injustice

> 20. But if...the tokens of virginity be not found for the damsel: 21. Then they shall bring out the damsel to the door of her father's house, and the men of her city shall stone her with stones that she die: because she hath wrought folly in Israel, to play the whore in her father's house: so shalt thou put evil away from among you. (Deuteronomy 22:20-21)

It sickens my stomach to think of all the innocent women and girls through the centuries who have died because of this atrociously chauvinistic injunction. God put his personal stamp of approval on punishing women with death for promiscuity—when in many cases, there was no promiscuity! The awful seeds of this commandment are still sprouting up bad fruits today, as countless women in the wasteland of the Middle East are having acid thrown in their faces and being set on fire for "becoming like the West."

The Conclusion

In studying the morality of the God of the Bible, what do we find? We find that the God of the Abrahamic religions is a perfect moral copy of other gods and peoples of the time. The examples set before us (among many others that could have been mentioned) tell us much about God's character. As Robert Heinlein put it, "Man rarely (if ever) managed to dream up a god superior to themselves. Most gods have the manners and morals of a spoiled child."

We would never dream of applying these morals today, and it's as though these passages weren't even in the Bible. They are ignored, and what is focused on instead of them are passages like John 3:16 and Romans 10:9-10. Believers tell us we are being unfair by holding ancient Israel to the moral standards of the twenty first century, but this is exactly why we are not being unfair—a God of higher virtue and superior knowledge, a God of perfect moral values can only be expected to guide and direct his people perfectly. And what do we find instead of this moral excellence? Cruelty, murder, debauchery, genocide, and insanity. Robert Ingersoll declared, "The Bible is not a moral guide. Any man who follows faithfully all its teachings is an enemy of society and will probably end his days in a prison or an asylum."

CHAPTER 9
Earth in the Scriptures

What the Bible Really Teaches About Our Planet

"All truth passes through three stages. First, it is ridiculed. Second, it is violently opposed. Third, it is accepted as being self-evident."
- Arthur Schopenhauer

"There is talk of a certain new astronomer who wants to prove that the earth moves and goes around instead of the sky, the sun, and the moon, just as if somebody were moving in a carriage or ship. The fool wants to turn the whole art of astronomy upside-down. However, as Holy Scripture tells us, Joshua bid the sun to stand still and not the earth."
- Martin Luther

Flat Earth

A theologian once said to me, "If God can't get it right on the age of the earth and the facts about earth, how can we trust him when it comes to our salvation?" I may not be religious anymore, but I'll say "amen" to that. Sadly, the majority of Bible believers are ignorant of the fact that the Bible just doesn't pass as a science book. In fact, it flunks like few students could. If the uninformed people of America knew what it really teaches about our planet, they would slam it shut and never crack it open again. I Samuel 2:8 says...

> He raiseth up the poor out of the dust, and lifteth up the beggar from the dunghill, to set them among princes, and to make them inherit the throne of glory: **for the pillars of the earth are the LORD's, and he hath set the world upon them.**

If you are a reader seeing this verse for the first time, you are probably shocked by it. I know I was. These were Hanna's words in a prayer to God, and we are told by apologists today, were a "figurative" reflection of the glory of God. The text seems to speak for itself, however. God set the earth upon pillars and this verse is not alone in saying so. Job 9:6 says...

> Which shaketh the earth out of her place, and **the pillars thereof tremble.**

Figurative? It is hard to see this as a figurative passage when this was exactly what the primitives believed back then concerning our earth. Were I to say, "The foundations of the building shook," or "the roots of the tree shook," only a literal interpretation would allow the sayings to make sense. The pillars of the earth might shake in some figurative sense, but pillars of the earth shaking would make no sense and could be figurative of nothing if the writer of Job didn't believe our planet to have pillars. The Bible clearly teaches a flat, structurally supported earth with a circular encompassing of waters (Proverbs 8:27), and four corners (Isaiah 11:12)...

> When he prepared the heavens, I was there: **when he set a compass upon the face of the depth:**

> And he shall...gather together the dispersed of Judah from the **four corners of the earth.**

There are those who insist that "four corners" was simply another way of saying "north, south, east, and west." This may be true, but they should consider how this doesn't solve their problem...

> I saw four angels standing on the **four corners of the earth, holding the four winds of heaven.** (Revelation 7:1)

Four corners are still four corners, whether from the direction of the winds, or in the shape of the corners of a table. The Bible uses the terms "four corners" literally, leading newer translations like the NIV to translate "corners" as "quarters." Concerning the construction of the alter, God gave the instructions for its making...

> The alter shall be foursquare, and the height thereof shall be three cubits. And thou shalt make the horns of it upon the **four corners** thereof. (Exodus 27:1-2).

"Foursquare" meant just what it described, why would it be any different when describing the four corners of the earth?

Jewels of Inspiration?

In time, I came to see that many passages I once thought were jewels of inspiration, foretelling of a spherically-shaped earth, turned out not to be. Isaiah 40:22 says...

> It is he that sitteth upon **the circle of the earth**, and the inhabitants thereof are as grasshoppers.

I was taught that the Hebrew word used here for "circle" meant "sphere." This is flatly incorrect. The word means "a disk." God sits upon the disk of the earth judging it the same way a child would set a toy soldier atop a record on a record player. God sitting upon a sphere makes no sense, but sitting upon a disk does. Consider Job 22:14; "Thick clouds are a covering to him, that he seeth not; and he walketh in the circuit of heaven." Another such passage was Job 26:7...

> He stretcheth out the north over **the empty space**, and **hangeth the earth upon nothing**.

To this day, I still get emails, many of them contending that God through Job spoke of the gravitational suspension of this planet when he mentioned the earth being hung "upon nothing." This is a wonderfully hypocritical claim on the part of contemporary Christians, who tell us on the one hand that the Bible is not a science book and shouldn't be expected to reveal modern, scientific findings, but on the other hand, tell us that this verse speaks accurately of the forces that suspend our earth, which was unknown at the time. This is a double standard for sure, but it is also a false understanding of the verse.

We have already seen from several passages that Job and other Bible writers understood the world to be upheld by pillars. And if that were not enough, this very chapter repeats the belief of a pillar-supported earth (Job 26:11; see also Psalm 75:3). If this is true, then Job cannot now be giving us a different position on the matter. The verse itself is one whole unit of thought consisting of two parts; (a) God stretches the north over empty spaces, and (b) hangs the land upon nothingness. When we visualize the meaning behind this verse, and when we understand the meaning of certain words, it isn't hard to understand.

The transliterated Hebrew verb "natah" used for "stretcheth out" is used in places like Exodus 33:7 and Judges 4:11 to the pitching of tents; to stretch out, to set up, or to spread is the clear meaning, but what is being spread? Any part of the earth, including the sky and winds, of the north (Genesis 28:14; Proverbs 25:3), which is why they are called "empty places." The masculine noun "tohew" is used for wilderness and deserts—any unoccupied patch of land (Genesis 1:2; Job 12:24), as is the condition of the far north. The ancients considered the arctic and sub-arctic lands desolate and lifeless, which is why Job poetically describes God who is the keeper and sustainer of the distant, lifeless territories.

It is this meaning Job has in mind when he refers to God who "hangeth the earth upon nothing." The word for "earth" used here is not a noun-specific word. It can refer to the whole earth, a field, soil, or a nation (Genesis 1:1; 4:12; Deuteronomy 4:38). The meaning then, based on the consideration of this context, is clear: God stretches out the northern sky over the barren lands below it, which are themselves suspended on nothing (on nothing but God's sustaining power). The sustaining God who blessed the fertile lands of his servants was the same one to uphold the most forsaken places on earth. This passage is actually poetic and beautiful when not adulterated with erroneous and misguided contentions.

The meaning here is similar to Psalm 139:8; *"If I ascend up into heaven, thou art there: if I make my bed in hell, behold, thou art there."* It was difficult for the Jewish mind to conceive of God creating something without a human-oriented purpose behind it. Everything that was made was made for man, and thus, "not in vain."

> For thus saith the LORD that created the heavens; God himself that formed the earth and made it; he hath established it, **he created it not in vain, he formed it to be inhabited**: I am the LORD; and there is none else. (Isaiah 45:18)

Job lets his readers know that even those places where no traveler dared explore, those places that seemed forever in darkness are fully understood and known by God. His hand is there too. That is the meaning here.

There is one more reason to know that this verse couldn't be describing gravity; as we shall see, in Jewish thought, the earth was fixed. It did not move, and to refer to "hanging" the earth would imply nothing more than a Christmas ornament hanging on a Christmas tree—a stationary hanging, not a gravitational orbit. How could that be said to be describing gravity or any detailed knowledge of our solar system?

To say that the Bible writers were ignorant of what we know today as basic astronomy is an understatement. How the stars gave off light, how the sky didn't "fall" to the earth, and whether or not an eclipse was an omen for doom occupied the minds of the greatest thinkers then living. To argue that Job chose this one occasion to reveal one secret scientific truth of the earth is to demonstrate a reckless and careless handling of the scriptures.

More Blunders

Revelation 6:13 says...

> And the stars of heaven fell unto the earth.

These are very small stars indeed! This verse is as uninformed as can be. And John is not speaking of meteorites or comets, but actual stars. Compare this to Daniel 8:10...

> And it waxed great, even to the host of heaven; and it cast down some of the host and of the stars to the ground, and stamped upon them.

Even though figurative language is being used, the problem with a writer speaking of stars falling to the earth doesn't go away. The Bible writers had no quarrels with stars falling to the earth because to them stars were only three or four chariots in diameter. A big enough giant could conceivably step on them. Had the ancient understanding of stars been better, a different metaphor would have been used.

Jesus' Flat Earth

In Matthew 4:8-9, we read...

> Again, the devil taketh him up into **an exceeding high mountain, and sheweth him all the kingdoms of the world**, and the glory of them. And saith unto him, all these things will I give unto thee, if thou wilt fall down and worship me.

The only way Jesus could see all the kingdoms of the world from a high mountain was if the writer of Matthew thought the earth was flat. Even the highest mountain, Everest, would only offer a shallow view of some of the earth's empires. In response to this, apologists will make plays on the word "world" to give it a local sense, a "world" in the limited sense of the Palestinian area, but this offers little to tempt Jesus with – the King of the Jews – whose father supposedly ordained him to rule over that area anyway. Jerusalem was the city of God already within Jesus' right and power. It would only prove to be a temptation if all the powers of the world's kingdoms Satan could package up and offer him. So the context seems to favor the more broad interpretation that the whole world is in focus here rather than a local part of it. The writer of Matthew just assumed the whole earth could be seen if one could be propped up high enough.

Geocentrism

The Bible gives us a picture of a stationary, flat earth, an earth with four corners, with a disk-shaped center-piece of some land and the seas, as well as an earth that dwells at the center of the universe...

> The Lord reigneth...**the world also is established that it cannot be moved**. (Psalm 93:1)

> Fear before him, all the earth: **the world also shall be stable**, that it be not moved. (I Chronicles 16:30)

> Who hath laid **the foundations of the earth that it should not be moved** forever. (Psalm 104:5)

According to the ancients, the earth was the center of the universe and everything (sun, moon, planets, stars, etc.) revolved around it. To them, the earth was made that it "should not be moved forever." As with all ancient writers who wrote at a time when science facts we take for granted were beyond human knowledge, we can forgive primitive ignoramuses for being uninformed about matters of astronomy, but we cannot forgive ignoramuses who were supposedly speaking by the inspiration of the almighty and who get the facts wrong! The earth and everything else in the known universe moves, and not only that, moves faster than we might think. The earth orbits the sun at an astonishing 67,000 miles per hour! To the ancients, it was an established truth that the earth was at the center of the universe, and lacking scientific knowledge, it became a powerful figurative description to say that the earth could possibly be moved with divine justice...

> Therefore, **I will shake the heavens, and the earth shall remove out of her place**, in the wrath of the Lord of hosts, and in the day of his fierce anger. (Isaiah 13:13)

Such descriptions were of course figurative, but this description would make utterly no sense if it is supposed that the Bible writers knew that the earth was always moving like we know it does—in orbit. The false belief of geocentrism was accepted for ages until the time of Copernicus and Galileo. Martin Luther, being a staunch proponent of geocentrism, knew that given a strict study of Bible passages without exterior biases (like the sciences, particularly astronomy), one will conclude that the Bible teaches a flat, geocentric earth.

The Bible is replete with geocentric passages. Joshua commanded the sun, not the earth, to stand still (Joshua 10:12-13)...

> 12. Then spake Joshua to the LORD in the day when the LORD delivered up the Amorites before the children of Israel, and he said in the sight of Israel, **Sun, stand thou still upon Gibeon; and thou, Moon, in the valley of Ajalon. 13. And the sun stood still, and the moon stayed**, until the people had avenged themselves upon their enemies. Is not this written in the book of Jasher? So the sun stood still in the midst of heaven, and hasted not to go down about a whole day.

In the days of Hezekiah, God moved the sun ten degrees backwards as a sign of his power (Isaiah 38:7-8)...

> 7. And this shall be a sign unto thee from the LORD, that the LORD will do this thing that he hath spoken; 8. Behold, I will bring again the shadow of the degrees, which is gone down in the sun dial of Ahaz, ten degrees backward. So **the sun returned ten degrees, by which degrees it was gone down**.

Other passages are every bit as plain spoken and need no explanation...

> The sun knoweth his going down. (Psalm 104:19)

> The sun also ariseth and the sun goeth down, and hasteth to the place where he arose. (Ecclesiastes 1:5)

Notice it says the "the sun riseth," not "the earth rotateth." Attempts are made to explain these passages as accommodative language, such as we would use the term today, "When the sun comes up, get to work." Did the Bible writers use the same sort of language when describing the motion of the sun as we do? This sounds like music to theistic ears until we remember that geocentrism was exactly what the people of this time believed—unlike those of us today who know better. In consort with the rule that a passage should be interpreted literally as opposed to figuratively if at all possible, we must stay with the spirit of these texts and read them as the authors intended them to be read—with a geocentric view in mind.

Moderate and liberal Christians will realize that the Bible makes a number of scientific blunders, that it cannot be championed as a science book, but ultra-conservatives and fundamentalists will not relinquish in their fight to deny the obvious meanings of the verses we have looked at. It is those in the latter category that I am writing this chapter for. I am not holding an archaic book of antiquated beliefs accountable to modern, scientific standards, but I am holding throwback biblical inerrantists accountable for trying to give credit to the Bible where it is not due. Every book will reflect the views of the day in which it was written, and the Bible is no exception. I do not expect a piece of ancient literature to be up-to-date by today's scientific standards, but I do expect religious believers to understand this and not try to support the lie that their holy book is infallible and inerrant, being the product of a miracle. The Bible warrants no such exaltation.

CHAPTER 10
Messiah Matters

The Truth About the Messiah of the Old Testament

"G-d does not suddenly decide to visit the earth in a human body. A G-d who fills and sustains all creation does not have to visit our planet in human form. The Jerusalem Talmud flatly states the Jewish view, 'If a man claims to be G-d, he is a liar!'"
- *Aryeh Kaplan*

"Jesus was a patriotic Jew, who loved his people, rebelled against the cruelty of the Romans, was put to death by Pontius Pilate, and brought spiritual knowledge to billions, but the Jews already had G-d, were already close to G-d, and needed no intermediary, and that remains the case."
- *Rabbi Shmuley Boteach*

I thought I was doing well. I was pretty proud of myself, as I sat, nine months old in the faith, discussing with a friend why Jesus must be accepted as the messiah. I was halfway through Acts 13, discussing the rapid growth of the Gentile church when this friend asked me, "Why did the Jews reject Jesus, Joe?" I didn't consider it a serious question back then. The gospels have a lot to say about the Jewish people and most of it is negative. Jesus said they had hard hearts, and that was good enough for me, but the question seemed to stick with me through the years. Why would those most familiar with the sacred scriptures their forefathers handed down to them not be convinced of the messiahship of Jesus? Why would those who knew the scriptures of their God best reject the anointed one sent by him? Why was the Christian movement regarded by the Jews as an apostate system of Judaism? I knew the New Testament's answers to these questions, but the Old Testament and thousands of years of Jewish history seemed to tell a different story.

Go and ask your local Orthodox Rabbi why the Jewish people reject Jesus as their messiah. You will be told that the Jesus of the New Testament in no clear way resembles the messiah spoken of in the Old Testament. Familiarity with The Torah and the writings of the prophets does not convince one of the messiahship of Jesus, but Christian indoctrination does. Jesus is supposedly the be-all-and-end-all of the Law...

> 44. And he said unto them, These are the words which I spake unto you, while I was yet with you, that all things must be fulfilled, which were written in the law of Moses, and in the prophets, and in the psalms, concerning me. 45. Then opened he their understanding, that they might understand the scriptures, 46. And said unto them, Thus it is written, and thus it behoved Christ to suffer, and to rise from the dead the third day: (Luke 24:44-46)

Here, Jesus has appeared in disguise to two of the disciples on the road to Emmaus and explains to them the scriptures that foretold of his death, burial, and resurrection. By "scriptures," we are referring only to the Old Testament because the New Testament also uses the term that way (Matthew 22:29; 2 Timothy 3:16-17). And do the scriptures speak of a Christ who died and rose again on the third day? Not at all, not even remotely. Jesus may be seen in the Old Testament scriptures, but only when the meanings of a great many passages have been mutilated beyond recognition.

Jesus also said...

> Search the scriptures; for in them ye think ye have eternal life: and they are they which testify of me. (John 5:39)

This I tried to do many times, but the more I studied the Old Testament, the more apparent became the gross inconsistencies and distortions in the handling of texts. Jesus does not – in any way, shape, or form – fit the scriptural picture of the Jewish Messiah. And that is why the Jews rejected him.

Who was the Messiah?

One thing to establish before we begin discussing prophecies of the messiah is the Jewish perspective of messiahship and how it is different from the one held by Christians, both in the nature of his identity, and in the nature of the term "messiah." Messiah simply means "anointed one." It referred to an elect individual, blessed and favored of God. The word brings up an image of royalty, of a king being anointed with oil by servants. When used by the Jewish people throughout every age up to the present, the word meant what it meant when applied to every man of God. The term applied to every King of Israel and Judah, and to every prophet and inspired messenger of God there ever was. For the time and for the purpose God called them for, a prophet was "anointed," handpicked to do God's will. So great was the esteem of such a rank that even after Saul tirelessly tried to kill David in bitter jealousy and rage, when at last David gained the advantage over him, he said, "The LORD delivered thee into my hand to day, but I would not stretch forth mine hand against the LORD's anointed." (I Samuel 26:23)

The notion of "The messiah" as we know it today is mostly a modern invention. Whether we went back in time to 750 B.C.E. or 750 C.E. and asked a Jew what they believed about "the messiah," they'd inquire as to which one we were talking about. Nevertheless, today they use the term the way Gentiles use it. The End of Days messiah (as he was known to the Jews) is the role Christians claim was filled by Jesus, but this messiah could not have been him—not if one values keeping the contexts of certain verses taken from the Law, the Psalms, and the Prophets intact.

Who was the End of Days Messiah to Be?

He was to be one "like unto your brethren" (Deuteronomy 18:20-21). He would be an anointed, hand-picked ruler by God, a son of man (not born of a deity, but with two ordinary, human parents) of the Jewish people (Deut 17:15). He would belong to the tribe of Judah (Genesis 49:10). He would be a direct descendant of David and Solomon (2 Samuel 7:12-13), not just any son of David, but through Solomon (and as we shall see, the gospel genealogies get it all wrong!) He would return dispersed Jews throughout the world to Israel and serve as a banner for all nations to see and rally around (Isaiah 11:12). He would rule the world and carry God's government upon his shoulders (Isaiah 9:7), and would bring about a time of peace (Micah 4:3). He would rebuild the Temple in Jerusalem (Ezekiel 37:26-27). The messiah would rule at a time when God's chosen people would be following all of God's commandments and abiding in faithfulness (Ezekiel 37:24). At this time, the whole world will serve the God of Abraham (Isaiah 66:23). If any candidate for messiahship does not meet every one of these conditions, then that person cannot be the messiah of the Jews.

Two Fallacies

Apologists will commit two fallacies when trying to argue Jesus into the role of the messiah; *first*, they butcher the contexts of the verses they abuse in trying to make connections to Jesus. The New Testament is literally packed with quotations of scripture, every one of them misquoted, misapplied, or else distorted beyond recognition in mistranslation. The apologist will take the gospel narratives and list pages of detailed similarities between the Old Testament and Jesus – *"Zechariah says they will look on him whom they pierced, how can you deny that that's talking about Jesus?"* – all the while never bothering to notice their reckless disregard for the contexts from which they steal these verses.

I had an instructor in seminary who warned me that "If you ask a text a question it was not meant to answer, the text will give you a wrong answer." Another would remind us, "Scripture out of context is pretext." Both statements are true. It's a shame they never applied them. So much is made of rival religions accusing one another of taking verses out of their contexts, and yet all adherents to the religion of Christianity are equally guilty of the charge.

The *second* fallacy of the apologist is to argue for what is usually called *dual fulfillment*. This is where an apologist argues that the Old Testament passages that apply to Jesus have two fulfillments; a passage can be fulfilled in one circumstance and then again in another. So, in example, Christians might acknowledge that when Isaiah spoke of a maiden with child in chapter 7 verse 14, or the suffering servant of Israel in chapter 53, these verses had immediate fulfillments in the times of their writing, and then secondary fulfillments many years later in the person of Jesus. This they say to dodge the charge that they are taking verses from the Old Testament out of context. It is a theologically futile attempt, however. Let it be stated with the utmost certainty that *the idea of dual fulfillment is altogether unknown in the Old Testament scriptures.* It is purely a New Testament invention to justify the monstrously inappropriate usage of selected, hijacked verses.

Problems with the Genealogies

One need write off Jesus as the messiah for no other reason than the fact that the gospel genealogies (Matthew 1; Luke 3) are contradictory and irreconcilable. The matter is summarized this way; the messiah could not come from Matthew's genealogy because Jeconiah (also known as Coniah) is mentioned in the lineage, and God decreed that no man of his seed could sit upon the throne of David (Jeremiah 22:30). Since Jesus was declared to sit on the throne of David (Luke 1:32), his legitimacy is demolished. And the messiah could not have come from the genealogy given in Luke as it has Jesus descended from Nathan, Solomon's brother, whereas prophecy demanded that the messiah be a descendant through Solomon. Moreover, Shealtiel and Zerubabel are descended from Jeconiah as mentioned in Matthew 1:12 (which is in line with the genealogies of Jeconiah found in the books of the Kings), but as we have seen, Jeconiah cannot have a descendant to sit upon the thrown, so for these reasons alone, the messiah of Christianity has no hope as a candidate for true Jewish messiahship. The genealogy in Luke is also worthless because if, as some say, it is the genealogy of Jesus through Mary, since kingship is only passed on through a male line, it is irrelevant anyway. The genealogy in Matthew is equally irrelevant for the fact that adopted sons could not partake of tribal lineage, and since Jesus was born of a virgin – even discounting all the other problems with Matthew's genealogy – Jesus still could not be legitimate. This means Jesus was not descended from Joseph, and therefore, has no claim whatever to the Davidic throne. So much for the genealogies then. In addition to Christ failing the initial qualifications as the messiah, not one of the many warped and perverted passages that are ripped out of their contexts will support Christendom's claims. Here are some of the highlight prophecy passages and why they fail to identify Jesus as Christ…

Genesis 3:15

> And I will put enmity between thee and the woman, and between thy seed and her seed; it shall bruise thy head, and thou shalt bruise his heel.

The heal of the savior was bruised at Calvary when Jesus was killed, but Satan's head was crushed upon his resurrection, so say the Christians. Since females are not recognized as passing on seed, the reference to "her seed" here must refer to Mary becoming pregnant with Jesus when she was a virgin, so goes the explanation. This is gross deception and plainly inaccurate. The Old Testament repeatedly refers to the seed of woman with the same Hebrew sentence structure and word of this verse. The word "zera" in three forms, always referring in scripture to physical, literal seed, appears and is used of women...

> And they blessed Rebekah, and said unto her, Thou art our sister, be thou the mother of thousands of millions, and let *thy seed* possess the gate of those which hate them. (Genesis 24:60)

> And Eli blessed Elkanah and his wife, and said, The LORD give thee *seed of this woman* for the loan which is lent to the LORD. And they went unto their own home. (I Samuel 2:20)

Genesis 3:15 refers to nothing more than the fact that Satan, the serpent, would be a pest, trampled under foot of man as part of his being cursed to stay upon his belly (Genesis 3:14). As the serpent beguiled Eve, part of his payback would be that her offspring (the whole human race) would keep him low.

Genesis 49:10

> The sceptre shall not depart from Judah, nor a lawgiver from between his feet, until Shiloh come; and unto him shall the gathering of the people be.

The scepter represented royalty (Psalm 110:2) and Shiloh meant something like "He who is to come." Jesus could not fulfill this verse anyway. Even if he was the lawgiver, the scepter had already passed from Judah before this time—in 586 B.C.E. Modern Orthodox Jews still view this as an active messianic verse. However, this appears to be a propaganda verse from a time when the Kingdom of Judah was still in power. The "scepter" of divine authority had not yet passed from Judah when this was written. The long-awaited messiah never came. The last king of the kingdom of Judah, Zedekiah, died, and when he died, he took the kingdom of Judah with him and voided this prophecy.

Deuteronomy 18:15

> The LORD thy God will raise up unto thee a Prophet from the midst of thee, of thy brethren, like unto me; unto him ye shall hearken;

This cannot be referring to Jesus for the simple fact that Jesus was not heard by Israel. The nation rejected him. Only the common people heard him (Mark 12:37), but nowhere in Old Testament scripture is it said that only some of Israel would accept him.

2 Samuel 7:12-16

> And when thy days be fulfilled, and thou shalt sleep with thy fathers, I will set up thy seed after thee, which shall proceed out of thy bowels, and I will establish his kingdom.13. He shall build an house for my name, and I will stablish the throne of his kingdom for ever. 14. I will be his father, and he shall be my son. *If he commit iniquity, I will chasten him with the rod of men, and with the stripes of the children of men*: 15. But my mercy shall not depart away from him, as I took it from Saul, whom I put away before thee. 16. And thine house and thy kingdom shall be established for ever before thee: thy throne shall be established for ever.

This cannot in any way apply to Jesus. The verses are speaking of Solomon and the carrying on of the throne of David through him (see also I Chronicles 17:11-12). In addition to being a physical descendant of David and Solomon, the subject of this verse is lined up to receive chastisement (vs. 14). It should be all too obvious why this can't apply to Jesus (see Hebrews 4:15). He was the only one who ever kept the law perfectly and would never need chastisement. Christian scholars have tried to equate "chasten" with the image of Jesus who bears our sins, but this can't be made to fit.

Psalm 22

> 1. My God, my God, why hast thou forsaken me? why art thou so far from helping me, and from the words of my roaring? 2. O my God, I cry in the day time, but thou hearest not; and in the night season, and am not silent. 3. But thou art holy, O thou that inhabitest the praises of Israel. 4. Our fathers trusted in thee: they trusted, and thou didst deliver them. 5. They cried unto thee, and were delivered: they trusted in thee, and were not confounded. 6. But I am a worm, and no man; a reproach of men, and despised of the people. 7. All they that see me laugh me to scorn: they shoot out the lip, they shake the head, saying, 8. He trusted on the LORD that he would deliver him: let him deliver him, seeing he delighted in him. 9. But thou art he that took me out of the womb: thou didst make me hope when I was upon my mother's

breasts. 10. I was cast upon thee from the womb: thou art my God from my mother's belly. 11. Be not far from me; for trouble is near; for there is none to help. 12. Many bulls have compassed me: strong bulls of Bashan have beset me round. 13. They gaped upon me with their mouths, as a ravening and a roaring lion. 14. I am poured out like water, and all my bones are out of joint: my heart is like wax; it is melted in the midst of my bowels. 15. My strength is dried up like a potsherd; and my tongue cleaveth to my jaws; and thou hast brought me into the dust of death. 16. For dogs have compassed me: the assembly of the wicked have inclosed me: they pierced my hands and my feet. 17. I may tell all my bones: they look and stare upon me. 18. They part my garments among them, and cast lots upon my vesture. 19. But be not thou far from me, O LORD: O my strength, haste thee to help me. 20. Deliver my soul from the sword; my darling from the power of the dog. 21. Save me from the lion's mouth: for thou hast heard me from the horns of the unicorns. 22. I will declare thy name unto my brethren: in the midst of the congregation will I praise thee. 23. Ye that fear the LORD, praise him; all ye the seed of Jacob, glorify him; and fear him, all ye the seed of Israel. 24. For he hath not despised nor abhorred the affliction of the afflicted; neither hath he hid his face from him; but when he cried unto him, he heard. 25. My praise shall be of thee in the great congregation: I will pay my vows before them that fear him. 26. The meek shall eat and be satisfied: they shall praise the LORD that seek him: your heart shall live for ever. 27. All the ends of the world shall remember and turn unto the LORD: and all the kindreds of the nations shall worship before thee. 28. For the kingdom is the LORD's: and he is the governor among the nations. 29. All they that be fat upon earth shall eat and worship: all they that go down to the dust shall bow before him: and none can keep alive his own soul. 30. A seed shall serve him; it shall be accounted to the Lord for a generation. 31. They shall come, and shall declare his righteousness unto a people that shall be born, that he hath done this.

A casual reading of this beautiful Psalm will reveal the obvious interpretation that the suffering of the Psalmist is the subject here. David, who is expressing the pain of his trials and tribulations as king, is speaking. He wants to be saved (vs.11), not crucified (vs.20): "Deliver thou my soul from the sword." This cannot be talking about a crucifixion. "They pierced my hands and feet" is a mistranslation. It reads *as a lion at my hands and feet*. Isaiah 38:18 and Numbers 24:9 are both evidences of the use of this word, and the multiple references to attacking animals in this Psalm confirm this with reference to aggressive dogs and bulls (vs.12-13,16). Of 79 uses in the Hebrew Old Testament, every time this word is used, it is translated as "lion." Why would this place in the Psalms be any different? Why would it mean "pierced" here and nowhere else?

It is sometimes argued that the Septuagint's translation of Psalm 22:16 has "pierced" as "oruxan," which supposedly means "to bore through," justifying the Christian position of a crucified savior, pierced in the hands and feet. But it must be pointed out that the 72 original Jewish scholars who translated the Septuagint would never have made such a mistake. Those scholars only translated the first five books of the Law. They did not translate anything but the Torah. Later, other scholars completed the translation of the Hebrew Old Testament into Greek, but the effort would not be finished until well over a century later. Since that time, many changes in the originally translated Jewish Septuagint continued to be added and made by Hellenized Jews and the church—the point being, there is no solace in looking for alternate translations in hopes to preserve the Christian rendering of Psalm 22:16. What is also interesting is that no New Testament writer or early Christian writer ever made reference to this passage as saying "they pierced" until well after the close of the Christian canon in the late second century C.E.

"They part my garments among them, and cast lots upon my vesture," is another troublesome reference to some. The Psalmist has described himself as being able to "count" all his bones (vs.17), denoting a fear of conditions of squalor like those of captivity. The Psalmist – fearing being stripped of his clothing and dignity to reveal a dishonored, dilapidated body, dethroned of his rulership – speaks of the honor among his captors as they jestingly fight for his royal garment. This was the fear of any ruler, not a prophetic description of any kind—much less of a crucifixion that was to take place hundreds of years later. Christians taking details from these verses and applying them ipso facto to a crucified savior centuries later totally disregards the context of the Psalm.

Isaiah 7:14

> Therefore the Lord himself shall give you a sign; Behold, a virgin shall conceive, and bear a son, and shall call his name Immanuel.

With the possible exception of Isaiah 53, no Old Testament prophecy has come under more scrutiny than has this verse, which supposedly foretells Jesus' virgin birth. The controversy begins with use of the Hebrew word "alma" that is used here and erroneously translated "virgin." Had virginal status been the thought the author was directly trying to convey, the word "bethulah" would have been a better choice to carry that meaning. Of 50 uses in the Old Testament, it always means "virgin," while the word "alma" can mean virgin, but usually means women *of marriageable age* (Psalm 68:25; Song of Solomon 1:3). This is a firmly established issue, with even a few pro-Christian Bible translations (like the RSV) including footnotes in their renderings of Isaiah 7:14, stating that "young woman" would be a more accurate translation. But when ideological comfort can't be found in Hebrew, the Christian seeks to find it in Greek. When quoting Isaiah 7:14, Matthew uses the Greek word for virgin, "parthenos" (Matthew 1:23), the same word used in the Septuagint—the Greek translation of the Hebrew Old Testament scriptures...

> Behold, a virgin shall be with child, and shall bring forth a son, and they shall call his name Emmanuel, which being interpreted is, God with us.

Both Matthew and the Septuagint equate the Hebrew "alma" with the Greek "parthenos," which we are told, unquestionably refers to a virgin. This contention meets a quick and brutal end, however; the word parthenos cannot exclusively mean "virgin" for the simple fact that the Septuagint itself uses the word to refer to the already raped Dinah (Genesis 34:2-3). So the equation of "parthenos" with "virgin" is false.

But let's concede that Isaiah was indeed talking about a virgin. Virgins can conceive on their first sexual encounter, so we needn't put up a fight over the issue. The question is, how can Jesus be the focus of this context? What is this passage saying? To answer this, we must familiarize ourselves with the surrounding verses and their message.

Isaiah was sent to inform Ahaz and the Kingdom of Judah that his enemies would not triumph over him in battle...

> And it came to pass in the days of Ahaz the son of Jotham, the son of Uzziah, king of Judah, that Rezin the king of Syria, and Pekah the son of Remaliah, king of Israel, went up toward Jerusalem to war against it, but could not prevail against it...Then said the LORD unto Isaiah, Go forth now to meet Ahaz. (Isaiah 7:1,3)

A young woman was to conceive and give birth to a child who was to serve as a sign to Ahaz and the House of David that God would not let his enemies (Syria and Israel), who had joined forces against him, to triumph over him in battle for Judah (Jerusalem). In order that Ahaz and his kingdom might be established in full faith, God through Isaiah offered Ahaz a sign of his own choosing, which could have been anything to assure him that God would indeed deliver him...

> 10. Moreover the LORD spake again unto Ahaz, saying, 11. Ask thee a sign of the LORD thy God; ask it either in the depth, or in the height

above. 12. But Ahaz said, I will not ask, neither will I tempt the LORD. 13. And he said, Hear ye now, O house of David; Is it a small thing for you to weary men, but will ye weary my God also? (Isaiah 7:10-13)

In pretentious and false assurance, Ahaz refuses a sign, so God gives him a sign of his own—a woman would conceive and give birth to a son, and before that son could mature, the plot of Syria and Ephraim would be foiled by God, rendering them no longer a threat to Judah. How was the child to be a sign to Ahaz? He would grow and learn the judgment of God, and he would eat butter and honey (likely denoting prosperity), but by this time, the opposing lands (Syria and Israel) would be forsaken of both her kings (Rezin and Pekah). The child was to serve as a sign that the alliance of Pekah and Rezin had failed just as God ordained...

> 15. Butter and honey shall he eat, that he may know to refuse the evil, and choose the good. 16. For before the child shall know to refuse the evil, and choose the good, the land that thou abhorrest shall be forsaken of both her kings. (Isaiah 7:15-16)

But things wouldn't be rosy for long. Because of Ahaz's lack of faith and his efforts to make a covenant with the king of Assyria to rally against his enemies, not only would the alliance fail and Assyria wipe out Syria and Ephraim, but the upsurging of judgment against those kings would overflow right up to the banks of Judah. God had warned against uniting with Assyria, but because this prohibition was cast aside by Ahaz, in the next chapter we see that Judah suffers the consequences...

> 7. Now therefore, behold, the Lord bringeth up upon them the waters of the river, strong and many, even the king of Assyria, and all his glory: and he shall come up over all his channels, and go over all his banks: 8. And he shall pass through Judah; he shall overflow and go over, he shall reach even to the neck; and the stretching out of his wings shall fill the breadth of thy land, O Immanuel. 9. **Associate yourselves, O ye people, and ye shall be broken in pieces; and give ear, all ye of far countries: gird yourselves, and ye shall be broken in pieces; gird yourselves, and ye shall be broken in pieces. 10. Take counsel together, and it shall come to nought; speak the word, and it shall not stand: for God is with us.** 11. For the LORD spake thus to me with a strong hand, and instructed me that I should not walk in the way of this people, saying, 12. Say ye not, A confederacy, to all them to whom this people shall say, A confederacy; neither fear ye their fear, nor be afraid. (Isaiah 8:7-12)

This event was the Assyrian captivity (721 B.C.E.) when Assyrian king Tiglath Pileser III came through and took captive the tribes of the Northern Kingdom of Israel and laid waste to Syria (2 Kings 15:29). If you are waiting for Jesus to show up in these verses, you'll be waiting a long time. Jesus is nowhere to be found. When were these events fulfilled? The fulfillment can be seen unfolding in the very next chapter with the prized child as a symbol of deliverance for the fast-approaching years of Judah's future. Isaiah began the fulfillment of this prophecy himself. The child was his own...

> 3. **And I went unto the prophetess; and she conceived, and bare a son.** Then said the LORD to me, Call his name Mahershalalhashbaz 4. For before the child shall have knowledge to cry, My father, and my mother, the riches of Damascus and the spoil of Samaria shall be taken away before the king of Assyria...And he shall pass through Judah; he shall overflow and go over, he shall reach even to the neck; and the stretching out of his wings shall fill the breadth of thy land, **O Immanuel**...10. Take counsel together, and it shall come to nought; speak the word, and it shall not stand: for **God is with us.** (Isaiah 8:3-4, 8, 10)

The child's name meant "the prey hastens," re-identifying God's orchestration behind the maneuvering of these power struggles. Before the child could cry out, the fortifications of Damascus and Samaria (the lands ruled over by Rezin and Pekah) would come to nothing. The king of Assyria would step in to thwart the purposes of Judah's adversaries. The resistance against God's people would fail, for "God is with us," as the name "Immanuel" declares. Isaiah's son was called Immanuel. Jesus was never called Immanuel by anyone except the writer of Matthew who uses the name as a means to subvert the Old Testament scriptures in a Christian machination. The text has nothing to do with Jesus whatsoever.

Trying to fit a prophetic virgin birth into the picture only renders pointless all that we have briefly brought to light. If Isaiah 7:14 was predicting a virgin-born savior many centuries down the road, how did it apply to Ahaz and Judah? We must also take issue with how a virgin giving birth to anyone could be called a "sign." Signs must be visible, verifiable, but a virgin conceiving is not such a thing. Understood in context, the miracle of Isaiah 7:14 was visible and verifiable in that its fulfillment could be seen in the lives of the nations around them.

Isaiah 9:6-7

> 6. For unto us a child is born, unto us a son is given: and the government shall be upon his shoulder: and his name shall be called Wonderful, Counsellor, The mighty God, The everlasting Father, The Prince of Peace. 7. Of the increase of his government and peace there shall be no end, upon the throne of David, and upon his kingdom, to order it, and to establish it with judgment and with justice from henceforth even for ever. The zeal of the LORD of hosts will perform this.

This is a real messiah passage, but it does not refer to Jesus. "Of the increase of his government and peace there shall be no end." Jesus did not have his own government, and in fact, he did just the opposite of set up a government or create peace. He taught submission to heathen governments and brought discord...

> Render therefore unto Caesar the things which are Caesar's; and unto God the things that are God's. (Matthew 22:21)

> Think not that I am come to send peace on earth: I came not to send peace, but a sword. (Matt 10:34)

The real messiah was to be a father-figure like unto God, a "mighty god," one worthy of awe and universal respect (Exodus 22:28). Jesus was not a "father," biologically or otherwise, and never portrayed himself as such (Luke 18:19; John 13:13; Matthew 24:36; I Corinthians 15:24-26). He was not called "wonderful," "counselor," "the mighty God," "everlasting father," or even "The Prince of Peace" until relatively recently. And Jesus did not bring forth judgment and justice forever. He was killed unjustly in a world that still fashions injustice as a running norm.

Isaiah 11:1-6

> 1. And there shall come forth a rod out of the stem of Jesse, and a Branch shall grow out of his roots: 2. And the spirit of the LORD shall rest upon him, the spirit of wisdom and understanding, the spirit of counsel and might, the spirit of knowledge and of the fear of the LORD; 3. And shall make him of quick understanding in the fear of the LORD: and he shall not judge after the sight of his eyes, neither reprove after the hearing of his ears: 4. But with righteousness shall he judge the poor, and reprove with equity for the meek of the earth: and he shall smite the earth with the rod of his mouth, and with the breath of his lips shall he slay the wicked. 5. And righteousness shall be the girdle of his loins, and faithfulness the girdle of his reins.

It is very odd that this would be referring to Jesus as a strongly sprouting branch when Isaiah himself, according to Christians, is describing Christ as a dying, bitter, unattractive root in Isaiah 53! Some of these verses might sound like they could apply to Christ, especially when it speaks of smiting the earth with the rod of his mouth, but there's more to this picture. When the real messiah was to come, the glory of his kingdom and power was to be seen everywhere. His banner of the nations would signal a time of glory and peace…

> 6. The wolf also shall dwell with the lamb, and the leopard shall lie down with the kid; and the calf and the young lion and the fatling together; and a little child shall lead them. 7. And the cow and the bear shall feed; their young ones shall lie down together: and the lion shall eat straw like the ox. 8. And the sucking child shall play on the hole of the asp, and the weaned child shall put his hand on the cockatrice' den. (Isaiah 11:5-8)

This is not even close to what we see today, so we are told by Christians that this paradise is a thing yet future, whereas the scriptures say that the arrival of the messiah and peace would be simultaneous. If the real messiah had come, we should already be in paradise. Efforts to bend these verses to make the animals refer to nations living in peace under gospel laws are vacuous.

Isaiah 28:16

> 16. Therefore thus saith the Lord GOD, Behold, I lay in Zion for a foundation a stone, a tried stone, a precious corner stone, a sure foundation: he that believeth shall not make haste.

This entire chapter is focusing on "the drunkards of Ephraim" and their covenant with idolatrous and rebellious lives of debauchery: "Because ye have said, We have made a covenant with death, and with hell are we at agreement; when the overflowing scourge shall pass through, it shall not come unto us: for we have made lies our refuge, and under falsehood have we hid ourselves." (Isaiah 28:15) What is this vile covenant being contrasted with? The tried and true foundation of Zion, "a sure foundation." Judgment would sweep through the wicked hoards (vs.17-21), resulting in the disannulment of their covenant with death. God is calling his people back to the tried principles of faithfulness— belief in and acceptance of their spiritual master who will not cut them off to face the oblivion of the grave. There is no reference to Christ here.

Psalm 118:22

> The stone which the builders refused is become the head stone of the corner.

It is very interesting how this verse is quoted by Jesus and used by evangelicals as though the Psalmist is supposedly speaking of Christ when the Psalmist declares a number of times, "I shall not die, but live, and declare the works of the LORD. The LORD hath chastened me sore: but he hath not given me over unto death." (vs. 17-18). Jesus died. He didn't live. Verses 10 and 11 speak of the Psalmist's deliverance from his enemies...

> 10. All nations compassed me about: but in the name of the LORD will I destroy them. 11. They compassed me about; yea, they compassed me about: but in the name of the LORD I will destroy them.

The context is addressing foreign nations who threaten the Psalmist. It is not directed against the nation of Israel of whom the Psalmist speaks on behalf of...

> 2. Let Israel now say, that his mercy endureth for ever. 3. Let the house of Aaron now say, that his mercy endureth for ever. 4. Let them now that fear the LORD say, that his mercy endureth for ever... 26. Blessed be he that cometh in the name of the LORD: we have blessed you out of the house of the LORD.

The Psalmist then goes on to encourage Levitical sacrifices as the Law commanded; "27. God is the LORD, which hath shewed us light: bind the sacrifice with cords, even unto the horns of the altar." The entire Psalm is describing the downfall of the wicked who plot against God's holy one. They will fail because the stone that the builders of iniquity "refused is become the head of the corner." How can this one verse be speaking of the rejection of Jesus when the entire rest of the Psalm has nothing to do with it?

Psalm 69:22-23

> 22. Let their table become a snare before them: and that which should have been for their welfare, let it become a trap. 23. Let their eyes be darkened, that they see not; and make their loins continually to shake.

The entire Psalm 69 is a prime example of how Christianity, picking and choosing from certain texts, plays on isolated words of scripture; "they hated me without a cause" (vs. 4), "the zeal of thine house hath eaten me up" (vs. 9), "in my thirst they gave me vinegar to drink" (vs. 21), and verse 25, "let their habitation be desolate and let no man dwell therein," are all pulled out of context and portrayed to be foretelling details in the life and passion of Jesus. Like Jesus, Paul, in Romans 11:9-10, sees the snare David calls for to be aimed at God's own people, as though the Hebrew God had some interest in seeing his people be deceived…

> 10. And the disciples came, and said unto him, Why speakest thou unto them in parables? 11. He answered and said unto them, Because it is given unto you to know the mysteries of the kingdom of heaven, but to them it is not given. 12. For whosoever hath, to him shall be given, and he shall have more abundance: but whosoever hath not, from him shall be taken away even that he hath. 13. Therefore speak I to them in parables: because they seeing see not; and hearing they hear not, neither do they understand. (Matthew 13:10-13)

> 9. And David saith, Let their table be made a snare, and a trap, and a stumblingblock, and a recompence unto them: 10. Let their eyes be darkened, that they may not see, and bow down their back alway. (Romans 11:9-10)

Christianity has God working out his heavenly plan to cause the Jews to stumble for the benefit of Gentile salvation (I Peter 2:8). The real meaning of the Psalm was to serve, like many of David's Psalms, as heartfelt appeals to God for deliverance. Throughout the Psalm, David is pleading for deliverance from his enemies, not foretelling a sacrificial death…

> 14. Deliver me out of the mire, and let me not sink: let me be delivered from them that hate me, and out of the deep waters. 15. Let not the waterflood overflow me, neither let the deep swallow me up, and let not the pit shut her mouth upon me. 16. Hear me, O LORD; for thy lovingkindness is good: turn unto me according to the multitude of thy tender mercies. 17. And hide not thy face from thy servant; for I am in trouble: hear me speedily. 18. Draw nigh unto my soul, and redeem it: deliver me because of mine enemies. (Psalm 69:14-18)

If David's prayer referred to Jesus, it must have meant nothing to David, for David wanted the exact opposite to happen to him from what happened to Jesus. David asks to be delivered from those who hate him, to be saved from "the pit" (an Old Testament reference to death/the grave), and for God not to hide his face from him, yet God supposedly turned his back on Jesus on the cross. The spirit of this Psalm in no way suggests a connection to Jesus. And what fate was pronounced by David for God's people here? Hard-heartedness? Blindness? Ignorance? Nay, but salvation! "For God will save Zion, and will build the cities of Judah: that they may dwell there, and have it in possession." (Psalm 69:35)

Jeremiah 31:31-34

> 31. Behold, the days come, saith the LORD, that I will make a new covenant with the house of Israel, and with the house of Judah: 32. Not according to the covenant that I made with their fathers in the day that I took them by the hand to bring them out of the land of Egypt; which my covenant they brake, although I was an husband unto them, saith the LORD: 33. But this shall be the covenant that I will make with the house of Israel; After those days, saith the LORD, I will put my law in their inward parts, and write it in their hearts; and will be their God, and they shall be my people. 34. And they shall teach no more every man his neighbour, and every man his brother, saying, Know the LORD: for they shall all know me, from the least of them unto the greatest of them, saith the LORD: for I will forgive their iniquity, and I will remember their sin no more.

According to the church, these verses predicted the coming of the New Testament age, and as usual, in trying to make their religious arguments stick, they resort to egregious contextual butchering to achieve the desired results. According to Christians, since the Jews broke God's Old Covenant, God got rid of it and has decided to make a New Covenant—this one "not according to the covenant" God made with Moses. First, this false view is based on a misunderstanding of the word, covenant; a covenant is a contract or agreement between two or more parties. The Old Covenant was not The Law. It was based on *the keeping* of The Law. Through idolatrous disobedience, Israel violated the old covenant—God's agreement with Israel to treasure her if she keeps his commandments...

> Now therefore, if ye will obey my voice indeed, and keep my covenant, then ye shall be a peculiar treasure unto me above all people: for all the earth is mine: (Exodus 19:5)

Obey whose voice? The voice of God through his commandments, upon which the covenant between God and Israel was based. The Old Covenant was indeed broken just as a marriage covenant is broken in a divorce because of the act of adultery. Since the Old Covenant was broken, a new one can be made. The Old Covenant was based on the written Law of Moses whereas the New Covenant would be written on a man's heart, but what was to be the content of this New Covenant? The Law: "I will put **my law** in their inward parts, and write it in their hearts" (vs.33), the same cherished law as before, only now it was ingested, a living part of every member of God's people who had forgotten God aforetime. They would remember him now and their former sins would be forgiven (vs.34). The Law was not to be new, only the covenant.

Second, these verses plainly refute the idea that this could be the "New Testament." Evangelists are trying to convert the world, telling everyone to "Know the Lord." This passage denies that such things will be said. This was to take place when both the House of Israel and the House of Judah were united again at that long-predicted time when "the earth shall be full of the knowledge of the Lord as the waters cover the seas." (Isaiah 11:9) This cannot be talking about Christianity for these reasons.

Zechariah 12:8-14

> 8. In that day shall the Lord defend the inhabitants of Jerusalem; and he that stumbleth among them at that day shall be as David; and the house of David shall be as a Godlike being, as the angel of the Lord before them. 9. And it shall come to pass in that day, that I will seek to destroy all the nations that come against Jerusalem. 10. And I will pour upon the house of David, and upon the inhabitants of Jerusalem, the spirit of grace and of supplication; **and they shall look unto Me because they have thrust him through; and they shall mourn for him**, as one mourneth for his only son, and shall be in bitterness for him, as one that is in bitterness for his first-born. 11. In that day shall there be a great mourning in Jerusalem, as the mourning of Hadadrimmon in the valley of Megiddon. 12. And the land shall mourn, every family apart: the family of the house of David apart, and their wives apart; the family of the house of Nathan apart, and their wives apart; 13. The family of the house of Levi apart, and their wives apart; the family of the Shimeites apart, and their wives apart; 14. All the families that remain, every family apart, and their wives apart.

It won't take very long studying matters of prophecy with evangelicals before Zechariah 12:10 is brought up. It is quoted in John 19:37 after Jesus' death: "And again another scripture saith, They shall look on him whom they pierced." The verses from Zechariah quoted above are from the Jewish Tanach (Jewish Publication Society, 1917) for clarity in meaning. The King James Version says, "and they shall look upon me whom they have pierced, and they shall mourn for him." The KJV text was translated to say that God was the one being pierced, but they left intact the second clause, "and they shall mourn *for him*," implying someone else was being pierced, and that someone obviously could not have been God. The one who was pierced was *not* God, but one whose death would serve as a turning point to cause the Jewish people to look towards God. Christian translators have no problem altering texts if it suits their purpose, and this is never truer than with these verses. To be more deceptive with the text, the King James translators should not have translated the second clause.

I have included the remote context of verse 10 because as with most verses claimed to be referring to Jesus, the context has been utterly ignored. Before we get to verse 10, we should start at verse 8 where it is said that God would defend the inhabitants of Jerusalem, and the one who can barely stand will be as physically vital as King David. This could not be a more different picture than the one history portrays of the first century, a time of Roman rule, where the Jews were subjugated and oppressed. The siege of Jerusalem under Emperor Vespasian took place in 70 C.E. This was not a time of great vitality or strength for Israel, and in no sense could it have been said to be. These verses speak of God's destroying the oppressing nations who come against Jerusalem. When did this happen?

What these verses predict is a time where God would induce a spirit "of grace and supplication." Precipitating end-time events would be a great battle wherein a certain individual would be slain. Who this person is we do not know, but it would induce a state of mourning like that brought on by the death of Josiah, spoken of in verse 12: "In that day shall there be a great mourning in Jerusalem, as the mourning of Hadadrimmon in the valley of Megiddon." 2 Chronicles 35:22-25 provides us with the background...

> 22. Nevertheless Josiah would not turn his face from him, but disguised himself, that he might fight with him, and hearkened not unto the words of Necho from the mouth of God, and came to fight in the valley of Megiddo. 23. And the archers shot at king Josiah; and the king said to his servants, Have me away; for I am sore wounded. 24. His servants therefore took him out of that chariot, and put him in the second chariot that he had; and they brought him to Jerusalem, and he died, and was buried in one of the sepulchres of his fathers. And all Judah and Jerusalem mourned for Josiah. 25. And Jeremiah lamented for Josiah: and all the singing men and the singing women spake of Josiah in their lamentations to this day, and made them an ordinance in Israel: and, behold, they are written in the lamentations.

The young, righteous king, rivaling even the righteousness and virtue of King David let his bright light shine on an otherwise dark line of kings who did not walk in faithful service to God. Zechariah makes note of this great loss and compares it to a day in Israel's future when God's people would be inspired towards faithfulness and holiness. It should be remembered that Josiah was killed ("pierced") by an arrow. The death predicted in Zechariah would also result from a piercing, but Jesus died of suffocation on the cross. He was pierced only after his death, which is yet another indication that the message of the gospel writers doesn't match up with the details of Zechariah's story.

Where is Jesus in all of this? The great mourning predicted by Zechariah was to be like the one in Josiah's day—universal. Jesus' own followers only partially mourned his loss, but hardly all the tribes of Israel as described (Zechariah 12:11-14). The event spoken of in Zechariah does not match the gospel story and cannot credibly be interpreted to describe a first century crucifixion.

Isaiah 53:1-12

> 1. Who hath believed our report? and to whom is the arm of the LORD revealed? 2. For he shall grow up before him as a tender plant, and as a root out of a dry ground: he hath no form nor comeliness; and when we shall see him, there is no beauty that we should desire him. 3. He is despised and rejected of men; a man of sorrows, and acquainted with grief: and we hid as it were our faces from him; he was despised, and we esteemed him not. 4. Surely he hath borne our griefs, and carried our sorrows: yet we did esteem him stricken, smitten of God, and afflicted. 5. But he was wounded for our transgressions, he was bruised for our iniquities: the chastisement of our peace was upon him; and with his stripes we are healed. 6. All we like sheep have gone astray; we have turned every one to his own way; and the LORD hath laid on him the iniquity of us all. 7. He was oppressed, and he was afflicted, yet he opened not his mouth: he is brought as a lamb to the slaughter, and as a sheep before her shearers is dumb, so he openeth not his mouth. 8. He was taken from prison and from judgment: and who shall declare his generation? for he was cut off out of the land of the living: for the transgression of my people was he stricken. 9. And he made his grave with the wicked, and with the rich in his death; because he had done no violence, neither was any deceit in his mouth. 10. Yet it pleased the LORD to bruise him; he hath put him to grief: when thou shalt make his soul an offering for sin, he shall see his seed, he shall prolong his days, and the pleasure of the LORD shall prosper in his hand. 11. He shall see of the travail of his soul, and shall be satisfied: by his knowledge shall my righteous servant justify many; for he shall bear their iniquities. 12. Therefore will I divide him a portion with the great, and he shall divide the spoil with the strong; because he hath poured out his soul unto death: and he was numbered with the transgressors; and he bare the sin of many, and made intercession for the transgressors.

This is heralded as the hallmark of all Bible prophecy passages, as the life and sacrifice of Jesus in prophecy. A lot has been written about these verses, and many congregations have heard these words, but unfortunately for them, they haven't heard much else from the book of Isaiah. Unfortunately for believers, Jesus is not to be found anywhere in Isaiah. These verses are describing Israel. Israel is identified a number of times in Isaiah as the servant...

First, let's consider the context of Isaiah 53. Isaiah 52 should have been added to what is chapter 53 because the subject is the same and will help to clear up the confusion in the next chapter...

> Awake, awake; put on thy strength, **O Zion; put on thy beautiful garments, O Jerusalem, the holy city**: for henceforth there shall no more come into thee the uncircumcised and the unclean. 2. Shake thyself from the dust; arise, and sit down, O Jerusalem: loose thyself from the bands of thy neck, O captive daughter of Zion...13. Behold, **my servant** shall deal prudently, he shall be exalted and extolled, and be very high. 14. As many were astonied at thee; **his visage was so marred** more than any man, and his form more than the sons of men: 15. So shall he sprinkle many nations; **the kings shall shut their mouths at him**: for that which had not been told them shall they see; and that which they had not heard shall they consider. (Isaiah 52:1-2, 13-15)

God is speaking of Jerusalem. He (Jerusalem) is described as a servant, a disfigured man, and an astonishment to other nations. It's not hard to see already the similarity to chapter 53. Israel is described as a marred, despised figure. Now we jump to chapter 54...

> 3. For thou shalt break forth on the right hand and on the left; and thy seed shall inherit the Gentiles, and make the desolate cities to be inhabited 4. **Fear not; for thou shalt not be ashamed: neither be thou confounded; for thou shalt not be put to shame: for thou shalt forget the shame of thy youth, and shalt not remember the reproach of thy widowhood any more.** 5. For thy Maker is thine husband; the LORD of hosts is his name; and thy Redeemer the Holy One of Israel; The God of the whole earth shall he be called. (Isaiah 54:3-5)

None too surprisingly, Israel is still the focus as these verses discuss a future time when the marred and maimed servant of God would stand proud and vindicated among the nations. So we have seen that chapters 52 and 54 of Isaiah are speaking of Israel, God's servant, and this compels us to ask the question: How can Isaiah 53 be speaking of Christ when both chapters before and after it are speaking of Israel? Lest there be any hint of confusion, let's spend a minute longer to nail down the language of Isaiah. Isaiah uses the language incorporated in chapter 53 all throughout his work, and every time, it refers to Israel…

> But thou, Israel, art my servant, Jacob whom I have chosen, the seed of Abraham my friend. (Isaiah 41:8)

> Ye are my witnesses, saith the LORD, and my servant whom I have chosen: that ye may know and believe me, and understand that I am he: before me there was no God formed, neither shall there be after me. (Isaiah 43:10)

> Thus saith the LORD, the Redeemer of Israel, and his Holy One, **to him whom man despiseth, to him whom the nation abhorreth, to a servant of rulers**, Kings shall see and arise, princes also shall worship, because of the LORD that is faithful, and the Holy One of Israel, and he shall choose thee. (Isaiah 49:7)

Since we have established that the language used by Isaiah is addressing Israel, how are we to assume Christ is being addressed in chapter 53? And now that we have established a language base for Isaiah, we can move on to the content of chapter 53, but before we do, we must ask who is speaking. God is not speaking, Israel is not speaking, nor is Isaiah. The Gentile kings are the primary speakers in Isaiah 53. We see this by referring back to chapter 52:15: "the kings shall shut their mouths at him: for that which had not been told them shall they see; and that which they had not heard shall they consider."

Consider how nicely the chapter reads with this understanding…

1. *Who hath believed our report?* [The non-Jewish kings of the earth speaking] *and to whom is the arm of the LORD revealed?*

The arm of the Lord refers to God's delivering strength with which he would redeem Jerusalem (52:9-10). When Israel would be redeemed, the kings would be confused, speechless (52:15), wondering how and why God was fighting for Israel when for so long the nation had been kept so low, so despicable, and so pitied. How now could he be delivered and standing with the strength of the almighty?

2. *For he shall grow up before him* [Israel, growing up before God] *as a tender plant, and as a root out of a dry ground: he hath no form nor comeliness; and when we shall see him, there is no beauty that we should desire him.*

Persecuted, captive, downtrodden Israel was decrepit and undernourished, a sorry image of how God's people should have appeared. Those nations who look upon him were astounded at the pitiable sight, but that pitied nation was about to be vindicated by God.

3-4. 3. He is despised and rejected of men; a man of sorrows, and acquainted with grief: and we hid as it were our faces from him; he was despised, and we esteemed him not. 4. Surely he hath borne our griefs, and carried our sorrows: yet we did esteem him stricken, smitten of God, and afflicted.

The Gentile nations bear the guilt of countless generations of persecuting God's people. So "acquainted with grief" was Israel that no one wanted to look upon him. Truly, he was "smitten" of God. Israel bore enough sorrow and guilt for the whole world—griefs that could have been laid on the heads of his oppressors – the Gentiles – but as we shall see, instead of punishing the nations that once wronged God's servant, salvation was to be spread; "all the ends of the earth shall see the salvation of God." (52:10)

5-8. 5. But he was wounded for our transgressions, he was bruised for our iniquities: the chastisement of our peace was upon him; and with his stripes we are healed. 6. All we like sheep have gone astray; we have turned every one to his own way; and the LORD hath laid on him the iniquity of us all. 7. He was oppressed, and he was afflicted, yet he opened not his mouth: he is brought as a lamb to the slaughter, and as a sheep before her shearers is dumb, so he openeth not his mouth. 8. He was taken from prison and from judgment: and who shall declare his generation? for he was cut off out of the land of the living: for the transgression of my people was he stricken.

Israel sat silently, without a voice in the world, while the nations around him abhorred and abused him. Because of his sins, it was by the will of God that Israel be rewarded doubly by the nations that oppressed him (40:2), and he was forgiven, but in the process, he bore the sins of the Gentiles who afflicted him; instead of being destroyed like Babylon (Isaiah 13-14), the Gentiles would be pardoned and allowed to partake in the deliverance extended to God's servant, and this deliverance was extended to every nation.

Additionally, we need to make a translational correction here; the text does not say, "with his stripes we *are* healed" but "with his stripes we *were* healed." Christian-biased translations want it to seem as though this forgiveness is ongoing, that this has reference to Jesus. Not so. The nations *were* healed, but the process will not be ongoing. Once forgiven, the Gentiles would partake in the universal peace that would commence thereafter (Isaiah 2:4).

9-10. 9. And he made his grave with the wicked, and with the rich in his death; because he had done no violence, neither was any deceit in his mouth. 10. Yet it pleased the LORD to bruise him; he hath put him to grief: when thou [The Gentile kings were speaking, but now notice how the voice changes, "thou." Isaiah is now speaking of God's purpose for Israel's future.] *shalt make his soul an offering for sin, he shall see his seed, he shall prolong his days, and the pleasure of the LORD shall prosper in his hand.*

Attempts to connect this chapter with the crucifixion continue as some point out that the suffering servant's making a grave with the wicked and with the rich in his death seems to describe Jesus' death on the cross alongside evildoers, and in the tomb of the rich man, Joseph of Arimathea. This is superficial, however. C. Dennis McKinsey, in his *Encyclopedia of Biblical Errancy* points out…

> When was Jesus with the rich in his death and when did he make his grave with the wicked? The outcome of this verse was actually reversed as far as Jesus is concerned. Christ made his grave with the rich by being buried in the sepulchre of the rich Joseph of Arimathea, and he was with the wicked, the crucified thieves, in his death. (p. 162)

We must point out that once again a mistranslation needs to be corrected. Many translations are guilty of not bearing this out; "death" here is plural—"in his deaths." The nation dies as its citizens are reduced in number. The biblical God's nation suffered as an evildoer, as though to die a deserving death. How did the nation die? If he made his grave with the ungodly and was cut off out of the land of the living, then this can only be speaking of the nation. Notice verse 10 says, "he shall see his seed, he shall prolong his days." A nation could "die" in a way an individual couldn't. Israel died in the sense that his influence, his voice, his power, and his presence in the world would be diminished beyond recognition during his years as a marred, despised, pitied vessel—he "died" as any diminishing people would, teetering on the brink of extinction. But all hope was not lost. He would see his offspring, his days of power and glory would return, he would "prolong" his days. The once great servant of God who suffered spiritual disfigurement would regain his glorious prowess. Jesus had no *seed* "zerith"—always used in the Old Testament to refer to literal, physical, fleshly descendants. Naturally, a nation has descendants (seed) to pass on. Jesus did not, and one cannot make the argument that the church was Jesus' spiritual "seed." The wording here does not permit that.

11-12. *11. He* [God] *shall see of the travail of his* [Israel's] *soul, and shall be satisfied: by his knowledge shall my righteous servant justify many; for he* [Israel] *shall bear their* [the Gentiles] *iniquities. 12. Therefore will I divide him a portion with the great, and he shall divide the spoil with the strong; because he hath poured out his soul unto death: and he was numbered with the transgressors; and he bare the sin of many, and made intercession for the transgressors.*

God is now satisfied. His servant has suffered enough. His days of misery and death will come to an abrupt end. What would be Israel's portion then? He would divide to himself a portion with the greatest and strongest nations, "and he shall divide the spoil with the strong." And how would the righteous servant justify many? Not by blood, but by knowledge! If ever there was a place to teach a blood sacrifice to redeem our souls, it would be here, but not a hint of such an idea is to be found. The many and long years of darkness God's people experienced, their unfair treatment at the hands of mightier nations, their enduring of suffering and death – instead of bringing them to an end – would cause them to be raised up as an intercessor, a shining light to all nations (Isaiah 11).

Staying true to the roots of the author and the intended message of the book, we can only conclude that this chapter is speaking of the suffering servant, Israel. It speaks of a time when the lowly nation we know today would be exalted above all others and serve as a light, leading the entire world to the God of Abraham. This position fits perfectly with many other passages in the Old Testament. This represents the position of Orthodox Judaism today.

If this, the hallmark of Bible prophecies of Jesus, falters under the heat of criticism, what other passages could possibly be brought to the table that could withstand scrutiny? Without spending hours, laboriously debunking all the other out-of-context passages believers use in support of Jesus and Christianity, we can rest in the firm conclusion that not one prophecy in the Old Testament has a thing to do with Jesus.

Believers in Christendom constantly remind us of the unbelievable odds of Jesus coincidently fitting so many biblical prophecies. Josh McDowell says...

> One could possibly find one or two prophecies fulfilled in the lives of other men, but not all sixty-one major prophecies! In fact, for years, if you could have found someone other than Jesus, living or dead, who fulfilled half of the predictions concerning Messiah, as listed in Messiah in Both Testaments by Fred John Meldau, the Christian Victory Publishing Company of Denver offered to give you a one-thousand dollar reward. There are a lot of men in the universities who could have used this extra cash! (*The New Evidence That Demands a Verdict*, p. 193)

McDowell goes on to list the odds against Jesus fulfilling just 8 of the major prophecies. This is one of those instances where we need to pull out the "figures don't lie, but liars figure" quote. McDowell is wrong. Jesus doesn't fulfill 61 major prophecies, and barely can he be said to fulfill several. Fancy calculations will do nothing to remedy this. An exhaustive refutation of every so-called prophecy in the Bible is not necessary.

Other Scriptural Abuses

I refer to Christian mishandling of the scriptures as abuse for the fact that the nature of the misuse is so grand that it requires tremendous deviance on the part of apologists to defend such views. Being indoctrinated like I was, I can see how one can become convinced that certain passages in Jeremiah, Isaiah, and Zechariah are speaking of Jesus. What I can't see, and what is theologically unforgivable, is the careless way the gospel writers mishandle the scriptures. Like wild banshees, the gospel writers (Matthew in particular) yank passages out of the Old Testament almost at random and apply them to Jesus. These misapplied scriptures can be seen for what they are by just casually reading the contexts of their origins.

Matthew 2:15 quotes Hosea 11:1, "And was there until the death of Herod: that it might be fulfilled which was spoken of the Lord by the prophet, saying, Out of Egypt have I called my son." Hosea is talking about the Exodus from Egypt, not Jesus. A simple reading of the context makes this as obvious as can be.

Matthew 2:16-18 incorrectly cites and then quotes Jeremiah 31:18 as though Jeremiah foretold Herod's alleged massacre of children two years old and up...

> 16. Then Herod, when he saw that he was mocked of the wise men, was exceeding wroth, and sent forth, and slew all the children that were in Bethlehem, and in all the coasts thereof, from two years old and under, according to the time which he had diligently enquired of the wise men. 17. Then was fulfilled that which was spoken by Jeremy the prophet, saying, 18. In Rama was there a voice heard, lamentation, and weeping, and great mourning, Rachel weeping for her children, and would not be comforted, because they are not.

If Matthew can make Jeremiah's words apply to a first century event we have no record of, then I can make it apply with just as much validity to a modern day Rachel who lost her kids in an automobile accident. Who was really weeping? Israel was weeping. Why? Because of the people's longing to be re-gathered to their own land...

> 8. Behold, I will bring them from the north country, and gather them from the coasts of the earth, and with them the blind and the lame, the woman with child and her that travaileth with child together: a great company shall return thither. 9. **They shall come with weeping, and with supplications will I lead them**: I will cause them to walk by the rivers of waters in a straight way, wherein they shall not stumble: for I am a father to Israel, and Ephraim is my firstborn. (Jeremiah 31:8-9)
> 15. Thus saith the LORD; A voice was heard in Ramah, lamentation, and bitter weeping; Rahel weeping for her children refused to be comforted for her children, because they were not. 16. Thus saith the LORD; **Refrain thy voice from weeping, and thine eyes from tears: for thy work shall be rewarded, saith the LORD; and they shall come again from the land of the enemy.** (Jeremiah 31:15-16)

Rachel (a metaphor for the spirit of the people crying out with care for their fellows) was weeping because not all her children were home, and God assures the people that they shall be. These passages have no other meaning.

Matthew 2:23 quotes a verse that exists nowhere in the scriptures. "And he came and dwelt in a city called Nazareth: that it might be fulfilled which was spoken by the prophets, He shall be called a Nazarene." There is no verse, nor a part of a verse that says anything like, "He shall be called a Nazarene," anywhere in the Old Testament. This one was made up out of thin air, it seems. Efforts to make this seem to be referring to the word "branch" in Isaiah 11:1 are not worth commenting on.

Matthew 27:9 quotes Jeremiah as saying, "And they took the thirty pieces of silver, the price of him that was valued, whom they of the children of Israel did value." The correct reference was Zechariah 11:12-13, though these have nothing to do with a crucified god-man.

Religious Systems That Do Not Match

The Christianization of the Hebrew scriptures has done more than serve the purposes of the church. In some ways, it has created little theological debates that are with us to this day. As a preacher, I was afforded many opportunities to discuss the differences I had with ministers of other faiths. Some of these differences were quite big, and more often than not, they had to do with eschatological matters, and I couldn't help but see the contradictions that kept showing up between our belief systems. The Old Testament and the conflicting ideologies of the New Testament factored into almost every one of these contradictions. For instance, the Old Testament teaches that when the end-of-days messiah comes, all the earth will unite to worship the God of Israel, but it also says, they would keep the Feast of Tabernacles and make animal sacrifices...

> And it shall come to pass, that every one that is left of all the nations which came against Jerusalem shall even go up from year to year to worship the King, the LORD of hosts, and **to keep the feast of tabernacles.** (Zechariah 14:18)

> Yea, every pot in Jerusalem and in Judah shall be holiness unto the LORD of hosts: and **all they that sacrifice shall come and take of them, and seethe therein**: and in that day there shall be no more the Canaanite in the house of the LORD of hosts. (Zechariah 14:21)

But according to the New Testament, no one can be judged by observances of holy days, and animal sacrifices are no longer necessary...

> 16. Let no man therefore judge you in meat, or in drink, or in respect of an holyday, or of the new moon, or of the sabbath days: 17. Which are a shadow of things to come; but the body is of Christ. (Colossians 2:16-17)

> 11. And every priest standeth daily ministering and offering oftentimes the same sacrifices, which can never take away sins: 12. But this man, after he had offered one sacrifice for sins for ever, sat down on the right hand of God; (Hebrews 10:11-12)

So we have a problem; according to Zechariah, feast days and sacrifices will still be in effect in the distant, spiritually glorified future that awaits the world, but according to Paul and the writer of the Hebrew letter, one need not observe Jewish feast days or offer animal sacrifices. We can either admit that the New Testament is a perversion of the Old and is not legitimate, or we must accept that the old Jewish feast days and animal sacrifices must still be offered, even if they mean absolutely nothing—and I have known a few preachers who tried to defend this latter position. Only one answer stands out. The religious systems of the two covenants do not match and cannot be made to fit together.

What the Old Testament Doesn't Say

Up to now, we have been concerned with clearing away the cobwebs of error by laying hold onto what the Old Testament actually says, but we should just as well be reminded of what it doesn't say. Nowhere in the

Old Testament do we find any of the core teachings that define the New Testament and Jesus. Nowhere do the Hebrew scriptures speak of a Trinitarian god. Nowhere in the scriptures do we find a death, burial, and resurrection of a god-man after three days in the grave. Nowhere do we find a suffering messiah or a rejected messiah. The more closely we study the Old Testament, the clearer it becomes that Christ is not a part of it.

CHAPTER 11
Puppets on a String

A Look at Biblical Predestination

"Believers are called in accordance with a settled plan and purpose of God, for whom He calls He had previously predestinated."
- Charles Hodge

"God preordained, for his own glory and the display of His attributes of mercy and justice, a part of the human race, without any merit of their own, to eternal salvation, and another part, in just punishment of their sin, to eternal damnation."
- John Calvin

One of the most sublime beauties of childhood is unrestrained creativity. In manner of thought, the bright, creative child is very much like a creating god. Being ignorant of the laws of reality and physics, the child is free from the hindrances which are the limitations of our world, and this enables the child to truly "create" as though they were a deity, having no conceptual limits. When children play, they are creating their own universes to house their battles and epics. In these universes, the laws of reality are not like our own. When a young mind thinks of a cosmically strong man able to lift a battleship out of the water, the child sees no problem with the scenario, but an adult certainly would. The set of hands trying to raise a sixty-thousand-ton object are going to go right through the hull of the ship, making it impossible to lift, but such predicaments don't exist in the world of fantasy. This allows children's minds to conceive more freely.

And the child is free in other ways too; the child is not interested in copyright considerations, trademark laws, or content originality or scrutiny, or what some double-chinned editor who sits behind a mahogany wood desk and makes forty grand a year might think of his ideas. It didn't matter what anyone else thought about my creations as a child. They were mine and that was all that mattered. As with sharing toys, children are selfish with their ideas, and selfishness also happens to be another similarity between children and the God of the Bible; free from all restraints and reservations, both children and gods control the destinies of their creations to whatever end they have planned for them.

As an honors English student, my first attempt at a horror story was at age eight. It was called, "The House on the Hill" and was the story of a boy my age who decided to take a shortcut over a certain hill on the way home from school. Out of curiosity, he decided to take a peek inside one particular old house. Upon entering, the door blew shut behind him and locked. After ten pages of eerie noises and suspense, a spike-headed monster in tattered clothes appeared and terrifyingly killed the boy. Not really original, but damn good for an eight-year-old, I'd say! The teachers loved it. One said to me, "Holman, I expect to see your name in print someday." I'm glad to know I didn't let him down!

I was proud of my story, but something about it bothered me greatly. The fate of the boy in the story was what bothered me. The story went through a revision—a revision I later tossed into the wastebasket only moments after it was written. In that revision, the boy made it out alive. I changed it because my family protested that the original was too negative. They wanted a happy ending, but I always thought good horror stories had to end badly to be worth reading, so I tossed the happy-ending revision without much deliberation. I was still a little bothered though. The boy from this story seemed to take on a life of his own, as though to say to me, "Give me a nicer fate. You wouldn't want to face this horrible destiny." But I shook off this fear when I remembered my purpose in creating him.

I was a cruel creator. I created this boy. He was an innocent, goodhearted schoolboy just like I was. I fashioned him as I saw fit, even gave him a face and a style of clothes in the dressing room of my mind. He was predestined by me, his creator, to die at the hands of a monster from the netherworld. Every fiction writer works the same way, creating characters as hosts to carry the messages of the story. The comedies and the dramas unfold in the theatre of the mind. The story is just the vessel, the setting wherein the ideas of the writer unfold, but the story doesn't come alive until the characters come alive within us.

The characters we create exist only for our pleasure, to cry or to laugh, to introduce an idea, to provide a motive or a plot twist, to create confusion, to bring fear, or to show pain. These characters might not exist in the real world, but as far as the life of the story goes, they exist on the same level as anyone ever has. The mental realities we give to our ideas could well be called realities all their own; after all, every invention of man that now exists in the material world once existed only in concept form.

When one speaks of the cruelty of the gods, one cannot help but speak of the cruelty of humans. Humans are cruel creators, and so it's no wonder the gods and goddesses we created out of fear and ignorance are equally cruel. The gods are products of our imaginations, which is why they are such intolerant and terrorizing monsters. They are no different than their creators. Even as I wrote the story, I almost felt the terror I chose to inflict on this specter of a boy, which had me wondering, had I possessed the power to create a real world and a real boy to suffer as described in the story, would I have done so? If creating worlds for my whimsical purposes was as easy to me as a child fashioning a horror story, would I have been as terribly cruel a creator as the one spoken of in the pages of Holy Writ?

The God of the Bible has his own horror story, and the terror and the drama of it has been playing out on the stage of tangible existence for at least the last fifteen billion years (only 6,000 years according to scripture). In the middle of a cold and inhospitable universe lies a cold and inhospitable world, a small, pitiable planet where social and moral chaos abounds. The sun is the spotlight, the stars are the stage lights, the moon is a background prop, the clouds are the curtains, and we humans are the fulltime cast in the drama/comedy/horror/action sitcom acted out on the stage of life. The plights we face we can only accept, for no amount of loathing, loving, or calling in sick at the last moment can get us out of playing our parts. We are locked into our particular roles in space and time as surely as a branch falls into a lake at the beckoning of gravity. We are – each and every one of us – imprisoned to fulfill our distinct destinies. The script is written. There are no last minute changes, and everyone always gets it right on the first take.

The Bible's Teaching on Predestination

The most comforting illusion inferred from the Bible is that of freewill. The Bible is held up as a book of justice and a declaration of freedom for the soul. The masses of America and the world see it as a book of liberty, a book to help make the right choices, when in fact, the Bible is a book of the exact opposite, a book of predestination. Many Christians believe in predestination, and well-known churches will defend it as an almost untouchable Bible doctrine, but overall, the churches of the world are split 50/50 on the issue. As a Christian and preacher, I defended the freewill doctrine, and some time after I became an atheist, I held that the Bible is contradictory because it both teaches and denies predestination, depending on which passages are consulted. Over the last several years, however, I have come to agree strongly that the Augustinian and Calvinistic churches have it right. Normally, this subject would be considered an in-house debate between believers of different camps, but I feel so strongly about it that I have decided to include this chapter on it. The Bible unequivocally teaches predestination, and the moral implications of that position show us much about the character of the God of the Bible.

As every wise and aged preacher knows, there are a good number of Bible passages that are not fit for public reading to a congregation. Only once in a blue moon will you hear a preacher quote from Song of Solomon or Judges during a sermon, and very seldom will you hear a minister quote from many parts of Exodus, Leviticus, or Numbers. Joining this rank are the Bible's predestination passages. Preachers realize it is difficult to explain them away, so like the many obscene Bible verses that aren't read from pulpits, these verses also get little attention.

Paul, in Romans 8:28-30, discusses the fashioning of an individual into a Christian...

> And we know that all things work together for good to them that love God, to them who are called according to his purpose. **For whom he did foreknow, he also did predestinate to be conformed to the image of his son**, that he might be the firstborn among many brethren. Moreover whom he did predestinate, them he also called, and whom he called, them he also justified, and whom he justified, them he also glorified.

Those who were called, the text says, were predestined so. In Ephesians, Paul again tells us that Christians themselves are predestinated to become so...

> According as **he hath chosen us in him before the foundation of the world,** that we should be holy and without blame before him in love. Having predestinated us unto the adoption of children by Jesus Christ to himself, according to the good pleasure of his will. (Ephesians 1:4-5)

Notice it says God chose us in him before the world was—meaning he selected who would be redeemed beforehand. You may think you have a choice in the matter, but you don't. As far as God is concerned, the final chapter is already written. You have been pre-selected to either bask in the glory of Heaven, or walk on the flaming coals of Hell. Evil itself comes from God...

> I form the light and create darkness: **I make peace and create evil.** I the Lord do all these things. (Isaiah 45:7)

Hear the words of Amos, the servant of the Lord...

> Shall a trumpet be blown in the city, and the people not be afraid? **shall there be evil in a city, and the LORD hath not done it?** (Amos 3:6)

The verse is clearly exalting God's control over the forces of this world, one of these forces being evil. The same God who created the forces of light created the forces of darkness...

> And it came to pass when **the evil spirit from God** was upon Saul that David took an harp and played with his hand, so Saul was refreshed, and was well, and **the evil spirit departed from him.** (I Samuel 16:23)

It is often said that the "evil spirit from God" referred to is just a figure of speech for anger produced from Saul's own envy of David's godliness and success. The text refutes this, however. "The evil spirit from God" was upon Saul. It was David whom Saul was angry at, so if "spirit" was just a euphemism for a state of anger, why doesn't the text say "evil spirit of David," (the person he was angry at) or "evil spirit of Saul" (angry within himself)? It makes no sense to say that the evil spirit was from God unless God was directly making Saul angry. If that is not enough, God sent a lying spirit to Ahab to persuade him to head into a losing battle...

> Now therefore, behold, the LORD hath put a lying spirit in the mouth of all these thy prophets, and the LORD hath spoken evil concerning thee. (I Kings 22:23)

Spirits did everything in this period of time, so it should not be a surprise if God sends an evil spirit to keep someone in a state of anger or to deceive someone. In preparation for the Exodus, God hardened the heart of Pharaoh. There is the temptation to think that God hardened Pharaoh's heart by simply giving him demands he was unwilling to meet. Thus, God hardened Pharaoh's heart (Exodus 9:12), and Pharaoh hardened his own heart (Exodus 8:15), but this is erroneous reasoning. Exodus 10:1 says *"Go in unto pharaoh for I have hardened his heart and the heart of his servants that I might show forth these signs,"* yet the fact that God keeps repeating this after every plague encounter with Pharaoh shows that God was working the situation directly, hardening Pharaoh's heart for the sake of more miracles and self-exaltation. Accordingly, the servants whose hearts God hardened along with Pharaoh are re-hardened after they became initially convinced that the Hebrew God was real: *"This is the finger of God,"* said Pharaoh's magicians, as they briefly became believers (Exodus 8:19), until God hardened their hearts again in chapters 9:34-10:1.

If it were not for all of this, both Testaments make very clear what we have said so far: God raised up Pharaoh to knock him down again for the purpose of exalting himself...

> And in very deed for this cause have I raised thee up, for to shew in thee my power; and that my name may be declared throughout all the earth. (Exodus 9:16)

> For the scripture saith unto Pharaoh, Even for this purpose have I raised thee up, that I might shew my power in thee, and that my name might be declared throughout all the Earth. (Romans 9:17)

A more indirect passage on the subject of predestination concerns Hophni and Phinehas, the two wicked sons of Eli the priest...

> If one man sin against another, the judge shall judge him, but if a man sin against the lord, who shall intreat for him? Notwithstanding they harkened not unto the voice of their father **because the lord would slay them**. (I Samuel 2:25)

That's right, you read the verse correctly; it says Hophni and Phinehas did not repent of their sins *because* God wanted to kill them. The RSV translates the last part of the verse; "for it was the will of the LORD to slay them."

In other words, God was so offended by them that he had them marked for death. They were impenitent because he had it in for them and didn't give them the freedom of mind to change. This is what the Lord meant in Proverbs 16:4 when he said, "The Lord hath made all things for himself, **yea, even the wicked for the day of evil.**" (Proverbs 16:4)

But by far the most expressive of the sets of predestination verses found in the Bible are found in Romans 9:20-23...

> Nay but, O man, who art thou that repliest against God? **Shall the thing formed say to him that formed it, why hast thou made me thus? hath not the potter power over the clay, of the same lump to make one vessel unto honor and another unto dishonor?** What if God, willing to shew his wrath, and to make his power known, endured with much longsuffering the vessels of wrath fitted to destruction: and that he might make known the riches of his glory on the vessels of mercy, which he had afore prepared unto glory.

This tells us the following: (a) God can raise up and cast down anyone so long as his purpose is served. (b) God cannot be questioned about whom he chooses to have mercy upon and whom he chooses to condemn, since the created can never answer back his creator anymore than a piece of pottery can inquire to its potter as to why it was made the way it was. (c) God has foreordained some vessels unto destruction and some unto honor, riches, and heavenly glory. (d) He will resist and bear with the vessels fitted to destruction for the sake of those he prepared for glory.

In an attempt to "answer" my claims about Paul's words here, freewill apologists run to the text where the potter illustration was first used (Jeremiah 18:7-10)...

> 6. O house of Israel, cannot I do with you as this potter? saith the LORD. Behold, as the clay is in the potter's hand, so are ye in mine hand, O house of Israel. 7. At what instant I shall speak concerning a nation, and concerning a kingdom, to pluck up, and to pull down, and to destroy it; 8. If that nation, against whom I have pronounced, turn from their evil, I will repent of the evil that I thought to do unto them. 9. And at what instant I shall speak concerning a nation, and concerning a kingdom, to build and to plant it; 10. If it do evil in my sight, that it obey not my voice, then I will repent of the good, wherewith I said I would benefit them.

Since Israel was admonished not to be a marred vessel in the hands of the potter, say freewill apologists, Paul in Romans must be using the same application. The application is wrong. Paul uses the same potter and clay illustration, but his focus is different from Jeremiah's. Jeremiah is discussing repentance, and Paul is discussing God's heaven-bound elect. Jeremiah was trying to sequester the penitence of a nation, but Paul is addressing more relevant, eternal matters; he is discussing the "Israelites; to whom pertaineth the adoption, and the glory, and the covenants, and the giving of the law, and the service of God, and the promises." (Romans 9:4) It would be fallacious to assume that because the same analogy is used by Paul and Jeremiah that the application is the same; it isn't. Jeremiah is encouraging repentance while Paul is explaining God's rational on those he favors and those he doesn't.

The Parable of the Wheat and Tares and Alleged Freewill Passages

In Matthew 13:24-30, Jesus gives the parable of the wheat and tares...

> 24. Another parable put he forth unto them, saying, The kingdom of heaven is likened unto a man which sowed good seed in his field: 25. But while men slept, his enemy came and sowed tares among the wheat, and went his way. 26. But when the blade was sprung up, and brought forth fruit, then appeared the tares also. 27. So the servants of the householder came and said unto him, Sir, didst not thou sow good seed in thy field? from whence then hath it tares? 28. He said unto them, An enemy hath done this. The servants said unto him, Wilt thou then that we go and gather them up? 29. But he said, Nay; lest while ye gather up the tares, ye root up also the wheat with them. 30. Let both grow together until the harvest: and in the time of harvest I will say to the reapers, Gather ye together first the tares, and bind them in bundles to burn them: but gather the wheat into my barn.

"From whence then hath it tares?" It was the work of the enemy. Notice Jesus addressed these tares for what they were—unwanted growths in his garden. Even at the start of life, the nature of the tare, a "bad seed," was different from that of the wheat. A person was born either as a wheat or a tare, and time would show who was what. A person could not have a change of heart and adopt another nature because the parable is dealing with the nature of the type of individual. Jesus' illustration demonstrates two distinct classes present throughout the New Testament, the elect and non-elect, the saved and the unsaved.

The significance of this parable is strong because it explains for us certain passages in the New Testament that seem to teach freewill.

These lose their force when we examine them more closely. 1 Timothy 2:4 speaks of God "Who will have all men to be saved, and to come unto the knowledge of the truth." If God wants everyone to be saved, then why isn't everyone saved? And if, as the doctrine of predestination suggests, only a limited number of souls will be drawn to God (John 6:44-45), why do the scriptures speak of God wanting all to be saved? 1 John 2:2 speaks of Christ being "the propitiation for our sins: and not for ours only, but also for the sins of the whole world." If Jesus died for everyone, how can everyone not be included in the elect? The parable of the wheat and tares tells us; passages in the New testament that have to do with evangelism are written from the standpoint of our outlook of the unsaved—from the beginning it is not apparent who is and who is not part of the elect. Only the trials of life will declare it. (1 Corinthians 3:10-15) The parable of the wheat and tares lets us know that God wants his people to make every effort to spread the redeeming word to as many as possible, because only God knows the identity of the elect, for "many are called, but few are chosen." (Matthew 22:14) So we find no conflict between so-called freewill and predestination passages.

There are many other passages in the Bible, including some in the Old Testament, that appear to teach freewill, but are found to tie right back into God's predestined plan for his people. Joshua 24:15-16 says...

> 15. And if it seem evil unto you to serve the LORD, **choose you this day whom ye will serve**; whether the gods which your fathers served that were on the other side of the flood, or the gods of the Amorites, in whose land ye dwell: but as for me and my house, we will serve the LORD. 16. And the people answered and said, God forbid that we should forsake the LORD, to serve other gods;

In every instance when God gives his people a choice, the "choice" always ties back into God's plan for his people. It was prophesied in Deuteronomy 30 that after numerous apostasies, Israel would eventually be returned by God to their homeland...

> 1. And it shall come to pass, when all these things are come upon thee, the blessing and the curse, which I have set before thee, and thou shalt call them to mind among all the nations, whither the LORD thy God hath driven thee, **2. And shalt return unto the LORD thy God, and shalt obey his voice according to all that I command thee this day**, thou and thy children, with all thine heart, and with all thy soul; 3. That then the LORD thy God will turn thy captivity, and have compassion upon thee, and will return and gather thee from all the nations, whither the LORD thy God hath scattered thee. (Deuteronomy 30:1-3)

Israel would come back to God no matter what! There are always options to choose from, but these are factored into the ultimate plan of God: "And the LORD thy God will circumcise thine heart, and the heart of thy seed, to love the LORD thy God with all thine heart, and with all thy soul, that thou mayest live." (Deuteronomy 30:6) A choice is only an option, but not freedom from divine will. The same can be said of every other alleged freewill passage in holy writ.

In Matthew 11:27, Jesus taught predestination when he said...

> All things are delivered unto me of my father: and no man knoweth the son but the father, neither knoweth any man the father save the son **and he to whomsoever the son will reveal him.**

From this verse, we learn that Jesus' enlightening influence is required to know God. Evidently, he won't have it so that everyone can know him. Mark 4:11-12 says Jesus spoke in parables because the knowledge of heaven was only given to those Jesus wanted to bestow it on (at that time, his disciples). He used parables to confuse his listeners...

> 11. And he said unto them, **Unto you it is given to know the mystery of the kingdom of God: but unto them that are without, all these things are done in parables: 12. That seeing they may see, and not perceive; and hearing they may hear, and not understand;** lest at any time they should be converted, and their sins should be forgiven them.

This is what Jesus meant when he said he would reveal the father to "whomsoever he will reveal him." There are other places in the scriptures where God plays an active role in opening hearts and minds to his word...

> And a certain woman named Lydia, a seller of purple, of the city of Thyatira, which worshipped God, heard us, **whose heart the lord opened**, that she attended unto the things which were spoken of Paul. (Acts 16:14)

Most hard-line sects of the Church of Christ are almost deistic in their thinking, rejecting any direct operation of God in the conversion process. To them, you are converted by reading and receiving the word and nothing else. I held and defended this position for a long time before concluding it was completely false. Church of Christ apologists see this verse as teaching that God opened Lydia's heart by her hearing the words of scripture and becoming opened to receiving them, but the verse has God opening her heart initially, so that she "attended unto the things which were spoken of Paul." See also 1 Corinthians 2:10-14.

God is said to open eyes and hearts all the time in the Bible. As in the case of Joseph and the eyes of his brethren being withheld from recognizing him as Pharaoh's viceroy (Genesis 42:8; 45:1), the creators of Jesus have him in the same position with his disciples (Luke 24:16, 31). Freewill is getting clobbered all the time here. A person comes to God when (and if) God is ready, not before! Concerning the fallen state of the Jewish nation and their spiritual blindness, Paul speaks...

> 7. What then? Israel hath not obtained that which he seeketh for; but **the election hath obtained it, and the rest were blinded**. 8. (According as it is written, God hath given them the spirit of slumber, eyes that they should not see, and ears that they should not hear;) unto this day. 9. And David saith, Let their table be made a snare, and a trap, and a stumblingblock, and a recompence unto them: 10. Let their eyes be darkened, that they may not see, and bow down their back always. 11. I say then, Have they stumbled that they should fall? God forbid: but rather through their fall salvation is come unto the Gentiles, for to provoke them to jealousy. (Romans 11:7-11)

God blinded them, caused them to reject the son of God so that the Gentiles could be included in the plan of redemption. Hear the words of Peter on the subject...

> And a stone of stumbling, and a rock of offence, even to them which stumble at the word, being disobedient: whereunto also **they were appointed**. (I Peter 2:8)

Foreordained to Hell

The scriptures speak often of those who were predestined to Hell. A passing reference to this is in Jude...

> For their are certain men crept in unawares, **who were before of old ordained to this condemnation**, ungodly men turning the grace off our God into lasciviousness, and denying the only lord God and our lord Jesus Christ. (Jude 4)

The ungodly will split Hell wide open. They don't have a choice in the matter. Another example is Judas Iscariot. Described in Acts 1, the apostles are selecting a replacement for Judas in the apostleship, "from which Judas by transgression fell, that he might go to his own place." (Acts 1:25) At no time and in no way did Jesus try to keep Judas from his infernal destiny, but said, "What you are about to do, do quickly."

(John 13:27, NIV) Judas had a destiny to fulfill, and God saw to it that his destiny was fulfilled...

> While I was with them in the world, I kept them in thy name: those that thou gavest me I have kept, and none of them is lost, but the son of perdition; **that the scripture might be fulfilled.** (John 17:12)

Foreordained to Heaven

As surely as we see an example of one who was predestined to Hell, we see Saul, a man destined to become Christianity's most virulent and authoritative saint. Paul, who was Saul of Tarsus, was converted against his will as he was blinded by a light from heaven when en route to Damascus (Acts 9:1-5). In his incapacitated state, he was instructed by God to go into Damascus for further instructions. He was led by the hand of the men who were with him, and when he arrived, he was met by a disciple named Ananias, who, when he expressed hesitation at approaching the former persecutor of the church, was told by God...

> Go thy way: for **he is a chosen vessel unto me,** to bear my name before the Gentiles, and kings, and the children of Israel. (Acts 9:15)

So many Christians make such a boast of freewill and God's preservation of it in the lives of men. God is limited in the ways he interacts with mankind so as to not violate freewill, we are told. This all goes out the window in the conversion of Saul. God not only violated Saul's freewill by granting him a physical manifestation of God (a thing many believers and nonbelievers would love to experience), but was coerced into submission by the blinding (if he wanted his sight back, he would have to obey). Being as good to others as God was to him, Paul struck Elymas blind for blasphemy and opposing the conversion of the deputy to the faith (Acts 13:8-11). I thought God was interested in preserving freewill?

Matthew 25:34 speaks of the saved...

> Then shall the king say unto them on his right hand, Come ye, blessed of my father, inherit the kingdom **prepared for you from the foundation of the world.**

God wanted Judas as his trophy of a fallen, wicked child of God, and Paul as one of the good guys, like Jeremiah...

> Before I formed thee in the belly, I knew thee; and before thou camest forth out of the womb, I sanctified thee, and **I ordained thee to be a prophet** unto the nations. (Jeremiah 1:5)

All debate on the issue of freewill and predestination can be put aside. Indeed, it was over before it started. If the soul-damning monster called the God of the Bible exists, and the very hairs of our heads are all numbered (Luke 12:7), how much easier are our words and deeds, our thoughts and our actions by a creator who "worketh all things after the counsel of his own will"? (Ephesians 1:11) We are nothing more than puppets on a string for his amusement.

CHAPTER 12
Lost Hope

Jesus Christ, the Deserter

"Let us pardon him[Jesus] his hope of a vain apocalypse, and of a second coming in great triumph upon the clouds of heaven. Perhaps these were the errors of others rather than his own; and if it be true that he himself shared the general illusion, what matters it, since his dream rendered him strong against death, and sustained him in a struggle to which he might otherwise have been unequal."
- Ernest Renan

"Among all forms of mistake, prophecy is the most gratuitous."
- George Eliot

That Christ will one day return to this earth in judgment has been the splendid hope of the Christian faith for 2,000 years now. Enough books have been written about the subject (Eschatology) to fill a decent sized library, and yet ignorance of what the Bible really says about the subject abounds. The early Christians believed in and expected a return of their Savior at some point in the first century. The Bible bears this out unmistakably, being replete with passages that leave no room for alternative interpretations.

As I began to experience doubts in the ministry, this issue became a heavily deliberated one. Why would Jesus wait to return some 2,000 years in the future? It made no sense. As my doubts worsened, this continued to play a part in the degeneration of my faith. I became terribly afraid; I began to doubt a return of Jesus, but at the same time, I feared that every next moment would be my last, and I'd face God in eternity unprepared. When I became a Christian, it didn't matter why the Lord was tolerating all the sin around me, or why he would wait for two millennia or longer before coming back. I so longed for this gloriously approaching moment that it didn't matter. As my mind and faith matured – and thereafter, soon began to die – I kept thinking back to when mom was getting her masters degree when I was young. Dad would be working late, and she would be leaving for classes, which left me alone for about five hours. Before leaving, she would charge me: "When I get back, you better have that room clean." It was kind of unpredictable when mom would get home. Classes might be let out early, so she might get home early or late. I never knew and got into some trouble waiting till the last minute to get things done.

Nowadays, I compare this to the second coming of Jesus. If a mother goes on a trip, and warns her son that she will be back at an unknown time, you have the same situation as the biblical second coming; if the mom never comes back, the command would still stand just as powerfully. Christians still feel the force of the scary command to "watch."

> Therefore be ye also ready: for in such an hour as ye think not the Son of man cometh. (Matthew 24:44)

But before my faith fall-off, when I was a faithful Christian and began hearing worldly people knock the idea of Jesus' return, wondering what was taking him so long, I remember honing in on the words of Peter...

> 3. Knowing this first, that there shall come in the last days scoffers, walking after their own lusts, 4. And saying, **Where is the promise of his coming? for since the fathers fell asleep, all things continue as**

> **they were from the beginning of the creation.** 5. For this they willingly are ignorant of, that by the word of God the heavens were of old, and the earth standing out of the water and in the water: 6. Whereby the world that then was, being overflowed with water, perished: 7. But the heavens and the earth, which are now, by the same word are kept in store, reserved unto fire against the day of judgment and perdition of ungodly men. 8. But, beloved, be not ignorant of this one thing, that one day is with the Lord as a thousand years, and a thousand years as one day. 9. The Lord is not slack concerning his promise, as some men count slackness; but is longsuffering to us-ward, not willing that any should perish but that all should come to repentance. (2 Peter 3:3-9)

These words of Peter seemed to be a picture-perfect prediction of the faithless generation I considered myself to be living in. Did not Jesus ask in Luke 18:8 that *"when the Son of man cometh, shall he find faith on the earth?"* Peter reminded me that my faith would be tested and that my Lord would someday return. I took comfort in that belief for a long time. Today, I realize how much of an eye-opener this is to the situation of faith in the church at that time. As these verses indicate, the saints were already questioning Jesus' return because they were taught and expected his return to be soon. The writer of Peter did his apostolic duty in calming them down and making them wait. Only, I don't think he intended on getting us to wait 2,000 years into the future! This became all the clearer the more I studied the scriptures.

John has done everyone a great disservice by not letting us know that the events of his Lord's coming were a great ways off. Hear him...

> Little children, it is the last time: and as ye have heard that antichrist shall come, even now are there many antichrists; whereby we know that it is the last time. (I John 2:18)

What is this "last time" business, anyway? It sounds like John means to tell us that he thought he was living in the last generation before the end times. If that's what he was saying, he was dead wrong, obviously. John sounds like a Christian in my time who lived to see the dawning of the year 2,000. Most of us look back with embarrassment on how we were duped by the whole Y2K nonsense (I, thankfully, was not in their number!) We were doing all sorts of crazy things – from stocking bottled water and toilet paper, to turning on the car and revving the engine through the turning of midnight – all in the name of a false scare! It seems that John bought into the same alarmist thinking that every generation since his time bought into—that their own generation was to be the last and the worst. Even the ever-so-wise Solomon was not immune from such fallacious thinking...

> 11. There is a generation that curseth their father, and doth not bless their mother. 12. There is a generation that are pure in their own eyes, and yet is not washed from their filthiness. (Proverbs 30:11-12)

Paul, following in his footsteps, said...

> 1. This know also, that in the last days perilous times shall come. 2. For men shall be lovers of their own selves, covetous, boasters, proud, blasphemers, disobedient to parents, unthankful, unholy, 3. Without natural affection, trucebreakers, false accusers, incontinent, fierce, despisers of those that are good, 4. Traitors, heady, highminded, lovers of pleasures more than lovers of God; 5. Having a form of Godliness, but denying the power thereof: from such turn away. 6. For of this sort are they which creep into houses, and lead captive silly women laden with sins, led away with divers lusts, 7. Ever learning, and never able to come to the knowledge of the truth. (2 Timothy 3:1-7)

Last days? I don't think so, Paul. Human behavior is no different now than it ever has been or will become. Populations grow, nations cycle through the adoption and rejection of different practices and customs, from conservative to liberal. Crime waves and wars move in and out like the tides (sometimes increasing and sometimes decreasing), but humanity always stays the same. Paul was an ignoramus. Of course, our alarmist Christian writers believed that things were changing, that the world was decaying, straying away from God the Creator, and "the end" was nearing, which is why "last days" is here used.

Let's allow Jesus to tell us his views on the "last days."

The Gospels of Mark and Matthew

> 36. For what shall it profit a man, if he shall gain the whole world, and lose his own soul? 37. Or what shall a man give in exchange for his soul? 38. Whosoever therefore shall be ashamed of me and of my words in this adulterous and sinful generation; of him also shall the Son of man be ashamed, when he cometh in the glory of his Father with the holy angels. 1. And he said unto them, Verily I say unto you, That **there be some of them that stand here, which shall not taste of death, till they have seen the kingdom of God come with power**. (Mark 8:36-38, 9:1)

The chapter break should have come at (9:2); that's where the subject changes. Back from verse 36 of chapter 8 to 9:1 is the same theme—the return of Jesus, which the writer of Mark thought would be in his lifetime. Jesus is speaking about the rewards of eternal life over gaining this world's blessings. He establishes the subject of his return in glory as he says, *"Whosoever therefore shall be ashamed of me and of my words in this adulterous and sinful generation; of him also shall the Son of man be ashamed, when he cometh in the glory of his Father with the holy angels." (Mark 8:38)* The next verse is what causes problems. *"And he said unto them, Verily I say unto you, That there be some of them that stand here, which shall not taste of death, till they have seen the kingdom of God come with power" (Mark 9:1)*. In the context of this chapter, Jesus can only be referring to his second return because that's what he's been discussing only two verses into the last chapter. I don't believe there are any living persons from this far-gone era who are still alive, waiting to fulfill this prophecy at the Lord's return. You probably don't believe that either.

Then, we have Matthew's presentation of these verses...

> 27. For the Son of man shall come in the glory of his Father with his angels; and then he shall reward every man according to his works. 28. Verily I say unto you, There be some standing here, which shall not taste of death, till they see the Son of man coming in his kingdom. (Matthew 16:27-28)

The similarities between Mark's account and Matthew's are too similar to dismiss. The same event – judgment – was the subject. Jesus would (a) *"come in the glory of his Father,"* (b) *"with his holy angels,"* (c) *"and then he shall reward every man according to his works."* Can anyone deny that the exact descriptions are used to speak of the return of Christ? (Matthew 24:29-31; 2 Corinthians 5:10; Romans 2:6) And as with Mark's words, so with Matthew's. (d) *"Verily I say unto you, There be some standing here, which shall not taste of death, till they see the Son of man coming in his kingdom."* Matthew makes the same statement Mark made. Again, the context leaves no room for escape: the creators of Jesus had him saying that he would be coming back in judgment in the first century—in the lifetime of some of his listeners. According to the gospels, Jesus was coming back very soon!

Jesus Gets It Wrong Again

Before we can proceed further in showcasing the apocalyptic errors of Jesus, we must deal with his prediction of the fall of Jerusalem. Did Jesus predict the destruction of Jerusalem? Yes and no. Using Daniel 12:11 as his proof-text, Jesus saw the taking away of "the daily sacrifice" and the coming "abomination that maketh desolate" as synonymous with the destruction of the temple. This was a very common Jewish school of thought—so long as the temple stood, God was with the Jewish people just as the possession of the ark of God was a sign of the same. So it should strike us as no remarkable thing that Jesus spoke of the demise of Jerusalem at the hands of foreign invaders based on his observances of the already heavy tensions between Judea and Rome. So yes, Jesus foretold of doom to befall the Jewish nation, but no, it wasn't original with him, and it certainly didn't require a divine hotline to heaven to predict. He interpreted Daniel to have foretold the event. The Jewish nation had suffered a great many invasions from invaders in the past. This was nothing new.

And bear in mind, we have no reason to believe that Jesus' prediction of Jerusalem's downfall was an after-the-fact write-in of history either. Jesus predicts the destruction of Jerusalem, but also falsely predicts how that would happen. Regarding the temple, he stated, *"There shall not be left here one stone upon another that shall not be thrown down."* (Matthew 24:2) This is as false as it gets. Many stones of the wall remained in tact through the siege, including The Wailing Wall, which still remains with us today. So it seems clear that had Jesus' foretelling of the Judean siege by the Romans been recorded after-the-fact, this pronouncement would never have been made. It would not have been said that no stone would be left standing upon another, and it certainly would have been stated that the temple was largely destroyed by fire. So Jesus was right, but also wrong.

But it was on this occasion that Jesus' words prompted his disciples to ask a question; *"Tell us, when shall these things be? And what shall be the sign of thy coming, and of the end of the world?"* (Matthew 24:3) Jesus answers the first question in his description of the destruction of Jerusalem, which occurred in C.E. 70. (Matthew 24:4-28)

> 4. And Jesus answered and said unto them, Take heed that no man deceive you. 5. For many shall come in my name, saying, I am Christ; and shall deceive many. 6. And ye shall hear of wars and rumours of wars: see that ye be not troubled: for all these things must come to pass, but the end is not yet. 7. For nation shall rise against nation, and kingdom against kingdom: and there shall be famines, and pestilences, and earthquakes, in divers places. 8. All these are the beginning of sorrows. 9. Then shall they deliver you up to be afflicted, and shall kill you: and ye shall be hated of all nations for my name's sake. 10. And then shall many be offended, and shall betray one another, and shall hate one another. 11. And many false prophets shall rise, and shall deceive many. 12. And because iniquity shall abound, the love of many shall wax cold. 13. But he that shall endure unto the end, the

same shall be saved. 14. And this gospel of the kingdom shall be preached in all the world for a witness unto all nations; and then shall the end come. 15. When ye therefore shall see the abomination of desolation, spoken of by Daniel the prophet, stand in the holy place, (whoso readeth, let him understand:) 16. Then let them which be in Judaea flee into the mountains: 17. Let him which is on the housetop not come down to take any thing out of his house: 18. Neither let him which is in the field return back to take his clothes. 19. And woe unto them that are with child, and to them that give suck in those days! 20. But pray ye that your flight be not in the winter, neither on the sabbath day: 21. For then shall be great tribulation, such as was not since the beginning of the world to this time, no, nor ever shall be. 22. And except those days should be shortened, there should no flesh be saved: but for the elect's sake those days shall be shortened. 23. Then if any man shall say unto you, Lo, here is Christ, or there; believe it not. 24. For there shall arise false Christs, and false prophets, and shall shew great signs and wonders; insomuch that, if it were possible, they shall deceive the very elect. 25. Behold, I have told you before. 26. Wherefore if they shall say unto you, Behold, he is in the desert; go not forth: behold, he is in the secret chambers; believe it not. 27. For as the lightning cometh out of the east, and shineth even unto the west; so shall also the coming of the Son of man be. 28. For wheresoever the carcase is, there will the eagles be gathered together.

The text describes perfectly the tension between Judea and Rome that resulted in Jerusalem's ultimate destruction in C.E. 70 at the hands of Roman Emporer Vespasian and his son, Titus. He also describes for us the historically confirmed religious atmosphere of the first century as one where self-proclaimed messiahs walked the streets, seeking to gain a following. It would be a time of "great tribulation." Jesus would "come" in judgment on Jerusalem, the nation that rejected him. Now Jesus answers the second part of the disciples' question...

29. Immediately after the tribulation of those days shall the sun be darkened, and the moon shall not give her light, and the stars shall fall from heaven, and the powers of the heavens shall be shaken: 30. And then shall appear the sign of the Son of man in heaven: and then shall all the tribes of the earth mourn, and they shall see the Son of man coming in the clouds of heaven with power and great glory. 31. And he shall send his angels with a great sound of a trumpet, and they shall gather together his elect from the four winds, from one end of heaven to the other. 32. Now learn a parable of the fig tree; When his branch is yet tender, and putteth forth leaves, ye know that summer is nigh: 33. So likewise ye, when ye shall see all these things, know that it is near, even at the doors. 34. Verily I say unto you, This generation shall not pass, till all these things be fulfilled. 35. Heaven and earth

shall pass away, but my words shall not pass away. 36. But of that day and hour knoweth no man, no, not the angels of heaven, but my Father only. (Matthew 24:29-36)

As we consider these verses, it is supremely important to remember three things: (1) In with their question about the end of the world, the disciples asked, "what shall be the sign of thy coming?" as well as "of the end of the world." The text makes no attempt to separate the "sign" and the "great tribulation" the Jewish nation would face from the "end of the world." The keen mind can only accept that the author of Matthew saw the end of the world as an event that was just right around the corner from the destruction of Jerusalem. It is also eminently significant (2) that the author of Matthew went out of his way to write, "This generation shall not pass away till all these things be fulfilled." (Matthew 24:35) "Pass away" means the same thing here as it does one verse later; "Heaven and earth shall pass away, but my words shall not pass away." According to Matthew, there were to follow no more generations because that same one would be the last! And (3) the phrase "immediately after the tribulation of those days" (Matthew 24:29) says a lot. Immediately means immediately. Jesus had been describing the turmoil to be faced by the Jewish nation under siege. Then the conversation changes to "after the tribulation of those days." How far after? "Immediately." So Christians have no wiggle room to split up the remainder of these verses and put them in the far distant future, like they do on the Trinity Broadcasting Network, talking wildly about a kingdom of Christ to be set up on earth and the rapture. The early Christian writers believed and understood Jesus Christ to be returning to earth not long after the desolation of the Jewish holy city.

To cover their tracks, the early Christian fabricators went out of their way to keep an element of mystery in this. "But of that day and that hour knoweth no man, no, not the angels of heaven, but my Father only." (Matthew 24:36) I guess it seemed a little too cocky to have Jesus know when the final day would come so he could lovingly warn his disciples. To protect the faith and avoid a grievous error, it seemed better for only God to know, and that way, no one can question him about it. But regardless, the damage is done—we can now see that the gospels spoke of an early return of Christ.

A Christian response to this would consist of claims that "coming in his kingdom" and "kingdom of God coming in power" refer to the establishment of the Christian church on Pentecost. Christ would endow the apostles with "power" from on high (Acts 1:7-8; 2:1-47). And there are plenty of instances in the scriptures where the Lord was said to "come" in judgment, and yet was not "coming" to judge the world as described in the "second coming" (Matthew 24:27; Revelation 2:5). And, according to some scholars, when Matthew and Mark are discussing eternal salvation and the rewards of faithfulness, and then jump right into the subject of the establishment of the church, Jesus is bringing up two different subjects based on *similarity of subject matter but not identity of subject matter*—this is how we were taught to explain these verses in preaching school. These claims, however, grossly disregard the local contexts of the verses covered. Those who are honest enough to come to terms about what the Bible really says on the subject will see things differently.

The Apostle Paul

The apostle Paul was a latecomer to Christianity, but nonetheless, contributed much to the Christian canon of scripture. He was a staunch Jew, yet preached a savior god-man like the pagans around him. He was a perfect example of the new age Jewish heretic, absorbing Gentile myths as he went along. Paul himself believed in an early return of Jesus and expressed so a number of times…

> 7. So that ye come behind in no gift; waiting for the coming of our Lord Jesus Christ. 8. Who shall also confirm you unto the end, that ye may be blameless in the day of our Lord Jesus Christ. (I Corinthians 1:7-8)

Paul's hope for the Corinthians was that they "come behind in no gift," that they properly and fully utilize their spiritual gifts "waiting for the coming of our Lord Jesus Christ." Since the Corinthian letter was to the Corinthian Christians, we must ask why Paul in verse 8 would instruct them to wait for an event that was 2,000 years off! Paul uses Jesus' confirmation of the saints before the Father on the last day to motivate them to stand blameless before the judgment seat of Christ. If we had no other, this would be a perfectly sufficient and all-but-spelled-out admission that Paul expected a first century return of Jesus. But there are others…

> 51. Behold, I shew you a mystery; We shall not all sleep, but we shall all be changed, 52. In a moment, in the twinkling of an eye, at the last trump: for the trumpet shall sound, and the dead shall be raised incorruptible, and we shall be changed. (I Corinthians 15:51-52)

Notice "we" (he is speaking to then-living Corinthian saints) "shall be changed." "We shall not all sleep!" Christian theologians apply this to the body of believers, as though Paul included us today. That is not the thought here. Such a position must be assumed, and we have no reason to make such an assumption. Paul was writing personal letters to people and congregations in the first century. To be honest in our study, we cannot apply his words to Christians today. Paul was speaking to Corinthian Christians. So when Paul says "we shall not all sleep (die)," he is telling a falsehood. And he continues giving false hopes...

> 15. For this we say unto you by the word of the Lord, that **we which are alive and remain unto the coming of the Lord** shall not prevent them which are asleep. 16. For the Lord himself shall descend from heaven with a shout, with the voice of the archangel, and with the trump of God: and the dead in Christ shall rise first: 17. Then we which are alive and remain shall be caught up together with them in the clouds, to meet the Lord in the air: and so shall we ever be with the Lord. (I Thessalonians 4:15-17)

Again, we see Paul's understanding of the return of Christ: "them which are asleep" and "we which are alive and remain" (then-living saints) would be transported to meet God in the air, who would come back in their lifetime! Paul manages to outdo himself...

> 8. Wherefore he saith, When he ascended up on high, he led captivity captive, and gave gifts unto men. 9. (Now that he ascended, what is it but that he also descended first into the lower parts of the earth? 10. He that descended is the same also that ascended up far above all heavens, that he might fill all things.) 11. And he gave some, apostles; and some, prophets; and some, evangelists; and some, pastors and teachers; 12. For the perfecting of the saints, for the work of the ministry, for the edifying of the body of Christ: 13. Till we all come in the unity of the faith, and of the knowledge of the Son of God, unto a perfect man, unto the measure of the stature of the fulness of Christ. (Ephesians 4:8-13)

Paul quotes Psalm 68:18 and applies it to miraculous gifts of the Spirit. With Jesus' ascension, miraculous gifts and holy offices were made possible, which included "apostles" and "prophets," "for the perfecting of the saints, for the work of the ministry" (Ephesians 4:11-12). What I find very interesting about these verses is that they mention apostles as given to the church "for the perfecting of the saints," etc. Yet, we have no instructions for qualifying or selecting new apostles today. Not a hundred years would pass before the apostles of the first century would need replacements—unless, of course, the world was going to end before their deaths! This is yet another subtle suggestion of what the early Christians believed about the end of the world.

The Apostle Peter

> But the end of all things is at hand: be ye therefore sober, and watch unto prayer. (I Peter 4:7)

In John 2:13, John said, "the passover of the Jews was at hand..." That meant eminent or near, just like it means here. So Peter thought the return of Christ was near, which was false.

> **Looking for and hasting** unto the coming of the day of God, wherein the heavens being on fire shall be dissolved, and the elements shall melt with fervent heat? (2 Peter 3:12)

Peter told the saints to anxiously await a day that would not occur for more than two thousand years. Why? It's one thing to tell your listeners to wait for something that will happen at some unspecified time, and it's quite another to be on the lookout because what they should be looking for is coming soon.

The Apostle James

> Be ye also patient; stablish your hearts: for the coming of the Lord draweth nigh. (James 5:8)

According to James, the time of Jesus' coming was nearing. James was a liar. If I lived in the year 1436, in the time of Gutenberg and the invention of the printing press, and said "Prepare yourselves because the days of cell phones draw near," I would be a liar too, just like James and the New Testament.

The Apostle John in Revelation

> He which testifieth these things saith, Surely I come quickly. Amen. Even so, come, Lord Jesus. (Revelation 22:20)

Bible defenders will point out that coming "quickly" does not necessarily mean coming "soon." To come "quickly" would refer to the manner in which the coming was completed; to come "soon" would describe the timeframe of when the coming was to occur. Apologists will tell us that this verse describes not when Jesus would come, but the manner in which he would come (quickly). But when you consider its usage in the context of the last two chapters of Revelation, it can only refer to Christ's return in the then-near future because it is used here as a comfort to the saints. John has Jesus saying: "Surely, I'm coming back quickly! You won't have to wait long!"

Conclusion

In John 14:1-3, Jesus said…

> 1. Let not your heart be troubled: ye believe in God, believe also in me. 2. In my Father's house are many mansions: if it were not so, I would have told you. I go to prepare a place for you. 3. And if I go and prepare a place for you, I will come again, and receive you unto myself; that where I am, there ye may be also.

This is why the New Testament message of Jesus Christ is a very sad message. Jesus did not come back for his early disciples, nor will he come back for us. Now, 2,000 years looking back, we see the remains of Christianity, a people subjected to heresies, divisions, persecutions, and costly conquests, and what do they have to show for it?

We live in a different world now, a much faster-paced world where saviors and prophets are woefully losing points with the people. Will the world still vainly be waiting for the return of an itinerant Jewish rabbi 500 or more years from now? Who can tell? Human gullibility is fathomless.

CHAPTER 13
The Cruel Commission

Why Christ's "Great Commission" Isn't So Great

"Death can bring us no terrors."
- *Lucretius*

"Who cannot overestimate the progress of the world if all the money wasted in superstition could be used to enlighten, elevate and civilize mankind?"
- *Robert G. Ingersoll*

I never will forget one hopelessly dreary Sunday in the summer of 2001. It was after the evening church service when my wife decided she needed to pick up a few things at the grocery store before heading home. I dropped her off at the front of the store, and because she said she would only be a minute, I parked the car and waited in the red zone up at the front. The wife took longer than was expected because the place was packed with people. While I waited, I kept the hazard lights on to draw attention to the fact that the car was not abandoned and that I would be moving it soon, but this didn't stop a nearby police cruiser from pulling right up beside me and rolling down his window to talk to me. I said to him, "Hello, officer." He responded, "Hello, Sir. I must ask you to please park in one of the parking spaces."

I thought about not saying anything, but being that I was starting to fight off a migraine (a condition I am no stranger to!), I said to him, "Well, sir, my wife is inside the store. She was only going to be there for a minute but is taking longer than was planned. I have my hazards on so that if an emergency vehicle needs to get in, I can always move. Besides, I can't see my wife if I am parked in a parking space." I may very well have come off a little disagreeable, but I didn't care. This Lord's day was not going to go down in history as one of my most spiritual, and so it was nice to run into a gentle and understanding public servant!

Like any good and reasonable man, he appealed not to his authority in the law, but to logic: *"I understand, sir, but this rule is in place not just to clear a path for fire trucks and ambulances, but to relieve congestion. If I make an exception for you and let you park up here, I would have to make the same exception for everyone else in your position, and then we would have the same congestion problem, you see?"* I understood. His reasoning was debasingly flawless. I felt quite the fool for resisting him and immediately complied with a smile.

Never in a million years could I imagine something as minute and ordinary as this experience going in any book I would write. However, it is often the case that many of the things that grab our attention in life tend to be small in nature, and these are often emotionally charged verbal exchanges, consisting only of the exchange of a phrase or a short sentence or two. Such was the case here.

What this extremely nice and patient police officer directed me to take notice of was fairness. Who doesn't want fairness? Who can deny its value? It's not something one can disagree with or flippantly disregard. It requires boatloads of selfishness to knowingly oppose it. Not everyone wants fame or money or power, but like happiness, everyone of sound mind wants fairness. And yet, as strangely as life would have it, I beheld a world where leaps and bounds of unfairness could be seen. It was in the Bible as well.

One of the earliest major doubts about Christianity centered around the Great Commission, the mission of salvation given by Jesus Christ himself. In all four gospel accounts, we find the command to evangelize the whole world (Matthew 28:19-20; Mark 16:15-16; Luke 24:46-48; John 20:21-23). Mark's account reads this way...

> Go ye into all the world, and preach the gospel to every creature. He that believeth and is baptized shall be saved; but he that believeth not shall be damned. (16:15-16)

This caused insurmountable problems for me, problems I could find no answers to. At the root of the New Testament's unfair message of salvation was one exclusive salvation plan. The instant God decided to allow a world where some of his creations are saved and some are lost, it was set in stone that we were going to have an unfair arrangement on our hands.

Judaism and Salvation

Under Judaism, the message of "salvation" was material; that is, being "saved" meant living wisely so that your days on the earth would be long, happy, and fulfilling...

> Honour thy father and thy mother: **that thy days may be long upon the land which the LORD thy God giveth thee.** (Exodus 20:12)
> **There shall be no more thence an infant of days, nor an old man that hath not filled his days: for the child shall die an hundred years old**; but the sinner being an hundred years old shall be accursed. (Isaiah 65:20)

Unlike their absolutist Christian descendants, the Jews believed (and still believe) in universal salvation; every nation had their own way on how to please God and be accepted of him—and this included the pagans who worshipped other gods besides Yahweh...

> And lest thou lift up thine eyes unto heaven, and when thou seest the sun, and the moon, and the stars, even all the host of heaven, shouldest be driven to worship them, and serve them, **which the LORD thy God hath divided unto all nations under the whole heaven.** (Deuteronomy 4:19)

Notice how in this passage God warns his people not to be drawn away into nature worship like the pagan nations around them, but in the same breath, lets his people know that the worship of nature was something God specifically allotted for the pagans. Solomon prayed for blessings on devout pagans who have no ill will towards God's people...

> Hear thou in heaven thy dwelling place, and do according to all that the stranger calleth to thee for: that all people of the earth may know thy name, to fear thee, as do thy people Israel. (I Kings 8:41)

All throughout the Old Testament, we find that even those Gentile cities that never submitted themselves to Jewish rule were nonetheless rebuked by God's prophets for moral wrongs committed, as in the case of Jonah and Nineveh, and Balaam the Gentile prophet (Numbers 22-31). This implied one all-encompassing moral law housed under differing religious systems.

For instance, 2 Chronicles 35:21-22 shows that the author believed Josiah's defeat in battle at the hands of Pharaoh Necho was because God was on his side—it didn't matter to the writer that Necho was an Egyptian and worshipped pagan gods. God was still on his side...

> But he [Necho] sent ambassadors to him [Josiah], saying, What have I to do with thee, thou king of Judah? I come not against thee this day, but against the house wherewith I have war: for God commanded me to make haste: forbear thee from meddling with God, who is with me, that he destroy thee not. Nevertheless Josiah would not turn his face from him, but disguised himself, that he might fight with him, and **hearkened not unto the words of Necho from the mouth of God**, and came to fight in the valley of Megiddo.

Then there is the example of Meesha, King of Moab. In the dire straits of war, he offered up his oldest son as a burnt offering to a pagan god to stop Israel, who had successfully defeated Meesha's troops. Strangely, Israel left him alone and went their own way, evidently because of the king's appeal to this deity. (2 Kings 3:4-27)

This principle applied to judgment in the same way. If you lived a sinful life of debauchery, if you displeased God, God either killed you right then and there (2 Samuel 6:7-8), or he might deliver you into affliction for the purpose of correction (Jeremiah 22:25). When the Old Testament speaks of judgment, it is not dealing with eternal judgment, but temporal judgments in the here and now based on the results of one's conduct (Ecclesiastes 11:9). Troublesome ideas like immortal souls and hellfire are completely foreign to the Old Covenant. Those ideas had not yet developed, and would not be until just before the writing of Daniel in 165 B.C.E. (see Daniel 12:1-2). Even in the New Testament where they are present, they cause problems. The idea of an immortal soul makes the concept of a bodily resurrection difficult to conceive, if not impossible. What the Old Testament had in mind when it spoke of death was...

> There the wicked cease from troubling; and there the weary be at rest. There the prisoners rest together; they hear not the voice of the oppressor. The small and great are there; and the servant is free from his master. (Job 3:17-19)

> For the living know that they shall die: but the dead know not any thing, neither have they any more a reward; for the memory of them is forgotten. (Ecclesiastes 9:5)

So it's fair to say that under Judaism, you lived life to the fullest, and if you were faithful to your god (whoever he, she, it, or them be), you lived a long and happy life. This conception of salvation doesn't present that many problems for the thinker because it is fair in its application; under this scenario, all people under all belief systems at all times and places are accountable in the same way to one and the same "saving" system. No one is left out and there are no changes in law or loopholes to contend with. The same cannot be said of the New Testament, however.

The New Testament and Salvation

Just as surely as the universalism of the Old Testament made us comfortable with things, the New Covenant makes us uncomfortable. Christianity is like your company's new boss who came along after the old one left and screwed up everything you knew and loved about your job!

In the New Testament, we have a change of covenants. This alone is a problem. The idea that God would create one religion, like Judaism, to teach principles of holiness and the nature of God as a "schoolmaster" (Galatians 3:24) to bring us to the savior, and then turn around and create another religion, a so-called "New Testament," which is supposedly established on "better promises" (Hebrews 8:6) deserves a chapter all its own! An eternal, all-wise God would not change religions for the same reason he would not do miracles; for God to have to work a miracle implies God didn't get something right in the natural order of things the first time around. And for a God to switch religions is even worse; it reflects corruption and changes in thought and perspectives over time—two very human elements that cannot be associated with any self-respecting deity. But this never stopped religionists from clinging to their beliefs—and this is only a minor problem created by God's creating a "new" covenant for mankind.

In the New Testament, everyone is amenable to one religious system, without subscribing to which, none can be saved...

> Neither is there salvation in any other: for **there is none other name under heaven given among men, whereby we must be saved.** (Acts 4:12)

> **In flaming fire taking vengeance on them that know not God, and that obey not the gospel** of our Lord Jesus Christ: Who shall be punished with everlasting destruction from the presence of the Lord, and from the glory of his power; (2 Thessalonians 1:8-9)

> And the **times of this ignorance God winked at; but now commandeth all men every where to repent**: (Acts 17:30)

Christianity is an exclusivist religion unlike universalist Judaism. Everyone, in order to benefit from the blessings of God, must subscribe to one particular set of beliefs in one particular savior. All men are sinful beings (Romans 3:23), and if we enter into eternity without the saving grace of Jesus, we must pay the penalty brought on us by our sins (Romans 6:23). God once winked at sinfulness and ignorance, but no more! (Acts 17:30) It's time for all men everywhere to adopt one set of beliefs, rejecting all others. Failure to do so will result in the loss of the soul.

So the New Testament imposes one very big restriction on the world that the Old Testament never did; it imposes one theistic system of belief on everyone. It must be received by all people, superceding all other belief systems, and all people at all times are accountable to it with no exceptions. Salvation is no longer a naturally acquired thing; it is now a doctrinally dependent thing. It has lost the beauty of equality and fairness that the Judaic and pre-Judaic systems had.

Problems with New Testament Salvation

The New Testament is constructed in such a way that it unfairly segregates mankind. It cuts off whole nations from receiving this "grace of God" through the message of Jesus and pronounces damnation upon them for not receiving it. It is cruelly divisive and restrictive. It is neither natural, nor universal. It does not apply seamlessly to mankind. Rather than offering satisfaction and peace of mind, it creates questions and dilemmas that cannot be solved, like *who* is under *what* covenant and *when*.

Accountability

As soon as Christianity came into effect at the death of Jesus (Matthew 27:51; Hebrews 9:16-17), all the world became instantly accountable to the Christian gospel, even though the New Testament message had not yet been preached on the first Pentecost after the resurrection (Acts 1:1-14; Acts 2). If the New Testament was already in effect, by what standard will those abroad who died before the preaching of the apostles be judged? If someone without the knowledge of Jesus could die and go to heaven while the New Testament was in force, at what point did all the world become dependent upon belief in Jesus for salvation? Debating this point endlessly was what we preachers did in the Church of Christ. These discussions were never nailed-down articles of doctrine, just speculation on our part because the Bible does not address these questions.

We were certain of our conviction that God judged those living before the death on the cross by what we called, The Moral Law. This, as we described already, is the principle upon which Old Testament salvation under Judaism rested. What we were not certain of was what happened to those who died in and around the time after Jesus' death. It didn't sound fair to us to say that the moment Jesus died on the cross, every pagan in the deepest and darkest parts of the world who died would wake up in Hell. So after a lot of debating, we concluded that once the finishing moment of Peter's preaching on Pentecost had elapsed, all men everywhere were finally accountable to the gospel since it had now been preached, and this meant that anyone who died ignorant of it from that point onward would go straight to Hell. As you might suppose, this never sat well with me, and this did not remedy the unfairness we were hoping to eradicate.

These questions were only made tougher by the time gaps present after the New Testament dispensation began. When the gospel was first preached, only the Jews were a part of it (Acts 2-9). Then in Acts 10 and 11, after prayers and visions and much consideration, the Gentiles were finally allowed into the fold. This was some 10 or 12 years after the New Testament had begun. This meant that for over a decade, no salvation was available to the Gentiles during that time. Was there a "grace period" for them, maybe? Hopefully, there was, but this grace period had to be very wide, for the gospel didn't reach many parts of the Gentile world for well over a thousand years, including many northern and southern territories far removed from the Palestinian area, many remote islands, and obviously, the Americas. The gospel took forever reaching these secluded souls, and yet accountability to Christ had been in effect for many centuries. This realization creates The Evangelism Dilemma.

The Evangelism Dilemma

The Evangelism Dilemma goes thusly…

If, after the New Testament is in force, an individual can be saved without knowledge of and belief in Jesus Christ, then out of fairness, God must make the same exceptions for everyone else who is ignorant of the gospel for whatever reason, for God is no respecter of persons (See Acts 10:34-35) (Recall here my experience with the officer). If this is the case, knowledge of the gospel becomes a detriment to an uninformed individual—because the individual, if he or she had just remained ignorant of who Jesus was, would still be safe from damnation. Then the Great Commission should not be heard, and preaching is the worst possible thing you could do to an individual because the person preached to might choose to reject the message, in which case, they are damned immediately upon hearing it and their sinfulness is implemented to them. If this be true, missionaries are wasting loads of money on trying to save the lost who are already "safe" through ignorance. They should just leave them alone and let them live their lives.

If, on the other hand, no one is saved without the gospel in the New Testament without knowledge of or belief in Jesus, then you have a monstrously unfair situation where those who died in the Americas and in the most isolated reaches of the earth are lost in sin, and will find themselves damned to the Lake of Fire for eternity. In this case, the un-evangelized, numbering well into the hundreds of millions (if not more), have lived and died in vain. They are nothing but "fuel for the fires of Hell," as it were. The unfairness here, the injustice, is unspeakable. The scriptures state that God's word cannot be broken (Isaiah 55:11; John 10:35). All that God decreed will come to pass. This means that when the Bible declares that anyone without knowledge of and faith in the Son of God cannot please him (Hebrews 11:6), and that without baptism one is damned to Hell (Mark 16:15-16; Acts 2:38; Romans 6:3-4), there are no exceptions. This makes God a monster who blesses only those who are geographically close to Jerusalem and surrounding areas—wherever a missionary can reach you before you die!

So, either the gospel is *useless and potentially dangerous,* or *mandatory and a mark of cruelty,* unfairly made available by a heartless deity. On the one hand, the gospel is useless to hear because all men are "saved" in ignorance, in which case, it is also dangerous to preach due to the fact that it might be rejected after it is heard, resulting in the damnation of the hearers. Or, on the other hand, the gospel is mandatory for everyone to have to get into heaven, in which case, whole nations of people are now burning in flames who never had the chance to obey the gospel to begin with. The Christian can have whichever horn of this dilemma he wants, but he can't provide a worthy solution to it.

The results of taking either horn give the same result—the gospel should not be preached. In the one instance, it should not be preached because it is not needed and because the hearer might refuse to obey it to be "officially" saved. Better off had we been if we remained under general moral law. In the second instance, the gospel should not be preached because it is a useless effort to enlighten *some* and not *all* people with it. If some never got the chance to obey the gospel, then no one should.

When I served as a missionary, I kept having to confront the fact that for every "lost soul" I encountered, ten thousand more had already died without ever running across a minister. Being a rational thinker, I had to prepare myself on how I would answer someone who asked me what had happened to their dearly departed pagan relatives who came before them. I found no satisfactory answers to give anyone, and this made me a wretched personal evangelist in my later years. I could never work past this issue, so while I still had a measure of faith, I resigned that God was calling me away from the mission field to do local preaching work.

I was shocked to find so many preachers who never gave much thought to this matter. They were content to tangle with the latter horn of the dilemma (they'd never even consider the first); they had no problem saying that millions were in Hell suffering who never had the chance to escape that fate! When I first began to struggle with this dilemma as a young Christian, I remember sitting around a table full of preachers at a catfish parlor. I was so anxious to discuss this subject with wiser men, only to find out that they had no better answers than anyone else had. One of them no doubt grew tired of hearing about the matter and said to me, *"Don't think about the souls that have been lost, Joe! Just don't let any more souls burn in Hell!"* This made me extremely angry. My brethren were so ready to believe that God was like a murdering kidnapper: *"I already blew the heads off of some of your friends. There's nothing you can do for them now. But if you want to save the lives of the rest of your friends, you'd better cooperate!"* No thank you! I want no part in spreading such a miserable message.

"It's your fault, missionary!"

In light of all this, to think that the God of the Bible has the audacity to call himself "just" is jaw-dropping, but believers will never blame their God for anything. In the eyes of some Christians, an infidel not hearing the gospel becomes the missionary's fault. Those who have perished have perished because of a missionary's failure to reach them with the word in time. I can remember the chilling feelings that would come over me anytime we sang that song in church, "You Never Mentioned Him to Me!" I was horrified by the lyrics...

> *You never mentioned him to me. You helped me not the light to see. You saw me everyday and knew I was astray, yet never mentioned him to me!*

I led this song, preached sermons on this topic, and participated in door-to-door missionary efforts for years. Then I saw how terribly wrong it was to proudly bow the knee in service to a deity who was willing to watch his children be damned over a simple matter of lax or poorly coordinated missionary efforts.

Of course, I wasn't the only one to find this a terrible thing. I found that many others struggled with the same issues I did. Evangelists went out of their way to find justifications for this. It didn't sound right to blame the missionary for the sincere sinner's damnation, and as a result, a number of absurd ideas developed, one of which is called Transworld Depravity.

This position is explained by Paul Copan in his book, *True For You, But Not For Me: defeating the slogans that leave Christians speechless*. Transworld Depravity is the term Copan uses to describe those with a hard heart who would never choose to obey the gospel even if a missionary was present. These souls are the ones whom God would place in parts of the world where no missionaries would go and would never be touched by the Spirit of God or his word...

> If no one were to go to, say, a particular tribal group in Papau, New Guinea, or in Gambia, West Africa, then God would place some of those afflicted with Transworld damnation there. On the other hand, if God knew that a missionary would go to this tribe, then he would place people in the tribe who would have accepted the Gospel. Persons can be saved through the labors of missionaries, but they are not condemned through the slackness of missionaries since, in the latter case, God would have placed different people—those suffering from transworld depravity—where there is no Gospel witness. (P. 131)

Like so many evangelical Christian thinkers, rather than just admit he has no answer to our dilemma, Copan follows William Lane Craig in the affirmation of one of the most asinine positions a Christian ever held—Transworld Depravity. Copan and those of his ilk have no problem concocting farfetched, unscriptural notions to explain the scriptures. Believers will do handstands and back-flips to keep their beliefs intact, and the manufacturing of this unbiblical idea makes this quite clear. This is desperation as its best!

One Big Justification

I have had many long and drawn out discussions over this through the years, some of them heated and serious, and some of them very comical, but not a one of them goes an inch towards making a dent on the evangelism dilemma.

More liberal apologists will very commonly run to Romans chapter 1 for help on this subject. Their goal is to use these scriptures to demonstrate that all men, even those without knowledge of the Christian God, incriminate themselves with the guilt of sin. They site this as proof of a New Testament moral law when it clearly isn't…

> 16. For I am not ashamed of the gospel of Christ: for it is the power of God unto salvation to every one that believeth; to the Jew first, and also to the Greek. 17. For therein is the righteousness of God revealed from faith to faith: as it is written, The just shall live by faith. 18. For the wrath of God is revealed from heaven against all ungodliness and unrighteousness of men, who hold the truth in unrighteousness; 19. **Because that which may be known of God is manifest in them; for God hath shewed it unto them.** 20. For the invisible things of him from the creation of the world are clearly seen, being understood by the things that are made, even his eternal power and Godhead; **so that they are without excuse:** 21. Because that, when they knew God, they glorified him not as God, neither were thankful; but became vain in their imaginations, and their foolish heart was darkened. (Romans 1:16-21)

Paul spends the rest of this chapter and some of chapter 2 describing the sinful rebellion of the Gentiles who once knew God, but strayed from him into reprobate ignorance. Then he denounces both Gentiles and Jews who are found guilty of transgression before God…

> For as many as have sinned without law shall also perish without law: and as many as have sinned in the law shall be judged by the law. (Romans 2:12)

This, however, only speaks of accountability to the moral law we spoke of earlier, a law that transcends provincial and transient laws to encompass all people at all places in pre-Christian times. As we have seen, this was in effect for the Gentiles during the Old Testament period. It does not solve our dilemma for us. It doesn't even touch on it. If anything, it only reaffirms the understanding that a system of universal morality is permanent in the Old Testament, regardless of religion or race. It does not clear up the difficulties that come with the Christian position that all human beings are accountable to the exclusive Christian salvation plan. These verses have nothing to do with the issue we are debating.

In many places in the New Testament scriptures, we see that God is no longer judging based on the old moral law of Judaism, but on faith in Christ. The Jews, for instance, are not justified under the moral law. If they don't believe in Jesus, regardless of their sincerity or moral turpitude, they will be condemned...

> Brethren, my heart's desire and prayer to God for Israel is, that they might be saved. For I bear them record that they have a zeal of God, but not according to knowledge. (Romans 10:1-2)

Sincerity in following some other religion or moral code will not do. Paul's praying for Israel to be saved meant that they were not saved in their present state of ignorance. So the teachings of the New Testament seem to deny that one can follow the dictates of his/her own conscience and live morally without the knowledge of the gospel and still be saved. But even if I grant that Paul in Romans 1 is telling us that God will judge every man according to their own level of knowledge of him, whether they know of Christianity or not, that only makes us take the first horn of our dilemma—that the gospel is useless and potentially dangerous to preach. Once again, if one is safe from the consequences of sin in ignorance, why not just leave everyone in ignorance? Why preach?

Other Justifications

One preacher with whom I sat down for tea believed that Paul and some of the other apostles actually managed to get the gospel over to the Americas only a few years after the first Pentecost. He claimed that the reason we have no record of such a visit was because God didn't want to shock the world by recording missionary journeys in the Bible to places that had not yet been discovered! This brother also claimed that the Indians were evil pagans who rejected the preaching of the apostles for their love of fiery feathered serpents and nature worship, and they wanted no part of the gospel. That is why none of them embraced it. He based this on Colossians 1:23…

> If ye continue in the faith grounded and settled, and be not moved away from the hope of the gospel, which ye have heard, and **which was preached to every creature which is under heaven**; whereof I Paul am made a minister.

"To every creature under heaven" was an expression describing the church's missionary efforts abroad. Paul believed he had all bases covered in the church's missionary efforts, but he was wrong. He was ignorant of many places of the globe which the church would not reach for a millennia and a half. While it is true that almost every society today has been touched with the influence of Christianity, this was most certainly not the case in Paul's day. And the idea that an Inuit family, residing somewhere in Canada's Northwest Territories, living in the first or second centuries of the common era, being approached by early Christian evangelists and taught Christianity is altogether laughable. Expectedly, however, I remember a few fellow preachers getting on me for doubting that things of this nature happened!

When the Ores Touch the Shores!

I argued with one preacher who was committed to the idea that nations of heathens who had never heard the gospel were safely sheltered by the protection of the moral law right up until the ores of the ship of a missionary hit the shores of the heathen's land! At that point, the tribe or nation would automatically bear their sins, and if they wanted to be saved, they would have to follow the instructions of the preacher on how to receive Jesus. But this is silly. Those believers who subscribe to any belief in a "grace period" before accountability can never give it an official stopping point. To preserve fairness, every unenlightened soul must be kept safe from damnation in ignorance for as long as they are personally ignorant. But as we have seen, this renders the gospel useless. The missionaries should never have come. They should have stayed home and allowed the heathens to dwell safely in the arms of religious ignorance!

Rabbit Out of a Hat

I only had one "answer" that satisfied me in attempting to resolve this difficulty, and that was to quote Matthew 7:6 and be done with it…

> Ask, and it shall be given you; seek, and ye shall find; knock, and it shall be opened unto you: For every one that asketh receiveth; and he that seeketh findeth; and to him that knocketh it shall be opened.

I could only resign myself to the conviction that if one sought after God long enough and hard enough, out of his divine mercy and fairness, God would lead that person to the truth in some providential way before their death, and if one died without ever hearing the gospel, that meant they weren't sincere and determined enough to be led to God's truth. Realizing that no missionaries visited the Americas for many centuries after the common era began, I was forced to conclude that no one sought God's truth during that time. Early on, I realized that this certainly could not be true. I have come to call this the "Rabbit out of a hat" position because holding it demands that we accept what amounts to believing in a magic trick, an absurdity.

Among millions of Native Americans, a handful of them would necessarily be philosophers, sages, wise men, wonderers of what lies above and beyond the temporal and the tangible. Among these would be a number of soft-hearted truthseekers—sincere, open-minded, and fit to hear the gospel. This should have brought on a decent number of missionary trips to the Americas, or trips of Native Americans to the Holy Land. We should have at least some record of these trips. But not only did these trips not happen, they couldn't have; the early church was not only ignorant of the Americas, but the Native Americans had not the foggiest idea of Jerusalem, the Christian faith, Jesus, or that they needed to accept a certain god-man as their personal lord and savior.

Indians were animists, nature-worshippers. They did not have identical concepts to Original Sin or a fall of man. In brief, Native American ideology did not match up to that of Middle Eastern religious thought. There would therefore be no spiritual connection to "seek out" the God of the Bible. To expect Indians to suddenly know to put aside their own native religions, together with their sacred chants and rituals, in order to receive the religion of a foreign people's God, or to travel across the world to seek out missionaries to save them, is as ridiculous as our earlier Inuit analogy.

For a Christian to think that not *one* Native American truth-seeker was deemed worthy of receiving a visit from a Christian missionary in the early years of the common era makes that person guilty of negligent and naïve reasoning. Every people has their share of philosophers and thinkers, those who want to understand the universe intimately, those who make their tribe or nation just as worthy as any other people of receiving heaven's message. But instead, we find generations of souls on this planet who never heard that message, souls who have long since died "in their sins," leaving evangelicals to solve a serious quandary.

CHAPTER 14
Evil Never Dies

The Problem of Evil is Still a Problem

"When you start out with the premise that everything God does is just, you are bound to reach the conclusion that God has mysterious reasons for his actions."
- Glenn Kachmar

"The only objects of practical reason are therefore those of good and evil. For by the former is meant an object necessarily desired according to a principle of reason; by the latter one necessarily shunned, also according to a principle of reason."
- Immanuel Kant

A Product that Sells Itself

I was in line at the checkout counter, frustrated from a fruitless day of shopping. Here it was, only two days before Christmas and I had no idea what to get dad. Everyone else's gifts were taken care of. Then, before having to uproot my tired feet to take another step forward in a long line of lethargic shoppers, there it was; it looked like a screwdriver, but it wasn't. I hadn't seen one before. It was a screwdriver handle with an extendable little magnet on the end to aid in picking up nuts and bolts that fall in crevices and hard-to-reach places where a hand would find it difficult, if not impossible, to go. "It's perfect!" I said. Dad loves to tinker with stuff in the shop. It'd be great! Problem solved! Dad now has a gift!

This little product sold itself. I didn't need some pale-skinned, acne-scarred college sophomore, wearing a Santa hat that's too big for him, lecturing me unenthusiastically on its features. It wasn't a hot commodity item, and it did not have a "Great for a Gift" sticker on it. It was just hanging on the display rack with a few other discounted tools, but it was the best gift in the entire store.

When it comes to an argument against the existence of God, an argument that "sells itself" on the philosophical market, one need only consider the problem of the existence of evil. This argument speaks to everyone, no matter their education level or their convictions. Even those who claim to believe in God despite the presence of evil in the world feel its power.

I have heard it said many times by those in the atheist's camp that the reason the problem of evil doesn't make more infidels out of believers is because they don't understand it. I disagree. I believe everyone understands this argument. I don't think it's possible not to understand it. Those who aren't convinced by it of the non-existence of God have never really thought about the issue (many cattle-like people), or have thought about it and are in denial of it (most people, and particularly religionists), or are too wound up in the defense of their beliefs to let it do any damage (apologists). In the case of apologists, the force of the argument is being combated by their preoccupation with possible answers to it. But everyone understands the problem of evil, and they squirm in their seats because of it.

The Searching Continues

As a minister, I can remember being asked a lot of questions on countless subjects, but never was I asked in my ministry: "Why do bad things happen to good people?" The reason I was never asked this is because the average person understands that ministers have no better answers than anyone else. This is a question everyone asks themselves, and subconsciously, they know that there are only a few possible answers, and all of them are within the reach of the average person's mind. A minister's responses are the same. Whatever answer might be given, the instability of it, the possibility of error, is always there, and no one is satisfied with any one response. So what does the average man or woman do with this question? The only thing they can do—move on with their lives without answering it.

We humans are a sad species. When faced with captivity for long enough, we just accept it. When beaten down, when abused, wronged, and ridiculed, we learn to swallow it. We accept defeat and our deflating human limitations. Like water, we take whatever shape we are given. In this, I am reminded of an old story about Dr. Sparks Gladman. Dr. Gladman was once asked by a doubting young man: "I long for the consolations of religion, but my reason forbids. Would you suggest a surgical operation to weaken my mind?" Dr. Gladman replied, "No, that is not necessary. Go to church regularly, cease to reason, and exercise the faculty of faith, and you will probably get relief. If these means are unsuccessful, time will help you out. As you grow older, you will become sufficiently feebleminded to accept religion." This is the case with our species: when faced with ignorance for long enough, our faculties of reason diminish and we just don't think about it anymore!

When our distant ancestors first began to tell stories, to fashion legends, and to sew together the first fabric of what would become organized religion, they did the next best thing to eliminating evil—they explained it away (or tried to); like the faith-filled of every age, since they couldn't remove the evils, they could only do their best to explain them away. At first, this wasn't hard to do. For thousands of years, man was more prone to believe unsupported superstitions than he is today. Today, man is more discerning. He looks around his world and sees a miserable picture (generally), a painful picture of suffering and agony on a level that is difficult to comprehend. Church members are moving away from church-based answers. They are looking for deeper answers, answers that satisfy the mind and the faculty of reason.

The problem of evil is an old argument. It was first formalized by Greek philosopher Epicurus (341-270 B.C.E.). Epicurus was one of the Post-Socratic philosophers who spent his days dispelling fear of the gods. Like many philosophers whose works have come to us through the ravages of time, most of Epicurus' works have been lost, but we have the following quote from Lactantius (240-320 C.E.) quoting Epicurus in Lactantius' work, *On The Anger of God,* in which Epicurus strikes a deathblow to all the gods—past, present, and future. Hear him...

> [God]either wishes to take away evils, and is unable; or He is able, and is unwilling; or He is neither willing nor able, or He is both willing and able. If He is willing and is unable, He is feeble, which is not in accordance with the character of God; if He is able and unwilling, He is wicked, which is equally at variance with God; if He is neither willing nor able, He is both wicked and feeble, and therefore not God. (Chapter 13, Of The Advantage and Use of the World and of the Seasons)

Since his time, theologians and philosophers the world over have tried – and abysmally failed – to refute the words of the erudite Greek. The argument stands like the Rock of Gibraltar. People commonly use expressions like, "I'd rather see a sermon than hear one," or "Actions speak louder than words." The same holds true for nature; the presence of evil in the world speaks louder than the theologians who are trying to explain it away.

The preacher will charmingly tell his congregation that death, insanity, sickness, disease, natural disasters, and all the other manifold pains of life are parts of a bigger plan, that God is watching, and ultimately, will make the suffering of his saints worth it in the end. Sounds good, but then I turn around and "see the sermon" of evil. I see no god, no comforting hand of a heavenly father, no help beyond the clouds, no angels, no evidence of celestial celebrations to come, and no relief from pain. The sermon I am seeing on earth is one far removed from that of well-dressed theologians.

Defining Evil

Contemporary believers in Christianity are not like they were decades and centuries ago. When confronted with harsh biblical criticism, they will not tell you things like "just have faith because nobody really knows anything," nor will they admit "I can't prove the Bible or Christianity, but I believe in them." No, those days of quaint and humble honesty are long gone.

What believers of today will tell you is a minimum of ten ways to explain the days of Genesis 1 and the snake of Genesis 3 as figurative rather than literal. On accepting Jesus, they will present the Trilemma (Jesus as a "Lord, liar, or lunatic") and try to buff it up with skewed logic. They will refer to Blocher's Thesis time and again, and wax eloquent quoting Alvin Plantinga and William Lane Craig on issues of common dispute. Concerning the problem of evil, instead of admitting that the existence of evil troubles them, they shine on asking skeptics to "define evil," as though this somehow helps to alleviate the problem. Looking to score points in a debate, believers want a formal definition, which is fine, though unnecessary. I suppose, if someone wanted me to, I could give them a definition of sadness, though we all know what it is. Even so, as stated, there is no one alive beyond the age of infancy who doesn't know what evil is.

Evil – any action(s), of nature or mankind, or omission(s) of action(s) thereof, that work against the life, health, happiness, and well-being of a species, society, and/or individual.

In providing our definition, we have just formalized what is already common sense. It doesn't take a formal definition to see that evil can be something passive (without malice or intent), as is seen in nature...predator-prey relationships, a bear killing a man, a volcano erupting and destroying an entire village, a plague spreading and wiping out thousands of inhabitants. Or, it can be something actively evil (with malice or intent) as committed by sentient, intelligent human animals, like the more obvious crimes...murder (the unjustified taking of life), rape, fraud, the torture of humans or animals and gratification received therefrom, etc.

It is also obvious that an omission of an action can be called evil. A governing body of people that fails to deliver on its promises – that failure resulting in a breach of contract and/or misfortune – is evil. A person of leadership or of great financial means refusing to use their resources to feed and help his people could well be called evil. Even the Bible acknowledges this, "He that withholdeth corn, the people shall curse him: but blessing shall be upon the head of him that selleth it." (Proverbs 11:26). An omission of good resulting in evil might well be citizens of a country harboring terrorists, refusing to turn them over to the authorities, or an individual refusing to testify against a known murderer to put that person away. Even nature can commit evil by omission of good; the village might not be destroyed by a flood, but by a lack of water—by a drought.

Some might well contest my calling a natural disaster evil, but the same people readily contradict themselves, as they would have no problem understanding someone who came to them and told them, "something bad has happened to me! My house caught fire!" We could replace bad with "evil" and the meaning is the same. We use this kind of language all the time, and the meaning is abundantly clear. No one has the slightest trouble understanding it...until God is attacked with the argument from evil, then suddenly we atheists are taken to task on how to define evil!

The issue gets more complicated, but not much more. Evil, as we have seen, is easy to define, and missing it is all but impossible. But applying it is somewhat more technical. Is it evil to inflict pain on a child by taking him/her to the doctor to get a shot if that shot will save the child's life and make the child healthier? Using common sense, this obviously isn't an evil thing to do even though some pain is inflicted, but there is still natural evil here. Where is it from and to whom lies the blame for this child having to be taken to the doctor? The blame lies on the theist's God. I may take a sick child to the doctor to save its life because it's the only option I have, but an omnipotent God has infinite options and is the one bearing the blame for allowing the child to get sick in the first place. Through the same understanding, I am not to blame for killing a man who sneaks into my house at night to do me harm. In such a case, I would be justified in preserving my own life by taking someone else's, but God would still bear the blame for allowing that to happen in the first place.

We humans find ourselves stuck with having to choose the least painful, least regrettable solution to a problem when a perfect one isn't to be found. Things like this we call "necessary evils", or "the lesser of evils" as we humans can often only choose from a small and disappointing array of options open to us. The same must be said of natural evils. When the sperm whale eats tons of fish a day, it is not "evil" as we commonly use the term. It is just feeding to sustain itself. The cheetah chasing down and killing the gazelle to survive is only taking the course nature plotted for it. But again, there is evil here, not by intent, but in result. Who is it that set up a system whereby a smaller, weaker animal is consumed by a stronger one? God created such a system, and it is he who bears the blame every time a predator's jaws and claws sink into the hide of a bison, struggling to escape its killer. No intentional evil need be committed to see when "a great evil" has befallen a city. The volcano doesn't bear the blame for leveling a town, but the theist's God does for constructing a dangerously quirky planet that must relieve its pressures in such a manner.

Defining evil in its many forms was never a problem. Evil is impossible to turn away from. Evil is all around us, and regardless of which side of the debate on the existence of God our convictions may fall, we cannot help but recognize it when we see it. An entire world is losing faith in God over the abundance of evils, and all the while, we are being told by Christian philosophers that we can't even define the term! I can, and just did, but don't have to. I see it every time I see a hospital, a police car, an ambulance, or when I turn on the local 6'o clock news. I see it every time I see a pair of reading glasses, a walking cane, or a sign on the highway that says "Buckle Up for Safety." I see evil, and everyone around me sees it too, even those who swear up and down that it doesn't shake their faith.

The buck of the existence of evil cannot be passed from God. He will never escape his appointment to stand forever convicted in the court of human reason as the most evil and fiendish being imaginable. The standard by which we convict is that of the senses, the same senses with which we judge all of reality.

Evil

As I write, a man is stepping to the edge of the roof of his apartment building. He has been suffering with cancer for quite a long time. His treatments are not working. He has gone to every faith-healer, every church service he could think of. He has maxed out every painkiller, every drug at his disposal. Nothing is helping. He has asked God many times to heal him of his illness with no effect. Finally, looking down some 300 feet, he stares at a black, lifeless parking lot where his diseased body is about to be. He says one last prayer, "Lord, if you will have me to live, please say something now. I can't take this anymore." All is silent. He takes the plunge. A minute later, the screams of a woman can be heard coming from the ground floor as she sees his mangled, twisted body lying motionless next to her car.

As I write, a man spends another day in prison, writing letters, opening mail, weeping as he tilts pictures of his daughters to stand them up against a wall in his cell. He has been working with his lawyers for an appeal to get a new trial, but things are looking bleak. He is serving forty years for a crime he did not commit. He may be over seventy by the time he gets out.

As I write, a woman is walking back to her car after a long day's work where she will be jumped by three men in masks and dragged into the back of a van where she will be raped repeatedly and savagely beaten. When they are through with her, she is killed and her body is buried in a landfill. Another woman in the same situation would not be killed, but dumped on the side of a road and left for dead. If she lives, she will be scarred for life with permanent, painful memories of the event. If she doesn't contract some sexually transmitted disease or die from AIDS, she'll count herself lucky.

As I write, a Christian couple is praying for a child. They are faithful, dedicated, prayerful, and patient, yet barren despite many years of intense prayer. They just got the news that the wife of a family down the street whose father was convicted of armed robbery is pregnant…again! Child Protective Services has already taken one child away on account of poor living conditions and abuse in the house. They get a fourth child and the Christian couple must try to save up a huge amount of money to adopt.

As I write, an angry, disgruntled employee is about to open fire on an establishment full of innocent bystanders. Panicking, frantically looking for a way out, some trample one another. Others sit in the fetal position and wet themselves, their hands covering their ears, shaking and quivering violently, hoping to make it out alive. Begging for their lives, these poor, unfortunate souls will eat lead before the disgruntled man's anger subsides. He will then look around and see the carnage he caused. Blood now covers his clothes and face. He then turns the gun on himself.

How long could we make this chapter? How many horrible experiences could we make note of if we chose? I dare say the number would match or surpass the number of possible Rubik's Cube arrangements.

The Objections

The real power of the problem of evil shines through ever more brightly when we see how easily it destroys the objections against it. A theologian can give his life blood trying to explain away the existence of evil, but when all is said and done, evil remains, and so does the question of why. Over the years, I have heard many reasons in an attempt to explain evil, so I have decided to let this chapter consist primarily of responses to the wholly inadequate bulk of theistic replies to the problem…

Objection #1) "God has a secret plan behind suffering. God's will is behind everything."

In order to make this objection, one must assume (a) that God exists, and (b) that God is just, compassionate, and concerned with human affairs as we would expect and understand him to be. If we go in assuming this, then naturally, the conclusion that God has our best interests at heart will be unavoidable. Indeed, the diehard optimism behind this contention is found to be at the heart of all religion. The reason people are religious to start with is due to their belief that their lives have meaning, that there is an ultimate sense of purpose behind everything that happens. To admit that God does not have a special reason for their suffering would be akin to admitting that God does not exist. It would be unthinkable.

And this position is a failsafe; when the theist dies, they expect heaven where God will pour out the answers to the question of why he tolerated the presence of evil, but if when the Christian expires no god or heaven exists, the believer will be dead and will not be around to be called on the carpet for his error. This has them accepting any and all tragedies without applying any rational criticism whatsoever. Blind obedience to a leader is what enables destructive cults to do terrible things. If a follower can never question the orders of his leader, that leader will have the best chance of completing his objective. If his orders are never questioned, he cannot be opposed. God can't be opposed either.

Though it's not rational, this is an understandable objection. I have found myself wondering what it would be like to hear God say, "My child, the reason I ordered the mass extermination of the Midianites was because...", "I allowed children to starve in Ethiopia because...", "I allowed the medieval church to ravage the world because...", "I allowed the holocaust because…". But I wonder if God's explanations for these things would be any better than the ones the apologists use? We will never know if we will even get these answers, but we are being asked to make the leaping assumption that such answers exist. And if I were to grant that a "secret plan" justifying evil did exist, but was not known, this does not diminish the potency of the problem of evil since this claim cannot offer up anything by way of intelligent thought to discuss the problem.

Objection #2) "God allows us to suffer to teach us lessons, to make us more spiritual, to make us stronger believers."

If humankind suffers for the sake of teaching us spiritual lessons and strengthening our character, this opens up a number of additional questions; (a) if mankind was intended to suffer, why was he created in a paradise garden to live free of suffering? Why did it take transgression to start us on the path to enlightenment? This seems to incriminate God's original destiny for man. And (b) if mankind is being taught lessons from suffering, why is it that so few learn the right lessons from suffering? And why is it that so many seem to be learning the wrong lessons? People are driven away from religion and spirituality as surely as they are brought to it. In fact, as per the scriptural declaration, few seem to be finding the narrow path (Matthew 7:13-14). Those who are not made stronger are torn down, made weaker by the manifold miseries of our being. The world is not benefiting from these struggles, but being ripped apart.

Telling me that when someone is driven to suicide because a man cannot silence the voices in his head, that it was because God was testing him and he should have handled it better, is insulting to the intelligence. Asking me to believe that one man killing another man and eating his flesh is an example of someone learning the wrong lesson in life is almost the equivalent of slapping me in the face.

If anything, these "lessons" which mankind is expected to learn, these trials he is expected to endure, prove to be too much. Despite the scripture's affirming otherwise, we are indeed given more than we can take. I Corinthians 10:13 is a lie. *"There hath no temptation taken but such as is common to man, but God is faithful who will not suffer you to be tempted above that ye able, but will, with the temptation also make a way of escape that ye may be able to bare it."*

This is a meaningless verse, a passage that exhibits no clear truth. Paul contradicts himself when he says that some temptations *will* overcome man, but that God will not allow you to suffer *too* harsh a temptation that will overcome your resistance against sin. You can't have it both ways; if the way of escape from temptation was not taken, then the temptation proved to be too much—period. This means the scripture is wrong and God is false to his promise. Any temptation that overcomes man is "common to man," since religious people are always falling short of their gods for the same assortment of reasons. According to this passage, man can overcome any temptation he faces, so why is the determined Christian not sinless? Surely there are Christians who are dedicated enough to take full advantage of this promise of absolute deliverance from temptation? Why don't we see them? Shouldn't the only sinners be the openly rebellious? Shouldn't the redeemed be truly sin-free?

As a minister, I had a number of hurting souls in my office who, in tears, told me, "God better help me out of this soon because I can't take much more." I committed one man who wasn't kidding when he said this. At what point will a theologian concede that something can be literally "too much"? What about convicted murderers or rapists who confess that an irresistible compulsion compels them to commit their crimes? How low must a person be brought before it will be obvious that God is not delivering anyone?

Finally, this demands that we ask (c) what percentage of suffering does this not explain, and what other explanations will be used to explain the rest? Surely all suffering cannot be God trying to teach us spiritual lessons on life? How is that suffering to be explained? As we can see, this explanation leaves much to be desired. It creates more questions than it answers.

Objection #3) "God allows us to suffer to offer us a reward beyond our wildest dreams in heaven."

I wonder what theologians think of fathers who beat their children and put out cigarettes on them, but then "to make up for it," get them good medical care and take them to Disneyland? Injustice is still injustice. The greatest possible compensation will not make up for evils committed. The most wonderful reward will not erase the fact that a wrong has been done. Even an infinite God who can give us pleasures unimaginable cannot be justified in permitting misery for a reward, no matter how grand the recompense. Humans might find themselves "making up" for the bad things they do, but for a supposedly just and omnibenevolent God, this conduct is inexcusable from the word "go."

Objection #4) "The argument of evil is presumptuous to assume that just because God has not eliminated evil now, that he won't eliminate it in his own time. God will get rid of evil when he is ready."

A number of years ago, I had a house debate with two prominent Mormon elders. When I asked them why so many of their church's older, no-longer-circulated prophecies had not been fulfilled, the response I got was, "There's still time." Islam predicts a future date when all the world will be converted to that faith. Ask an advocate of any religion why their faith is not *"the faith"* of humanity, and they'll tell you that it will be; "There's still time."

This response is very similar to Objection #1 in that it demands our playing a "waiting game" on God. How are we to differentiate between these claims? And when will be the cut-off point? If God will someday eliminate evil, what's to stop him from stretching out justice a thousand more centuries, or a billion? I appeal to the believer's sense of justice when I ask what they would do if I were a judge, and a criminal stood before me who had been convicted of murder. Without hesitation, I pronounce the sentence of the man to be death by lethal injection. But what would the community think of me if, before I hand him over to die, I postpone his sentence for two thousand years? A lot of angry voices would be heard over the injustice, and they'd be justified. But God has decided to let criminals run free until judgment day (whenever that will be). Theists themselves are much more just than the deity they serve. Even if Satan has already been convicted by God, there is no reason for his sentence to be postponed. He should be serving his sentence now, and the atrocities he brought into the world should have been wiped away at once. To allow an entire world to become corrupted by his influence and his presence is a crime on the part of God himself.

Objection #5) "God allows suffering to rebuke us of sin, to chastise us."

There are those preachers and churches that teach that suffering in all forms is the result of sin we commit, but I wonder if they really believe this since their own leaders end up suffering just as much as anyone else. This is an incomplete answer at best. It does not account for suffering experienced when no sin was involved, which has to be most of it. It sounds good for Christians to say that if God sets a standard and we depart from it, then we face the consequences of our actions, but this does not explain all other suffering, and more importantly, it does not explain how these chastisements are different from the materialistic consequences of our actions; for instance, if I walk into a bar and insult someone's mother and get knocked to the floor for it, how is this any different from learning the consequences of making a stupid mistake? Would not the same thing have happened if no chastising higher power was in the picture? Trumped up excuses like this are nothing more than afterthoughts of religious irrationality.

Objection #6) "God allows suffering because of the sins of others."

The problem here is twofold: (a) as with a number of others in this list, this response only covers a small amount of the suffering a person endures at the hands of others. Another reason will have to be provided to account for the other causes of evil. And (b) there is no reason why God cannot be benevolent enough to let one bear only the consequences of their own sins (if any).
    A drunk driver may run off the road and hit a child playing in his front yard, crippling him for life, but in a world of justice, we would never see such a thing. First of all, there should be no drunks, but if there were, there should be no injurious accidents because of them. We are not talking about forbidding the drunk from choosing to become a drunkard, but we are talking about having God send an angel to move the car out of the way before it hits and forever ruins the life of a child, or better yet, to not provide the means to become a drinker in the first place.

Objection #7) "God allows suffering because of violations of natural law. God must allow suffering when his physical laws are broken."

So if I put my hand on a hot stove, I can only blame myself for it burning me, and it has to burn me, otherwise exposure to the flame could kill me if direct exposure to it was sustained. If I fall off a ladder, I must fall to the ground, and if I land wrong, I will break my tailbone because of gravity—because gravity must be in place for the sake of the whole planet. This is not an explanation of why we suffer, only a restatement of the fact that we suffer, and how. Telling me that heat and gravity are responsible for pain in a certain circumstance doesn't explain why pain has the often irreparable physical and psychological effects it has on us.

Speaking of heat, why, for instance, can someone break into my house and force my face against a hot stove? If violations of natural law are operational laws for our wellbeing, how could an omniscient deity not have foreseen the need to equip us with the mental hardware to "turn off" pain sensations when they are misused (such as in instances of torture)? The theist is so busy talking up the benefits of natural law that he thinks he's got something when he says, "Can you fault God for using pain as a means to save your life?", when more than half the time, our pain is not saving our lives. But what about those situations where pain does save our lives? Can I fault God for that? I can.

God is thought to be an infinite God. The theist will gladly affirm as much, which means I should be able to stick my hand on a hot furnace and have it not burn me. This furnace should cease to be a furnace at that moment and regain its furnace properties when my hand is removed. If I try and chase my fellow man with a garden hoe, the hoe should lose its properties as a hoe until my anger subsides. Then it would become a useful tool again. If I try to commit suicide, the water around me should not be able to drown me. If I walked so that I would trip over a stone, the stone would cease to retain its properties as a deadweight object and I would pass through it, and not be caused to fall. Why not have a superior system of natural law like this? Instead of natural law, we should have "supernatural law."

The scenarios above should in no way be considered unrealistic. They are not. An infinite God has infinite resources, and therefore, we lose nothing if every single thing that could harm us is eliminated or modified so that it poses no threat. You don't need a crude set of "natural laws" when there is an all-knowing, all-seeing, all-powerful eye looking out for you!

On this very subject, the late Apologist Thomas B. Warren wrote in *Have Atheists Proved There is No God?*

> If a man were dying of thirst, water would have to have the properties which it now has, but if a man who could not swim fell into a lake, in order for the man not to drown, water suddenly would have to take on another (different) set of properties. Or, if a man were using an axe on

> a tree it would have cutting power which an axe now has in our present world, but if one man were to try to use an axe on an animal or another man then the axe would have to lose its property of being able to cut through a man's body. *It might be questioned whether such 'laws' are really law. At any rate, it seems clear that such a situation would be really another form of chaos, and a world characterized by such conditions hardly would be an ideal environment for such moral decision and development. What rational man would argue for such chaos to be characteristic of man's environment?* (p. 54)

To answer Mr. Warren's question, the answer is: a truly rational man! Why should some find it queer to demand that God tap into his infinite resources to create our world in the best possible way? God, as creator, is responsible for the material structure of the universe. For him to have constructed a universe without the limitations of a "material" world as we know it was an option he could have pursued…but he didn't. Instead, he constructed a universe where accidents and death are the norm. That is the problem. Apparently, God thought it was worth it to create a world where misery and death are everywhere.

Objection #8) "God allows suffering to weed out the unfaithful, to test men, so that only righteous, dedicated, worthy souls dwell with him in heaven."

I like this objection because it brings out the very cruel nature of the God of the scriptures. This is not just a man-made objection. The Bible actually says this...

> Now if any man build upon this foundation gold, silver, precious stones, wood, hay, stubble; every man's work shall be made manifest for the day shall declare it, because it shall be revealed by fire... (I Corinthians 3:12-13).

What Paul is talking about is not works in the sense of good deeds, but works in the sense of converts. The converts were the "work" of the preacher. "The day" (this life of trial) would declare it (see which souls would be faithful and would endure—gold, silver, and precious stones, and see which souls would be unfaithful and would not endure—wood, hay, stubble.) But God doesn't need to weed out weaklings. When he created us, he knew beforehand those of us who would pass and those of us who would fail the test. By moving forward with the creation of erring children, God made himself responsible for populating Hell.

Objection #9) "God allows suffering because it can be a blessing in disguise. Good can come from suffering."

Yes, good can come from a recovering alcoholic who may learn from her bad experiences with alcohol how to help others. And yes, a cancer survivor may learn how to help others fighting cancer, but these are only examples of creating problems to solve them. Wouldn't it make infinitely more sense to never have anyone face alcoholism or cancer in the first place? This reminds me of a preaching friend I had years ago; he expected me to believe that babies are born deformed so that doctors can learn how to treat other deformed babies!

And what about those many instances where suffering is clearly not a "blessing in disguise?" I'm sure a rape victim who contracts AIDS would not consider that a blessing, nor a visitor to a foreign country who contracts an incurable disease. Since man will always adapt and fortify his means of survival, it is inevitable that a great many bad things will have good endings, but this hardly suggests that a smart creator would use such troubled means of bringing about improvement. I could choose to water my garden by wetting my hair and slinging my head around until drops of water hit the leaves, but there are better ways of getting the job done. Why not just give us the improvements without the pain, which is a much better way?

Objection #10) "Life would be boring without suffering. We need troubles to appreciate the good we have."

This objection is not very well thought out. If man had not sinned in the garden, would life in the paradise garden have been boring? Will heaven, without suffering or evil, be boring? Why must peace and tranquility be accompanied by pain to be appreciated? This does not speak well of heaven, nor of God for planning it. Can we not appreciate heavenly peace for its own sake? If heavenly peace alone cannot be appreciated without suffering, then this makes the creator ten times worse for designing it this way. Again, God is at fault for not getting it right! A life without any pain and suffering would be just that—a life without any pain and suffering, characterized only by contentment. There would be no drawbacks to living in a perfect paradise, only we can't do it.

Objection #11) "Suffering occurs because we are not spiritual enough. God will allow mankind to suffer until this whole world is a spiritual place dominated by Christians full of faith."

This is the same sort of thing the faith-healers tell those who are not healed by them. "You would have been healed, but you lacked faith." If we suffer because our society is not spiritual enough, because it is immoral and evil, then the theist has a fail-safe position; while the world stands, there will always be heathens, so there is no way we will ever see a lifting of evil on this earth because according to scripture, God is coming back to judge a sinful world. By the liberal distribution of guilt, preachers and theologians have their craft. They use guilt to their advantage, and if they can't classify you as a disgusting sinner, consumed by the forces of darkness, they'll cast aspersions on the rest of humanity.

Objection #12) "You atheists only find fault with suffering because you are incorrectly judging God by the exceptions, not the rule. Suffering is not all there is to life. It is possible to take suffering in stride and live a productive, happy life, rising above it."

Try telling this to someone who has been paralyzed from the neck down, or someone with a botched fusion who lives with an implanted morphine pump to manage the pain. To those who don't suffer very much, this might be hard to understand, but there are fabulous numbers of people who are trapped in bodies they only wish they could escape from. The truth is, it is the theist who judges by the exceptions. Those who live adventurous, pain-free lives with a minimal amount of suffering—*they* are the exceptions.

Most of us will spend a good portion of our lives patching up these miserable bodies, and this is not counting suffering that comes our way from accidents and natural disasters and violence. Those who object to the existence of God based on suffering are not overemphasizing anything. We are addressing what is ignored by those willfully blind optimists who refuse to see life as it really is. It is true that most suffering does not completely squeeze the life out of all joy we might have. Suffering can usually be overcome (at least, most of the time. Human beings are good at that because we have to be!), but *minimizing suffering does not take the focus off the fact that it exists*. Suffering exists, and it has not been adequately accounted for, so the argument stands.

Objection #13) "God allows us to go through suffering and sin as a sort of vaccine against evil. A taste of the devil's medicine makes us immune from its affects. By being exposed to sin and suffering, we are safe-guarded from falling away in heaven like Satan did, securing eternal life for us."

I used to champion this line. The objection was cut and pasted from an old article I wrote as a preacher. I'll give the explanation credit for being the most creative, but beyond that, it gets no credit at all.

For a moment, let's go with the flow of this argument and grant that it could be true. Every soul of man or woman born into this life is "vaccinated" from sin by experiencing the hard nature of living and overcoming the world through faith amidst trials. What about those young babies and aborted fetuses who die not having this "vaccination?" Even if they die in a sinless condition, will it not be possible for them to be in heaven and apostatize like Satan did since they were never spiritually fortified like the rest of us? Why did God create angels, all of whom (like Satan) are "unvaccinated"? This reflects poor planning on God's part.

Objection #14) "The question of God permitting suffering only deals with the character of God, and therefore, is irrelevant to the question of his existence."

This objection is eerily similar to our first objection, and you've got to admire it. It tries hard, and it *would* be valid. It is certainly true that my neighbor exists despite my estimation of his character, but the same can't be said of God. In the case of my neighbor, he exists. I have no doubts about that, but in the case of God, all I have of him are his alleged words from a book, from myth. The only way I can examine him are through the surety of his ways and principles, the fidelity of his promises, and the credibility of his prophecies. This opens up the question of God's existence to arguments from plausible claims.

Why would a deity who has mankind's best interest at heart allow evil and human suffering? Either God has a plan behind suffering, or he does not; if God has reasons for allowing suffering, why are we not finding them? Why are we spending an entire chapter demolishing the oft-given-but-poor-quality responses from God-supporters? Why don't these responses stand up to scrutiny? The only way for believers in God to argue that a deity *might* have hidden purposes behind suffering is to forfeit the use of logic and reason—there is no point in debating *might bes* and *could bes*, and what otherwise cannot be known, is there? At such a point, the believer in God has conceded the debate.

On the other hand, it may be that God has no plan behind suffering; it may turn out that he is an openly fiendish galactic entity who doesn't have mankind's best interest at heart. It may also be that God is of a deistic persuasion and doesn't really get involved in human affairs. Maybe he just doesn't care about us? But there is one other possibility—that no capital "G" god exists, that this universe is a godless one, and all suffering experienced is for purely mechanistic reasons. So, either God exists and has a plan behind suffering, he exists and does not have a plan behind suffering, or God doesn't exist at all; a benevolent God cannot meaningfully and logically be said to exist *and* have a plan behind suffering, and a wicked god who intends suffering, or a deistic god who couldn't care less about our suffering means nothing to humankind, which leaves us with only the last option—that no god exists at all, which means our suffering is a natural phenomenon in a godless existence.

What have we done here? We have come right back to the initial problem of evil. We have effortlessly demonstrated that the existence of evil has everything to do with the question of God's existence.

Objection #15) "In order for the atheist to say that God does wrong in not eliminating evil, the atheist must assume an objective standard of right and wrong, but if he assumes a standard of right or wrong, then God must exist."

Standards exist for pragmatic, comparative reasons. It is childish to suppose them to have *a creator*, per se, as opposed to an observant body of people to formulate and abide by them. When it comes to moral standards, both the Christian and the atheist employ the same standards, though they arrive at them through different means. The god-believer is convinced that a murderer will roast in Hell, and therefore, should not murder; the atheist believes murder to be unworkable in an intelligent, peaceful society, and therefore, one shouldn't murder. When the theist objects to murder, the atheist objects to murder, and in just about every circumstance, the two agree. Rapes, burglaries, and scams should be stopped as much as is in our power to do so. None of these evil occurrences are considered desirable by atheists or theists of any persuasion. There is strong consensus on almost every issue between theists and atheists when it comes to the health and wellbeing of mankind. As there is among standards employed by humans – be they religious or secular – they tend to have almost universal value and acceptance.

This objection represents a pathetic attempt on the part of the theologian to standard-plead, to make a distinction where one doesn't exist. Both the theist and the atheist draw the same conclusions about the natural world around them. It doesn't take deep scholarship to see that a hurricane is not good for humanity. This reasoning applies all across the board, from stopping a rape or assault, to putting out fires and keeping laws. Whether a god commands it to be done, or whether a counsel of intelligent humans determine that said deed needs to be done, the result is the same. The same standard exists, and therefore, we can hold the God of the Bible accountable to that standard. By what standard is God evil? By the believer's standard and by my own—by the same standard that allows us to know evil when we see it.

Objection #16) "God allows evil because God allows freewill. It would be a violation of God's nature not to preserve freewill. Therefore, God allows freewill, and the commission of evil results from that."

The freewill objection is like a young couple in a heated argument when the girlfriend throws up the name of an old lover: "Bobby was better than you!" Frustrated and not wanting to argue, the boyfriend says to himself, "Is that guy always going to be with us?" I would be having lunch with Steve Forbes right now if I had a dime for every time a believer in God said something like, *"But God gave us freewill. He didn't want to make us robots."* The simplicity of this retort, the profound shallow-mindedness of the thinking behind it is perplexing, but like the old boyfriend who just won't go away, it seems that this objection is another thing that will not be going away any time soon!

And of course, we *are* like robots. On a philosophical level, freewill does not exist. Every action or decision you've ever made you made because causality led you to do so. Given your knowledge at the time, your influences, and your causal conditioning, you made every decision you made because you had to. Things had to happen the way they happened. This is classic determinism. We are in every sense slaves to the forces of causality, and no theist has yet explained how any of us cannot be.

While freewill is seen as an answer to the problem of evil, it is in fact what actually proves my point concerning the deplorable nature of the God of the Bible—he is so evil that he subjected his creation to all manner of unspeakable miseries in the name of nothing more than a staring contest. That's what freewill is, just a staring contest, an opportunity for God to sit up in heaven and stare down at his creatures as they toil and labor under the sun. He's just staring at us. He already knows what we are going to do before we do it, but he wants to give us the freedom to do it anyway…to screw up and make mistakes— needless, countless, painful mistakes that ruin lives. God will let a carload of gangsters spray bullets into a crowd of children at a church picnic, and he'll allow a pedophile father to rape his kids for a decade, and for what? So that God can stand by and watch, and so that he'll be able to say to the perpetrators of these crimes on judgment day, *"You had freewill. You did that. I didn't make you do it. Now to Hell you go!*

There you will be forever!" What doltish glory! What wicked indifference! The freedom to rebel is without a doubt the single greatest curse God ever unleashed on this world.

Evil in the Church

In the quest to take the kick out of the problem of evil, we hear so much about "accepting God's will" for our lives. But what about when we know all too well that "the Lord's will" is only being undone by evil? Just when you think it can't get any worse, just when you think you've seen it all, something else happens that surprises you. What always unsettled me was not just the random nature of suffering in the world, but suffering in the church too. I have been in the middle of church services when the power was knocked out by lightning. Had I not had my material memorized, I would not have been able to finish the sermon! I have seen one awfully violent seizure during a morning worship service, and have known of three flat tires members had to stop and fix on their way to church. One family was involved in a wreck that nearly resulted in the amputation of a foot. I have witnessed one stroke and one heart attack during and right after services.

In 2005, news broke about Pastor Kyle Lake, minister of a large Baptist Church in Waco, Texas, just 32 miles south of where I preached. I believe I met the man once. He was electrocuted as he grabbed a microphone to say some words before performing a baptism. He died then and there, serving God and saving souls. If ever divine help was to be given, if ever man was to be blessed by God to do his will, if ever there are opportunities for modern day miracles, those opportunities would come during the worship services of almighty God, would they not? Apparently God doesn't think so. Efforts in the furtherance of God's message and the conducting of his services mean nothing to him, it seems. Chances of running into misfortune then and there are identical to falling into calamity at any other time. God treats his ministers like he treats an ugly circus midget or a wino sleeping on a bench in a public park. The clergy sees no suspension of the laws of nature. Even righteous Polycarp was provided with no providential protection as his body was consumed in flames for refusing to denounce his savior before Roman authorities.

Couldn't God have at least waited until services were over to let the power go out? Shouldn't he have preserved his worshipping church members from flats, wrecks, seizures, heart attacks and strokes, at least while his children went to and from worship? This would have been the ultimate demonstration of God's power. The avoidance of incidents like this could have been hailed as the most undeniable line of evidences of the divine power: while you are worshipping the lord, all will be well! And can you imagine what would happen if everyone knew that on the Lord's side, health and happiness would be theirs? A suspension of the unequally distributed suffering of mankind for the people of God could have been a step towards vindicating God of the problem of evil. If only it was the ungodly who endured the curse of sin, no one would ever have any excuse to complain. But this is exactly what we don't see, and as things are now, we would expect them to be so only in a godless world.

God's Will and God Incriminated

When it comes to a willingness to accept the providential will of God for his world, it shouldn't raise any eyebrows when atheists have problems with God's will, but it definitely should when believers themselves do. Titus 1:16 speaks of those who profess to know God, but by their works deny him. This almost seems to apply to faithful believers themselves who, though claiming to believe in God and God's sovereign will, end up fighting him by undoing the wrongs he allows to happen. Every time a decently-minded Christian man tries to stop a rape in progress, he is incriminating God by putting a stop to a bad act that God was content to sit by and watch happen. Every time a Christian fundamentalist couple vote for an activist local judge who promises to make stricter laws for sex offenders, they don't take the time to realize that they are doing something God has not bothered to do. They are changing the natural course of things, and in principle at least, thwarting God's providential will. They incriminate God by their refusal to do what they tell us atheists to do—to accept that God is in control of his world.

If God is in control of this world, why are we fighting so hard to change it, to make it better? Why are we having trouble resigning ourselves to being complacent with regard to whatever happens? The idea that mankind must fight to end world hunger, to ward off diseases, to stop crime, to combat natural disasters, while God himself does nothing about these things is the ultimate kick in the pants to humanity.

Denial is Not a River in Egypt!

While at my second church, I had a friend who came to me one Sunday afternoon in my parsonage. He urgently asked to discuss with me the problem of evil because he was certain that it was making him seriously question his faith. Although this was before I began to experience my own doubts, I remember feeling how unsettled he was. Over a cold glass of iced tea we discussed the issue. I laid it all out for him, using many of the attempted justifications included in this chapter. We met up again a month later and he was even more disturbed about it. He said to me, *"Explain the problem of evil again?"* Frustrated, I fretted within myself why this troubled soul hadn't absorbed the information I had given him. Looking back on the event years later, I came to see just how honest this young man was to see through the smokescreen-ish doubletalk I'd subjected him to in an attempt to explain away a problem that was unexplainable.

That is how things are with the problem of evil; the believer has much to say to justify evil, but when the wordiness has stopped, and the longwinded conglomerations of thoughts cease, all we are left with is the same feeling of emptiness we began with. When all the vain arguments are put to rest, and all of the excuses for God's fiendish conduct are used up, we walk away as disturbed as ever. There will never be an answer to the problem of evil because the benevolent God hypothesis cannot meld with the existence of evil. I have to believe that any creator of the universe would be able and willing to fashion for us the ideal world, a fixed and permanent paradise, just as he allegedly planned from the start. But instead of this, we get excuses to explain why things are not this way; we get substance-less tales about fallen angels, about wrong choices being made by two sheepish humans who knew not right from wrong, about depravity, and about witch-like curses—all earmarks of denial and egregious lies.

CHAPTER 15
Stolen Goods

From Tantalizing Tall Tales to Mythologically Morphed Messiahs

"The reasonable man adapts himself to the world; the unreasonable one persists in trying to adapt the world to himself."
- *George Bernard Shaw*

"The Christian Theory is little else than the idolatry of the ancient mythologists, accommodated to the purposes of power and revenue."
- *Thomas Paine*

The Making of a Mighty Myth

For nearly as long as I can remember, I have been fascinated with the Bible story of Samson. Some time around my conversion, I recall watching the 1950 film "Samson and Delilah" with Victor Mature. It made such an impression on me.

Ordinarily, I suppose I have a somewhat theatrical mind and enjoy a good drama, but there's a problem for me; if whatever I'm watching is of outrageous fantasy, I tend to mentally grind to a halt and not be as entertained by it. Immediately, I start picking out the faults to the extent that if the flick is not exceptional enough to compensate for its blemishes, I'm inclined to quit watching.

In the case of the story of Samson, this one has it all...drama, forbidden love, lust, betrayal, racial tensions, a flawed hero arising from humble beginnings, comic book style action and fighting, and even a good measure of science fiction. Samson is every powerlifter's dream. World record holding bench-presser Scott Mendelson has nothing on this guy! And even to the rest of us who couldn't care less about weightlifting, we are still moved to wish like anything that we could transcend the clutches of normalcy and earth-boundness to be our own supermen and women. I am entertained by quality comics and science fiction, and a story like this one definitely fits the bill. It is worth sidestepping realism for a while to enjoy. There's always something fascinating about a place where the mundane, boring rules of our material world do not apply. Who can deny that?

Samson and the Solar Myth

The Samson myth is a regurgitation and modification of the older Greek myth of Herakles (Hercules to the Romans), sandwiched together with obviously veiled characteristics of Assyrian and Egyptian solar deities. Egyptologist Gary Greenberg offers the following comments...

> Samson's name means something like 'little sun' or 'sun man.' His long hair (like the manes of the lion and horse) symbolized the rays of the sun. In the Near East, especially in Egypt, the lion was often used to symbolize the power of the sun. Fire plays an important role throughout Samson's story. The angel who announced his birth ascended to heaven in a flame, Samson scorched an entire field, and when his arms were bound the ropes burned. (101 Myths of the Bible, p. 265)

Concerning solar symbolism, Greenberg continues...

> Samson's circular path in the grinding mill corresponds to the circular routes of the daily and annual suns. In one episode of the Samson story, he is shown with thirty companions, a number suggesting the solar

> month. The blinding of Samson has been compared to a solar eclipse, but more significantly, the blinding of Samson recalls an episode from the conflicts between Horus and Set, in which Set, the enemy of the sun, blinded Horus, the sun figure. Herakles, too, reflected solar symbolism. In one of his famous feats, he killed a lion and wore the skin like a cloak, with the animal's head and long flowing mane forming a helmet. The lion head's cloak was the standard icon used to identify Herakles in Greek art. (p. 266)

While some may well take issue with a few of the comparisons Greenberg makes (I, for one, do), note that in the most prominent Herculean myth, Hercules ascended in the flame from the alter to heaven just as the angel ascended from the campfire after announcing Samson's birth before Manoah (Judges 13:20). And as a display of power, both Samson and Hercules were shown to kill lions with their bare hands. Plus, both Samson and Hercules favored blunt weapons (Samson killed with the jawbone of an ass and Hercules with his trusty, wooden club). So the mythical overtones of the story do seem rather hard to ignore.

The stronger pagan connection with Samson is the Assyrian sun god, Shemesh. Temples were built to Shemesh in the same area where Samson was said to have been born, "between Zorah and Eshtaol" (Judges 13:25). Beit Shemesh and Ain Shemesh were two villages in this story in the same area, and both cities were places that honored the ever popular solar myth. It cannot be denied that the name Samson itself, "Shimshon" is a take off the root word "shmsh," which means "sun."

But Biblicists will not give in easily, as you might imagine. They point out that the name may be figurative of shining strength and the radiance of God. *"The Lord God is a sun and a shield"* (Psalms 84:12). Sounds good to a believer, but doesn't hold water when compared not only to the universality of the solar myth at the time, but to the events in Samson's own life, which are clearly solar in nature. But believers will not let their God be tarnished; if Samson's name had meant "Moon man," this would not have deterred them from saying something about how the moon is a celestial testament to God's glory! Count on Christians to set things up so that even the most damning facts appear not to be so.

Recurrent Similarities

One big giveaway to a myth is not only similarity to other obvious fabrications, but the recurrence of life details of other characters, situations, and events. Samson's mother was barren, just like Sarah,

Rachel, Rebecca, and Hannah. Samuel's mother, Hannah, was spoken to by God and commanded to abstain from wine while pregnant with her child of promise, just like Samson's mother (Judges 13:3-4). Both Manoah and Abraham were commanded by God to follow the words of their wives in regard to their children (Judges 13:13; Genesis 21:12). Both Manoah and Jacob asked the names of the angels sent to them and they are told in the exact same language that their names are secret (Judges 13:17-18; Genesis. 32:29). Samson himself was remarkably similar to other biblical characters. Both Samson and Samuel were Nazarites, required never to cut their hair (I Samuel 1:11; Judges 13:5). Both Samson and Absalom had long hair, the non-keeping of which managed to be their undoing (Judges 16:19; 2 Samuel 18:9), and both set fire to a field (Judges 15:4-5; 2 Samuel 14:30). Both Samson and Saul are figures with glaring faults, who lose God's Spirit in their falls from grace (I Samuel 28:15; Judges 16:20), and both request that their deaths not be at the hands of the Philistines – and they succeed – albeit through what amounted to suicide (I Samuel 31:4-5; Judges 16:28-30). One has to ask how and why these similarities with other Bible characters keep popping up?

The Shamgar Connection

Another tremendous giveaway of a myth is the recurrence of heroic themes. The Bible is lipping full of this. Before there was Samson, there was Shamgar, who killed 800 men with an ox goad (a device used to prod oxen along in herding) (Judges 3:31). Further on into the Bible, we read about Jashobeam, who could take on 300 men at one time with just a spear (I Chronicles 11:11). And Adino, the Eznite, a spearman who victoriously took on 800 men at once (2 Samuel 23:8). Why do we keep getting these fabulous heroic accounts? Because we are dealing with stories – legends – not historical facts or accounts.

Add to that, the Old Testament prophets were basically political cheerleaders for their own ideals and beliefs. One can see this similarity by just casually reading through the major and minor prophets; their writings have a cheery message for the believers in the Yahweh cult...

> For the LORD will have mercy on Jacob, and will yet choose Israel, and set them in their own land: and the strangers shall be joined with them, and they shall cleave to the house of Jacob. (Isaiah 14:1)

The creators of the Samson myth were doing the same thing here, and even softly relying on the words of Moses and Joshua as an encouragement...

> One man of you shall chase a thousand: for the LORD your God, he it is that fighteth for you, as he hath promised you. (Joshua 23:10)

This is exactly what the fabricators had happen in Samson's great battle with a thousand Philistines (Judges 15:15), and why they created it in the first place. Storytelling has always been a most trusted way to teach and give hope.

Putting a lid on the mythical nature of this story is Samson's portrayal in traditional and Rabbinic literature as a giant, strong enough to lift the mountains of Zorah and Eshtaol and grind them together as easily as we can handfuls of dirt (The Talmud, Sotah 9b). Samson could also leap across mountains in one stride (Sotah 10a).

Of course, it does little to quote from sources to critique an obviously fictitious biblical account when the logistical problems with the story itself are so much more interesting to focus on.

The Logistical Mechanics

Suffice it to say, the logistics here just don't add up. If God wanted a judge to deliver Israel from Philistinian oppression, he needed only send this Old Testament superman to smash a few strongholds to the ground and kill a few hundred soldiers in demonstration of his unmatchable power. The Philistines – like all other human animals – have this thing called a survival instinct; when faced with extinction, the Philistines would humbly drop to their knees in awe and meet any demand God gave them, including leaving Israel alone. Anyone who is strong enough to bare-handedly rip a lion to pieces without effort (Judges 14:5-6), to kill thirty Philistine soldiers (Judges 14:19), to have the speed and cunning to snatch up 300 foxes and tie their tails together to mischievously ruin a wheat field by setting it on fire (assuming, of course, there were that many foxes – or possibly a similar animal, like jackals – in the area, and that Samson could acquire them, store them, feed them, and tie their tails together and set the rope on fire in a timely enough manner!), to slay yet more of an unknown number of soldiers (Judges 15:8), before demolishing a fully equipped army of a thousand trained warriors, would have no problem making demands! Real life isn't like those cheesy 80's ninja flicks where the enemies fight to the death at every encounter. People have this tendency to want to live, you know!

Besides this, I have always wondered why the lords of the Philistines did not offer Samson a job as their elite soldier. They had already seen he was a greater warrior than they had ever faced. Would it not be far more cost-efficient and expedient to have him on their side? Salary, plus all the women Samson could ever want would have been a good offer to make him. He obsessively loved Philistine women anyway. But whatever the reason, their leaders seemed to think they could safely risk losing more troops at the hands of someone strong enough to rip out of the ground and carry a 12 ton gate about 38 miles up to the top of the rock which stood before Hebron (Judges 16:3)!

This, however, is all secondary to the super science fiction that lies behind the mechanics of this fabulous encounter. As we shall see, contemplating the physical abilities of Samson is nothing short of breathtaking. Samson is known for his strength, not his speed, but that ought not be. Samson must have possessed unearthly speed if he was able to accomplish what the Bible says he accomplished. And we are not talking about just speed, but about absolutely inhuman levels of dexterity! We've got an awful lot of fantasy to overlook in the legend of Samson.

The Overbearing Principle

I don't set myself up as an accomplished fighter by any means, but I have a decent understanding of applied physics. The principle of overbearing refers to a combat situation where a given individual or group of combatants are physically overpowered by their opposition by means of a greater number of people and/or weight of an individual.

Dealing with individual scenarios first, weight is an issue. Police officers use, in part, the overbearing principle to determine whether or not to call for back up, which is why a 911 operator will relay to officers the approximate weight of a potential assailant. If a 5'4, 120 pound man is making trouble downtown, one police officer should be sufficient to handle it should the man become physically unruly, but chances shouldn't be taken with a 6'4, 280 pounder. In summation, as a wrestling coach once told me, *"There are exceptions, but as a general rule, if someone is heavier than you, they can kick your ass!"*

So greater weight of an opponent is a problem, and this is never truer than with multiple opponents. Because Team Red has only 20 people, going up against Team Yellow with 200 people, Red will quickly be overborne by means of weight, number of attacks, resources, and strength, even if Red's fighters are far superior by way of skill and experience. One man might be able to physically beat down another of equal size and ability, and could certainly whip someone weaker with less effort, but put the stronger man up against two weaker opponents and he will likely lose. Put him against three and the man is just about certain to be whipped. Even in cases of truly great fighters, two or three ordinary men will provide sufficient power to beat them. Evander Holyfield and Bob Sapp are both tremendous fighters. Individually, they could easily whip the average, able-bodied man, but doubtfully 2 or 3 people at once. Why? Because the principle of overbearing has it that the greater sum of power and number of attacks will determine the winner. The amount of time a fighter spends striking one attacker is the same amount of time his two opponents will take tackling him and grabbing his throat and squeezing. There's just not enough one man can do to defend against and attack multiple opponents.

The point I am making is this; the very best fighter in the world is still subject to the laws of reality like everyone—his constitution, dexterity, skill, and strength notwithstanding. The laws of reality will firmly dictate his limits. I belabor the point only to emphasize that there are physical limits that cannot be exceeded, yet if we are to believe the Bible legend of Samson, human physical limitations mean absolutely nothing.

God must have had to somehow animate Samson's body with Godhood to enable it to do what we are told he did (i.e. considering here, his slaying of 1,000 soldiers—Judges 15:15-19). For believers to say things like "God was with Samson," or "God helped Samson win," is not accurate. Let me correct these statements: to do what the Bible says Samson did, God wasn't just helping Samson, but actually doing the fighting for him. Because of the way our laws of nature are set up, Samson's body would only have gotten in the way. In every area, Samson would have needed the physical abilities of Superman to accomplish what the scriptures say he did. He would also have had to possess fighting technique and skill like the world had never seen, dwarfing the accomplishments of Achilles many times over.

Can you imagine this battle? It would be an incredible sight to see; one man, dodging and parrying flurries of attacks, routing the mob of angry soldiers surrounding him...and with a most crude, unreliable weapon—the jawbone of an ass! This little detail presents another problem because even if it was fresh like the scriptures say it was, the density of it would only be good for a few hits to any well-crafted steel body armor before the jawbone broke—unless of course, you are Samson, who could apparently swing the bone three or four times the speed of sound, so as to allow it to cleave solid steel and flesh, like a sharp piece of thin, wooden debris, hurled by a tornado into a barn door! But even there, the problem doesn't go away; if someone could swing this makeshift club that fast, the club would break from the sheer force of the air opposing it.

If, by now, your mind is not prompting a grin of amazement as you contemplate this, you aren't quite honing in on the outrageous details involved. Let's look a little closer at them...

An army has gathered around one man to take him into custody. The soldiers are experienced killers in full body armor, equipped with lethal military weapons, which they have used many times to kill whole armies of equally armored opposing forces, but now they feel compelled to go through the expense and trouble to put their efforts on just one man. They know he is a threat like they've never had to face. The soldiers took up their most astute defensive postures, relying on the skill of their own battle-hardened experiences to help ensure the most fortunate outcome for them. Samson is surrounded and studied, then studied some more. Every move he makes, every turning of his head, is noticed and scrutinized.

The first wave of fighters make their attacks, the great leaders, the honorable warriors, the Philistinian Rambos and King Arthurs. They lunge first, hoping to send everyone home early from a fight quickly ended. Their efforts are to no avail. Their speed and power, their gumption and war-seasoned countenances are not enough to stop Samson. They are quickly slain, despite their best and most valiant efforts, and despite their skills in wielding two-handed weapons, and despite their abilities to read their opponent and spot weaknesses. They aren't good enough.

Now the secondary elites move in, the 20 foot pole-arm-bearers and their shield-men, the elite soldiers, and a swarm of footmen, all eager to prove their worthiness to the generals. Sounds of armor rustling, of swords being unsheathed, of assortments of blades slicing through the air, of axes swooping down, and the throwing of daggers and spears can be heard. The soldiers close in for what should be a sure and easy kill. For anyone else, it would be certain death, but not for Samson. He manages to kill his opponents, row by row, section by section.

Next, the archers stand focused and ready from a distance, ready for the slightest pause, the slightest hesitation on Samson's part. Had he given them the chance, Samson would have been plugged with a milieu of arrows in both torsos, crippling him and making him a finished opponent. But the archers have it the toughest, because as fast as Samson must keep moving to avoid a quick death by long and short swords, knives, flails, spears, daggers, axes, rocks from slings, and war-hammers, he is a human blur and it is hard to even see him, much less get any sort of aim on him.

If you listen carefully, you can make out, echoing through the noisy mass of soldiers, the generals and tacticians barking out orders; "Fall back, fall back." "Swordsmen to the front." Rows upon rows of slain soldiers pile up, and as men move in and out, trying to re-group and save the lives of their injured comrades, sending in more mounted soldiers and fresh bands of troops, the tacticians re-strategize, this time employing their back-up plans, but they are quickly running out of options. The fall-back plans keep failing. They've never seen anything like this. They instruct the soldiers on the front lines to wedge their huge shields side by side, with the weight of their fellow soldiers to back them up as they march forward to push him away. Mouths drop open in absolute dismay as Samson manages to shove back a combined weight of soldiers many, many times that of his own. Samson can push them back, but he has not a moment to rest, for while this is happening, more cunning warriors swoop in and around him from all sides. Their blades glimmer with speed and technique. Still no success! Any nearby onlooker would see a person swamped in a sea of bustling soldiers, covered from head to toe in shiny steel and red splotches of blood...all being defeated by one man!

Bodies of slain men fly through the air, sometimes five and ten at a time, as Samson's powerful arms crash into huddles of resolute soldiers who try to rush him. Swords and shields are hurled out of tightly-clutched hands and fall to the ground. Broken pieces of armor lie scattered in the dirt. Blood is everywhere. Heads and limbs come flying off and are sent sailing in all directions. In a domino effect, once-confident, lengthy lines of soldiers are knocked off their feet into each other, and into panic and confusion. The battle reaches its climax and Samson manages to overcome the odds. This brutalizing, jawbone-swinging tower of power is met with the remaining waves of military might, still intent (amazingly!) on thinking they can win against him. Though much of the army is now dead, soaking the ground in sticky blood, air-cutting blades can still be heard seeking their target. Instead of intelligently running in fear for their lives, these Philistines stayed around to see the last of their friends die painful, brutal deaths.

Finally, the intimidating sounds of metal-clanking and fighting begin to die down. Only a few stragglers remain, and Samson wastes no time silencing what few grunts, gasps, and groans for survival remain to be heard. Slings and stones and flaming coals and sweeping staves, and the melee of a thousand men proved no match for him. Team after team, regimen after regimen, took their tenacious turns, charging him vigorously and unrelentingly from every angle. Without fail, Samson managed to avoid laid traps and ambushes, pits and berserker's rages of determined soldiers—and even unorthodox tactics, like thrown rocks or sand being kicked in his face. Nets were spread, desperate tactics were resorted to as this Jewish Hercules managed to break free from every predicament. Samson won, his jawbone miraculously remaining intact all the while.

One would think that just a solitary thrust of a sword might have gotten through his flesh and punctured a lung, or that just a single blow might have been successful in seriously drawing blood. One would think that with all that twisting and turning and pivoting and dodging and jumping around, and exerting unearthly feats of strength and dexterity for that extended length of time, that just one major wound would have been inflicted, or maybe just one footstep would have been ill-placed, causing him to fall or trip over a dead body, allowing soldiers to rush in on him. Or maybe a soldier played dead and quickly stabbed him by surprise. But the only thing Samson appeared concerned with when the battle was over was getting water (Judges 15:18), so he was evidently untouched in all this commotion!

From this description, we can see that the battle didn't last very long. How long can someone go without water while sustaining super vigorous activity? Maybe 6 or so hours? Samson did not strategically or stealthfully take their lives, but used brute force from miraculous power, which kind of makes me wonder why – since the Lord had to give Samson unearthly abilities to win this fight in the first place – he didn't also keep his body from dehydration instead of having to perform the additional miracle of giving him water from a jawbone after the fight? And since the Lord obviously wanted these unclean Philistines dead and had to work a miracle for Samson to be able to kill them, why didn't he just send his Angel to cut off their heads as they slept as he did with the Assyrians (2 Kings 19:35)? But I'm glad the Bible doesn't read that way. That would be far less entertaining.

Now it goes without saying that this account is far beyond remarkable, and since no matter how we look at it, God is involved, and therefore, the laws of reality must be suspended, we may as well consider a couple of other crazy options; maybe Samson was not fast at all. Maybe he was just impervious to attack. But this doesn't seem to go well with the fact that the text implies he is a normal man with the common lusts and passions thereof. And since Samson's hair could be cut, and judging from the fact that he made the people of Israel swear not to kill him when they took him into custody, I have no reason to assume he was invincible. We could suggest that perhaps Samson was able to slay his enemies the same way the ropes came off his arms—by his sun-like powers of heat (Judges 15:14). But the text says he killed them with the jawbone, not from heat, so we're back to the speed position again. Samson had to be really, really fast! And Bruce Lee's record-breaking 111 mile-per-hour punch would have been nowhere close to sufficient!

Yep, this is a tall tale if ever I've heard one! I put it right up there with Captain America and The Fantastic Four. But in the spirit of cinematic fun, I would love to see The Hulk and Samson go at it. With Samson's speed, I'm no longer sure the Hulk would emerge the winner!

Where have I seen that before?

Suppose, for a moment, that I am a Hollywood director, and I have it in my head to make an action movie. You are a critic and scriptwriter hired by me to critique my work and supplement ideas. So, after months of brainstorming and idea-prodding, I finally find the discipline to put together a working script. When it is completed, I bring you in. Your job: to give me your honest opinion on the quality and potential acceptance or rejection of my work. You are listening to me expound on the plot…

> The flick is about a tough FBI agent named John Chambers who works in the fraud prevention department, which in his slummy New York neighborhood, puts him on the streets, tracking down high-end thieves, counterfeiters, and crooked businesses. He is tall and scary looking in an attractive sort of way, and wears distinct, jagged-edged type sunglasses. He carries around a big and powerful gun, and he's been known to brag about it being the most powerful handgun in the world just before he kills an argumentative scumbag. Right when he's about to pull the trigger, he says, "Go ahead! Make my night!"

You sit, squirming in your seat, trying to think of a nice, tactful way to tell me, the dumb producer, that the idea is not only piss-poor and unoriginal, but has been lifted from another movie almost verbatim, from the Dirty Harry series from the 1970s and 80s. Stumped and completely at a loss for words, you finally realize that there will be no easy way to tell the director that this simply will not work. You tell him how you feel, and to your surprise, he's prepared with a calm, collected answer: *"There may be similarities to Dirty Harry, but my character is different from that character; for instance, one is a cop, mine is FBI; Dirty Harry worked in San Francisco, John Chambers is in New York; and as far as my character being tall, carrying a big gun, wearing sunglasses, and making a "tough guy" line just before he kills someone, well, those are general descriptions that could apply to anyone. And besides, a lot of police dramas use tough-guy lines, and since mine is different from Dirty Harry's line, there are no problems here."*

In a state of nervousness, your palms beginning to sweat, you find the strength to again point out: "Uh, um…uh, sir, those differences you pointed out are not differences at all. The idea is the same, and your finishing tough-guy line is only one word removed from being Dirty Harry's exact line." The director replies, *"Alright then. I'll change the 'Go ahead! Make my night' line to 'You just go right ahead and see if I don't make my night killing you!'"* Frustrated and angered, you reply, "That's even worse, sir. Now you have a wordy line that sounds ridiculous and unintelligent, plus, it still sounds like a cheap knock-off of the original." After a few more bad attempts to salvage this cliché-ridden, fit-for-the-crapper script, you realize that the director is a mind-blowing imbecile and you don't want your good name to be tarnished by having it associated with this project. So you cut ties.

The scary part is not that directors like this really exist and work in Hollywood today, putting out non-creative bunk for near-brain-dead, weed-smoking teens, and for general audiences in the form of knock-off ideas, but that in the realm of religion, a copy-cat instance is not picked up on by believers when one is seen. Like this dimwitted director, Christian apologists defending the Bible will point out many differences between pagan myths and the Christian myth without ever addressing the strong and undeniable similarities between them. "The Copy-Cat Theory" is often the phrase used by apologists and freethinkers to describe debates on how much of the Bible (and particularly the person of Jesus) was stolen from heathen myths. We will be discussing this here, but before we begin, we should stop to consider the scope of the discussion.

Where Have I Seen That Before?

Much debate about biblical mythology has run its course through the academic world in the last few years, and much of it centers on the pagan nature of Jesus and his similarity to older pagan gods and god-men. I am not an expert in such fields, but I can recognize a pattern when I see one.

I do believe that the biblical Jesus is without a doubt the product of regurgitated myths from heathen imaginations, and I believe I can prove that in this chapter. Here, I plan to demonstrate that the Bible itself abounds with mythologies stolen, in part and parcel, from other faiths. One need not be an expert to spot a pattern in things. When we come across a Bible reference and notice a similar reference or theme in pagan mythologies, this makes us ask the question, "Where have I seen that before?"

Christian apologists have had varying degrees of success defending Christianity from charges that it consists of the stolen goods of a non-Christian religious nature, and to some degree, this was justified. It must be remembered that not only can it be demonstrated that Christianity was influenced by paganism, but paganism was also influenced by Christianity. It is worth stating that some of the sources used by infidels to demonstrate a Jesus coming from pagan origins date only to a time contemporary to (or in some cases later than) Christianity, not before it. This is why an expert is needed to delve into these items to side-step the controversy and determine what is genuinely pre-Christian and what is not. That is not my job here.

What will separate my material will be the depth of the content I cover. Most of the things I will be presenting will be things that just about all scholars will very easily agree upon. A casual examination of many of these claims will reveal that they are not heavily disputed and can be verified with little effort. What I am doing is establishing a pattern; where one myth is to be found, others will likely be found as well. The whole Bible draws its substantive content from various mythologies of the times in which the different books were written, making it a compilation of stolen goods.

I. Enuma Elish and Genesis

Enuma Elish, the Mesopotamia/Babylonian creation epic, is much older than the creation tale of Genesis. While being remarkably different, some key similarities run between them.

From The First Tablet, the very opening words (L.W. King Translation)...

> When in the height heaven was not named, And the earth beneath did not yet bear a name...Their waters were mingled together, And no field was formed, no marsh was to be seen.

And now the more common Genesis creation myth...

> In the beginning God created the heaven and the earth. And the earth was without form, and void; and darkness was upon the face of the deep. And the Spirit of God moved upon the face of the waters. (Genesis 1:1-2)

Throughout the two creation accounts, the following similarities can be seen; first, the world in both accounts was created and sat in a watery but lifeless form; second, both accounts refer to the creation of a firmament between heaven and earth "to separate cloud from silt." Third, both have stars, light, and mankind created, followed by a celebration among the gods.

To explain their similarities, apologists tell us that both the creators of Enuma Elish and Genesis simply had access to the same literary source from which to take details. Why would this be the case? How would this be the case? If Moses was guided by inspiration to record the words of Genesis, why would an earlier creation tale have such similarities? Why would Moses' words in Genesis be needed? If God inspired an earlier document, why not just use that one? And where is this early, inspired literary source today? The fact that the Babylonian narrative is older than that of the Hebrews doesn't speak well for those who believe in the inspiration of the Bible.

II. Sargon I and Moses

Written on a cuneiform tablet, we learn of Sargon the Great: "I am Sargon, the powerful king, the king of Akkad. My mother conceived me and bore me in secret. She put me in a little box made of reeds, sealing its lid with pitch. She put me in the river. . . .The river carried me away and brought me to Akki the drawer of water."

This venerable folk-tale is quite well known in the ancient world. Stories of a secretive birth of a ruler were extremely common. The Sargon legend was well-known and dates to as far back as 2500 B.C.E., much earlier than the story of Moses in the biblical record which was written no earlier than 1000-700 B.C.E...

> 1. And there went a man of the house of Levi, and took to wife a daughter of Levi. 2. And the woman conceived, and bare a son: and when she saw him that he was a goodly child, she hid him three months. 3. And when she could not longer hide him, she took for him an ark of bulrushes, and daubed it with slime and with pitch, and put the child therein; and she laid it in the flags by the river's brink. 4. And his sister stood afar off, to wit what would be done to him. 5. And the daughter of Pharaoh came down to wash herself at the river; and her maidens walked along by the river's side; and when she saw the ark among the flags, she sent her maid to fetch it. 6. And when she had opened it, she saw the child: and, behold, the babe wept. And she had compassion on him, and said, This is one of the Hebrews' children." (Exodus 2:1-6)

There is very little dispute on the dates of these texts—the one is clearly older than the other. And as big as this old myth was, there is little wonder why it was used in the Moses character—to add age-old prestige. As hard as apologists insist that this objection is old and obsolete, I cannot help but be stunned at how obvious it is that this part of the Moses story (if none other) has to be pure myth. It is easily possible for stories to have many common elements between them, but these are seldom disputed by anyone. Those that are tend to be fabulous tales like this one, emotional exaggerations, what we now call, urban legends.

If you tell me that you bumped into an old friend at the mall or you were in a car accident on the same day you suffered a broken wrist, or even that you won the lottery, I will not dispute your words, but tell me that you stayed in a hotel and went to a bar, where a very attractive woman began to have drinks with you and took you back to her room for a good time, and then proceeded to drug you, and when you woke up, you'd had a kidney removed, I'd know you're repeating a very popular urban legend that has been around in my country since the mid-1980s. It is an interesting and eerie tale, but nothing more. As false as this story is, I still hear people telling it as though it were their own. This is the modern equivalent to the Sargon/Moses legend. Other stories of children sent down rivers at or near birth include the legend of Karna of the Indian Mahabharata epic, and that of Telephus, son of Hercules. We could cite others as well.

It might have sounded cool to embellish the accounts of ancient rulers this way, but today such embellishments will bring them no praise whatsoever. They will only bring scorn.

III. The Bible and the Book of the Dead

Similarities of thought are very territorial. In exactly the same way we can determine the approximate era in which a book was written by judging from its content, we can look at mythical tales and see similarities between contemporaries. If you lived within six to eight hundred years of the common era, you would be familiar with the newly popularized doctrine of angelic beings and you would see the rise of the mystery cults, like those of Attis, Dionysis, and Mithra. It was in this period of time that worship of "unknown gods" began to take off; if you lived one to three thousand years before the common era, you would grow up hearing tales of dying and rising vegetation gods, gods of the harvest, one of which is even mentioned in the scriptures—Tammuz, who died and was resurrected annually, for whom sinful women were condemned for weeping in Ezekiel (Ezekiel 8:14). If you lived in the Neolithic period (between 8,000 and 12,000 B.C.E.), you would hear about goddess worship, ancestor worship and god-woman-worship, and sun worship.

During a time when the Old Testament books were still being written, it is hardly surprising to see similar themes in many old religions. Take this quotation from The Book of The Dead...

> Homage to thee, O my divine father, Osiris, thou hast thy being with thy members. Thou didst not decay, thou didst not become worms, thou didst not diminish, thou didst not become corruption, thou didst not putrify, and thou didst not turn into worms.

Then, in Psalm 16, we read...

> For thou wilt not leave my soul in hell; neither wilt thou suffer thine Holy One to see corruption. (Psalm 16:10)

This verse is quoted by Peter in the book of Acts...

> Therefore being a prophet, and knowing that God had sworn with an oath to him, that of the fruit of his loins, according to the flesh, he would raise up Christ to sit on his throne; He seeing this before spake of the resurrection of Christ, that his soul was not left in hell, neither his flesh did see corruption. (Acts 2:30-31)

In the old world, when you thought of vegetation cycles, you automatically thought of the idea of a bodily resurrection. As crops return in the spring and stay strong through the end of summer, and then die, their return became analogous to human resurrection. If you doubt this, consider Egyptian Osiris Beds. They were wooden boxes that date back long before the common era, boxes placed over the tomb of a fallen one with vegetation growing up from the top of the box, symbolizing a future return to life. This was as common back then as a cross placed on a tombstone is today.

IV. Sun Worship

Exodus 27:13-16 shows us that the Tabernacle faced the East like the temples and shrines of the sun worshipping cults. Had instructions for the building of the Tabernacle been to build it with the entrance facing the West, this would have been hailed as a jewel of Bible inspiration for disassociating itself with paganism, but since this wasn't the case, it is glossed over in silence.

What does this little tidbit tell us? It at least suggests to us that either Judaism in its infancy had sun worship at its roots, or perhaps that the creators of the God of Moses gave no thought to how much their deity looked like their pagan neighbors.

V. Stoicism, Platonism, and Christianity

One of the strongest pagan themes in the New Testament is the presence of Stoicism that creeps out of certain passages of scripture now and then.

Stoicism was one of the core philosophies of the ancient world, known far and wide. Paul himself quoted almost word-for-word from a Stoic writer named Aratus in his famous sermon on Mars Hill (Acts 17:28), removing any doubt of his familiarity and usage of the cult's ideas. Briefly, the basics of Stoic belief were; (a) Fatalism: everything that happens is fate and must be accepted, and even embraced as such. (b) Pantheism: the universe is God and its physical manifestation is his body. This implied a form of (c) Materialism: the "spirit" aspect of things was not above nature, but alongside it; so when a Stoic referred to the operation of God, they were speaking of causal fate, not an eternal deity who is outside of time.

Scenting many Greek schools of thought in the old world was Dualism. With the arrival of thinkers like Plato (490-399 B.C.E.), the belief in a spiritual and physical nature of man had come to full strength, and this led to the thinking that the flesh – along with the tangibles of the corporeal world – were evil, and that our bodies were prisons for our souls. This can only be where the New Testament writers pulled out the idea of Original Sin. The entire New Testament is saturated with this very Greek-like belief.

Original sin was not a Jewish doctrine, mind you, but a Christian one. Christians tell us that depravity is different from the pagan's ostracism of the flesh as evil, but in reality, they are grounded in the same soil. Any differences between them are miniscule…

> For what the law could not do, in that it was weak through the flesh, God sending his own Son in the likeness of sinful flesh, and for sin, condemned sin in the flesh. (Romans 8:3)

When Paul referred to "sinful flesh," he meant exactly that. Christians don't even know it, but every time they refer to all being sinners, having fallen short of the glory of God, they are – in root form – seconding a pagan belief. As a Church of Christ believer, we rejected the idea of original sin based on a number of passages (like Ecclesiastes 7:29; Psalm 58:3), but futile debate aside, the vast majority of believers subscribe to and defend that view. To the average believer, sin is like a cold, a disease; it's an illness, and it's contagious. You got it from mom and dad, who got it from their mom and dad, etc. How this is supposed to be different than a sinful, material universe I cannot see, other than the fact that Christians don't believe animals or inanimate objects are sinful, just human beings. But beyond that, the similarities are pretty stout. The New Testament testifies to this implicitly, as we shall see.

So pervasive was the Greek belief of the wickedness of matter that this became an issue of fellowship for the early Christian church. Deducing from the belief that matter is evil, that God and spirituality are above it, and that God cannot be harmonized with it, the idea arose that Christ – who was reported to have come in the flesh – could not *really* have come in the flesh; he just appeared to have so come! But the leaders of the Christian movement denounced this conclusion, and in the book of First John, we see the apostle's unequivocal repudiation of it...

> Beloved, believe not every spirit, but try the spirits whether they are of God: because many false prophets are gone out into the world. Hereby know ye the Spirit of God: Every spirit that confesseth that Jesus Christ is come in the flesh is of God: And every spirit that confesseth not that Jesus Christ is come in the flesh is not of God: and this is that spirit of antichrist, whereof ye have heard that it should come; and even now already is it in the world. (I John 4:1-3)

Note his addressing Jesus' having "come in the flesh." Audiences read these words as they sit in congregations today and fail to get the context. John was denouncing this understandable thinking that Jesus couldn't have come in the flesh because flesh was sinful. John says that he did come in the flesh. It's just we humans who are sinful (how's that for consistency?)!

It should be stated that while the church and the Bible writers rejected this extremely Grecian idea, debate still ravaged the church. The birth of the Gnostic heresies was not unrelated to this same pool of conviction. The central Gnostic heresy was that since God is all good, no evil could come from him, which means the material, evil world must be a thing totally unrelated to God, and therefore, not created by him. This meant that the flesh, along with the entire material world, had to be hated and despised. This belief augmented hatred of the material world and produced in large segments of the Christian population either asceticism or unchecked hedonism, both of which Paul condemns as sins in Colossians 2:20-23 and Galatians 5:21.

Having an understanding of these things, it is not so difficult to see how these views gave rise to scholarly thinking in the early church. Descarte's version of the Ontological argument has an eerily Gnostic ring to it, as Descartes argued that the reason for evil in our world was on account of the fact that our creation had to consist of a lower level of perfection than God himself (if God is to create at all and is to remain the supreme being, he must create a universe and beings of lesser stature and power than he)—and those lower levels of perfection gave birth to what we call evil. Descartes turned an old infidel heresy around and made it into an argument for the Christian God's integrity. The point is made, however: one can no more divorce the Bible from its pagan philosophical flavors today than could church fathers and Christian scholars throughout the Middle Ages.

This led to great divisions in the early (and to some degree, the later) years of the church. All kinds of issues developed, like this one; if man was "born in sin," a depraved sinner by nature, then something had to happen in the case of Jesus and his coming in the flesh to keep him pure at his birth; after centuries of fighting and having heated debates about The Virgin Mary, the Roman Catholic Church decreed what we know today as The Doctrine of The Immaculate Conception. This does not refer to the virgin birth itself, but to the Roman Catholic position that when Mary was conceived, she was conceived *without a sinful nature*—so in turn, she would be "pure" to bring to term the eternally pure son of God. This doctrine reeks of pagan thought.

Though not exactly, the Greek idea of our bodies being prisons for our souls also stands to be counted in the Bible...

> For I delight in the law of God after the inward man: But I see another law in my members, warring against the law of my mind, and bringing me into captivity to the law of sin which is in my members. O wretched man that I am! who shall deliver me from the body of this death? (Romans 7:22-24)

I would include just the twenty-fourth verse were it not for the fact that apologists will say that I am misusing the verse. The "body of this death" that Paul seeks to be delivered from is his own, and not a general description of death—as in a "body" of articles or a group of people. The Darby Translation puts it this way; *"O wretched man that I [am]! who shall deliver me out of this body of death?"*

Paul, like all believers seeking to escape a miserable existence of pain to a heaven of bliss, was opting for deliverance from his corrupt, fleshly confines...

> Who shall change our vile body, that it may be fashioned like unto his glorious body, according to the working whereby he is able even to subdue all things unto himself. (Philippians 3:21)

Romans 8:21 says, "Because the creature itself also shall be delivered from the bondage of corruption into the glorious liberty of the children of God." It will be observed that the "creature" in this context is the church. The long awaited and glorious liberty of those who would be called "children of God" would be bestowed on the church—God's predestined vessel to escape the "bondage" of corruption from dying, "vile" bodies. If Paul is not touching on the very same thread of the Stoic's notion of a wicked, jailhouse body, then I am Sally Struthers! This idea is found throughout the New Testament in a number of passages. As this connection is obvious, I shall move on without belaboring the point further.

Lastly, another aspect of Stoicism was the concept of the Logos. Though the word is used very loosely by writers like Philo, the Logos was nature's embodiment of action, energy, power, the underlying, eternal "seed" of all mechanistic forces. Stoics would call the universe "alive" with the Logos; it was the "soul" of the universe.

None too shockingly, the concept of the Logos itself is alive and kicking in the pages of the New Testament. Hear the words of the Apostle John...

> 1. In the beginning was the Word [the Greek word, logos], and the Word was with God, and the Word was God. 2. The same was in the beginning with God. 3. All things were made by him; and without him was not any thing made that was made. 4. In him was life; and the life was the light of men...And the Word was made flesh, and dwelt among us, (and we beheld his glory, the glory as of the only begotten of the Father,) full of grace and truth. (John 1:1-4, 14)

Based on what we know of Stoicism, it is a pretty tall order to deny that the New Testament writers could not have been in some way influenced by it. The Logos permeated all things. It was the underlying reason behind existence and thought and fertility and vitality. The Logos was with and of God, and it was God, via the apostle's own admission. Exploding-full churches refer to Jesus as "the Word" and don't even know what they are saying.

In an attempt to show that there existed no connection between the pagan concept of the Logos and John's referring to Jesus as the Word, Spiros Zodhiates in his work, *Was Christ God? An Exposition of John 1:1-18 from the Original Greek Text,* says...

> The term *logos* was in common use when John wrote his Gospel. One Jewish philosopher in particular, Philo, born in Alexandria, Egypt, in 29 B.C., employed it profusely, which made some believe that John had borrowed from him. We do not believe John did anything of the sort. Undoubtably, what John had in mind was the Hebrew word *memra*, translated in the Septuagint as logos. In using the Greek word *logos*, he did it with its Jewish background in mind. (P. 55)

One would think that if John had a particular Hebrew word in mind, he would have used it. But instead, he used a word that was consistent in meaning with an overwhelmingly prominent pagan philosophy of his day. This is puzzling. And why does Zodhiates say this expression was chosen for Jesus?

> John wants to tell us that Jesus Christ existed before the beginning of the world. The Creator was before the creature. And the first thing that occurs to him, as a logically thinking man, is that this Creator must have been possessed with intelligence, with a mind. How could he

express that? Where could he find an adequate word? He could find it only in the Greek words 'ho logos,' which cannot be translated adequately in any other language. (P. 55)

This seems like an explanation, but it does not explain the terribly noticeable coincidence of how the Stoics spoke exactly the same way of their logos being at the heart of the universe, as John does. To the Stoics, the logos was the force behind the form, the concept behind the construction, and this is exactly the sense in which the word is used here by John, thus, confirming for us a pagan association.

VI. Jewish Dietary Laws

Rabbinic thought holds that consuming dung-eaters and carnivores is beneath the dignity of man, so unless one needs to survive, eating shellfish and pork (among other things) is forbidden for Orthodox Jews (Leviticus 11:9-12).

It was also common wisdom in ancient times that herding swine often resulted in mosquito upsurges and the spread of certain diseases. We are not told in the Bible why the Hebrew God forbade the consumption of these meats, but we are told by many believers in the Bible that God was providing his people with dietary advice for health's sake. But if this was true, then why was the advice not reiterated in the New Testament? And why did Christianity revoke Jewish dietary laws? We are informed that the eating of clean and unclean meats is of no importance anymore, and nothing is unclean of itself in the New Testament age (Acts 11:8; Romans 14:14). So it seems to be that only religious reasons can account for the idea of unclean meats. Health concerns were never an issue.

From Genesis 32:32 we learn that Jews do not eat a certain sinew of any animal in commemoration of God's injuring Jacob's leg in the wrestling incident. This is a good insight into how ancient religious minds reasoned; it was wrong to consume any edible thing that was holy or of a sacred nature.

Swine were worshipped in Egypt. They were regularly sacrificed to pagan gods, to Osiris and to Adonis, and it was said that a wild boar slew the pagan god, Dionysus. His followers were forbidden to eat it. To the followers of the Attis cult, swine were considered the embodiment of divine presence. To them, it was "communion." The swine and the boar were very sacred animals in all parts of the ancient Palestinian world, which suggests to us that early Jews revered the swine, causing later Jews to deem them unclean as a safeguard against lapsing back into animal worship. Isaiah himself mentions the offering of swine's blood as a great abomination (Isaiah 66:3).

VII. Sons of God and Virgin-born Savior-god-men

From the very first book of the Bible, the idea of gods mating with human women and producing great offspring is found...

> And it came to pass, when men began to multiply on the face of the earth, and daughters were born unto them, That the sons of God saw the daughters of men that they were fair; and they took them wives of all which they chose...and also after that, when the sons of God came in unto the daughters of men, and they bare children to them, the same became mighty men which were of old, men of renown. (Genesis 6:1-4)

The Christian denomination from which I hail was extremely critical of these verses. A good Church of Christ preacher, when accosted about them, will deny any supernatural element here. They explain these verses as the righteous sons of Seth choosing wives, but this view is obviously fallacious. Old Testament usage of the phrase "sons of God" is used in reference to angels...

> Now there was a day when the sons of God came to present themselves before the LORD, and Satan came also among them. (Job 1:6)

> Where wast thou when I laid the foundations of the earth?...When the morning stars sang together, and all the sons of God shouted for joy? (Job 38:4,7)

The "sons of Seth" position is a very new idea, totally lacking in credibility. A few have run with it, but largely, it has fallen by the wayside. A very simple reading of the verses in Genesis implies that these "mighty men" of renown were not of the Adamite stock. These verses could be used to describe the origins of Hercules, and the fit would be perfect. Genesis was written in a time when it was believed that some men were the products of gods and women; Alexander the Great, for instance, was believed to have been fathered by an incubus, and so it shouldn't surprise us when Bible writers possess the same ideology. The idea of a god having a son was as common to them as opening a jar of pickles is to us.

As mentioned earlier, the vegetation god motif was extremely popular. It is based directly on the Solar Myth; the sun is born, then he comes to terms with himself, is tempted with defeat and weakness, and must learn that it is his destiny to climb higher and higher in the sky to defeat the darkness; he embraces his destiny and defeats the night (the days become longer than the nights) and the land is blessed with good crops; the people rejoice; the sun is then given over to die for his people as he is claimed by the longer nights (winter descends and the sun's death is mourned); the new year arrives and the savior is reborn; the sun comes to power, and darkness is again defeated, starting the process over. This motif was the life-blood of every major mystery cult and every nature cult in the old world.

With some major overhauling, we see the same pattern in all sons of gods in every old religion, including Christianity. It should be remembered that in the mind of the Old Testament pagan, the concepts of vegetation, fertility, and resurrection couldn't be separated. And now we come to the resurrection of Jesus...

> And, behold, thou shalt conceive in thy womb, and bring forth a son, and shalt call his name JESUS. He shall be great, and shall be called the Son of the Highest...Then said Mary unto the angel, How shall this be, seeing I know not a man? And the angel answered and said unto her, The Holy Ghost shall come upon thee, and the power of the Highest shall overshadow thee: therefore also that holy thing which shall be born of thee shall be called the Son of God. (Luke 1:31, 34)

As has been pointed out by not just infidels, but by Muslims, Orthodox Jews, and older religious critics of Christianity from the past, the savior of the New Testament is like all the other savior/deliverer-god-men of the pagan religions in that he also is half-god and half-man – was a son of God and wielder of miraculous powers – and would be a deliverer, a savior of his people. This idea is nowhere close to new. It is, as they say, "as old as the hills."

Giving us a nice summation of this point, Thomas Paine in *The Age of Reason*, offers the following comments on how and why the Christian mythology took off...

> It is not difficult to account for the credit that was given to the story of Jesus Christ being the Son of God. He was born when the heathen mythology had still some fashion and repute in the world, and that mythology had prepared the people for the belief in such a story. Almost all the extraordinary men that lived under the heathen mythology were reputed to be sons of some of their gods. It was not a new thing at the time to believe a man to have been celestially begotten; the intercourse of gods with women was then a matter of familiar opinion. Their Jupiter, according to their accounts, had cohabitated with hundreds; the story therefore had nothing in it either

new, wonderful, or obscene; it was conformable to the opinions that then prevailed among the people called Gentiles, or mythologists, and it was those people only that believed it. The Jews, who had kept strictly to the belief of one god, and no more, and who had always rejected the heathen mythology, never credited the story. (p. 25)

When Christianity began to grow radically among the Gentiles in the latter half of the first century, it naturally started to get some attention. Among this attention came that of the critics. Thanks to dark centuries of Christian intolerance, most of these works have been destroyed. Only a handful of their writings have survived the stretch of time, and those in questionable condition. One very famous critic of Christianity was the unbelieving pagan philosopher, Celsus, who published a famous work, "The True Account." This work has been lost today, but it is known and referred to in the work of his Christian opposition, Origen (185-254 C.E.) who wrote *Contra Celsum*, in 248 C.E.

Even from the second-hand references to his words by Origen, this keen-minded critic put his stamp of approval on everything thus far stated. Speaking of a god taking on the form of a man, Celsus was reported to have said...

> Who, then, would make choice of such a change? It is the nature of a mortal, indeed, to undergo change and remoulding, but of an immortal to remain the same and unaltered. God, then, could not admit of such a change. (The Anti-Nicene Fathers, Volume 4, Book 4, Chapter 14, 1867-1872)

In this next quotation, Origen (not Celsus) is commenting on Celsus' comparison of the Christian Son of God to heathen deities. In one of Celsus' original works, he created a Jewish character and put in his mouth words of opposition against Jesus...

> But these stories are really myths, which have led people to invent such a tale about a man because they regarded him as having superior wisdom and power... to the multitude, and as having received the original composition of his body from better and more divine seed, thinking that this was appropriate for men with superhuman powers. But when Celsus has introduced the Jew as disputing with Jesus and pouring ridicule on the pretence, as he thinks, of his birth from a virgin, and as quoting the Greek myths about Danae and Melanippe and Auge and Antiope, I have to reply that these words would be appropriate to a vulgar buffoon and not to a man who takes his professed task seriously. (Contra Celsum, Henry Chadwick translation, 1953)

According to Celsus then, advocates of Jesus simply re-quoted and reapplied the myths of older pagan deities. When Celsus says savior-god-men were nothing new, was he right, or was he just a crusty infidel whose heart was hardened to the gospel? Turns out, he was right. Church Father Justin Martyr (100-165 C.E.), in his famous defense of Christianity and plea to end Roman persecution, entitled *Apologia I*, tells us so. In Chapter 21, Justin wrote...

> And when we say also that the Word, who is the first-birth of God, was produced without sexual union, and that He, Jesus Christ, our Teacher, was crucified and died, and rose again, and ascended into heaven, we propound nothing different from what you believe regarding those whom you esteem sons of Jupiter. For you know how many sons your esteemed writers ascribed to Jupiter: Mercury, the interpreting word and teacher of all; AEsculapius, who, though he was a great physician, was struck by a thunderbolt, and so ascended to heaven; and Bacchus too, after he had been torn limb from limb; and Hercules, when he had committed himself to the flames to escape his toils; and the sons of Leda, and Dioscuri; and Perseus, son of Danae; and Bellerophon, who, though sprung from mortals, rose to heaven on the horse Pegasus. For what shall I say of Ariadne, and those who, like her, have been declared to be set among the stars? And what of the emperors who die among yourselves, whom you deem worthy of deification, and in whose behalf you produce some one who swears he has seen the burning Caesar rise to heaven from the funeral pyre?

Justin Martyr says, in effect, "Yes, my dear Roman readers, we do say that Jesus was born of a virgin and was a Son of God, but you say the same thing of the sons of Jupiter, Perseus, and Hercules, why are we so queer then? In this respect, our Jesus is no different from your gods." Justin continues in Chapter 22...

> And if we assert that the Word of God was born of God in a peculiar manner, different from ordinary generation, let this, as said above, be no extraordinary thing to you, who say that Mercury is the angelic word of God...And if we even affirm that He was born of a virgin, accept this in common with what you accept of Perseus. And in that we say that He made whole the lame, the paralytic, and those born blind, we seem to say what is very similar to the deeds said to have been done by AEsculapius.

Justin says, "Hey, it's no big deal that Jesus was born of a virgin. You have virgin-born gods, and not only that, you pagans have miracle-working gods." Well, how does Justin Martyr explain these similarities? Hear the man in Chapter 54 of the same work...

> But those who hand down the myths which the poets have made, adduce no proof to the youths who learn them; and we proceed to demonstrate that they have been uttered by the influence of the wicked demons, to deceive and lead astray the human race. For having heard it proclaimed through the prophets that the Christ was to come, and that the ungodly among men were to be punished by fire, they put forward many to be called sons of Jupiter, under the impression that they would be able to produce in men the idea that the things which were said with regard to Christ were mere marvellous tales, like the things which were said by the poets.

So there you have it; a well-respected and highly quoted man of God who lived during a time when these myths were alive and still taken seriously tells us that the reason for these similarities is because demons, knowing Jesus was the one and only Son of God, decided to thwart the plan of redemption by screwing things up! Retroactively, the son-ship of Jesus was sabotaged by imposters, the mythical products of lying devils.

While not all Christians accept Justin Martyr's explanation, many do. Those who don't will often be heard to make the opposite contention—that not the devils, but God put pagan similarities between Jesus and pagan gods for the purpose of "softening" the pagans up for an easier conversion to Christianity. This explanation sounds a lot more believable and intelligent than Martyr's, which will simply not fly as a credible explanation to a thinker in the West today.

Of the more credible position, we still have problems. C.S Lewis was one of the most expanded theistic minds of his time. I say this because traveling to Greece in the 1960s, he was moved to admit that at one point it was hard for him not to pray to a statue of Apollo the Healer. (*C.S. Lewis, a biography,* see pages 30, 62, 235, and 274, Roger Green, 1974). Lewis was of the mindset that in the person of Jesus, pagan prophecies were fulfilled by Jesus, as well as Jewish prophecies. According to those who embrace such a view, God hadn't forgotten about the pagans. He threw them a life-preserver in the form of precursory Christs.

But this explanation of Copy-Cat-ism isn't that much better. It only raises the question of which religion, if any, is the "true" religion. Staying with sound reason demands that we give the credit to the oldest proponent of the Son-of-God motif—and that award doesn't go to Christianity. When someone writes a book and someone else comes along and steals the theme and claims it as his or her own, you don't favor the one who swiped the idea; you favor the original creator of said idea. Worshippers of Zeus could just as easily (and with more credibility) argue that Christianity is the knock-off version of their myths, and not the other way around. It is also unbelievable to think that the openly jealous God of the Hebrews would put stink on his name by sharing his glory with infidels in the form of heathen myths. It just wouldn't happen.

Before we move off this very revealing point, we should make mention of the fact that it is a common ploy of apologists to gloss over the present contention by claiming that Justin Martyr was wrong, that no pagan ever taught a virgin-born god-man. In response to this already-refuted-by-what-we-have-seen point, one need only use a little common sense to seal the deal; how could the credibility of any god-man remain intact while having their mothers give birth as non-virgins? If the woman – the god's chosen vessel to give birth to the god-man – was "pre-owned," what was to keep non-believers from claiming that a certain god-man was merely the product of an ordinary birth? Obviously, the legend of the birth of a god-man had to include a chaste and holy woman. A birth-giver of a god-man had to be pure and undefiled.

VIII. Marked for Death at Birth

Going along with the virgin-born savior-god shenanigan, we have the marked-for-death-at-birth legend. That is, many of these gods narrowly avoided death at or before their births. Hercules was marked for death at birth by the snakes sent by Hara to kill him. Perseus was the son of Danae, who was the daughter of King Argos, who was told by an oracle that he would be dethroned and killed by his daughter's man-child. To avoid this fate, Acrisius (as the king was named) locked his daughter in a secret chamber to keep her from being approached by a man. This didn't stop Zeus from coming down and mating with her. Angrily, Danae and Perseus were locked into a chest and thrown into the sea where, providentially, they were later delivered. Dionysus was almost killed by Zeus himself who had been manipulated into taking the life of Dionysus' mother, Semele, while she was still pregnant with him, but he was delivered and preserved by his father in the nick of time.

Other gods were delivered from their own deaths in various ways. Like Moses, Jesus was also spared from the wrath of an angry adversary…

> And when they were departed, behold, the angel of the Lord appeareth to Joseph in a dream, saying, Arise, and take the young child and his

mother, and flee into Egypt, and be thou there until I bring thee word: for Herod will seek the young child to destroy him. When he arose, he took the young child and his mother by night, and departed into Egypt. (Matthew 2:13-14)

It is worth restating what others have brought to light concerning this before—that to date, in the plentitude of Herod's well-known crimes, absolutely no record of this supposed massacre has been uncovered. But it would be impossible to conceal an event of this proportion, which tells us that this probably never happened.

IX. The Trinities

One of the oldest of the surviving heathen myths comes to us straight from its polytheistic roots. I am referring to Trinitarianism. All believers do not accept this doctrine, neither today, nor in the past. Modern Jehovah Witnesses, for instance, live in peace with their denial of this position while in the second century, theologians like Arius (250-336 C.E.) and his followers, many of whom were well known bishops and teachers all over Rome, were excommunicated by Constantine. This, the Arian controversy, was the first of the most devastating divisions the church would face. They denied the eternal God-ship of Jesus and the trinity, for which they were censured. Though this is not a big issue today, the debate on the Christian's three-in-one god of trinitarianism has never been made sense of. Believers simply quote the Nicene Creed and hang on its wording to stir up as little debate as possible on the subject, lest they be taken to task on it.

Like Christianity, Hinduism has a trinity with its three comprising gods being different from Christianity's, but alike in form. Despite centuries of debate, the trinity is as acceptable to the orthodox believer as a birthday cake. (Matthew 28:20) The Hindu Trinity comprises Brahma, the creator of all life, and Vishnu, the preserver and sustainer of life, and Siva, the destroyer. While these Trinitarian members do not have parallels to the triune Christian deity, they wear the same size shirt. We could kill many trees in bringing out the details of the scores of pre-Christian, Babylonian gods. They consist of swivel-headed gods with three, and sometimes more members. It is not remarkable that as the gospels were written, this pagan element began to surface and eventually was championed by the mainline sect of the religion.

There are also small similarities between the holy books of Hinduism and Christianity, between the Bhagavad-Gita and the Bible; Krishna road a white horse as a status symbol of great honor like Jesus. (Bhagavad-Gita 1:14 and Revelation 6:2; 19:11), and both Krishna and

Jesus exhibit their deity in much the same way as so many other god-men...

> I am the Ultimate Consciousness situated within the heart of all living entities, and I am the beginning, the middle, and the end as well of all living entities. (Bhagavad-Gita 10:20)

> And he said unto me, It is done. I am Alpha and Omega, the beginning and the end. I will give unto him that is athirst of the fountain of the water of life freely. (Revelation 21:6)

If we listed all such similarities, this chapter would be much longer!

X. The Apologist's Responses

Asking the question with which we began, "Where have I seen that before?" our highlight study of these Bible legends has shown us important similarities. While a few of these similarities might barely raise an eyebrow, when we put them all together, we see that indeed a good amount of religious copy-cat-ing has been going on. Like the hypothetical and moronic movie director we began our discussion with, it is originality which is in question here.

In this chapter, we have pointed out undeniable similarities that demand explanations. It won't do for apologists to gloss over the issues and list boatloads of differing aspects between the religious figures and faiths involved. That there are grave differences in the stories and legends was never an issue; what is at issue is why we see the similarities between them that we do! I don't need to prove complete mythological theft, only a few lifted religious notions...and I've done more than that. I don't need to show that every single aspect of the Christian religion was swiped from some other source (which I have never said and do not believe), just that the adoption of a single doctrine or position, a rank, or a place of power or privilege came from a neighboring faith. This should be more than enough to give us serious cause for concern.

CHAPTER 16
Corrupt and Scandalous

A Look at the Oppressive Church of Jesus Christ Throughout The Ages

"To disbelieve in witchcraft is to disbelieve the Bible."
- John Wesley

"Man will never be free until the last king is strangled with the entrails of the last priest."
- Denis Diderot

Smith

The year was 1928. The place was Arkansas. Charles Lee Smith, President of the American Association for the Advancement of Atheism was arrested "on charges of blasphemy." What was his crime? Passing out atheist tracts in a local town. After spending one night in jail, Smith was released with one charge dismissed, and the other charge was never set for trial. Like the famous blasphemy trial of C.B. Reynolds decades earlier, Mr. Smith was just one more victim of the American legal system, hijacked by Christianity.

Inoculation

The year was 1722. The date: July 8th. The place: St. Andrew's Church in London, England. A bold, determined preacher walked up to his pulpit and delivered a heartfelt sermon entitled, "Against the Dangerous and Sinful Practice of Inoculation." The sermon was published and became widely famous. His text: Job 2:7; "So went Satan forth from the presence of the Lord, and smote Job with sore boils from the sole of his foot unto his crown." His contention: that Job was suffering from Smallpox (the epidemic of the time) and yet he endured it, and therefore, so should Christians the onslaught of Smallpox in his day. The masses took this advice. Smallpox killed and maimed and ravaged hundreds of thousands of people. It spread and spread some more. The new and experimental scientific practice of inoculation was an abomination, which the preachers proclaimed, "usurped God's providential authority." This preacher was none other than Reverend Edmund Massey, who pleaded from the bottom of his heart, along with scores of Catholic and Protestant church leaders everywhere, not to tolerate the "diabolical operation." God wanted man to suffer for his sins and to endure his punishment, so said University of Cambridge's Reverend Ramsden no less vigorously. He and other Bostonians formed the Anti-Vaccination Society in 1798. The result: an incredible death toll among both Catholics and Protestants, particularly the Catholics, some of whom almost came to bloodshed out of the pious desire to trust in God and not let some physicians make the procedure mandatory...

> Is any sick among you? Let him call for the elders of the church; and let them pray over him, anointing him with oil in the name of the Lord: (James 5:14)

> And Asa in the thirty and ninth year of his reign was diseased in his feet, until his disease was exceeding great: yet in his disease he sought not to the LORD, but to the physicians. (2 Chronicles 16:12)

This attitude towards medicine was not by any means new. Since the year 1248, the Council of Le Mans had concluded that experimenting with surgery was wrong because "the church hates the shedding of blood" (the irony here is pretty intense since the church caused more bloodshed than just about any other institution). Pope Honorious III extended the ban. Pope Alexander III forbade his monks from even studying medicine. Along with all the sciences, the Dominican Order outlawed any practice of medicine.

So there you have it—God does not recommend amoxicillin! What God wanted mankind to do when sick was a simple matter. Very few dissenting voices expressed themselves, until later when yet a greater number of lives were lost because of this foolish zeal.

Bruno

February 17, 1600. Giordano Bruno, an Italian philosopher, astronomer, ex-priest, and freethinker, was burned at the stake for the crime of heresy. His Copernicanism, Arianism, his contentions that all churches should tolerate their schismatic disagreements, along with his somewhat materialistic belief that the universe was infinite and contained many worlds, could not be tolerated. He really crossed the line when he decided Jesus was nothing more than a skillful magician! Talking like that back then would get you killed. Bruno's defiance and distinct individuality made him seas of enemies. On May 22, 1592, he was arrested, and by January of 1593, his trial, which lasted almost 7 years, began. He was tortured and delivered up to be killed, repudiating images of the cross along the way. Lest any be seduced by his heretical words, a large spike was driven through his jaw just after proclaiming his last words. He then painfully awaited his silent consummation by fire. Giordano was a man bigger than the time in which he lived. The world was not worthy.

Servetus

October 27, 1553. Michael Servetus was burned at the stake for the crime of heresy. He committed serious "crimes," such as disbelieving in the trinity, dabbling in astrology, calling the Holy Land infertile, and denying the need and validity of the practice of infant baptism. His irate, argumentative tone, much like Bruno, made him plenty of enemies among both Protestants and Catholics. Having been burned in effigy after escaping from Roman authorities in Vienna, he fled to Geneva where he was spotted by reformer, John Calvin, who had vowed to God that the heretic, Servetus, would not leave the city alive! True to Calvin's vow, it was not the Catholics who killed him, but the Geneva Council, who decided he should meet his maker by way of the flames.

The impenitent, stubborn Servetus soon lost his pride as the slow-burning flames engulfed his body. Blood-curdling screams for mercy were rumored to be heard throughout the crowd of onlookers, and thus ended the legacy of a brilliant mathematician and quite able physician.

Corrupt and Scandalous

Christianity – like nearly all religions – is an albatross to humankind, this small list being scarcely a microscopic fraction of what could be cited to prove the point. It should be noted that these are modern and not-so-modern examples of Christian oppression. They emanate from Catholic and Protestant groups, and therefore, cannot be so easily swept under the rug of willful ignorance by suggesting that the above examples were merely the result of "false Christianity." For centuries, believers have been disagreeing with each other, telling each other that they are wrong on this and that—and therein lies the problem when a believer tries to deny that Group X is a "True Christian" group, but not Group Y. The dispute on what constitutes "genuine" Christianity is as unsolvable a puzzle as partisan politics.

Christianity is not a religion of progress, nor is it a religion of open-mindedness. It does not tolerate, nor appreciate free inquiry. It condemns it, if not in word, in spirit (I Timothy 6:20-21). It sets up the classic clergy-laity system by setting up few as teachers (James 3:1) and the rest as dumbbells, members who sit in the pews like wooden Indians and take in what their spiritual leaders tell them. Like the ancient mystery cults, Christianity claimed infallibility, and so vilifies everyone and every school of thought to be at odds with it...

> If any man love not the Lord Jesus Christ, let him be Anathema Maranatha. (I Corinthians 16:22)

> If there come any unto you, and bring not this doctrine, receive him not into your house, neither bid him God speed: For he that biddeth him God speed is partaker of his evil deeds. (2 John 1:10-11)

This, of course, did not stop with infidels. It went right on into the splintered camps of Christendom and wreaked havoc there.

Believers Attack Their Own

In the middle of the sixteenth century, a man named Isaac de La Peyrere, a Protestant, wrote a book called "The Pre-Adamites." In it, he expressed his belief that a race of men lived before Adam. Once the book was published, he was feverishly attacked by the church. Tons of "answers" to his arguments were printed, and his book was burned by the Parliament of Paris. That wasn't all. He was thrown in jail by the Grand Vicar of the Archdiocese of Mechlin. Not only was he forced to recant his heresy, but to convert back to the Catholic Church.

Most everyone knows of Galileo and the duress he was under from the church to denounce his works, but not many know of Comte de Buffon, the French naturalist who dared to disagree with the Bible's account of creation. Buffon believed in science, and upon stating his views, he was removed from his role on the faculty of Sorbonne and forced to print his recantation. Under immense pressure from all sides, he gave in. The recantation was widely publicized, in which he was made to state that he denounced "all which may be contrary to the narrative of Moses."

Oppression of Women

The years were 1437 and 1445. Pope Eugene IV issued bulls commanding punishment of witches who caused bad weather. The penalty for witches? Death, of course—unless a convincing, forthwith confession was made. A number of Popes followed suit. Pope Innocents VIII, Julius II, and Adrian VI did much to further the killing of thousands of women.

The year was 578. The Council of Auxerre strictly forbade women from receiving the sacraments with their naked hands. They were far too sinful and unclean to be allowed to touch anything as holy as that little wafer known as Jesus' body, much less to be allowed to put it into their mouths.

The crimes against women are too numerous to mention. Women were given the normal speeches from church leaders and pious parents about how menstruation was evil, and during this time, they were excluded from taking the sacraments. As fervently as any teenaged boy was warned, the women were reminded that masturbation was a sin. The female body was filthy and indecent.

Without the aid of an evolving, progressive culture, Christianity would still have us in the dark ages, prattling off the pious nonsense of Tertullian on the subject of women…

> The sentence of God on this sex of yours lives in this age: the guilt must of necessity live too. You are the devil's gateway: you are the

> un-sealer of that (forbidden) tree: you are the first deserter of the divine law: you are she who persuaded him whom the devil was not valiant enough to attack. You destroyed so easily God's image, man. On account of your desert – that is, death – even the Son of God had to die. (Tertullian, "On Women and Fallen Angels," Book I)

The most dreadful of all resistance movements against women came in the form of a work written in 1468 by James Sprenger and Henry Kramer, two obscure academics of the Middle Ages. The book was called *Malleus Maleficarum.* It is called today, "The Hammer of Witches." For nearly four centuries after it was written, it was relied upon by the Catholic Church as a crime and punishment handbook on detecting, capturing, trying, torturing, and killing witches. This work is quite graphic, with detailed questions on how to spot a witch (women who live alone, who dabble in herbs, who teleport from house to house, who fly above rooftops, who make men impotent, etc.), and how a judge should proceed when bringing one to trial. Take this paragraph, for example…

> First they are to be brought face to face, and their mutual answers and recriminations noted, to see whether there is any inconsistency in their words by reason of which the Judge can decide from her admissions and denials whether he ought to expose her to torture; and if so, he can proceed as in the third manner of pronouncing a sentence, explained in the Twenty-second Question, submitting her to light tortures: at the same time exercising every possible precaution, as we explained at length towards the beginning of this Third Part, to find out whether she is innocent or guilty. (Part III, Question XXXIII)

The book points out all the avenues to get to "the truth" of whether or not she was a witch, but far too often, just the accusation was enough to bring about the death of a suspected witch. Professional "prickers" were paid well, much like today's bounty hunters. They were sent across kingdoms to discriminately prick certain warts, moles, or marks on a woman's body to look for "signs" of demonic infestation.

Torquemada and Anti-Semiticism

The year was 1420. The place was Castile, Spain. A crusader was born who was to claim his place in human history as a man of exceptional cruelty. We are talking about the infamous church inquisitor, Thomas de Torquemada. He was a nephew to the renowned theologian and Cardinal, Juan de Torquemada. Torquemada became a learned man and a well-respected Dominican priest. After a number of years serving as

Assistant Inquisitior, he was promoted to Grand Inquisitor of Castile. His quest was to purify Spain of the Jews, some of whom had converted insincerely to Christianity (mostly out of compulsion). Torquemada discovered something very disturbing about himself – that his grandmother was a *converso* as they were called – a converted Jew to Christianity. This did not sit well with him as he prided himself on "sangre limpia," being of pure, white, Christian blood. He sought to root out the impure and heretical Jewish forces that threatened the economic stability of the Catholic Church.

Torquemada was the primary push behind the expulsion of the Jews from Spain. When Ferdinand and Isabella would have taken the Jews' offer to allow them to stay if they paid 30,000 ducats, it is said that Torquemada came to them with a cross and held it aloft saying, "Judas sold his Master for thirty ducats. You would sell him for 30,000!" It worked. When the Edict of Expulsion was passed in 1492, the Jews were given till the first of July to leave. Any Jew who stayed after that time would be killed. Some fled to Portugal, North Africa, and others remained in Spain and came to be called, "Secret Jews."

Of those that remained, at least 2,000 ended up paying with their lives (more according to some historians). Most of these were burned at the stake. Others were tortured so inhumanely, so maddeningly that false confessions became rampant. Torquemada's cruelty and abuses were so heinous that even Pope Sixtus IV, a man in favor of the inquisition's torture methods, spoke out against him in 1482. Torquemada was called by the Spanish Chronicler Sebastian de Olmedo, *"The hammer of heretics, the light of Spain, the savior of his country, the honor of his order."*

The darkest day in English-Jewish relations came during the reign of King Richard I. On March 16, 1190, 159 Jews barricaded themselves inside York Castle and committed suicide to escape an angry mob that stood ready to kill them. Of those few who surrendered in an attempt to have their lives spared, intending to later recant their conversions to Christianity, were subjected to a horrible death at the hands of the rioters. The church's massacre of the Jews swept far and wide. The "impenitent Christ-killers" (the people the church had the least success converting) paid with their lives in atrocity after atrocity.

Opposition to Science

Without the aid of an evolving, progressive culture, Christianity would still have us forbidding surgery lest we defile a dead body and dishonor God. Mankind would have no doubt progressed medically beyond where we are today had we had access to biological experimentation

700 years ago. But in exchange for life-saving medical advances, they were given the sanctified decisions of medically ignorant church councils. In 1299 C.E., Pope Boniface VIII issued a papal bull that decreed the penalties for anyone with the ungodly gall to dissect a corpse—excommunication and possible imprisonment. The hurt that this has done to the fields of anatomy and biology is quite incalculable, but I'm sure Boniface felt more than justified in this move and even felt he could support it with the Bible…

> Thus saith the LORD; For three transgressions of Moab, and for four, I will not turn away the punishment thereof; because he burned the bones of the king of Edom into lime. (Amos 2:1)

Christianity fosters intolerance and suspicion, a most dreaded and undying fear of change. As we have seen, it opposes science, it opposes medicine, it opposes logic, and even common sense. It makes man's way difficult, burdened down with needless concerns and worries. It lays at the feet of society an alarmist mentality of spotting trouble where there is none and always stands ready to reject sensible solutions to problems. These handful of examples by themselves show us that when mankind is morally motivated and indoctrinated by a religion that claims to embody "infallible truth," the tendency to bind those "truths" on others always ends up being hurtful.

I find it interesting how Christians will so readily site Newton and Galileo as examples of believers demonstrating scientific refinement, while silently glossing over the long, cold, dark years of Bibles being chained to pulpits, women being forced into convents (as was the case with Marguerite Delamarre in 1752), the mentally ill being locked up and tortured for fear of their being possessed, and forbidding marriages in local towns because of expressed defiance from the common people. The Church expressed her complete contentment with the "Earth, Wind, Fire, and Water" theory of elements as taught by the ancient Greeks, until the likes of Priestly and Scheele came along and set us straight on the matter with the groundbreaking discovery of oxygen. Christians are every bit as capable of discovery as anyone else, but the question is, if Christianity promotes science and free inquiry, why did it take Christianity many centuries to produce only a handful of great thinkers? The answer is: it didn't (and doesn't).

Christianity has never directly produced a single freethinker. Mankind finally broke away from the stranglehold that the infamously oppressive Church had on the world. With that came flourishing minds who could begin to experiment and question and think on their own without fear of the guillotine (or as much fear of it, at least). As the

Church began to lose grip of the world, slowly but surely, objective learning could begin to be exercised. Christianity remained, by far, the most dominant faith throughout Europe, so it would be a shock if at least some scientists and thinkers were not of the Christian Faith. But those good scientific minds were scientists and Christians; they were not scientists *because* they were Christians. We cannot give credit where credit is not due.

Christianity, unleashed on the world, has done many terrible things throughout the ages, far outweighing any good it managed to accomplish. Only when faith in the church's infallible dogmas began to decline did we see increases in liberty. Today, the church displays only a glimmer of her former snarling, mad dog image. To make better inroads infiltrating societies, she now uses the stealth approach.

This, however, is the freethinker's perspective. It is not the believer's perspective. The proud, white, middle-class Protestant of today is utterly perplexed at how the freethought movement could dare suggest that Christianity is a vice against humanity. They live in their own Christianized world and attribute every little semblance of pleasantness and decency to their God. Christianity takes credit for everything even remotely good and runs away, like a caught-cheating husband, from any hint of bad publicity. As Woolsey Teller so eloquently put it...

> But leave it to Christianity to bedeck itself in stolen plumage. After blocking the cultural progress of the world for hundreds of years, it now poses as the champion of civilization, when, in plain truth, its behavior has been like that of the chameleon, changing colors and blending with the background whenever it is expedient. Let a people gather a few crumbs of culture in spite of Christianity and Christianity will claim the credit. Christianity upheld slavery for over a thousand years, yet no sooner was emancipation achieved than it posed as "the black man's friend". It spat on woman suffrage, then, when woman's rights were won, it posed as the "liberator" of women. It fought tooth and nail the doctrine of evolution, but now assures us (from "liberal" pulpits, at least) that there never was any "real" conflict between science and religion. It opposed anesthesia in child-birth; it now proclaims it as God's "gift" to womankind. Before the war, it worshiped "the Prince of Peace"; it is now singing the song, "Praise the Lord and pass the ammunition." (Woolsey Teller, Essays of an Atheist, "Chameleonic Christianity," 1945)

This is why Christianity stands condemned in the council of freethinking humanity as a mischievous trespasser, a migrant troublemaker, stirring up ruckus and unrest everywhere she goes. With useless regulations and hindrances, she does nothing but crush the life out of an observant, budding, and experimental society. Like a cruel, dry, second grade teacher who berates her students for innocently choosing to color outside of the lines, Christianity is a detriment to the progress of any society. Christianity operates by manipulation – befriending the mighty, seizing their power, and when finished using them – casts them out like spoiled goods. Like a crooked but sharply dressed politician, Christianity vainly points to a bright, appealing future, replete with promises of a Utopian tomorrow, while cleverly maneuvering her believers to keep from noticing the plentitude of horrendous injustices, allegations, and scandals of her past.

Chapter 17
God's Shrinking Living Room

A Journey Through Time

"God exists in the gaps of our knowledge of the world."
- *Epicurus*

"As the spirit derived from truth is superior to that based upon credulity, the new doctrines that supplant the old may be expected to excel any that have preceded them."
- *William Floyd*

Let's take a journey through time. Go with me in your mind one thousand years from now. We are going to experience life as a Christian in the distant future. Meet Sylomekra. He has a last name, but it is a long series of numbers (000.076.997.531.1112). We'll just call him "Sylo" for short. He is a prospective convert to one of the very few remaining sects of the Christian faith still in existence. He is going into a Bible study with a well-known minister who is a part of the Mars Ministry Coalition, one of the largest councils of churches that are responsible for directing evangelistic affairs on the red planet. This world happens to be where Sylo has lived since birth. The minister – in this age called an Embracer – presents his study program in what we know as a holodeck simulation, not unlike those from Star Trek The Next Generation. The downloading of cortical implants are also used to more effectively teach the nuances and doctrines of the church without confusion.

Before we begin with the details of Sylo's story, let's first lay down some groundwork of this time period. There are twelve surviving Christian denominations, and unlike churches in our time, all of these denominations are almost totally at peace with the natural sciences. They don't dispute evolution. They embrace it. There are no Young Earth Creationists, Flat-Earthers, or Geocentrists anymore. The Christian church in this age makes up one eighth of the solar system's population. Counting from Earth, the colonies on Mars, and fifty-three other made-habitable moons of Earth, Jupiter, and Saturn, the total is 16.9 billion.

Believers in this time are usually young instead of old, short, thin, and almost effeminate-looking. Their bodies have been enhanced both biochemically and cybernetically. They are stronger than a peak-human powerlifter of our day and in better condition all-round than Jack La Lanne was in his prime. All are genetically prescreened at birth from harmful gene arrangements, like deformities, retardation, and learning disabilities, and the parents now choose the abilities, the talents, and even the inclinations of their children before conception, much the same way an online role-playing gamer in our world chooses the strengths and weaknesses of their character by the simple click of a mouse.

By this late date, most races have merged into slightly dark-skinned, fair-featured beings—I say "beings" because the sexes have been done away with. Reproduction is done in clean, specialized laboratories. By way of genetic manipulation, these humans have had brought out in them both masculine and feminine features and qualities—the best of both worlds. People are still sexually active, but the acts vary in kind and preference, and they are much cleaner and are impassioned by more emotional engagement, rather than out of physical need.

In certain low-lying areas on Earth – the "slums" of our world, one could call them – some human families fall under the radar and are born "the old fashioned way." To steal a popular science fiction term, we'll call these *free-borns*. Though they are few in number, they can still be found. This is because four centuries ago, their ancestors chose to head back to life in the woods in protest of the new world's use of various technologies. Free-borns are viewed by the new mankind as barbaric, dangerous, impulsive, and animalistic, given to urges and beastly calls of nature. In this age, the church is heading up legislation that would make it flatly illegal to allow the continuation of free-births due to the fact that in their societies, instances of rape, alcoholism, incest, and domestic violence abound because of the untamed masculine element and the horrors it causes.

The political climate in this age is not quite as volatile as it was in our day. The Islamic religion has died out almost altogether, except in unnamed, desolate areas, like in the area that used to be called The Gaza Strip. The Middle East was bombed off the map almost seven hundred years earlier by what became a Neo-Iraqi/United States of America proto-nation that itself subsequently dissolved before ever becoming a nation of its own.

Big debates and mysteries in this age include but are not limited to…*Should free-borns be allowed to reproduce as barbarous as they can be? Should all remaining earth predators (most, like the big cats, are extinct already) be converted to grain-eaters for humanitarian reasons, even though doing so would be at great expense? Should a parent have a choice in refusing optical light implants that are given to all children before birth to prevent accidents from walking in the dark? Should expensive perfumes be released onto the market that have been made with a rare, moss-like bacteria found on a planet orbiting Alpha Centauri even though it is considered wasteful? Was the outlawing of flesh-food in 2158 and the infamous Ampsterdam Riots that followed the work of the political manipulation of Denmark's The Vega Order? Should we proceed with Operation Sombrero—our plans to open a new wormhole to that galaxy, even though serious funding and safety issues remain? How should the dispute among scholars in the historical records concerning America be settled?* Two major schools of thought are defended on this controversy; one says the dispute that divided the now defunct U.S.A. was on the issues of Artificial Intelligence (A.I.), the debate on whether or not the new order of droids were truly "alive." The second school of thought said that it was the slow merger of Mexico into America that weakened her leadership and destroyed the morale of the nation to the point when China (which still exists in this age) was able to bring about her defeat. This is Sylo's world. Now, we move on to his discipleship into the faith.

Sylo's great grandparents migrated to Mars Colony Sigma three hundred and fifty years earlier. They were charter members on the new colony. Sylo is not a free-born, but just like the Ethiopian eunuch in the chariot in Acts chapter 8, he is like everyone else and has a longing for the universe, a desire to understand it. Like most religious minds in this era, Sylo is a very pantheistic thinker. He sees the world and the whole universe as an extension of God, not as being apart from or beneath him. Like almost everyone else, he looks for happiness and enlightenment in the form of codes and highly complex music that would sound like silly gibberish to humans in our time. People in Sylo's period of history are fickle, observant, refined, high functioning, and incredibly sophisticated. He (if I may call him that) would be quite out of place in today's world, a bizarrely intelligent freak of nature. After all, he is not a homosapien but really a *hypersapien*—a drastically upgraded human being.

In the downloads given him by the Embracer, Sylo learns about the believers in Christianity. Even these cherished beliefs have evolved over time. Christians no longer worship a militant, evangelically-minded God who is above the universe, but one who is wise and compassionate, and "in" the universe. He *is* the universe, you could say. Christ was a great and noble mythical figure who was created by God through the creative agency of mankind to identify the traits of God, giving us an example of compassion in personhood. He is not God. He might not even have been a historical figure, but he was the embodiment of love. Just as the creation story of Genesis has taken on new meanings in our time as the knowledge of science increased during the middle ages, even so now Christ is viewed differently. He is seen as a triumphant force, a force over negativity and the gloom of the grave. Jesus didn't really rise from the dead. No one did, and for the most part, no one trusts the Bible historically anymore. In fact, the cortical downloads believers have of the Bible contain only the Psalms, Proverbs, the Gospels, and select portions from the epistles of Peter and Paul.

In the study, Sylo learns of Peter and John arriving at the empty tomb to find no Jesus inside. The lesson: this represents the intellectual side of man, and there is no satisfaction there. We must view life and the scriptures spiritually, which is to say, allegorically. If you look for Jesus with the mind, you won't find him. You've got to seek him with the evolved spirit! This part of the story is followed by an almost condescending apology for the church's ways of the past. The church in this age fully denounces intolerance and violence of any kind, and also divisiveness over doctrinal issues, like the archaic Nicean Creed (or the "Apostle's Creed" as it is also known) from the year, 325 C.E. This cruel creed is now denounced as being the cause of all the terrors that the medieval church brought on the ancient world. "This was the intellectual phase of Christianity," says the Embracer, "which has passed." The disciples finally having their eyes opened on the road to Emmaus (Luke 24) is said to be the spiritual part of man, realizing for the first time the love of the mystic, transcendent God of the universe. The Embracer then goes through what it means to have the fruits of the spirit. These haven't changed, but other moral issues have.

Sexuality is no longer an issue at all, neither is abortion. Those decisions God gave mankind his own authority to make. They were issues of a more base mankind, a state humanity has now risen above. Good and evil, right and wrong, are situationally determined with a healthy use of reason. Though death is hardly an obstacle anymore, it is not unknown, even with Utopian-like technology – and when death presents itself, prepared people willingly end their own lives – they defend and appreciate sensibly applied euthanasia. Capital punishment is no longer an issue as well. Believers in this area understand that in those rare instances when someone commits a brutal crime, the person committing the act is sick and needs help. He is not evil and does not deserve punishment, only correction—why punish the criminal when you can fully rehabilitate him? The idea of Hell is only the sad mental prison we make when we refuse to open our minds, to fulfill our dreams. No longer do believers fight over the use of words or interpretations of scripture, at least not very often. God is the real guiding authority, and he leads us by the perplexing forces of nature.

For tradition's sake, communion is still done in some churches, and when it is done, even the A.I. droids (who are wholly embraced as equal spiritual beings to the biological ones) partake in communion and storytelling, but other faiths choose to leave it behind as it is an unpleasant reminder of a time when men worshipped horrific sky figures who drank blood and ate flesh – both items that have been illegal for a long time. Worship services are more or less like a whole episode of The View.

But even in this new and radical age, things still aren't perfect. One of the bitterest issues of the day among the churches is over the invention of a new technology, as it concerns the church's use of brain-mapping technology in the ministry. Normally, technology is very aggressively used by the church and is seen as an extension of the universe—God himself. But like the realizations of science and technology in ages past, the discovery of this one device has proved to be troubling and worrisome to the faithful. It has resurrected age-old hatred for science and human progress.

About one hundred and ten years ago, a famous Christian apologist hailing from the United Federation of Canada by the name of Nuemurdan made an invention. For this invention, he is heralded as C.S. Lewis is among Christians today. He took secular brain-mapping technology and made it into a spiritual technology called Brain-mapping Apostasy Prevention (BAP). What does this technology do? It is a perfect comb-over of a scanned brain. Through the secular breakthroughs in completely understanding the inner-workings of our brains, every operation of the organ is clearly understood. This makes it possible to predict with perfect accuracy when someone will go through a midlife crisis, become terminally depressed, become reclusive or self-destructive, become obsessed or phobic in anyway, and it can go much deeper; for instance, it can predict what your tastes and moods will be when you reach fifty, how often you will desire sexual relations, and with what type of person, future life ambitions, and on and on we could go. In the process of these breakthroughs, this notable apologist/scientist discovered a way to map out which brains respond best to religious claims and which do not, who will make a life-long convert to the faith and who will not.

So nailed down is this technology that it can predict how one will turn philosophically through every achievement, tragedy, and milestone of life. In summation, this technology enables a church to know for beyond a 99 percent certainty whether or not one will apostatize from the faith. In almost every opposing sect, each potential church member must submit to and pass this test before membership will be granted. If you fail the test, the church no longer pursues your conversion, but they give you the option to undergo a mind alteration procedure that reroutes your brain in the appropriate area(s) to match the brain-structure of the rest of the faithful fold, thus, eliminating any chance you will ever have of wanting to de-convert or apostatize for any reason. Of course, having the procedure will change various aspects of an individual's character, and that makes this a very debatable decision that requires a lot of time and devotion before it is agreed upon. Still, a great number of people decide to go through with it.

In all but one of the remaining Christian factions, Nuemurdan is considered the greatest saint of all. In the opposing sect, he is seen as a misled individual who took technology further than the scriptures intended it to go. He is viewed as an apostate, as it were. Exchanges over the use of this item prove to be bitter and often degenerate into character attacks, not unlike the old barbaric man they consider themselves above. Speaking of infidels, the biblical dispute centers on the affirmation that it would have been better "for them not to have known the way of righteousness, than, after they have known it, to turn from the holy commandment delivered unto them." (2 Peter 2:21) And, "Jesus said unto him, No man, having put his hand to the plough, and looking back, is fit for the kingdom of God." (Luke 9:62) And, "But I keep under my body, and bring it into subjection: lest that by any means, when I have preached to others, I myself should be a castaway." (I Corinthians 9:27)

Pro-BAP advocates point out that for the first time in history, mankind has the ability to actually prevent wayward souls from falling away and displeasing God. "Just as we have and use many great technologies," say they, "we should utilize our ability to stop wayward souls from joining the fold, knowing they will not complete their spiritual walk." They argue that God would expect such prudence and diligence on man's part. Use of this technology would be fundamentally no different than using lights or medicine.

Those who are Anti-BAP point out that this misses the whole point of conversion to begin with. They highlight how Jesus said, "He that hath an ear, let him hear" (Revelation 2:7) They point to Peter's exchange with Jesus in the book of John, "Then said Jesus unto the twelve, Will ye also go away? Then Simon Peter answered him, Lord, to whom shall we go? thou hast the words of eternal life. And we believe and are sure that thou art that Christ, the Son of the living God." (John 6:67-69) Sounding like dinosaurs from the twenty-first century, the backward anti-BAPs argue the freewill argument which believers used to harp on until the simplistic notion was abandoned by the body of Christ way in the past. They maintain without hesitation that God wants men to have a choice to walk away from Jesus or follow him as they choose. Those from the Pro camp fire back without missing a beat, "But this has nothing to do with freewill. Man was incapable of preventing apostasy back then. He would expect us to use every means at our disposal to ensure faithfulness today. To say that God doesn't want us to prevent a sheep from straying away from the fold is to make him cruel and insensitive." Then they quote I John 2:19, "They went out from us, but they were not of us; for if they had been of us, they would no doubt have continued with us: but they went out, that they might be made manifest that they were not all of us." Say they, "We are preventing unfaithful converts from offending God. We are doing his will as we can. This is God's world. He gave us this technology to use." They go on to point out that using technological means to ensure faithfulness is no different from using (in our case) a drug to help control mood-swings and other personality glitches, or (in their case) a brain-scan procedure to help get the right mental balance. The Pro-

BAPs hold the majority position in the end, and the more rigid old timers are viewed as "just not with it."

That is the way it is with churches in every age; it's always the young whippersnappers verses the old traditionalists. They fight, but they never come to a meeting of the minds. Their scholars will battle it out for generations, and in the process, come to hate each other to no productive end. Even the most sagacious church member becomes incensed discussing this controversy. It has the church in an upheaval, just like science and progress in technology have always done to religious believers of every shade.

Getting back to Sylo, he takes the BAP test and fails it. He assures the Embracer that he will be faithful and that he is interested in following the sacred path, but the preacher informs him that it just doesn't work like that. Upon hearing that he has an option to get a mind alteration procedure to secure his future faithfulness, he feels too violated by that and decides to walk away, valuing the sovereignty of his mind over the faith. And that is the end of Sylo's story.

Coming back to our time, there are some lessons here, important lessons that should have been learned by the civilized world no later than the publication of The Origin of Species in 1859. The story of Sylo shows us how belief in God as pursued through Christianity or any other religion is out of place today and cannot be brought into harmony with the free-flowing naturalistic mind. Progress made in the furtherance of science will always prove threatening to any system of faith. If you doubt this, then I have some questions for you.

To which passage will you direct me to provide me with the Bible's take on cryonics? Will it be a scriptural practice with humans once we learn how to safely freeze, and in the future, unfreeze a human to find a cure for a disease? Or are we dodging God's will on the fact that he wants us to face the consequences of any condition/ailment he sends our way? To which passage will you direct me to show Bible authority for the cyborgization of replaceable/repairable body parts? If I lose a hand, I do have Bible authority to replace it with a genetically engineered one, no? If I don't, are all the old people with pacemakers and artificial joints going to Hell along with me? Surely not, right? For that matter, why not show the Bible authority for removing a non-life-threatening mole or deformity, or for allowing an extremely homely person to undergo plastic surgery? If our bodies are the temple of God, how dare we alter them in any way, right?

To which passage will you refer me in an effort to show me that life begins at conception? Which passage(s) deal with artificial insemination, invitro fertilization, test-tube babies, contraception, etc? I, for one, would love to know just how a Christian determines that when the first cell division occurs at conception, you have a life. I would have thought that perhaps it is after the initial cell divisions occur and the embryo splits in two...say, into twins or triplets, and that is the point at which life really begins, but I'm not a Christian. You tell me, and please don't fail to direct me to the Bible passage from which you arrived at your conclusion. To which passage of scripture would you advise I adhere to, to provide a doctor with counsel on how to deal with a baby born with the anatomical parts of both the male and female sexes? Would there be any authority to surgically fashion a newborn baby into a complete man or woman? Which passages deal with how we should treat transgender people? I would really like to know.

To which passage would you lead me to find authority and the motivation to pursue a space program? Should we even try to visit far distant worlds? By what authority? As far as the Bible is concerned, we shouldn't even expect to find pond scum on those distant worlds, and there certainly wouldn't be any sentient, intelligent life out there, right? So why should we even bother investigating those lofty matters when earth was created as our portion for life and well-being? Should we ever discover aliens from another world who are sentient, what should we do? Evangelize them? Do they have souls? Do they have sin? On the one hand, if they have no souls and are to be considered as mere sheep and oxen, what if they are capable of doing the same moral things we humans do, like exhibiting advanced forms of love and compassion? What if they are truly moral beings? What if their morality actually exceeds our own? On the other hand, if we say yes, that they do have souls and sin, and need to be evangelized, have all those who died on their planet thus far without the gospel of Jesus headed to a place of torment?

Then, of course, there is the issue of cloning; where in the Bible do we find the go-ahead to proceed with this branch of science? Was it wrong to clone Dolly, the sheep, like we did back in the nineties? Will it be wrong to clone humans? Does cloning somehow encroach on God's plans for man? Will these future human clones have souls? Will they be able to go to Hell for sins? Will they get off scot-free for wrongs committed? If these soulless things reproduce, will they be capable of having offspring with souls if one of the partners is a normal, "ensouled" human? Won't the children have to get the soul from the non-clone parent who has a soul? Or is the soul sent down from heaven at conception? Might God decide to send down souls for these clones since, for all practical purposes, they are still created in God's image? Also, what about DNA banks, sperm banks, and egg banks? Please give me the scriptures on these deep topics. I have other questions on the creation of artificial intelligence, but I think I know what the answers will be. All I want is a good and hearty "Thus saith the Lord" from the word of God to help mankind on these morally crucial matters.

As a former minister, I tried many times to find the answers to these questions in the "good old book", but never could. I gave up. I am curious to see the Bible's teaching on how to proceed on these subjects from some current believers who are confident that they can do better than I did. I am now fully convinced that the Bible doesn't have these answers, and therefore, is a book that is far from fit as a reliable and applicable guide for matters of life today.

Now I do hope that any wayfaring Christians who take time to answer these questions will realize how much I appreciate their effort in doing so, but I also hope they realize that if their answers don't match up with the answers of their fellow believers, then this suggests that their book does not clearly offer these answers at all. Either all that is in the Bible is only what we have authority for (then we'd have to eliminate anything extra-biblical, like cars and planes, pacemakers and medicines, etc.), or the Bible implicitly authorizes and guides us today, authorizing a number of extra-biblical things that must be carefully and tediously studied out. However, it is worth stating that the latter has proven to be an impossible task to complete, since no one has yet reached a consensus on these "answers" provided by the Bible.

Stereo instructions for a particular model of stereos might be well written, useful, and relevant for a whole product line of a given stereo type, but as time passes, those instructions will inevitably become obsolete. Time and learning will render them useless. The same, I contend, is true of the Bible. It cannot be a valid means of answering today's complex questions and issues. We must look for answers elsewhere.

Just when we want the fighting to stop, it only intensifies. Through vain determination and tireless foolishness, the religious mindset is what keeps the myths of today growing and changing, taking on increasingly difficult dilemmas, pigeonholing them into the crevasses of Christianity. Generations will pass and the fighting will continue until one day, someone, somewhere will decide to throw down the gauntlet and call it quits, and when this happens, the rest of humanity will be ready to follow. Someday the curtain will fall on religion forever. God will have moved out of his shrunken living room and into the condemned, one-room apartment of shameful relics of our past. But in the mean time, preachers will go on trying to answer questions that neither the Bible, nor religion in general can answer. These same preachers, given to fight the tides of human progress, are the same ones who step into their pulpits each and every holy day and talk to their congregations about how God and his church haven't changed, but they are wrong. The gods change just as surely as the believers in them change. Every church you drive by will someday be boarded up.

Boarded Up Church

I see a glimpse from the road driving by, nothing glorious, just something that catches my eye…

A boarded up church, with fallen tiles and a faded hull, a memory of a church that used to be full.

Inside those doors, laughter and shouting could be heard, with a zealous, young preacher proclaiming the word.

Baptisms, restorations, emotions, and healings, souls saved, alter calls, and precious, warm feelings.

If you stand in the center of the room for a while, you can see the happy people, each with a smile.

One by one the members died, moved, and fell away—slowly but surely, here we are today!

But a church is a place of delusion, of sanctified lies, really not worth the space it occupies.

But tough it will be to get that believed, with as many decent people who have long been deceived.

A boarded up church is a church of the best kind, one that doesn't make you irrational and blind.

Hard as it may be, the past must be forgotten, with the memories at the church and the wood that now stands rotten.

Chapter 18
A Spooky Kooky World

My Experiences Investigating the Paranormal

"The savage belief in magic and the later barbaric belief in conscious invisible beings gave a degree of assurance in striving to overcome evil by rites, ceremonies, and worship."
- Charles Lee Smith

"The candle flame gutters. Its little pool of light trembles. Darkness gathers. The demons begin to stir."
- Carl Cagan

I was probably eight years old at the most. Mom got me a cup of water and proceeded to tuck both my brother and I in our beds for the night. My brother (almost four years younger than I) was not content with just being tucked in. He wanted a story read, so he jumped out of bed, ran down the hall, and went back to tugging on mom's nightgown, begging her to read us a story. I was still alone in our room while this was going on. I distinctly remember this like it was yesterday.

I went to take another swig of a cup of water. The water was in a memorable little Kool-Aid cup that sat on my dresser, when suddenly, the cup moved all by itself. It slid about an inch closer towards the front of the dresser. My heart started pounding like I couldn't believe and I was scared so incredibly that my voice couldn't scream, though as I recall, I tried. The hair on my head and all over my body stood straight up. I couldn't react for a whole five seconds at least. My mind kept trying to get a handle on what had happened, but it couldn't. Finally, I found the composure to turn around and run like a bat out of Hell down the hallway to mom's bedroom where brother and mom both were. I told mother what happened and she humored me as though she believed. After a while of getting to stay up later, she escorted us back to the room where she and I studied the cup for a moment.

At first, I thought that maybe the condensation of the cup accumulating on the dresser acted as a slippery surface causing the cup to slide a little. This had happened to me before, so I looked for signs of it, but there was no ice in the glass. The cup was not wet and the dresser top was dry. Then I took note of the position of the cup in relation to where I thought it had moved. I noticed it was in exactly the same place as I observed it earlier (before I saw it move). I know this because there was a stain on the dresser which I compared it against before it supposedly moved.

Suddenly – amazingly – now it looked like it didn't move at all. "You see, it was just your mind playing tricks on you," mom said. "No, it had to be real!" I thought to myself. I had never experienced such a convincing mind trick, and even still, I wasn't fully ready to just except that it was a specter of my imagination. Then I realized something else: the water didn't move in the cup. A cup of water instantly moving would have made the water swoosh around in the glass, but I was certain that was not in my recollection of the event. This confirmed for me, after going over and over the experience in my mind, that it was in fact my mind playing tricks on me. At first, I was as sure as I was alive that the cup did indeed move. I would have bet my life on it a hundred times over. It was so real to me. The human mind can be a powerful trickster.

Fast-forwarding to more recent years, I find these mind games showing themselves in other, less troublesome ways. If I am in the shower, sometimes I can just barely hear my cell phone ringing. I'm instinctively wondering who is trying to reach me. The ringing stops. They hang up since I am temporarily indisposed. Then I keep wondering whether or not the phone is still ringing because the melody of the ring-tone is still jumping around in my head. I think I hear it still. Is that person calling back, or is it just my mind again?

Unlike many, I tend to have an exceptional memory, so it has periodically bothered me through the years when I watched an old movie or listened to a song I hadn't heard in ages and noticed that the dialogue wasn't exactly as I remember it. Some words are out of order or missing, and my mind replaced other words with words that were never there. Just goes to show how even the best of memories are not always loyal to their owners.

What I have taken the time to point out is a simple, observable, and self-testable fact that applies to all human minds; (a) even in the sanest of people, the human mind is subject to delusion, no matter how sober and alert we might be. (b) We are capable of misconstruing and blowing out of proportion our knowledge of facts and experiences to the extent that our minds turn them into false images or experiences. I am not now, nor have I ever been mentally unstable, yet my experience with the cup as a child and other keynote misperceptions were every bit as real to me at the time as was my own name, but I was wrong about them. The truth – the reality – was not what I perceived it to be. The human mind is capable of delusion and outright error. (c) Our minds piece together sensory experiences, forming living images. A movie is nothing more than a series of pictures, freeze-frame images flashed successively. Our minds put these together and this makes the movie the experience that it is. A bland series of pictures becomes a "motion picture," to which we can relate. In life, our minds do the same thing. They distort reality as surely as they do interpret and make sense of it. Unknown noises, eerie feelings, things that go "bump" in the night, turn our calm into confusion and worry. We face our "demons," the undesirable products of our overactive minds. Experiences can be deceiving, as can be the senses that make them possible.

When we take into account the deceptive nature of our minds, our still gross ignorance of nature and science, the possibility of potentially false experiences, and the often-faulty operation of human memory, it should not surprise us how on the subjects of religion and the supernatural, delusion and misperception threateningly creep in. Like all emotional experiences, religious ones are nothing to laugh at. They are very real to a lot of people, but are they categorically, objectively real?

And if so, do these experiences constitute evidence of something divine, as opposed to merely "unexplained phenomenon" that could come to be understood by unraveling the intricate workings of nature? This is the heart of the controversy.

Two Major Criticisms

Religious experiences suffer from two major defects, the first one being that *they cannot be independently subjected to a battery of critical tests and physical observations.* While psychics, spiritualists, and ardent believers in the supernatural will not agree that not having physical evidence of a claim weakens its likelihood of being true, they will admit that these paranormal events we hear so much about are hard to get evidence for. Someone may have seen a ghost at grandma's old house, but one might go back over there and invest a lot of fruitless time waiting for it to reappear with no success. But "absence of evidence is not evidence of absence," so the debate continues.

However, the fact remains that any position that cannot be validated or invalidated we must be extremely suspicious of by reason of the fact that the lines of reality are distorted and rendered void when supernatural claims are made. If we are to accept notions as truth which cannot be demonstrated to be either true or false, we are left with the fact that we are incapable of separating truth from error. That means a great chasm of uncertainty exists. What remains is only a maze of maybes and maybe nots—not a satisfying groundwork for the building blocks of knowledge to say the least!

To believers in it, the world of the supernatural is a spooky, kooky place, a place where gods and goddesses sit on their thrones, a place where demons and angels fight it out in the heavenly realm, where prophets are shown images of heaven, where the relics of dead saints remain uncorrupted, and where dead relatives await the joyful reuniting of their long-lost loved ones. Theirs is the place of doppelgangers, Alaskan shape-shifters, spiritually ascended masters, the donkey lady, Chupakabra, and astral beings. There too, virgin-born savior-god-men and perpetual virgins with their exalted saintly consorts in company abide. These unseen and un-seeable super-beings dwell in heaven, but their messengers are here on earth. The psychics, the prophets, the faith healers, the miracle-workers, the telepaths and remote viewers, the exorcists, the ghost hunters, the wiccans, the witches, and other spiritualists, are the ones who are convinced they are talking to heaven. They are of the number of those who email me, trying to prove the existence of the supernatural by recounting credulous stories and wild tales, and so it will be my focus to briefly address the rationality of those claims here.

The second major criticism believers in the supernatural must face is *the blatantly unfair way in which they classify their experiences*. Believers will swear up and down that their seeing a ghost was real and that no one will ever come along and convince them otherwise. But watch them bend over backwards to avoid crediting someone else's spooky experience, if indeed, they happen to disagree with the theology behind that person's experiences. They will explain it away or call it a lie just like we crusty skeptics they tend to abhor. The visions of Islam *and* Catholicism cannot be true at the same time. The revelations of Mormonism *and* the Jehovah's Witnesses cannot be reconciled, so one or both of them must be counterfeit. All of the sudden, skepticism is not the religious man's opponent—other competing religious revelations are! Amazing how the tables turn!

In the year 1917, three young children were said to have seen the Virgin Mary and even received revelations from her on three separate occasions. These revelations were held as secrets to be revealed at certain times. But more than just visions of the Virgin Mary, believers in this tale accept that visible signs in the sun were observed on October thirteenth of that year, though scientists and astronomers reported nothing different about the sun that day than at any other time. The Virgin Mary is called "The Lady of Fatima" in recognition of this event, which took place in Fatima, Portugal, where the Virgin Mary appeared to the three children, Lucia Santos and Jucinta and Francisco Marto. Mary revealed secrets to the children. She commanded them to make restitution for their sins and for all other sinners in the world, and to afflict their bodies in the name of "penance," which they did. In such a highly religious climate, you can imagine how in only a short time, miracles and similar visions were reported. Now everyone was experiencing miracles. In total, it is estimated that some 70,000 people were "witnesses" of God's power as the sun supposedly descended in the sky with a manifestation of brilliant, glorious, divine light.

And another site has become famous. Our Lady of Lourdes Basilica in Lourdes, France has become one of the world's leading cities for Marian apparition admirers to visit. On the fourteenth of February of 1858, a young girl by the name of Bernadette Soubirous was visited by the Virgin Mary. Not just once either, but eighteen times! Since then, every good Catholic and his family of seven kids has visited the site, and among many of these were claimants stating that they had been healed by God of their diseases, just as we would expect. At the time of this writing, the Roman Catholic Church has officially recognized some sixty-six official "miraculous" healings from the holy ground.

Do you believe these stories? How many people would you say believe them? Quite a few. Of what religious persuasion are they? They are almost exclusively Roman Catholic, and to some degree, Greek Orthodox. The Greek Orthodox Church has amassed its own radiant collection of miracles through the centuries, and quite recently, has become militant in campaigning for their universal acceptance...

To the devout Orthodox believer, miracles happen all the time. We cannot neglect to mention the incorrupt holy relics of the church, including the incorrupt right arm of Saint John Chrysostom from the 4th century, the left foot of Mary Magdelene herself, which we are told, has remained at body temperature for the past 2,000 years! Then there's the skull of Saint John the Baptist, and those portions of the true cross of Christ that keep popping up all over the place!

Yes, to this crew, angels regularly appear during religious services. At the Solovki Monastery, a tree has grown in the shape of a cross. A bleeding jug of holy water can be found in one church. The descending of a holy cloud and reappearances of revered dead men are quite common, and many of these holy men are not dead, but alive! Elder Ephraim came to America from Mount Athos of Greece. He was the one to inherit the spiritual legacy of Saint Joseph the Cave Dweller. Elder Ephraim has a monastery in Arizona (Saint Anthony's Monastery). He is said to be clairvoyant. He can read your thoughts and see your sins without you telling him a thing! He can also reveal God's destiny for your life. He has also been known to bi-locate and work miracles, even levitate! He is often spotted bathed in an unearthly light! But if you're a traditional, white, middle-class Protestant, you chalk this up to hooey, plain nonsense from overzealous believers in pagan-ized, apostatized versions of Christianity. That's what the average Church of Christ, Baptist, or Community Bible Church member believes anyway. The apparitional experiences described by non-Catholics differ from those described by Catholics. The Protestants have their own miracles, like Joseph Smith and the delivery of the golden plates for the writing of the Book of Mormon. Seventh Day Adventists have the writings of William Miller, and later Ellen G. White, the so-called prophetess who was taken to heaven and shown that the Ten Commandments are still binding on Christians today. Mary Baker Eddie spoke words of "divine healing" for members of the Church of Christ Scientist. Charles Taze Russell, and later Joseph F. Rutherford, a fill-in Missouri judge, gave birth to the Dawn Bible Students, or as they were later known, the Jehovah's Witnesses.

To atheists and skeptics like myself, we are only one step removed from the stance of practical religionists, like Baptists, Methodists, and the Church of Christ, who accept only Bible miracles as being true. We believe in none of these things. To the rationally-minded, head-scratching affairs and events of the unknown have the potential to be explained rationally. We have no reason to assume otherwise.

The Religious Domino Effect

Supernatural claims by believers cause a domino effect behind them. If not one, just a handful of devout religionists need be present to convince an indiscriminate mass of the "truth" of something. The telling of the littlest events are blown up with word-of-mouth religious and media hype so that they tear right through an unsuspecting populace, creating a state of hysteria. A statue is said to bleed, one parish reports. Suddenly, more statues start bleeding and "revelations" on the meaning of the signs are given by monsignors and priests everywhere. Crop circles appeared in the 1940s and 1950s, and suddenly, the world was full of them, with more elaborate designs being spotted as time went on. Then there are books to explain which of them are hoaxes and which are not. Instead of getting together to decide which supernatural claims hold the most weight, believers ignore their competing groups, get in their own circles with those who are likeminded, and spout off about the undeniable integrity of their claims. If you happen to agree with them, your eyes were opened by God himself, you are blessed. If you are a doubter or a disbeliever, you are a dark heart, an infidel, unenlightened by God's Holy Spirit.
   Despite the impassible walls put up between religious competitors, disputes can get really ugly, but more often than not, they don't. They just ignore the claims of their opposing lighthouses and seek to save others who are open to receiving their particular brand of life raft.

What's Good for the Goose

Had you lived in the ancient world, you would probably have believed and even counted on séances to direct your way. Spiritual seers, sages, priests, and witchdoctors have always had plenty of business. They lack none today, but some were more popular and trusted than others.
   The Oracle of Delphi was believed to be the heart and soul of the entire cosmos, the gateway to the will of the gods and the afterlife. From beyond Greece, all the way to Egypt, the Oracle was revered. Politicians, warriors, and common people alike flocked with offerings to the priestess (the Pythia) who ministered to the masses, telling fortunes, and giving precious advice. Channeling heavenly powers, destinies of deceased loves ones were made known, advice was given on war and business affairs, and divine healing floated through the air. Recountings

of a thick, divine presence were spoken of, and over the passing of many thousands of years, people from all over the world still come to the oracle for more than sight-seeing reasons.

Of course, the track record of the Oracle's "predictions" were none better than today's James Van Praag or John Edwards, but you wouldn't know the difference the way believers in both peddle the accuracy of their predictions. After heavy editing is done, after scenes are spliced, and the right audience members are selected and their readings honed in on, the psychic comes off looking credible to believers in the phenomenon. Beyond vague generalities and typical hit-or-miss cold reading techniques, no one in the séance crowd is a cut above the rest. But don't tell that to believers.

In the end, the fact remains that no real distinctions exist between supernatural claims beyond the hazy walls camps of believers put up between themselves. If we are to believe a spiritualist's or a Christian's claims of seeing angels just before going into life-threatening surgery, then the same must be said of a Mormon or a Catholic, a Muslim or a Hindu in that situation. If we are to believe that God spoke to an Assembly of God preacher and revealed that gossip was ripping apart a church, and that the members of the church must repent, then so must we give the same acceptance to the pagan African tribesmen who chains up the women of his village because God revealed to him that their gossip has deprived the land of precious rain. If we are to believe that a ghost levitated an object in someone's house, then we must believe all such claims that appear even remotely credible. If we grant that one psychic is genuine and not a fraud, we will be hard-pressed to sift through them all to determine who is a fraud and who is not. But now we have a serious problem; in a tumultuous sea of debate, we will quickly be lost in efforts to find what can reasonably be determined to be genuine.

I have had good discussions with some levelheaded people over various pseudoscientific topics, like near-death-experiences. I could state that I was less than impressed with the evidences for them, but that doesn't need to be stated. I am concerned more with the hypothesis in the first place. It is possible for a rational person to get interested in near-death-experiences and be persuaded by evidences he or she finds, while it just as well could have been that had the same person been exposed to a battery of books on out-of-body-experiences or psychic surgery, they would have been sucked into one of those beliefs instead of the one they hold. Anyone can get lost in the mire of debate and remain unable to see just one or a few claims standing out from the rest as true. Even if one becomes fully convinced that the legend of Loc Ness is more than a legend, the arguments for that position may have him falsely convinced, lost in the convincing minutia of a fantasy. If he studies another claim, such as the claims of the Pana Wave Cult of Japan, he may get entrenched in those "evidences" and become a believer and follower in one more unfounded set of beliefs.

I have no objection to someone studying out any of these positions and coming to different conclusions. What I have a problem with is the fact that it doesn't often come to this. No one has the time to thoroughly investigate every position out there before picking one to believe in. But the believer has a preference anyway—usually whichever belief came wrapped up with the stork that delivered them to mom and dad.

What is needed is a consensus of truth. Maybe one day things will be different, but in the fight for being accepted as truth, such myths have lost out time and again to verifiable fact. At present, skepticism reigns supreme. Supernaturalism and the beliefs of the pseudoscientific disciplines are still the underdogs who haven't fought their way to the top to become contenders to take on real science, the champion.

My Own Experiences

On my exit from Christianity, through my investigation of liberal Christianity, and on into my consideration of spiritualism, I went through a desperate time in my life where I grasped at straws in an effort to believe that mankind could actually talk to the dead! In a diehard effort to reclaim my withered faith, I gave myself over to the advice of the séances. I figured that if Christianity wasn't true, maybe some other divine form of communication was. Maybe I could transcend this cumbersome body and sail across space and time into the netherworld. I didn't believe it, but embarrassingly, I humbled myself to follow psychic James Van Praag's instructions on how to contact my spirit guide. Well, there was no payoff!

I meditated over and over and kept waiting for an inner-awakening inside to enable me to see the unseen. After a while of trying, I gave up because – needless to say – it didn't work! The only "contact" I made was with my sanity again, letting me know I would no longer be embarrassing myself in such a manner. My days of waiting for a knock at the door from some prophet of God, who would save my emaciated soul were over.

The Sylvia Brownes, the John Edwards, and the Anthony Carrs of this world are unimpressive enough for even a somewhat casual religionist to write off. Their generalities, word-baiting techniques, and constant misses are a giveaway of their manipulative nature, but when an audience has already fallen head-over-heels for the psychic, when almost every single audience member present came to contact a dead loved one, it doesn't take much to convince the crowd. Skeptics and atheists don't go to these meetings. They have better things to do. Like preachers and other religious leaders with great charisma, the typical wiles of a psychic derailing the average person can sometimes be impressive. The psychic con artist is a master of the verbal manipulating of words, details, and situational exchanges to his or her favor, and sometimes this isn't done consciously. The psychic actually believes in their own abilities. A number of police departments use psychics as help for investigative work, but it is staggering to consider how often they fail. The success stories are the big ones you hear about on Court TV and news specials. Of those, the psychics themselves became detectives by following clues already made public in local newspapers. Revealing that "the boy is laying near a grassy field" is not spectacular, nor is giving directions to the spot as "in a hilled area," or "over a ravine by a river." If you were an abducting murderer and had to dispose of a body, where else would you take your victim? In the city? By a highway? Not if you had any sense. Of killers caught and kidnapped or deceased children found, *someone* has to make the right guess based on the clues. Detectives worldwide are waking up every morning to a cup of coffee and another hard day of trying to track down killers and rapists who have successfully evaded law enforcement for years. How are the psychics helping this? They aren't, but let one fortunate outcome of a rescue effort involving a psychic come about, and the endless songs of praise come the psychic's way, not the detective's.

When employing common sense to determine just how effective these psychics should be, we are disappointed. You would think that the psychic could give a full name, address, and detailed physical description of the offenders, just as you would think that every faith healer would be able to go down the line healing everyone of any and every disease, condition, and ailment they are afflicted with. But that is what we do not see. Instead, we get excuses, clever and creative reasons as to why this doesn't happen. I dare say that if it were possible, Osama Bin Laden would have been in custody long ago if remote viewing powers existed (as we are told by some that they are used by the U.S. government in covert operations). It would be a cinch to get a military ESP team together and put them to good use. Yet, psychics and soothsayers are as worthless in such matters as they are for using their powers to get winning lottery numbers—if they could do it, they would! This is no different from the alarmist Christians who tell us that the events of September 11, 2001 were predicted in the Bible and sent as visions to prophets beforehand (Where were they on September 10th?)

On Ghosts and Apparitions

In the ministry, I came across a few occasions that were purported to be genuine hauntings. To sum up, here are the observations I came to flush out when dealing with these unknowns…

First, the setting of a haunting is usually typical and myth-fitting: To me, this consideration proved to be an important part of investigating a supernatural claim. What was the event? In what setting did it happen? Chances are, someone had a spooky experience during a Ouija board experiment, noticed an all-too-common crop circle in a wheat or corn field, went to a séance for a reading, or stayed in an old house where people have been reported to have died tragically. What you don't hear about are the more off-the-wall events, such as a haunting in a brand new house, a ghostly rustling of papers in a closed office building in a business meeting, or a public appearance of an object levitating. The typical haunting scenarios are too expected, which begs consideration that perhaps said ghostly phenomenon was read into an already "spooky" setting.

Second, the one who recounts a ghostly encounter has a genuine belief in the supernatural: The most memorable of my short-lived ghost-hunting experiences occurred while I was at my second preaching work. There, one Friday evening, I received an almost frantic call to come and pray over "a definitely haunted house." I remember the anticipation I felt driving over there to investigate. I think a part of me was hoping to take back some material proof of the spirit world. Upon arriving, I walked in to be met by two excited and scared parishioners who walked through each room of the house with me, describing the spooky things that happened in each one. The most intriguing part of it all were the photographs, taken with three different cameras over a three-and-a-half year period in the same house. The photographs revealed orbs of light in star-like points and in strung-out "arms," near and around the second youngest boy in the family. I was given the pictures to take with me to investigate. I took the time to show them to an affluent camera operator friend who assured me, "I have seen things like this before…I'm sure there is a natural explanation for them." He suggested that dust particles, condensation, and lighting conditions of the area offered many possible explanations for their presence, making them unremarkable. While getting the details from them on the unexplained events that had been happening, I was barraged with continual affirmations of their belief in the supernatural and exorcisms. They even asked me if I had the power to exorcise the demons if need be. I reminded them that I would have to look into this. The Church of Christ did not believe in exorcisms or live, active "demon possession," so I told them I would just pray over the house and family. These congregants were obviously ready to believe this was ghostly phenomenon. Even before this time, they were always of a superstitious vein. It seemed as though they kept bringing up the supernatural, and now something like this happens?

Third, a legend develops or is adapted to explain or give a context to the haunting phenomenon: On this particular occasion, these talkative brethren finally came up with a reason for why this haunting was taking place. Supposedly, an angry maid was having an affair with the husband of a wealthy family who lived in their house back in the 1920s. They fought bitterly over the adultery and the man eventually chose to divorce his wife. She left the house, and allegedly, consulted a dabbler in the Occult to put a curse on him. A month later, he died in that house. Sounds like a fantastic enough story. I did manage to get sound information on the house and the situation. A wealthy family did live in that house, and the man died while living in it, but beyond that, nothing else was true. They said they "heard" the rest was true, but I "heard" from more numerous and reliable sources (people who were alive and knew the old owners) differently. There was no satanic curse, no cheating maid, or any of the other embellished details that the family managed to cook up. Knowing the all too human tendency to exaggerate, I have no doubt they heard the same details of the story I heard and blew them up into a mostly fictional tale.

Ghost stories are like health problems—everyone has plenty they are ready to talk about. In 1993, when an aunt and uncle moved into a new house, strange things began to happen. They weren't even settled in when sightings of a young man walking around the house in a white t-shirt were reported. My aunt said this figure saved one of my little cousins from having an asthma attack at night. Another ghostly figure in that house was evil, a floating presence in the form of a shifting, black trash bag that slithered from room to room, choking certain family members and waking them up at night, causing them to gasp for breath. Pots and pans were heard in the sink moving by themselves, and strange sightings down hallways were seen. My uncle and one cousin noticed none of these things, however. But when the spookiness reached its height, lo and behold, a story appeared to explain it. The house was built on an Indian graveyard and a man fitting the description of the one seen in the house had committed suicide there! Wrong on both counts. Neither tale was true. My superstitious aunt and mother surmised them into reality after my uncle first suggested it as a joke. We did not find any truth in these stories. We did, however, later find a gas leak in that house. This may well account for the distinct hallucinations that some of them experienced—encounters with spirits that behaved, looked, and felt differently. In just about all cases where I looked, stories or large details of stories were concocted alongside an unexplained event.

Fourth, the ghostly phenomenon is accompanied by a possible alternate explanation(s): I always found myself being led away from accepting a phenomenon as divine or supernatural because I found an at least equally plausible explanation running alongside the supernatural model. The family in the house with the orb pictures and my cousin's house could all be explained neatly by staying with natural assumptions. It is far easier to believe that a lot of minds are having tricks played on them than to just assume that these bewildering events are all supernatural in origin. I am obligated as a rational creature to draw only those conclusions that are warranted by the evidence, and since outrageous claims demand outrageous proof, I cannot intelligently go out on a limb to grant a divine occurrence without airtight evidence for the case. Call it being a little too cautious, maybe even closed-minded, but if we lower the standards of proof, we will certainly be driven with the wind and tossed with every spurious claim that comes and goes our way.

Fifth, details of a ghostly encounter are often erroneous or exaggerated: Here, we are talking about the telling and *re-telling* of an experience. I have found that details and crucial points of a story were at first exaggerated, then recounted in a different order, or flatly negated or omitted at a later time. Going back to our excited couple with the orb pictures, out of caution and an attempt to come away with an accurate understanding of the events, I asked them for what they thought was the most telling assurance to them that this event was indeed paranormal. They proceeded to inform me that the dryer has a timer alarm that goes off for a very short time and never any longer. But on this occasion, the ghost must have gotten to it because it went a whole hour without stopping and without even being plugged in! After affirming several times, *"No, seriously. There is no way that dryer timer alarm could have gone off like that. It wasn't plugged in and even if it was, the buzzer couldn't run that long,"* I was almost halfway persuaded there was some sort of electromagnetic field in the house responsible for both the pictures and this quirky dryer, but asking him about the event two days later, the man told me that the dryer was indeed plugged in, and the couple discovered by reading the dryer's handbook (when all else fails, read the instructions!) that there was a way to readjust the buzzer setting for an hour. This detail had conveniently been forgotten about (or purposefully omitted, I do not know). Now, I have to scratch the dryer experience too. One by one, the pieces of the puzzle became much less captivating and far less deserving of my time and effort.

Lessons from Thor's Hammer

Drawing on knowledge, we know much more about our world now than we did millennia ago, and we know that ignorance of our natural world promotes confusion and superstition. It is truly shocking to see the ignorant notions that were once believed by a fearful populace and how these notions have been thrown by the wayside with the findings of science. Lightening was what was produced when Thor's hammer struck a great object out of holy wrath in the heavenly realm. The stars were once thought to be points of light from the realm of the gods to shine down upon mankind. Thunder was the result of the last roundtable discussion that turned into a heated argument amongst the most high gods. Floods and droughts punished the prideful, blizzards the irreverent, volcanoes and tsunamis the impious. Vegetation died because not enough children were sacrificed to the crocodiles of the Nile. Rainbows existed because a deity took his finger and drew a symbol of his covenant he made with man in the sky. That was the way things were. Now we know better. Now things are different. Oscar Wilde said, "Science is the record of dead religions."

Chapter 19
On Morality

Morality from a Godless Standpoint

"Doing good to others is not a duty, it is a joy, for it increases our own health and happiness."
- Zoroaster

"Let us be careful in dealing with those who attach great importance to being credited with moral tact and subtlety in moral discernment!"
- Nietzsche

Perhaps the second biggest concern to anyone investigating atheism is in regard to the subject of morality. If an atheistic worldview is assumed by an individual – that person being confident enough to conclude that any evidences for the existence of a deity are insufficient to warrant belief in – the next subject considered in connection with unbelief is moral accountability. Why be moral without God? What incentive is there to do right verses wrong? What is "right" and "wrong" without a concept of a supernatural god anyway? If God does not exist, then isn't morality completely relative, with no principles of ethical guidance and directional stability whatsoever?

For some, these are the really big questions that burn to be answered. I say, for some, because it is mostly religious people who feel like they need answers on this matter. Having been a theist, I understand these questions. Some believers honestly do not know how and why non-religious thinkers live stable, upright lives, and how we can call a thing "good" or "bad" with any sort of meaning. To atheists and other grades of freethinkers, morality is a very simple subject, explained completely by naturalistic principles.

A secular morality is composed of two core components. Those components are *Contract Behavior* and *Enlightened Self-interest*.

I. Contract Behavior: the basis of all morality

Contract behavior is a mandatory arrangement of standards or rules which must exist to keep a society in order. This is not a layout of any particular set of laws or moral regulations, per se, but a simple principle that allows societies to remain intact when all the members of a group agree to abide by certain ethics and rules. Generally, all intelligent animals – not just humans – honor this principle without thinking about it or putting a name on it.

Humans have rules that say stealing is wrong and that murdering one's own kind (without cause or provocation) is wrong. The entire human family has these rules, but so do bears, wolves, lions, and baboons. So too with each and every intelligent form of life in existence which happens to be higher than mindless bacteria or base organisms that operate on instinct only. Granted, the specifics of the morals are different from group to group, from species to species, but the high points of contract behavior are the same. Try stealing a lion's food— you will find out the hard way that they have a principle against stealing as well!

And despite what some would have us believe about the animal kingdom, animals seldom kill outside of necessity. They kill based on their own systems of morality and need. Wolves will attack any one member of their pack who tries to mate if he is not the alpha dog. One bear will attack another to safeguard their cubs. Lions will kill the offspring of another male to preserve his own seed and to protect himself when he is older. Baboons may well kill each other fighting over a mate. Peacocks, despite possessing colorful beauty and mobile grace, carry out vicious, competitive bouts to claim their highly prized mates. However terrible these "laws of the jungle" may seem to civilized you and I, they are rules nonetheless, rules that remain constant and help to enhance and preserve the species that adopts them. There is method behind the madness!

The more complex a society or species becomes (i.e. humans over lions), the higher the form of morality that society or species adopts. Humans face multifaceted issues that lions don't face. A human boy must determine what he should do when he is dumped by his girlfriend. In a rage, he can kill her, or he can seek the affections of someone else and try to make her jealous, or he can cut his losses and move on with his life. A father must decide whether he should have an affair with his secretary and risk his wife finding out, or whether or not he can live with himself, knowing that by having the affair he is breaking her trust. He knows he would be disappointed if she did the same to him. A boss must decide how to reprimand an employee who breaks the company rules. He can fire him and tell him to get his stuff and get out of the building and risk coming off like a hard ass, or he can sit him down calmly at his desk and politely tell the man that for the sake of the company and himself, it would be best if he started looking for a job elsewhere.

But since animals don't face complex issues like we do, this sometimes gives us the illusion that we are not animals, but something "higher." This simply isn't true. It is typical human arrogance that causes us to see ourselves in that light. We are every bit just as much animal as our primate, meat-eating cousins, despite our enormous 1400 cc brain sizes. We have the same basic emotions, like love, confusion, excitement, and anger. We play and show juvenile aggression in games of competition and challenges. We kill members of our species (sometimes without a worthy cause). We break laws and contracts we make with each other, whether verbal or written. We fight over mates and show egotistical tendencies in relationships with our fellow man. On and on we could go. We might look down on our distant animal kindred, but their issues are just as significant to them as ours are to us. A wolf who refuses to dismount mating because he is not the alpha dog with rites to mate, must defend himself or be killed. Occasionally, that wolf leaves the pack and decides to start his own—most of the time a very dangerous maneuver! That wolf is ostracized or ex-communicated, much like a shunned, impenitent church member who leaves the fold. In a simplistic way, animals, like humans, break contracts—the agreements they make to live with each other.

Chickens have a "pecking order." Should any chicken peck out of that order, they will be chastised. That is their way. The members in the wrong must suffer the consequences for their actions (wounds, ostracism, death, etc.). They have an evolved working order to which they hold, a basic form of morality, the beginnings of culture even. So the same principle that tells lions not to steal from one another teaches humans and bears and baboons the same lesson—a society cannot exist without social structure, and therefore, a "wrong" and a "right." These terms have differing meanings between species, but they are always constructed out of the need for social order and survival. Regulations supporting these socially ordered behaviors are contracts, and contracts upheld and contracts broken form the basis of moral or immoral behavior. Thus, I refer to the principle as Contract Behavior.

So it should go without saying that animals are completely "moral" in their respective ways without a god. They don't go around unsatisfied about how their acts of compassion and aggression are useless because a spirit is not commanding them. Animals conform because their society and their identification with it demands that they conform so. The incentive is acceptance by the fellow members of their group, and the purpose behind it is that they find satisfaction in doing what makes them useful units to their groups. Emotional creatures need the love and support of their kind. If they do "wrong" they are ostracized, if "right" they are praised. The terms "right" and "wrong" only have meaning according to the accepted ways of the given species. The animal kingdom is full of species that feel need and significance in honoring the standards of their own societies without the slightest feeling that their ways are more or less meaningful without a deity. They have not the faintest knowledge of the existence of a god, no fear of burning in a place of fire for refusing to live a certain way. They don't for a moment suppose that if there is no chicken or wolf or lion god, that their ways are useless and that they can do whatever they want without fear of consequences. There is nothing more natural than the development of moral systems of order.

Is there a single reason why the answers above do not equally apply to human animals? If naturalistic drives and the erecting of primal laws to keep a society of animals together is sufficient for animals, why would this be insufficient for humans? Not only is God not needed for morality, but the idea of a god-ordained system of authority only gets in the way of a naturalistic morality.

The highlights of morals were made to keep social order and maintain the status quo. Even if it could be conclusively shown that no god existed, this would not make stealing or cold-blooded murder one bit more acceptable to a society; and if it could be indisputably demonstrated that a god exists, this would not make conforming to principles of social order as we know them one bit more right. Morals exist apart from a divine being. At least as far as morality is concerned, a god is superfluous. The existence of such a being adds nothing to the mix of what humankind determines is good or evil.

Humans are complex creatures, living in complex and diverse cultures. It cannot be a fair statement to say that there is anything simple about the species, Homosapiens. But one thing unites us all – not a god – but contract behavior. The Head hunters of Borneo are a warrior people, and though they have been recently touched with a hint of civilization, tribal violence still occurs in their homeland of Malaysia. These warriors are taught from birth that to be a "good" head hunter and to earn the right to mate as an adult, you must take the head of one of your enemies. This has been their way for thousands of years, and no matter how terrible it may seem to us westernized Americans, it has worked well for them, much like human sacrifices in the old world. These were not reckless, uncoordinated murders. They were ritual executions, important and cherished rites.

I would love to step out and take a long look down on these people and call them "evil." I believe they are, but not from an anthropological point of view. They are not "evil" by their standards, though they would be considered so by my own. But despite the drastic moral differences between more civilized peoples and the Head Hunters, contract behavior still joins us. Many states and countries still impose the death penalty for certain crimes in place of beheadings. While I see serious differences between this and hunting heads, the value of each practice serves a purpose to each society. These are not examples of chaos or lack of moral order, they are regulations, regardless of whether an individual considers them morally upright and civilized or not. We could spend quite a long time listing examples of regulated third world cultures which, aside from falling short of our expectations for humanitarian excellence, manage to maintain a working culture where chaos does not abound. In order to survive, contract behavior had to be in place or the society could never have survived.

My Critics

Naturally, the points made thus far are not beyond criticism. My critics will argue that my comparison of animal and human moral systems is invalid, that animals cannot be called "moral or immoral" in any true sense of the word because humans have the ability to conceptualize, to think ahead and make decisions between options, whereas animals are limited to not much more than instinct. This objection is moot.

The difference between the advanced decision-making abilities of humans and the instinctual actions of animals is one of degree only. The complexity of human morals and the ability to choose between many options comes from evolution; our intellects surpass those of the animal kingdom, but we still operate like animals. Our drives are primal; love, hate, anger, excitement, curiosity, embarrassment, fear, and jealousy are animal emotions. And it is humbling to consider that despite our species' complexity, we are every bit as predictable as any other animal species.

It cannot be denied that it is because of our intelligence that humankind affects the world in a more extensive way than do animals. Humans are capable of saving wildlife and committing genocide on a much larger scale than the animals ever could, but the fact remains that the principle of what is morally sufficient for the animal kingdom is sufficient for the kingdom of man. Contract Behavior is sufficient; societies can survive in degrading conditions, so long as the basics of morality are intact (prohibitions against murder and theft). Moral precepts of man beyond these are merely additives.

The Additives

Being that we have conceded man's animal nature, his complexity, and his incredible diversity, we must be careful to distinguish between contract behavior and false additives to it, which are extraneous as far as survival is concerned. Moral necessity and utilitarian thinking is not the only means by which ethics are established. Religion provides the rules for many people. These rules, believed to have been spoken by God, are considered ultimate laws. They cannot be broken without suffering the consequences. God makes the rules and we have to abide by them, so they say. But religious laws are superfluous; Muslim Shariah law is one example; Christian-based laws, as set up during the colonial period, is another.

In 1682, Pennsylvania's Great Law declared that only Protestant Christian worship was to be allowed, and if this law was violated three times, death was the penalty—so much for the idea that the colonists came to America to set up a society of religious liberty! In fact, all laws – including almost all secular laws – are the particulars of every human society, and are thus additives. Man loves to employ policies and laws in the name of keeping order. He sets up state, federal, and local laws to improve the quality of life, but these are not absolutely necessary for survival. They only help out.

Distinguish between the natural principles of contract behavior and those contracts made out of religious piety between gods or religious leaders. They may all involve agreements, but when we speak of contract behavior, we are speaking of strictly utilitarian laws. Religious teachings are not. They rely on submission to a spiritual leader. They are extraneous, and more often than not, useless, but contract behavior and religion can sometimes overlap. That is, religion is seen as a means to preserve moral order. In reality, it is not needed, but it can act in conjunction with natural principles of contract behavior underneath the religious garb.

For instance, in many parts of Afghanistan, the police enforce religious ordinances *along* with prohibitions against theft and murder. To them, Muslim law should be bound on all people just as surely as principles like "thou shalt not steal." Here is where the secularist draws the line. We don't serve a god. We refuse to submit ourselves to the laws of one. Why should I submit myself to the laws of a god I have no faith in? I put no stock in Hindu rules for life. Such rules are needless to me, but for the people that submit themselves to this system of religious authority, the rules are important because, in their case, Hinduism attaches to itself the enforcement of contract behavior, which, as we have seen, binds and directs lives. It has power over them like our own beliefs do over us, and the world continues to go round—morality intact. I already have a respect for contract behavior, for naturalistic principles of moral conformity. Men may disagree on the particulars, specifically where devoutly religious people are involved, but we can keep order in our disagreements. We don't need the laws of a higher power to preserve moral order. Therefore, as an atheist, I will bypass the gods and go straight to the morality they supposedly represent.

Relativism, Government, and the Iron Rule

About now, a theist accuses the naturalist of belief in moral relativism, the idea that what has been presented here is nothing more than my opinion, and that without a god, I am left with no decisive answers on what is good and what is bad. I can, after all, say "to hell with society" and decide to take a baseball bat to everyone I don't like! Much hogwash has come from religious and irreligious people alike as they discuss "objective" verses "subjective" morality, when those on both sides use the terms only at the expense of understanding morality. Call it a product of relativism or absolutism, but true morality comes ultimately from *need*. The individual and the society both play a part; the individual searches out the moral side of things. He follows his own moral compass, but society doesn't work that way. Societies and governments are concerned with utilitarian and pragmatic concerns. Governments are not moral or immoral—they are effective or ineffective. It is their job to enforce what works, not what is "right."

Because contract behavior-based morality deals only with the bare essentials of surviving, when we speak of moral considerations beyond mere survival, we are "going off the map," so to speak, into uncharted moral waters. Life on an island may be simple as a small group of men and women do what they must to preserve moral order, and this will consist of making non-complicated moral calls. There is simplicity in a small society, but this simplicity is thrown out the window with a nation and a government. In preserving themselves, societies and their governments become lone wolves. It is sometimes in a nation's best interest to wage war on another nation in efforts to preserve their way of life. At this point, we are not talking about "moral" or "immoral," only feasible and unfeasible. Contract behavior doesn't help us anymore.

By what standard is a suicide bomber to be judged? Under what law are we to prosecute the leader of a foreign land for "war crimes"? When heinous acts are done selflessly and in the name of a greater good, what wrong was committed? The suicide bomber who blows himself up because he believes he is killing the enemies of his people who are trying to steal his land is not doing a bad thing—except in the eyes of outsiders who do not understand his plight. A president or a king who defeats his opposition may be a murderer in the eyes of his enemies, but he is serving and preserving his country as many would see it.

When we began this chapter, we examined the simple moral connections between intelligent animals and showed how basic wrongs and rights in nature run through each species. But now we present the limitations of contract behavior. Murder is a defined term. It can only be committed in view of a society's definition of it because what is murder to some is not murder to others. The same with theft. In war, plundering the enemy's camp and taking weapons is good strategy, not "evil." But when terms like murder and theft are defined in the eyes of societies and applied within, we find that they are identical in each society. Every society must have these prohibitions or they will not survive—that is what objective morality is. All other moral convictions are essentially subjective, changing with times and cultures. There can be no agreement on these things. As complex as the human species is, with its brain-bending problems and ethical dilemmas, there are not, nor will there ever be easy answers to our problems. Having bigger brains than primates often doesn't help us in goodness and virtue. It only complicates our decisions and drops us in the center of a confusing and elaborate maze of decisions from which we cannot escape.

Godless Morality and the Balancing of Societal Morality

The dogmatically religious (particularly those of the Christian persuasion) tend to view godless morality in a very childish way. They seem to think that upon becoming an atheist, a formerly decent person will be more inclined to become a morally dissolute thug. But people do not forget their upbringing and moral conditioning because they lose faith in a religion. People do not suddenly decide to go on a pick-axing spree because mom and dad's old time religion didn't pan out for them. Anyone of any belief system is capable of doing horrible things, and people do such things; rape, extortion, bank robberies, murders, domestic violence, muggings, and hate crimes happen all the time. Anyone can become a criminal if they choose to, and when they do, they mark themselves as enemies of the greater good who must be dealt with accordingly. So should I decide that I don't care about others, but only myself, and decide that it is in my best interest to rob a bank, thinking I can get away with it, I become an enemy—a lawbreaking, contract behavior-violating threat to society. I must then be stopped, like all other moral threats.

There will always be criminals, those who fight against the status quo, malevolent individuals who must be stopped, but few of us stop to consider how few people choose to totally disregard the safety and wellbeing of others. In a world of 6.1 billion people, only hundreds of thousands of serious crimes take place per day. This is a strikingly small number, given the population. No police force can operate without the backing of a supportive civilian populace; rioters are dispersed, only a few of them are arrested. A whole city can't be arrested. People can and do maintain a secular status quo morality. It is not as though lacking churches would throw the world into a state of utter chaos. Even in situations where leaders like Hitler orchestrated many horrible acts, we find that only 3% of Germans claimed allegiance to the Nazi party.

It is interesting how some refer to the balancing out of powers in the universe as The Boomerang Effect. It would have disastrous consequences to drastically modify any aspect of this world. Kill one kind of bug and the bugs which were supposed to be kept in check by it stay around, eat, and overpopulate. But in not too long, nature rights itself so that the struggle for survival balances out. Species go extinct over time, but it is rare in the short term because of nature's tendency to preserve. Nature rights itself so that struggles reach a standstill. One empire might conquer another for 400 years, but after some rebellions and a few bad rulers, by the next millennium, that empire becomes just one among many contemporaries, a big but brief blot appearing in the history books. Diseases, natural disasters, and wars wipe out large portions of societies, but since people keep dying and being born at a comparable rate, the population does not diminish and life goes on as normal. Viewed over the long term, an average is obtained. Society keeps going. A murderer can only take so many lives until the more numerous opposing forces against him get the upper hand. Justice returns. The wrong is righted. Life goes on.

Generally, it can be said that mankind demonstrates great compassion for others of his kind. It can therefore be called a "natural law" when humans exhibit emotional and moral concerns, strongly promoting preservation, instead of the destruction of other races and peoples. However, we would be remiss if we left our discussion without facing the ultimate truth of naturalistic morality: the Iron Rule (that might makes right) is true, in the final analysis.

Suppose another race of beings visited our world. Suppose they came down, and for whatever reason, decided that they needed to learn more about human anatomy. So they find an isolated human, fishing in a lake. They abduct that person and perform whatever experiments on him they choose. The poor human is screaming bloody-murder to be released. Naturally, he feels violated and terrified beyond words. He endures what amounts to sheer torture, and if he lives and is returned to earth, will never be the same again. According to this man, these beings are "evil," perhaps even "demonic," but do you really suppose these beings would care what this lower life-form thought?

What law could we hold them accountable to? Being that they are more powerful and obviously working according to the best interest of their species, is not their morality higher than ours? Logically, we must say that it is, the same way our morality is higher than the fried chicken dinners we consume so thoughtlessly. That chicken had its own will to live, but your morality had a higher say in the matter. The higher/greater/more powerful good must always be served; you are less important than your race as a whole. When one acts according to the best interest of their species (no matter what species that happens to be), how can they be faulted for it? The cheetah is not evil when it consumes the gazelle as his meal. It is feeding, a thing that ruthless nature put into play. This is certainly not encouraging to think about, but it is indisputably true. We must remember that we live in a universe that doesn't give a damn about our hurt or our wellbeing, either way. Sad, but true.

As with any hypothetical alien species, even so with mankind: when push comes to shove, it is our dominance, our power, our own pursuit of ideals and sense of preservation that determines right and wrong, though this only applies to collective powers (species, races, factions, groups, causes, etc. It does not apply haphazardly and individually to mere "bullies").

II. Enlightened Self-interest: the second principle of morality

Egoism

Enlightened self-interest is the second principle of a freethinker's morality. When all is said and done, we live for ourselves. We are egoists, each doing what ultimately makes us happy and brings us some sort of fulfillment. The most humbling, noble, and selfless efforts manage to give something back to the one who does them. The religious believer searches for the comforts of eternal salvation, and when he thinks he's found it, it gives him mental satisfaction to believe that others might receive the same thing once he tells them about it and persuades them to receive it.

One has a hard time wondering how selfless one can be, but even these acts are ego-driven. Those who do so operate out of the desire to reap the rewards of heaven some day, to get an extra star in that shining crown. Yes, humans are selfish creatures, as are all animals. We can't help but be so. But if all actions are ego-driven at their source, then our primal instinct to survive is at the top of that pyramid.

Self-preservation

Nothing is more precious to us than our lives and the lives of our loved ones, and when our lives are threatened, we choose to preserve our lives over the ones threatening to take them. Individuals fight to save their lives. Communities and cities have local systems of law enforcement to preserve life and domestic tranquility. Nations go to war to preserve their ways of life. This is the height of preservation, and it is more than justified. Someone who kills in battle or in defense of their own life is not looked at like a degenerate addict who murders to get money for a cocaine fix.

But morality goes beyond this to social situations, complex social situations where societies have grown as large and as complex as they are today. Michael Shermer, in "The Science of Good and Evil," p. 41, observes...

> Sociologists know that once groups exceed 200 people, a hierarchical structure is needed to enforce the rules of cooperation and to deal with offenders, who in the smaller group could be dealt with through informal personal contracts and social pressure. Still larger groups

need chiefs and a police force, and rule enforcement involves more violence or the threat of violence. Even in the modern world with a population exceeding six billion individuals, most of whom are crowded into dense cities, people find themselves divided into small groups. Studies on optimal group size (in terms of finding a balance between autonomy and control) by the military during the Second World War found that the average-size company in the British Army was 130 men, and in the U.S. Army it was 223. The 150 average also fits the size of most small businesses, departments in large corporations, and efficiently run factories.

Smaller is better; the smaller the community, the more intimacy there is between members, and consequently, less crime. But with population increases, there are increases in crime. It is quite a pleasant thought to imagine living in a world where we wouldn't need to worry about locking our doors when we go out or safeguarding the passwords to our bank accounts, but it wasn't to be. Extreme measures must be taken to ensure that justice and social structure are upheld. Remember this next time you are pulled over for speeding, or stopped on the way out of a department store and your bags checked because you set off the theft alarms. It is the price we pay for living in big, impersonal nations instead of small, spear-wielding tribes.

Enlightened Self-interest

So far, we have demonstrated the rationale behind moral behavior of the individual. We have seen that conducting ourselves properly is natural and reasonable, but how do we go from serving ourselves to serving others and looking out for their interests? The principle of enlightened self-interest with applied egoism states that I will serve myself *except* when it is in my best interest to serve and help others. I will look out for myself first, but I will also look out for you if it is in my best interest to do so—and it usually is.

If, living 50,000 years ago, I needed to chase a wooly mammoth off a cliff, I would be a fool to try it on my own. Two hunters on the hunt work better than one. I would rather have more friends and less enemies. I don't go around looking for trouble. On the contrary, I am looking for help, for a community to aid me in my survival, and not to be struggling on my own against all odds. Apply this to social situations, big and small. By exchanging nice words standing in a line at a coffee shop, I could be making a friend who will someday save my life, bail me out of debt, or become one of my best friends. The same reasoning would apply to any stranger I meet. Humans are naturally social animals, just like our chimp cousins, but beyond that, we look for friends because it profits us, and scratching each others' backs is what friendship is all about.

What about those situations where it doesn't profit us? Why don't we club someone over the head who disrespects us? Why don't we attack anyone whom we find disagreeable? Again, reason comes to the rescue for those who are normal and rational and sane. In cases where we would become angry and violent with someone, we remember what the consequences of our actions would be. Does hitting a waiter with an attitude put us in a favorable position? Is there a better solution to getting back at a corrupt business colleague than threatening to kill him if he does it again? What avenues does the law provide to rectify this wrong? Even if no options for payback seem to stand out, is it really worth pursuing just for the diminishing returns of sweet revenge? Beyond your satisfaction, what will it profit you? Is it worth it? The wise pick their battles. They don't pick up the sword and fight at every challenge, and often enough, the sword never has to leave its sheathe! So it is enlightened self-interest that serves as a rational basis for morality.

But how do we explain natural selection giving us the ability to put ourselves in harm's way for the sake of someone else? Isn't that contrary to nature? If we see someone drowning and we know we could join them in death by trying to save them, why do we risk it? Where do the virtues of compassion and sacrifice come from in man? From rationality, from contract behavior, and from enlightened self-interest.

As we can see in nature, even the "lesser" animals can sacrifice themselves for the sake of their kind. An older male baboon will throw himself at a predator, surrendering his life to the beast, so his troop can escape the jaws of death. The baboon does not need to be told to love his neighbor as himself to do that. A herd of bison, attacked by a lion, will at first try to flee, but if enough are prepared, they will line up side-to-side to fight off their attacker. The lion will retreat and await a better hunting opportunity in order to avoid being gouged by a mob of horned beasts with tremendous weight advantages. And these bison need only be of the same species to help each other—not necessarily immediate offspring. Love, nature, and rationality enables us to endanger ourselves to help each other because that helps our species to survive.

III. The Alternative: morality through a theist's eyes

Now with theists, morality is quite different. God-based morality tells us that all morality can only stem from a supernatural creator. God is in the heavens, making rules, laying down ordinances and commandments, constantly shaking his finger at man, warning him not to cross the line by doing something he forbids. It is as though man is incompetent of doing anything good were it not for this "godly" influence in the clouds. To a believer, it's not enough to live a moral life. You can't just pay taxes, hold down a job, help the world by excelling in your career, give to charities, raise a family, donate your time and resources to a good cause, or just live a quiet life by yourself in search of knowledge. No, you must acknowledge the right Spirit and keep his ordinances. These ordinances usually have nothing to do with living a more productive life, and are useless as far as improving the world is concerned. But regardless, you've got to do what this deity says.

There was a time when almost every believer in Christianity held that one cannot in any way be moral without the adoption of that religion or its principles, but times have changed. Most theists today will concede that one can in fact live a perfectly good and moral life without being of a certain religious background, only the morals they are living by are not really theirs, but "borrowed" in principle from God. So all secular morality that we atheists follow is simply borrowed from the Christian God, so they say, who originally made all things. America is only law-abiding because it gets its principles from Jehovah. That's what we're told.

I will go on and point out what should be astoundingly obvious thus far—long before Judeo-Christianity was around, laws and moral order were kept just as they are today. And all countries who fail to identify themselves as Christians haven't the slightest concern that the laws they have been living by all these years (Jewish and Muslim countries, for instance) are lacking in some way. So the claim from believers that Christianity is the highest and best form of morality is reduced to nothing but an arrogant breath of hot air. Christians, Muslims, Jews, and believers in any other world religion or no religion at all will likely respect and abide by similar moral precepts. When believers in any religion stand up and declare themselves more moral and just than their spiritual counterparts, we have spiritual snobbery. Though she is by no means alone, Christianity has been exceptionally guilty of this throughout the church's history.

It is this sort of smirking pride which proves to be one of the least desirable qualities of a faith. Morality is morality. It is not mine or yours, nor does it belong to the guy down the street. No temple can claim to have a monopoly on it, and no priesthood can claim to bring it down from the mind of their god and bind it upon the masses. It does not belong to any one race or species or nation. It stands on its own power. Rather than being elusive and complex, it is everywhere and simple. It need not be deciphered or decoded, or translated, or declared by some pious individual, decked in ritual garb. It stands by itself, whether you like it or not. It was not created. It does not come to be, but in our struggle to survive, its presence becomes known. It has no preference to anyone. It does not take sides or play favorites. It cannot be manipulated by councils and seminars. It speaks to all living beings and befriends all with common sense. Living beings often stray from her, but like a tried-and-true best friend, it welcomes us back to its side when our sense of reason returns.

IV. Tag-along Morality: three ways god-based morality is inferior to a reason-based morality

The *first problem* with a god-based morality is that it commits the believer to any and all actions a god commands. "All thy commandments are righteousness," says Psalm 119:105, which means whatever God commands a believer to do is right. We haven't the luxury of determining whether or not a commandment is humane and decent. The follower of God must be as faithful to God's will as Abraham was, who was prepared to offer up his son on the alter (Genesis 22). No matter what action God commands, it must be followed without question—from murder and torture, to rape and mutilation. God decides what is right and no one else can object.

Christians, like all of the civilized world, hated what happened on September 11 of 2001, but they would do the same thing if they were faithful to God and he commanded them to do it. The Muslims obey their violent God's commandment to wage holy war on the world, and it is wrong, but had the God of the Bible been the one to command it, the same act would have been right, and to refuse to go through with it would have been wrong!

The freethinker's morality is not based on such unprincipled reasoning. Morality does not operate so. We are not committed to blindly following the whims and ways of a dictatorial deity, which change from time to time, from religion to religion, and from interpretation to interpretation. Killing is never done so heartily and without remorse as it is in the name of God.

The *second problem* with god-based morality is that what little good Christianity manages to promote (like charity) is limited and offsets itself. Mother Theresa's charitable work in India was motivated by her religion. In her case, something good came from her faith. Though she was at first met with resistance from the Hindu people who disdained conversion to Christianity, when it became apparent that she would be charitable regardless of whether or not they converted to her faith, she was praised for her work. I don't believe her religion was responsible for her good works. I believe that good was in her to do, but

I'll not contest that point here. Let us say without argument that she was good because of her faith. What was her attitude towards science? What was her attitude towards stem cell research and abortion rights? The religion that brought out her benevolence also made her oppose science and use her good name and influence to impede the progress of learning. Her compassion for her fellow human being didn't extend to the mother who was forced to carry a mentally retarded child to term. How can we grant that religion is a benefit to society when its moral reach is merely a trade-off with error? A man who gives to charities but opposes evolution is not doing a good thing. He is trading one good for one bad. Even granting that Christianity can be at times, and with select individuals, a morally productive religion, if its motivation for good is being offset, if it is not complete and balanced across the board, how can it be called a good thing?

Who is really more of a saint? Is it a devout religious man who opens his home to some orphaned children, or a stingy, atheist scientist who never gives a dime to his fellow man, but uses his education to build earthquake-sensing devices, enabling millions of lives to be saved all over the world? A benevolent atheist can compassionately give to the poor while *not* setting back the cause of science. Christianity is motivationally inferior because it does not provide the proper motivation for moral excellence in all areas, whereas an atheist can be equally or more benevolent than a believer. And charity is not all there is to goodness. There is more to decency than feeding starving children. Using our minds to ingeniously make this world a better place is also part of what it means to be called "good."

If we want a superior system of ethics, neither Christianity, nor any other religious belief system need be consulted to achieve this. A compassionate, science-minded individual can be every bit as moral or more so than any believer in superstition. We need only look within ourselves to find the goodness that is already there.

The *third problem* God-based morality exhibits is that it proves to be motivationally inferior. It has to do only with the consequences of our actions. The Christian does good things for a bribe, for a reward (Heaven), and avoids doing bad things to avoid torture, a punishment (Hell).

I will consent that the laws of our land operate this way (that is, people have to know how to act). There must be punishments to a certain degree, but one should not have to be spiritually motivated by rewards or punishments. To do so strikes at the heart of all that can be called "spiritual." One who keeps the law only to get a reward, and one who abstains from an action out of fear of punishment is not a principled individual. That person is operating out of intimidation. Who is to be commended? Would it be one who does great deeds out of the desire to be paid a large amount of money, or one who does so because he believes it is the right thing to do? It doesn't take a Solomon to see the glaringly obvious selection that just about all of us would pick. A criminal who is sentenced to prison, makes life changes, and is paroled, is to be desired over one who regrets getting caught, and intends on maintaining good behavior and a sense of humility just to get paroled so he can try to wrong the world again.

I am not going to "be good" to get some awesome prize up in the sky, nor because of a bully's threat that eternal hellfire awaits me if I refuse to comply. Though most God-believers will claim to serve God out of a "higher" desire to love him, when push comes to shove, it is still basically a fear-motivated service. Should they apostatize from their faith by reasoning their way out of it, their deity becomes a galactic bully who punishes with eternal damnation. This is clearly an inferior system of morality in every conceivable way.

Chapter 20
God's Little Shop of Horrors

The Biblical Message of Eternal Damnation

"Hell is an outrage on humanity. When you tell me that your deity made you in his image, I reply that he must have been very ugly."
- *Victor Hugo*

"The doctrine of eternal punishment is in perfect harmony with the savagery of the men who made the orthodox creeds. It is in harmony with torture, with flaying alive, and with burnings. The men who burned their fellow-men for a moment, believed that God would burn his enemies forever."
- *Robert Green Ingersoll*

Whether or not God wants to torture you is not the issue—that God *will* torture you is. If you do not please him in this life, if he does not deem your conduct acceptable to him, then you are going to face the Alpha and Omega's eternal retribution in the next life. Should you die in an unsaved condition, you will face the unchecked wrath of an infuriated, emulous God who will stop at nothing to make sure his enemies pay for their crimes against him. So says the New Testament of the *loving* Lord and Savior, Jesus Christ.

Ten thousand centuries will come and go, and not one day in Gehenna will have ended. In the amount of time it takes a new universe to expand and collapse, not a single evening in the furnace of Hell will have gone by. In Hell, you'll have nothing to do and nothing to think about except your past and how you were nothing but a terrible disappointment to your creator. In addition to all the unceasing and unspeakable pain you'll be feeling, you will have the added despair of knowing that the life you lived in the flesh was completely in vain. You will be fully awake to experience a nightmare above any nightmare you ever experienced while alive. And just when you think you can't take anymore, an eternity of suffering awaits you still.

At least, that was the traditional view of Hell. For totally understandable reasons, this view is losing out in popularity. Today, you can attend some churches for 30 years and not hear a peep about Hell. People are ashamed of this merciless idea. They are ready for something new, for what modern apologists think is a better take on the destiny of the unsaved. They are championing the acceptance of what they consider to be a more merciful form of suffering in the afterlife, one that is better in tune with a warm and loving Jesus with outstretched arms and a great big smile, like the one portrayed in that painting on your parent's wall in their bedroom or living room.

I am convinced that the doctrine of eternal damnation has always been what makes more infidels out of men than any other bestial ideal of scripture. It makes the God of the Bible a villain like nothing a Hollywood producer ever brought to life on the big screen. And what we have here is a whitewashing; the superstitious mindset of the populace used to be one that could accept a "merciful" deity who casts swarms of people into a lake of fire, but not anymore. That won't fly. So Christian apologists are asking you to just forget what every unrefined country Roman Catholic, Baptist, Methodist, or Pentecostal preacher ever told you about Hell. Just listen to these new oracles of the brotherhood! This is not really a new view as much as it is revitalized for the likes of the educated minds of today. Many defenders of the faith tell us that the fires of Hell are figurative, and so is the actual suffering experienced in the home of the damned.

During my preaching years, I participated in discussions on the nature of Hell, and some of these were quite entertaining. Some of these spats came down to preachers affirming that hell contained "a spiritual form of fire that tortures sinners eternally," or "some sort of spiritual pain in another dimension that Jesus described as physical burning." Others went the traditional route, "Real fire awaits sinners in the next world." So does this mean that God established that spirits would retain some form of a nervous system that enables them to feel pain sensations even when they are disembodied?

Old and problematic as this last belief is, it should be said that some preachers still fervently maintain that it is correct—sinners are literally barbequed all day, everyday! This is not an exaggeration. I once had a member of a church hand me a tape of a preacher woman from a holiness church in Alabama, who said she went to Hell in a spirit journey so she could describe its horrors firsthand. She stated that the unsaved are trapped in gloomy darkness on very small islands that they are chained to. At the end of each day, these lost souls are "burnt to a crisp," after which time they are again made whole, only to have the process start over and over again for all eternity. Very sadistic thinking, I must say!

If what modern apologists say is true, centuries of learned gospel preachers have been dead wrong in affirming the reality of such a place. These contemporary Christian thinkers tell us that the suffering experienced in Hell is just suffering in the mind (in the spirit mind) of a deceased unbeliever. As he passed into eternity, his body died while his spirit (and therefore consciousness) lived on, but now his soul was separated from God into the "blackness of darkness" of the absence of the Almighty (Jude 1:13). This creates misery all by itself, and this likewise alleviates God from actually creating a Hell or inflicting pain personally. God just made sinners immortal as he has all human beings, and they chose to live in such a manner as to make God separate himself from them so that his righteousness would not be compromised.

This might sound a little nicer than the traditional view of a fiery Hell, but it is just as bad as the first. Upon further consideration, the position meets a quick and brutal end. Of all the dying and struggling theological positions out there, this one actually makes you feel sorry for modern Christians as they face the embarrassment of having a God who openly approves of everlasting torture. There's really no way to water it down, though theists try with the help of a fire hydrant.

For starters, this new position denies some pretty plain scriptural language that seems to teach a literal place of torment (Luke 12:4-5). While good arguments can be made for a Hell with figurative fire, it is undeniable that Luke 16:19-31 portrays the existence of a place of real suffering, the kind we were used to in our living bodies. If this is not the case, then the writer of Luke woefully misrepresented the facts—under inspiration of the Holy Spirit no less! But regardless of the presence of fire, we need not get bogged down in disputed details. The scriptures teach some form of suffering of the ungodly beyond the grave.

Regardless of the how, the God of the Bible still makes it clear that he wants disobedient souls that will never be redeemed to stay around for eternity and be miserable. Sure, it wasn't his original will for them, but he doesn't feel for us sinners enough to actually deliver us from all possible suffering. God decided that it was fine with him if we suffer for a lifetime of mistakes, no matter how sincere those mistakes may have been in their making. We infidels are headed to a place of agony to grope in the darkness of damnation. Our unending groans for mercy will not cause him to have pity on us and deliver us from the pitiful condition we will be in. It would just be too much for him to put the sinner out of his misery, to blot him out of existence when he dies.

God has declared that "there will be a resurrection of the dead, both of the just and unjust" (Acts 24:15), and "them that sleep in the dust of the earth shall awake, some to everlasting life, and some to shame and everlasting contempt" (Daniel 12:2). God may have wanted all to be saved, but since they "chose" not to be, he is pleased to see them suffer unimaginable pain. The fact that he can stand by and watch as some of his children endure endless centuries of anguish – anguish a man or a woman could not possibly deserve from a single lifetime of bad deeds – is what makes him a hideous, indescribable presence. To call him an exceedingly cruel cosmic tyrant makes him sound much nicer than he really is!

Getting an unbeliever to accept the concoction called Hell is the hardest thing for a believer. The problem for the Christian is that they are always better, kinder, and more compassionate than the deity they serve. They would never dream of leaving even a small animal to die a prolonged death out in the street, much less suffer forever, and yet they are compelled to defend their God's employment of this indefensibly merciless treatment of the unsaved. He knew when he created man and gave him an "immortal soul" that this would forever seal the fates of sinners to an eternity of unspeakable miseries. He went right on with our creation anyway.

The search for truth is not without its ironies, however. In this case, the irony catches the believer off guard; this new perception of Hell is an even more fiendish one than the traditional fiery view they are trying to get the whole world to abandon. It is not difficult to think of how the nature of each person's "hell" would be distinct and varying according to one's spiritual vices.

Advocates of this "more compassionate" view tell us Hell's suffering would be in the mind, the result of being away from the light of God, presumably feelings of loneliness, shame, hopelessness, and perhaps other agonies. So we could surmise that one who lived a life of pride might suffer an eternity of humiliation, and a person who belittled his fellow man with verbal abuse and degradation would forever be ridiculed as he ridiculed others. I suppose the same would be true for those who lived lives committing rape and murder. They would mentally experience for eternity the hurt they caused others. This would be directly in line with the Bible's teaching that we reap what we sow according to what was done in the body (2 Corinthians 5:10). Or would this be a fear-based mental Hell? While we're considering alternatives to the fiery Bible Hell, we might as well get creative and go a step further. Why not a personal, Freddy Krueger-inspired Hell where we face our worst fears, and not just spiritual vices?

My earliest fears of Hell did not consist of fire at all, but of being confined to a featureless bright white hallway that goes on forever in two directions. It is small and narrow, has no doors or windows, and has no places to sit or lie down. The punishment was to walk forever, enduring loneliness. It wasn't until a certain sincere but misled family member I loved took me aside and told me, "Joe, that idea of Hell is wrong. You will be covered in the flames of fire in Hell, so you better not use the Lord's name in vain!" that I began to be afraid of the fire notion. Someone else might have a fear of worms, or spiders, or being torn apart by a huge demon, in which case they would mentally suffer such things in their minds. This type of Hell would be incomparably worse for each individual than one standard place of suffering for everyone. So if either of these derivations describing the "real" Hell are true, then Hell is not really a place, just a sort of mental/spiritual/psychological software that automatically uploads to the hard drive of our minds when we die to create for us the worst possible afterlife!

Picture a man strapping you down to a chair and attaching a device to your head. It probes your brain to find out where your worst fear lies. When it finds your weakness, it exploits it, subjecting you to the most heightened level of misery conceivable. I fail to see how such an intellection would be any more merciful than Dante's description of a hell with pits of fire and horned demons, punishing naked and tormented souls, buried in pits of dung and boiling blood! Regardless of the details of exactly how it is administered, suffering is suffering and torture is torture, no matter what form it takes.

At the base of all this terror is the fact that none of this can be called justice by any stretch of the imagination. No one, not even the devil himself, could be worthy of truly eternal suffering. Eternal torture is worthless. It does not bring about correction or rehabilitation. It is no means to an end. It does not serve a practical use, unlike governments that apply torture to terrorists to get them to divulge the location of weapons of mass destruction. It is nothing but a cruel and vindictive invention, like the cold, germy, sharp, steel instruments found in the basement of a psychopath used to disfigure his victims.

Hell is a purely brutish payback perpetrated by a powerful barbarian who rules the skies with an easily bruised ego. The slightest thing pisses him off. He runs around with his giant war hammer, scaring the crap out of everyone. But amazingly, he wants to make friends! He is surprised when people run from him and see him as an evil ogre. He apparently doesn't understand why intelligent, decent people want nothing to do with him. No one likes a bully! But now the bully pretends to be compassionate; he throws everyone for a loop by creating the greatest contradiction anyone ever saw; he sends his son to bring a supposed message of peace and mercy. But should you reject his son and his message, the barbarian father again pulls out that trusty war hammer and takes care of business the old fashioned way! You *have* to befriend him…or you get the war hammer!

Any two-bit numbskull might even realize that this logically destroys any real "choice" that God assures us we have. We are told that God only sends those to Hell who have chosen to go there, but this is just ridiculous. I could offer you the "choice" of a million dollars or cancer, but even the dumbest halfwit would understand that such a choice would not be a very good one!

This reminds me of a certain Simpson's episode where a cult worshipping "The Leader" comes into Springfield and indoctrinates the whole town into following him. When they put the people into their convent and the people start to express the desire to leave, they say, "You are free to leave at any time." But the moment they try to leave, they are met with attack dogs and spike pits! The God of the Bible is every bit like these funny cartoon characters, offering unbeatable hope and bliss on the one hand, and misery and torture on the other.

The doctrine of Hell will never be compatible with a merciful deity. A nice, smiling preacher in a suit, writing smooth articles, trying to make the position sound refined and graceful won't work. Taking literal fire out of the picture will not do it either. The smallest fiber of common sense tells us that we put a sick dog out of its misery. We don't torture it because it bit us on the leg. Hell defies decency, civility, morality, compassion, and sound judgment. I am glad to see modern Christians becoming ashamed to profess belief in it.

Chapter 21
What if I'm wrong?

Another Look at Pascal's Bad Wager and the Subject of Death Through the Eyes of an Atheist

"In man everything depends upon the soul, but the things of the soul itself depend upon wisdom."
- Socrates

"Instead of enjoying our five minutes in the sun, we allow our religions to hobble us with fears and shame and pangs of guilt. Guilt for what? For being human. Religions put a sick spin on the human experience, making death the primary focus of life. Most religions are nothing but continuous reminders of the Grim Reaper."
- Judith Hayes

Pascal's Bad Wager

Allow me to cover some old ground in this chapter. I say this because the material we are going to briefly cover has been covered a great many times by different authors over the course of many years. I would rather not waste time on it, but it appears some worn out pieces of lingo will always remain with us, much like that annoying phrase, "knock on wood." So it is with Pascal's material.

Blaise Pascal (1623-1662) was a 17th century French mathematician and theologian, and in his own right, quite an honest one as I see it. He did what too many modern Christian theologians refuse to do—admit when an argument cannot prove something. Said Pascal, "The heart has its reasons, which reason does not know." [Pensees, 277 (1670) translated by W.F. Trotter]. This quote sounds almost unlike theologians of my time who think they can prove everything. I find such an admission refreshing. Pascal was famous for a number of accomplishments in different fields, but most relevant to us now is what he is most famous for, the "wager" wearing his name...

> Yes; but you must wager. It is not optional. You are embarked. Which will you choose then? Let us see. Since you must choose, let us see which interests you least. You have two things to lose, the true and the good; and two things to stake, your reason and your will...Let us weigh the gain and the loss in wagering that God is. Let us estimate these two chances. If you gain, you gain all; if you lose, you lose nothing. Wager, then, without hesitation that He is. [Pensees, 233]

So, says Pascal, the unbeliever has everything to lose and nothing to gain. The believer has nothing to lose and everything to gain; if God does not exist and I believe in him, I lose nothing. But if God does exist, and I don't believe in him, I lose everything.

The First Problem

From the outset, let me emphasize that no one who understands what it means to doubt the existence of God or Christianity would make this argument. It is always offered from the standpoint of a believer. An atheist who became a theist would see its powerlessness and avoid using it to convince anyone else. Among those few occasions where an atheist manages to reclaim faith in the divine, this argument would never have a part in that conversion.

If one does not believe in the God of the Bible, then one does not believe in the God of the Bible. We have a word for someone who insists to themselves that they believe something contrary to the way they truly feel—denial. A person is in denial who refuses to admit how they really feel and what they really believe, yet this is what proponents of Pascal's Wager are inadvertently asking the doubter to do—to tell one's self that they still believe in a particular belief system. It is the equivalent of asking doubters to choose to believe, hope to believe, strive to believe, to exercise those "faith muscles," fighting back whatever doubts he or she has. If this notion is not fallacious and futile, it is difficult to conceive of what would be. The contention is insulting to doubters and thinkers alike who value honesty in reasoning.

The Greek word for hypocrite, found throughout the gospels, and particularly in Matthew 7, is a word that means literally, "actor," like play actors, not dissimilar to today's Hollywood stars. Actors are pretenders, people playing a role not connected to their actual selves. The sort of actors Jesus has in mind are religious actors, those who follow the rituals and observe the teachings, but have no inward faith, no inner convictions to accompany their outward actions. How much more applicable could this be to this sort of "faith substitute" that advocates of Pascal's Wager expect us to have? The Bible makes it clear that "without faith it is impossible to please God." (Hebrews 11:6) This is expressly clear and in direct opposition to this have-faith-without-really-having-faith idea, as are other passages, "let him ask in faith, nothing wavering." (James 1:6)

Before my resignation from the ministry, I was "undercover" as an atheist for the last two years before finally defecting. I was pretending then. I was merely going through the motions. I haven't met a believer yet who heard my story and would have the gall to tell me I was saved in that unbelieving, pretentious state. I faked faith, but faith never came. I could keep faking faith, but faith would not develop. This is true for doubters of all religions.

The believer's groping hopes and prayers for unbelievers to develop faith are naïve at best, and that is the vain hope of those who make Pascal's Wager. They somehow think that a thought-out, enlightened atheist might one day decide to forget about all the major biblical and doctrinal issues that caused the unbelief in the first place, and just mysteriously become "faithful" again. This doesn't happen to atheists who reject the Bible for valid, logical reasons. It should be apparent to anyone who is familiar with the Bible that pretentious service to a god would not even be as good as no service at all. In this case, outright atheism would be more preferable to God than fake theism…

> No man can serve two masters: for either he will hate the one, and love the other; or else he will hold to the one, and despise the other. Ye cannot serve God and mammon. (Matthew 6:24)

> 15. I know thy works, that thou art neither cold nor hot: I would thou wert cold or hot. 16. So then because thou art lukewarm, and neither cold nor hot, I will spue thee out of my mouth. (Rev 3:15-16)

With that in mind, it seems that instead of God aiding doubters back to faith, he is pushing us away from the fold because of our "sin" of unbelief...

> So we see that they could not enter in because of unbelief. (Hebrews 3:19)

Unbelievers are not very comforted by this, even when believers show us passages that appear to sympathize with doubt...

> Lord, I believe; help thou mine unbelief. (Luke 9:24)

> Jesus saith unto him, Thomas, because thou hast seen me, thou hast believed: blessed are they that have not seen, and yet have believed. (John 20:29)

Jesus removing from a man's son an unclean spirit and granting doubting Thomas an opportunity to believe by examining his wounds still doesn't help us. The truth is, there are a lot more doubting Thomas' today, people who realize a story is just a story until it is backed up with proof. This is all cold comfort for the unbeliever.

The Second Problem

The second problem with Pascal's Wager is that it is completely selfish in its application when used by believers. For instance, a Christian will ask an atheist, "Is it worth risking going to Hell because of unbelief in Jesus?", but they fail to apply the argument from the standpoint of other faiths. In *Why I Became an Atheist: a former preacher rejects Christianity*, John Loftus has the following to say...

> Muslims claim that you will go to Hell if you don't convert to Islam too, but you cannot be a Muslim and also a Christian. Both religions offer some evidence to believe, but Christians think their faith has more evidence on its behalf than Islam, and one billion Muslims think otherwise. But according to both religions the other group is going to Hell. So choose wisely. The risk is the same because a lot is at stake. Both are calling in a proverbial bomb threat. On the one hand, one claims if you stay in one building you will die, whereas a different one claims that if you leave and go into another building you will die.

> How Pascal's wager helps us with this quandary is itself a quandary. (p. 56)

So a dominant religion replaces the thrust of this argument from Christianity to any religion a religious teacher chooses to get his hearers to "wager" on. "Is it worth wagering against the existence of Allah when you have nothing to lose by believing?" We can apply this to any religion that is judged acceptable and tenable to a people. In all cases, the application is the same; the Christian wants the atheist to wager on the acceptance of a deity, the Christian God, but forgets that this applies to any and all gods since they are all equally drenched in the unknown. When all the back-and-forth of religious competition for truth is put aside, the wager is made by the individual based on whatever religious preference they happen to have!

Taking this yet another step, we must ask, "Is it worth risking burning in Hell because belief in the wrong god might offend the right one?" The problem now becomes pissing off the true god by mistakenly wagering on the wrong one! This begs the question of which deity is the right one, and this filters down into the disconcerting feeling that we are again having to make a "leap of faith" into the dark, uncharted waters of uncertainty.

The world of *could bes* is infinite; any form or thing or conception could be called a god. The thought of accidentally offending a "true God" becomes too much. I am being asked to gamble when the stakes are unknown. I might be gaining eternal life or eternal damnation. In the volatile and unpredictably scary world of the gods, anything can happen. The God of the Bible once killed a man for touching the ark of the covenant with the best of intentions—to keep it from falling off a cart (2 Samuel 6:6-7). You don't wager based on how you feel such harsh and temperamental beings might react! But the Christian God is not alone in this. All gods were and are more or less the same way—vengeful, vicious, and easily angered at the slightest things. I am frightened at the nightmarish possibility that any sort of being even remotely like this could be real! I don't want to risk pissing off an angry, jealous being with the temperament of a bipolar seventh-grader fit for alternative school.

I am not about to wager on one unknown above another just because my culture and my parent's religion happened to land right in my lap. By the Christian's own logic therefore, I *shouldn't* wager on the Christian God because that God is only one, whereas any one or all of the many hundreds of thousands of gods adored by mankind since antiquity might well be real. The odds are now too great that I might be wrong. Doesn't it make perfect sense then to stay neutral on the issue?

Wagering on unknowns at the casino is bad enough—just ask anyone who lost their money gambling!

The Third Problem

The third problem with Pascal's Wager is that the Christian God may indeed be real every bit like the Bible describes him, in which case, me and every other atheist, pagan, heathen, deist, and anti-Christian religious or irreligious person who ever lived will roast in a hot, fiery furnace for a ceaseless eternity, screaming in bloodcurdling agony every second of every minute of every hour of every day of every year of every century of every millennia, forever. If Joe Holman stands before an angry God on the day of judgment, and if it is true that all unbelievers must burn in Hell regardless of their sincerity or honesty in their search for the facts, and if it is true that one cannot repent on that final day, then I will stand speechless before my monstrous creator and accept my sentence—remember, I won't have a choice in the matter! The problem with this horrible scenario is that it displays all too well the terror and brutish nature of the God of the New Testament who punishes with not the slightest hint of mercy, those who disagree with him.

Pascal's Wager brings to light every intolerant and hateful attribute of this bully in the sky called Jehovah. This God is like a mob boss who kills those who oppose him in the most hideous ways imaginable. In my case, I thought too much and asked too many questions, so God resolved to have me silenced, "knocked off." Pascal's Wager makes a man think about the eternal anger, the divine and supreme level of unimaginable cruelty, unleashed from a being who could simply blot out of existence those who wrong him, but instead, chooses to watch them suffer forever in a chasm of painful separation from him.

But perhaps I can wager on a god without wagering on one? If I am going to wager on anything, is it not much easier and more desirable to wager against the existence of an infinitely evil entity like the God of holy writ, heartless and vindictive of a monster as he is, and instead, throw off that hypocritical shroud of faith, and in its place, wager on compassion and human dignity? Does it not make vastly more sense to wager on a god who would understand the honest motives of a person who must follow the mind in the pursuit of truth, even if that pursuit happens to lead him away from the notion of a transcendent deity?

If I, as an atheist, can understand that there are people who legitimately doubt the existence of any god, is it so surprising for a supreme being to understand that as well? If the transcendent, all-knowing source of power and glory the Christians call "God" exists, does it make sense to believe that he would damn me to Hell, even though I did my best to preserve my walk with him? According to his holy book, he will. But even assuming such a scary being exists, I know that he would know what I know—that there are many who simply cannot believe in him. Such knowledge means that a God with any amount of compassion would know that the idea of damnation for disbelief is a hideous idea, a holdover from the dark ages, an idea that is mentally oppressive and best left forgotten. So while I am not going to believe in such a being, it would be up to him (in a manner of speaking) to believe in me!

Apologist Josh McDowell once said, "The heart cannot accept what the mind rejects." I agree. So I am going to wager that if a supreme being could and does exist, then it is a compassionate and smart enough being to know what we enlightened atheists know—that people are made the way they are by their genetics, their experiences, their cultures, their upbringings, that it is a combination of many factors which make a person who and what they are, thus, eliminating the idea that man is an "evil," "sinful," or "depraved" creature who deserves an eternity of torture. Should such a god of compassion be up there hiding, he knows I have tons of questions for him, and I hope he will someday answer them. However, I presently do not believe a god can exist, and I am wholly convinced that the god idea is so highly contradictory and ridiculous on every level of thought that I can safely throw off my belief in him. Like any and everyone, though, I could be wrong about the God question, but I have not the slightest reason to alter my belief system or life to make some "wager" in the nebulous world of intangibles, where spooks walk and goblins dwell. I leave that miserable world of ghouls, gods, and goddesses alone. I want no part of it. Reason, common sense, and wholesome humanistic values demand that the ignorance of the past remain in the past where it belongs.

Facing Death as an Atheist

A heart attack is a scary thing. I was never so scared! I was a believer and a minister at the time. It was June of 1999. I was right in the middle of a "blood, sweat, and tears" work-out at my local gym, hoping to drop a few pounds. Unwisely, I was on a steady diet of Dexatrim, plus one meal per day—not exactly a dietician's recommended wait loss plan! First, I hammered out six sets of squats, and then another three of leg lifts with 640 pounds. It was slow to dawn on me, but finally, I realized I'd pushed myself right past the breaking point.

Becoming noticeably winded, my body decided it was time to rest. My heart was racing, pounding out of my chest, and it seemed not to be slowing down, even now that my activity level was down. It wasn't long before I noticed a slight tingling in my left arm. It kept getting worse. Wiping away the sweat running profusely down my face and arms, I resigned to going out to the waiting room and resting in a more relaxed position. Before I got up to make the move, I felt a sharp pain on the top of my heart, a weighty feeling. I rested on a wicker sofa, which, thankfully, was semi-secluded from view. Had anyone glanced over by this time, they would have seen a big, sweaty man grabbing his chest and gasping for breath. I was taking in air, but couldn't catch my breath ("air-hunger" as a paramedic would refer to it). Looking in a mirror, I saw my beet-red face and newly forming drops of sweat on every visible surface of my body. Tunnel vision finally set in and the fear and shock of oxygen deprivation began to give way to a blackening delirium of semi-consciousness.

By now, my life started flashing before my eyes. I never imagined the human mind could run through so many images in such a short time! I began praying, preparing to meet my Maker. At this point, I was one hundred percent sure I was headed to see him. I was at peace with myself as far as eternal matters were concerned, but no one wants to make an embarrassing scene! That was exactly what I was thinking about now. Among the flickering thoughts blazing through my mind over the next several minutes was a statistic I heard on how a good number of people a year run to the restrooms to save themselves embarrassment when choking on a piece of steak or cornbread. They die there. Not wanting to err in the same way, I decided I could care less about embarrassment and resolved within myself that if 10 more seconds of this horror continued, I would stumble up to the counter and tell them to call 911. That ten seconds came and went, and it seemed now that I couldn't get up.

I tried to sit up and go to the counter and found out that it would take everything I had left in me to do it. I had no strength. I was quivering madly. Then, just as I was blacking out for what I thought would be my closing moment of life, I noticed my lungs seemed to be getting a little more air than I was getting seconds earlier. I was still gasping for breath, but it wasn't as bad. The shooting pain in my left arm began to lessen and the black tunnel that was consuming my vision began to level off. I knew then I would probably be alright. A crippling feeling of weakness and sleepiness hit me like I had never experienced before. All I could do was rest for about 15 minutes. My body was trying to fall asleep badly. Every ounce of strength in me had gone. My wife, who had dropped me off to work out while she shopped at the mall, was back to pick me up. I fell down trying to walk out to the car to meet her. I went home and I slept like a slab of limestone from 5 pm until 11 am the following day.

I don't know why now, but I didn't go to the doctor until much later. Even though all symptoms pointed to it, he told me that in fact I did *not* have a heart attack. So despite all the drama, I was fine. Back when it was happening, however, this didn't matter. I believed I was dying, and that was enough to make a big, sobering dent in my life outlook. My family has a history of heart trouble and deaths at an early age. We shall see how fortunate or unfortunate I will be!

I faced the prospect of death back then as a believer, looking forward to a heaven. Now, I am an unbeliever with no expectations or hopes beyond the grave. Having seen my life flash before my eyes, having taken in the utter shock of my own mortality, I can see life from the most sober of perspectives. Unlike many who go through life without getting the harsh wake-up call of their terminality, I know all too well my own. I believe the earmark of mental and psychological maturity is determined by whether or not we have learned the somber lessons life teaches us—that we are not immortal, that we should not expect to be exempted from the pain and brutality of being. Any horrible tragedy can ensnare any of us at any time. Pain is more pronounced for those who thought it could never happen to them than for those of us who see it coming afar. It is one thing to cognitively "know" that we are going to bite the dust, but quite another thing to truly take in the gravity of exactly what that means.

How do I approach death now that I am an atheist? After years of mental turmoil and debilitating fear of a tormenting afterlife, at last, I enjoy peace of mind. I approach the subject with the utmost contentment. Death is no longer a terrible thing, the result of evil, but one can't help but be afraid of it because it is a rough transition in its very nature. It is a natural part of life, and I have no more reason to fear what lies beyond the grave than does a stray German Shepherd getting hit by a bus.

I know life doesn't owe me anything. Calling upon a ghost to deliver me from my hour of calamity will have no more effect than calling upon a ghost to ease the pain of a sprained ankle. Calling upon God will not prevent your death anymore than it did the poor souls on the Titanic who drowned in the icy cold waters of the Atlantic. It is simply our own selfishness that makes us think we are somehow entitled to be enrolled in God's special care plan. And this arrogance is tenacious; we figure, God may have let several thousand people die hot, crushing, choking deaths in the smoldering ruins of two burning, collapsing buildings on September 11, 2001, but God would surely deliver us, right? This is the same sort of selfish thinking that enables religionists to believe that God will help their soldiers win a war against the opposing army.

Partly, we are to blame for this highly selfish tendency, and partly we are not; we *are not* to blame in that nature is what compels us to regard our lives higher than those of everyone else. We can, in a self-defense situation, choose to save our lives over one trying to take ours from us. We *are* to blame, however, when this misplaced ideal spills over into the realm of common sense reasoning: God is with us and not with our enemies. God may not answer the prayers of a hundred thousand people asking for war to end, but God may answer just one prayer—ours. This is uncritical ignorance and it is inexcusable. We are at fault for not educating ourselves and using the faculty of reason to think through the emotion-driven madness of self-serving, agenda-catering-to religionists who are no more interested in rationality than getting bubonic plague.

It is the ego-driven comforts of religion that compel so many to put reason on the backburner. Reason is like a useful giveaway item; in a marketplace or garage sale, if you put out some items listed as "free," you will have a harder time getting rid of them. People assume something is wrong with them and pass them by. Not much is free in life…*accept the best things*! But we pass the best things by because we are accustomed to paying for things we think are worth it—"you get what you pay for" is the slogan that comes to mind here. Now take another item and put "$1.00" on it, and you will get rid of it before you can blink!

Religion is the $1.00 item. It's worthless, but people buy it because it's a steal, even though that metaphorical one dollar goes to a deceiving preacher or priest who gives nothing in return. Reason is the item marked "free." Only a few takers are interested in it if they are looking for that particular item, much like a worn out rocking chair put out to the garbage is wanted by just the right person who comes to your doorstep and says, "Can I have this? I've always wanted one like this!"

Go to your local drive-thru restaurant and ask for a cup of water. It's free at most places, and much better for you than soda, but damned if more people won't pay that overpriced $1.75 for a large Pepsi at a corner store! It's more expensive, but worth next to nothing. The best things in life are free indeed, but the buyers just aren't there who see the value of them.

Reason may be the better, free item, but when death becomes the topic, reason becomes too tasteless as a source of comfort, much like that cup of water. Once you've had enough water, you want a more ambitious drink because the taste of the water loses appeal. Concerning an afterlife, we prefer the selfish, comforting fantasy over the cold, hard reality, and who can be blamed for this? But all we have is cold, hard reality, and that reality tells us a few things about life and death…

Regarding life, reality tells us that we want life to be as pleasant as possible. Reality tells us that life is short. Reality tells us that we only live once. Therefore, since this life is short, and we only get one shot at it, and since we want to make it as pleasant as possible, we ought to reject future worlds and lofty notions of an eternal home beyond the clouds, and instead give our all to making this life as pleasant as can be.

Regarding death, reality tells us that death is eminent. Reality tells us that death is natural for everyone. Reality tells us that when we die, we die all over. We have no reason to believe that any part of us survives the grave. Reality tells us that we have nothing to fear in death. Troubling and unsettling as it is, and as painful as death can be to go through, it will happen. We should accept it, and even learn to appreciate it, and more importantly, to love our little moment in the sun when we are alive.

As an atheist, I view death as a great equalizing of the natural forces that resulted in my creation. The life force is a strained unit, a departure from the monotonous norm, an extension of the universe itself, but soon that extension will be retracted, and all that will be left of me is whatever memories happen to remain. I will not be playing harps or racket ball with Moses and Jesus, and the rest of the good old boys in togas, eating grapes for eternity, around a jeweled throne on streets of gold in a city foursquare. My end will come, as will yours, and when it does, you won't know the difference.

CHAPTER 22
Articles of Anti-Faith

An Assortment of Godless Articles

"Any intelligent fool can make things bigger, more complex, and more violent. It takes a touch of genius – and a lot of courage – to move in the opposite direction."
- Albert Einstein

"There is a concept which corrupts and upsets all others. I refer not to Evil, whose limited realm is that of ethics; I refer to the infinite."
- Jorge Luis Borges

* A number of these articles have appeared on the Debunking Christianity Blog and on different freethought sites throughout the internet.

Jesus, Omniscience, and the End of the World

So much has been written about Jesus' second coming. So many mistakes have been made in efforts to predict when Jesus will return, embarrassing mistakes that remain etched in human history forever, like the "track marks" on a drug-user's arm. One such mistake was made in the year 1099 C.E. It marked what believers far and near perceived would be the definite return of the Lord. Thousands of people sold their possessions, quit their jobs, stood on housetops, waiting for Jesus, while some made desperate pilgrimages to Jerusalem to meet the savior. By all accounts, it was nothing short of mass hysteria.

Commenting on this event, in *Extraordinary Popular Delusions and the Madness of Crowds,* (1841) Charles Machay wrote...

> It was universally believed that the end of the world was at hand; that the thousand years of the Apocalypse were near completion, and that Jesus Christ would descend upon Jerusalem to judge mankind. All Christendom was in commotion. A panic terror seized upon the weak, the credulous, and the guilty, who in those days formed more than nineteen twentieths of the population. Forsaking their homes, kindred, and occupation, they crowded to Jerusalem to await the coming of the Lord. (p. 290)

Long story short, at least some Christian date-setters have learned their lesson by now not to attempt to predict when Jesus will return, but some remain stubborn and continue the tradition, confidently blaming any mistakes they make on "miscalculations." At the time of this writing, 2009, 2012, and 2016 are being passed around as prominent dates for the Lord's triumphant second coming. When these fail, we'll get a new batch of excuses once again, along with new dates for the future. It will be quite fun to tear them apart. But for those Christians who have learned not to set dates for God's return, we still get a fair amount of optimistic theological doubletalk; instead of giving a specific time when the Lord will return, we are told we can know *the season* of Christ's return, though the Bible denies this too...

> But of the times *and the seasons*, brethren, ye have no need that I write unto you for yourselves know perfectly that the day of the Lord so cometh as a thief in the night. (I Thessalonians 5:1-2)

Yet again, we find deep-seated arrogance and foolhardy emotion taking over, causing God's little messengers to say things they will later regret. But the second coming of Christ has created other problems for believers. For starters – and what concerns us at the moment – is the matter of Jesus' omniscience in relation to the second coming and the end of the world.

> 31. Heaven and earth shall pass away: but my words shall not pass away. 32. But of that day and that hour knoweth no man, no, not the angels which are in heaven, **neither the Son**, but the Father. (Mark 13:31-32)

This brings up a tricky question: Can Jesus be called omniscient while lacking a component of knowledge? How can the second member of the Godhead be omniscient and not know when his father will return to end the world? Could it be that Jesus is omniscient with the sole exception of this one truth? Believers would like to think so, but here is where the logical problems start coming out of the woodwork. As we shall see, if Jesus is limited in knowing when the end of the world will be, he must also be limited in other knowledge as well, and this further erodes his omniscience.

For instance, we must ask, can Jesus see into the far distant future up until the end? I haven't met a Christian yet who would claim he couldn't. But to say that he couldn't would mean that Jesus could not share in knowledge of predictive prophecy shared by the other two members of the Godhead. Now if indeed Jesus has knowledge of the distant future, but not all of it (saving only his second coming), you run into another logical problem; whenever the world will end (say, for the sake of example, one thousand years from now) Jesus would be powerless to see beyond this point, because if he could see and predict exactly one thousand *and one* years down the road, he would be able to deduce when the universe had been ended by His Father, and thus, would know what Jesus said that only the Father could know. Picture Jesus popping his head into the future and seeing the New Jerusalem, angelic beings, redeemed saints worshipping before the thrown of God, etc. So having the ability to see into the future would mean Jesus could figure out when the end was to be, even if he did not have that exact date given to him by his Father.

Now let's go further; suppose God informed Jesus that he would be curtailing his abilities of foreknowledge to ensure that he doesn't stumble onto this one truth which was kept from him by God. So Jesus would now know that he could still see into the future, but only up until some point close to when the world would end, and no more. This way, Jesus wouldn't be able to deduce anything about the end-times, and the secret would be preserved.

Well, now we have not only the already bad problem of an eternal God lacking in knowledge, but the awkward predicament of how the savior of the world is supposed to be able to supernaturally act as an all-knowing intercessor/mediator for man with compromised access to his omniscience. Jesus' being limited in omniscience makes him useless as a guiding force for our lives—since he is now without the ability to predict future events up to a certain point, he is unable to answer prayers and providentially guide us away from potential spiritual hazards that would be more than we could handle: "God is faithful, who will not suffer you to be tempted above that ye are able." (I Corinthians 10:13) The only way he could make good on this promise is if he knows all future events, but as we have seen, his knowledge of end times would have to be kept limited in order to maintain God's exclusive knowledge of the last day. Jesus must be able to hear the groaning heart to know just what every soul needs to deliver us from pain…

> 26. Likewise the Spirit also helpeth our infirmities: for we know not what we should pray for as we ought: but the Spirit itself maketh intercession for us with groanings which cannot be uttered. 27. And he that searcheth the hearts knoweth what is the mind of the Spirit, because he maketh intercession for the saints according to the will of God. (Romans 8:26-27)

"Spirit" should not be capitalized here. A careful study of these verses, and the context of Romans 8 will reveal that what is being discussed is not the Holy Spirit, but the human spirit, facing pain and suffering (See Romans 8:18-22). What these verses are saying is, the yearnings of our own spirits help us in those trying times when we don't know what to pray for, when the pain of life begins to seem unbearable and inexpressible. We cry out "with groanings which cannot be uttered." And Christ, the heart-searcher (Acts 1:24) and the one and only intercessor/mediator we have (I Timothy 2:5), the one who "makes intercessions for the saints according to the will of God," hears this inner agony and renders aid as we have need. But someone living around the time before Christ is to be sent back would necessarily have compromised access to the Lord's tender loving care—if indeed his knowledge of what is to come is limited. Granted, this would effect only those Christians who lived in this time where Jesus' predictive powers had to be capped off. Nevertheless, the fact that we are even having to make such mental leaps to keep this myth intact is amazing.

None of this makes a lick of sense, I know, but let's just assume it's true. We still have the initial problem created when a "Son of God" humbles himself to take upon the form of a lowly human (Philippians 2:7)—the problem of one being called "God" without having the full abilities of God. As a matter of logic, an omniscient deity cannot be ignorant of even one thing and maintain his omniscience; if Jesus never knew the day when he would be sent back to reclaim the earth for himself, then he was never omniscient, and therefore, never an omniscient God; if Jesus once knew and chose to forget this piece of information, then you have a deity renouncing his omniscience, and therefore, his claim to true Godhood. And what about all the oblong troubles this presents for those who defend the trinity doctrine except to say that if Jesus is at any point not fully omniscient, then he renounces his rank as "the second member of the Godhead," and since the "three in one" nature of the trinity *is* God himself, Jesus' compromise of omniscience means the compromise of the entire nature of God. Infinite deity cannot be shuffled around. You cannot have a *part* or a *piece* of the Trinitarian God losing his claim to deity for any length of time.

As a minister, to make this problem go away, I took the position that during Jesus' ministry only the Father knew when the world would end, but now this truth has been revealed by God to Jesus since he has ascended, thereby solving some of these logistical problems. Unfortunately, the Bible offers not an ounce of credibility to this position, and it doesn't actually solve anything. Jesus was glorified with the Father before the world was created (John 17:5), so if God was going to inform Jesus of all his plans, he would have done it then and Jesus would have been able to answer his disciples about the burning question of when the world would end when he was alive with them. That being the case, in order to keep from making Jesus a liar, we have to say that God erased the date of the return from Jesus' mind before sending him to complete his earthly ministry! Now we've clearly stepped into science fiction: "Smile, Jesus! You've just been erased!"

Add to that, the text seems to imply that God the Father wanted to keep some authority under his belt and no one else's (see I Corinthians 15:24-28); if God wanted to convey the idea that Jesus would never know when the world would end, how much plainer could he have said it? And why did the Holy Spirit choose to put this in God's inspired book if it was not a truth of eternal duration like all the other cherished biblical affirmations? So it makes no sense to say that Jesus *now* knows the time of the second coming, but didn't back then. Is there a way to resolve this quandary?

Let me help by offering a better explanation, one we infidels think makes perfect sense out of this whole mess…

In this scenario, the writers of the gospels are all ordinary religious men without the slightest hint of divine inspiration. They are, as Voltaire put it, "ignorant fishermen," and nothing more. Now since the writers of the gospels are mere finite beings, when they come across a big, burning question that no one has the answer to, just like everyone else, they are stumped and forced to find a convenient reason as to why the question cannot be answered. This was precisely the case with the question in Matthew 24:2, *"What will be the sign of thy coming and of the end of the world?"* That's a big question! Every religious cult for thousands of years has been trying to guess when the world will end, and every time they've tried, they failed abysmally. So rather than disqualify themselves by giving a likely inaccurate date and time, they decided to have Jesus pass it off with cryptic messages of signs and seasons, and then, to make the Lord not appear spiritually stingy with his all-divine, all-authoritative knowledge, the convenient way out of this trap was, "I do not know exactly when the end will be. Only my Father knows."

Well, daddy's not around to be accosted for answers, is he? God was so holy to the Jews that he dare not be questioned or approached without a priest, and as far as the disciples were concerned, without Jesus. So we appear to be dead-ended for answers. Jesus no doubt was supposed to come off as though he asked His Father for answers and daddy refused to be forthcoming (for whatever reasons we will never know). Jesus, the warm side of God's love, as opposed to the Father in heaven, who always manages to stay at arm's length from everyone, doesn't know, which means we are just plain out of luck. We will never know when the world is going to end. We have Jesus' word on that!

It is interesting how Jesus struts around his authority in the scriptures. He is said to have all authority whatsoever (Matthew 28:19; John 5:22). But then, on the one part that matters most, when it comes to the super big question that mortal man longs to know more than anything else, the story changes. Jesus goes from "I have all authority," to "I have almost all authority except in this one area!" As much as I hate to be the killjoy cynic, I've got to be one here and point out that Jesus isn't scoring any points for himself! The one thing that would demonstrate perfectly Jesus' testable accuracy as a divine prophet of God is missing. In a world full of religious excuse-makers and flimflam artists, anxious to explain brilliantly why a prophecy or a date for the return of God didn't come to pass, I cannot be liberal or lax in my demand for proof. I have to put Jesus on my list of those who waste their breath, avoiding tough questions.

Wars and rumors of wars will not impress me, nor will claims of earthquakes or religious persecution and power shifts between nations. These have always been around for as long as we have record of human history. What I wanted more than anything was to be able to put a date on that glorious appearing of the savior, but I could not. Instead, I am condemned to wonder why the savior of the world would not possess that knowledge if he was legitimate and his claims real, and why he would not give faithless humanity a "heads up" on just when he will return to prevent a huge percentage of humanity from being lost.

Why Does the Universe Bother to Exist?

To some, it seems that the most sincere and provocative question for an atheist is the question in the title of this article; if there is no God, no ultimate power, no eternal first cause and creator of the universe, a power from which all other powers and forces are derived, why is there something rather than nothing? Why do we observe a universe at all? How can we account for the existence of matter and energy? Why does *anything* exist?

I don't want to sound like a spoiled sport and bow out of answering a million dollar question such as this, but I must, and I shall explain why. I don't like special pleading, and I don't believe I am doing so when I say that this question is nebulous at best and insignificant at worst. Yes, I think the question itself is flawed. It has no fundamental meaning. As sincere as this question is, as original and encompassing as it strives to be, it is unanswerable, an unqualified question—that is, a question which has no logical basis for its asking.

If I were to ask you why the color green appears to be what we know as green and red appears to be what we know as red, what answer would you give me? How about if I asked you why a square describes the shape we know it to have and not what we know as a circle? Suppose I asked you why an "i" is dotted and a "t" crossed, and not a "t" dotted and an "i" crossed? What kind of answers could you give me? I dare say a thinking, levelheaded person would just say, "Joe, that's just the way things turned out to be." I would agree. This is a sufficient answer because the questions I asked were unqualified. They demand only that we accept them as sufficiently self-evident facts.

Growing up, I was obsessed with questions about my existence. For instance, I would ask my mother, "Why am I me and not somebody else?" Don't dismiss it. It's a damn good question. My mother would say, "You *just are* you, son!" I was never satisfied with this answer. Why is Joe Holman's consciousness not in some other person's body, asking the same questions? Why am I not a Chinese peasant living ten centuries ago, a German business man, a Mayan Indian priest, a Roman bricklayer, or an African cheiftain's wife? Why do I not answer to the name Kimchasa and chop wood for a living? I finally had to accept mom's answer because this, like the previous ones, is an unqualified question, one that shouldn't logically be asked and can't logically be answered. Go ahead. Keep thinking it over. In the end, you will come to the same conclusion I did, that we are each at the center of our own personal universes, and that is just the way it is. No other answer can be given. That is the meaning of an unqualified question, a question that cannot be answered because the question involves accepting something as an inherently brute fact.

With this observation in mind, we now proceed to the question we intend to discuss, but in order to do that, we must first answer what it entails to say that something *exists*. When I ask why the universe bothers to exist, I am essentially demanding that in order for something to be said to exist, we must be able to see or verify it in some way. I challenge anyone to give me a more cogent definition than this. We are deep within the realm of metaphysics here, and nothing "exists" (as far as we are concerned) until we can detect a thing, but something may very well exist and not be detected. So when we discuss the existence of a thing, we are discussing our ability to detect it.

In the case of the universe, we detect it and we judge it to be real. But what if we didn't? Could the universe still exist? Certainly, it could. Three conceivable universes (or states of being) are possible…

First, the universe could have existed, but been lifeless. Conditions could have been unfavorable for even the smallest type of life to take root anywhere in any galaxy on any planet. It could have been that the surface of every heavenly body was as sterile as the surface of the sun. Second, the universe could have existed (as it does), containing at least one planet with life on it, a planet with beings on it with high enough intelligence to determine and appreciate the fact that they exist. Third, the universe could have been as a theist pictures a godless universe being—completely non-existent altogether. I can't really imagine this as an option because I find that my mind is incapable of conceptualizing a "nothing" of any kind (the term is philosophically dubious), but I can consider it as an option anyway. The theist thinks that if no deity existed, there would be "nothing" because nothing would exist, period. No stars, planets, space or time, nothing in the strictest and most defined sense of the word.

Any three of these universes could have been, but we know the second option turned out to be the way things are. But now a problem has emerged; the only big difference between a lifeless universe that exists, a universe that exists with life on it like ours, and a non-existent universe altogether, is observation—our ability to detect existence. Since it is possible for a universe to exist without our knowledge of it, by asking why a universe exists, we are only asking why we see it. Who is to say what "is"? Who determines what it means to "be"? How can we possibly define existence without appealing to our knowledge of things? So the question of why there is something rather than nothing is unqualified, a thing that must be accepted as brute fact because questioning it is to dwell in a metaphysical no-man's-land from whence there is no escape.

I am arguing that without consciousness, nothing exists (as far as human understanding goes). There is no real difference between the theist's perceived universe where *literally* nothing exists, and my conception of a universe without life and consciousness where *practically* nothing exists. Without intelligent consciousness, it is impossible to tell the difference, and therefore, the question of man's existence is unqualified. It has no basis for its asking whatsoever.

So my answer to the theistic inquirer as to why something exists rather than nothing hinges upon observation; it might well have been that no universe came to exist, but it also could have been that a universe of matter came to exist without life in it, in which case, because of the absence of life, it would still "not exist." We would never know the difference between an existent or non-existent universe were it not for consciousness. So the question, "why does the universe exist?" is rendered meaningless.

Obviously, we observe a universe that exists (consciousness being the only rational standpoint from which we can say this), but I contend that this universe does not show divine handiwork, but instead, signs of a natural, unintelligent arrangement and operation—an arrangement I believe we would expect to see if there were no omni-max deity. But this conviction concerns judgments on the material world, and is therefore debatable—alas, we are back in the land where terms make sense and debates can have meaning!

What must we do now? We must ask a more direct question, a sensible question that can be answered. There are many types of questions that are valid and answerable, like "How did life arise from dead matter?" or "What processes had to take place to give us our current universe?" If a theist wants to take an atheist to task on his position, many questions like these can be asked.

I can ask a question that pertains to the operation of things in the universe, to the reaction and properties of things within the universe, but I cannot ask a question that envelops the existence of the universe itself. We simply have no logical framework for answering such questions.

In conclusion, since we are made of the same matter that composes the universe, we can only search for the material causes behind our being, and when these causes are found, accept them. This is as far as human understanding can take us for now. Life is full of unknown variables; we might figure all of them out one day, or maybe not. To those who are still unsatisfied with my answer, they are free to propose a better one, but why stop there? Why not answer all the other unqualified questions I asked here? If you can do that for me, I will reveal to you why you are not a fur trader who crossed the Bering Strait twenty thousand years ago!

The Line Must Be Drawn Here!

I believe correct reasoning is definitely an acquired characteristic. It is something we develop if only we are fortunate enough to start life with the basic cognitive abilities nature provided.

I believe a good analysis on a position comes by knowing where to draw a line and whether or not a line has been crossed. What constitutes A? What constitutes B? What are the deciding differences between A and B? At exactly what point does A end and B begin? Then there is the ability to troubleshoot one's own thinking. How blurry is the line between A and B? Do A and B really deserve separate categories? Are the distinctions I have drawn between A and B to constitute a categorical change in thinking warranted, or am I drawing a distinction without a difference? Making a distinction without a difference happens to be a very common fallacy.

What made my departure from Christianity possible was the time I had to think and re-think the quandaries that troubled me. When I found no resolutions, it was only as my faith began to erode that I was finally able to see why I couldn't resolve the issues—because I was unable to draw satisfactory lines between the available positions I was compelled to choose from...

I considered how the faith-healer and the charismatic Christian who prayed at a revival meeting for someone to be healed of cancer, expecting "a miracle right now," differed little from the traditional Catholic or Protestant who believed in God's healing providential hand over time. The aggressive evangelicals who demand an immediate healing are saying little different than what any average Christian believes, that God will somehow bend the laws of reality to heal them of their infirmities.

I considered how the same militant charismatics who believed in modern miracles differed little from those of my former religious persuasion, who believed in just the Bible miracles. The only difference is the time period, and realizing that, it only followed to wonder why God would perform miracles back then and not today when they would be no less needed.

I considered how the extremist flat-earthers and geocentrist Christians differed little from the literal creationists who argued for a 6-day creation, or those progressive creationists who accepted an ancient earth, but rejected classical Darwinism—all were in support of supernatural perversions of natural evolution; the literalists basically denied evolution altogether, accepting only "micro-evolution" occurring between God's created "kinds," and in the case of the progressives (depending on which breed you talk to), the evolution only occurred in the animal world, and some time later, God decided to transform an ape into a man and call him Adam, employing a hoky form of God-directed evolution.

I considered how those who maintained belief in modern day Jesus and Virgin Mary apparitions were no different than those who believed that Samuel and Moses heard and spoke to God, or that Constantine saw a cross in the sky and received a commandment to conquer in its name.

I considered how the Catholics esteeming the pope and the church authoritative, and the Mormons following their own "12 apostles" of the new age, whom they consider to be authoritative, are fundamentally no different from my former belief that the original 12 apostles (14 if you count Matthias and Paul) were authoritative as they spoke the will of God on earth.

Similarly, I found that those who stood in the more liberal Christian camps and who held to the position of a local Noahic flood, as opposed to a global one, that the days of Genesis 1 were figurative as opposed to literal, or that the Preterist's view of Revelation was correct, tended to differ little from secular commentators and higher critics, the same class of thinkers who might subscribe to later dates for the Bible books or accept the idea of Thought Inspiration instead of Verbal Plenary Inspiration.

I get asked all the time why I didn't accept a more liberal version of Christianity when I defected from the faith. Well, the answer should already be apparent, but if it isn't, here it is: I found it impossible to identify with any one liberal or conservative alignment of beliefs. I couldn't properly draw the dividing lines that allowed me to make the necessary distinctions to preserve some, and not all, of that superstitious scrapheap known as the Bible. Consequently, I had to reject it in full faith.

I cannot put myself in the same camp with someone who denies Mosaic authorship of the Pentateuch, and *then* claims that such a position is consistent with the New Testament's Jesus, "If you believed Moses, you would believe me, for he wrote about me." (John 5:46) I cannot put myself in the camp with those who have no problem lopping off the first 12 chapters of Genesis as mythical, while accepting only the other parts of the book that are more believable to the modern world, and yet hasten to tell me I should believe in a crucified and risen savior-god. It just doesn't jive! I am respecting neither Christianity, nor science (not to mention myself) by half-heartedly trying to believe them both.

And one must ask, is there any real incentive seeking out solace in a dethroned Jesus, a Christ robbed of his deity, one who's ass has been kicked by reason and modern science? If I want to learn from and admire a humanitarian, I'll read Gandhi. If I want a self-help specialist,

I'll read Dr. Phil. Jesus is ok too, so long as he doesn't get risen to the level of a deity.

For me, the findings of assessing Christianity had only one consistent pull—away from being considered the products of any divine origins at all. The pieces of the puzzle had to fit, and they finally did; I was forced to naturalize what had been pounded into my head as supernatural. Those horses and chariots of fire that took Elijah to heaven had to mean something that would click with my rational mind. Well, in time, they did, but the answer I came to did not bring God glory. The Bible was a complete work of fiction; that was the answer I came to embrace.

I believe the matter boils down to this; if I'm going to fudge the laws of reality to make room for the possibility of a supernatural god who intervenes in nature, then there are lots of gods to choose from, less defined gods to whom I can assign whatever positive attributes I see fit. But if I want to stay with the Christian God, even preferring a nicer, more scientifically pliable version of him to posit as my creator, I cannot find the consistency to do so; if I can fudge some laws of nature to make room for a supernatural being, then I can fudge a few more to preserve the Bible's testimony of who this God is and what he has done—and indeed, I must do so.

If I want to start a new line of Superman comics, my readers are not going to be very happy with me if my rendition of Superman doesn't have X-ray vision, heat vision, and the ability to fly because those are three of the characteristics of Superman. If I am going to expect people to identify with my portrayal of the character, the image I portray of him must be characteristically identical with he who is known as "Superman." Otherwise, I would just be stealing his name and creating a new character.

In precisely the same way, one should not be expected to identify with a new version of the Christian God, a deity divorced from the characteristics that make him who he is known to be. But this is exactly what modern theologians want you to accept, a re-made Yahweh for the new age, severed from his barbaric past, one who cares more about science, about having his believers set up abortion protests, racial equality, and preachers in suits and ties, praying non-judgmentally and with tightly clutched hands at social events and the dinner table. This is clearly not the God of the Bible.

Contemporary apologists want you to forget that it was this same God of old who has been an opponent of science (I Timothy 6:20-21), the cause of abortions and child murder (Hosea 13:16; 2 Samuel 12; Numbers 31:15-18), racism and slavery (Genesis 9:24-27), and a fierce bringer of judgment on his many enemies (homosexuals, Leviticus

20:13, witches, Exodus 22:18, Sabbath breakers, Exodus 31:14, and those who worship other gods, Exodus 22:20, see also Luke 19:27). Yes, today's refined theologians are trying to sell you a new and improved Jesus, one who cares less about crusading against Jews and Muslims, and more about tolerance and compassion for the infidel. This is definitely not the God I read about in the Bible! Yet if the Bible itself is what serves as the basis for one's belief in the God of the Bible, then how can I but rely on that same testimony to define who he is?

Realizing this, I am now compelled to go down the list of less-than-admirable qualities and fantastic ideas attributed to this being and accept the biblical testimony about him. The God of the Bible made the sun stand still (Joshua 10:12-13), an ax head float (2 Kings 6:6), and a chariot of fire, led by actual *horses of fire* (2 Kings 2:11) to take Elijah to Heaven. But since all of this smacks of nonsense and savage cruelty, I cannot square these things with sensibility or civility, so I am compelled to go the only other route I can find and accept that the Bible is not of divine origins at all and must be rejected as the testimony of a god in its entirety. The line must be drawn here!

Good Old Christian Morals!

Brad is a good kid. He is 24, a college student with a straight A-average, and a young man who makes his parents proud. He goes to church too. Every Sunday he's there, singing hymns and "lifting up holy hands," praising God. He even gets together with the church youth group and travels to see famous Christian singers and performers, like Rebecca St. James and The Power Team. He goes to the Lord in prayer and asks to be a better person. He feels led of the Spirit of the Lord to do this and that. He feels that God is with him, giving him guidance and direction in life.

Now Brad isn't perfect. He's just human like the rest of us. Sure, he has his fraternity buddies over to party once in a while, and he tends to annoy some of his more straight-laced, gray-haired neighbors by playing loud pop/rap music, but he's a good kid. Like most Christian young people, Brad believes that other forms of sexual activity, minus direct intercourse, are not sins, and that God is okay with them. Plus, he thinks God won't mind if he has premarital sex with his girlfriend at least once to see if they'd be compatible in the long term. When he finally marries the girl, and several years go by, he runs into an attractive "other woman" and quickly shacks up in an affair at the local Motel 6. But he breaks it off afterwards, knowing that he is a Christian and Jesus forgives him. After this happens about 4 more times, people get concerned that he has problems, but he finally quits fooling around for good. God has been patient with him to restore him to the grace of the faithful, as has his longsuffering wife, and for that, Brad is thankful and resumes his Christian walk.

A year goes by and Brad again shows his sinful human nature. He is at a huge football game and his favorite team just won. Fans are so excited that a massive riot ensues. Thousands of crazed, inebriated fans take to the streets, turning over cars, throwing rocks through store windows, looting businesses, climbing up street signs and tearing off the names, causing great harm and tens of millions of dollars in damages. Just that morning, Brad was in church singing, "Oh How I Love Jesus," and "Shall We Gather At the River," but that night he was being arrested and hogtied by the police and thrown into the back of a police van, along with 71 other pieces of human garbage. But Brad still knows Jesus loves him. Jesus loves him so much, in fact, that Jesus gave him a wealthy father who will get him a damn good lawyer. The attorney will argue that Brad was the unfortunate victim of Riot Consciousness Syndrome, a fancy term describing how the moral resolve of an individual weakens in the highly charged emotional atmosphere of a large group. Brad will get off with a slap on the wrist for smashing that department store window and stealing that nice Italian leather jacket. Yep, Jesus really loves him, as he does all the rest of those rioters—the majority of whom are churchgoers, ardently claiming Christianity as their faith!

But Brad was not happy about what he did or getting caught. Brad headed back to church, as you probably imagined he would. The following Sunday, he could be found sitting attentively in those pews, listening to the preacher tell him that "without God, your life will be empty and evil will come in to fill the void." His pastor tells him, "Put God in your life, and you'll be good. Put the devil in your life, and you'll be bad." and "There is no good without God." But Brad notices a number of non-religious friends he has and how they are perfectly moral people, so he inquires as to how they can be moral without God. His pastor told him what any good minister would, *"Some are more moral than others, and Christian people are not perfect, but imagine how evil the world would be if there was no religion!"* This satisfied Brad, so instead of considering that many of the irreligious people he knew would be considered morally superior to him by a long shot, he just chalked up his sins to "weaknesses of the flesh" and moved on, giving God the credit for his restoration to the fold.

I changed the name and tweaked a few details, but "Brad" is based on a real Christian man I know. Quite honestly, Brad well represents the moral integrity of the average Christian, albeit not counting the faithful fanatics, who have no lives outside of crossing the T's and dotting the I's of their religious dogmas. Brad, like so many other unfortunate religious dupes, bought into the false idea that religion – Christianity in particular – equals good (or at least, not as much "bad"), and if people don't have it (religion), they will surely do evil.

Sort of reminds me of the old story of a woman who was visiting a seaport, and while riding with a captain, asked, "What do the people of this town eat?" The captain replied, "Mostly fish." The young lady continued, "I thought fish was a brain food, and yet these seem to be the most stupid people I ever saw." The captain responded, "Imagine how stupid these people would be if they didn't eat fish!"

Christian apologists offer us the exact same rationale; Christianity tells us faith in Jesus produces good morality, and when we point out that Christians are no more (and, in fact, are sometimes less) moral than those with no faith at all, they tell us how immoral the world would be if we had no religion!

The Dangers of Fundamentalism (Part I of IV)

"Be afraid...be very afraid!"

One of the more entertaining recreational aspects of being a preaching student was the work we did at Camp Hensel. Camp Hensel is a well-known Church of Christ Camp in Austin, Texas. We preaching students helped to teach and work there once per year while in school. My preaching companions and I even attended there as youngsters before entering the ministry. For us, it became a home away from home. Everyone had fun there. There was so much to do, so many activities. The good times seemed never to end, and any kids who came expecting their experience to be a bummer left pleasantly surprised and couldn't wait to come back the following year. It was a great way to win souls to Christ.

When the summer of 1996 rolled around, we students were facing yet another opportunity to reach out to the lost. A lot of planning was done, and this year promised to be the best year yet for number of attendants, and we hoped, for number of baptisms too. Turned out, it was one of our better years for conversions, and here's why.

Each night, one selected speaker would hold a sermon all campers were required to come and hear. After an exhausting day of godly and educational activities, the kids didn't mind. Their energy was gone, and before their eyes began to close to retire for the night, we seized the occasion to teach the words of the Lord to these delicate souls. I spoke one night, some other students spoke the following nights, and then one night in particular, one of my instructors from Southwest spoke. The subject? You guessed it...the awful horrors of Hell!

Each year, one of these lessons – usually the parting lesson before everyone went home for the year – was intended to be an especially soul-searching lesson, a "beyond the comfort zone" message held around a bon fire to commemorate the experience and reach out one last time to save the lost. We were told before the meeting began to make the fire extra big this year. I recall the words of the instructor: *"I want this fire hot, blazing hot! Maybe we can get some more baptisms this year as these youngsters think about the heat from the flames. And make sure all the kids are sitting extra close to the flames to enhance the effect."* I thought it was a swell idea at the time. I gladly gathered the wood for this fire. At the time the services began, the fire was lit and it roared beyond our expectations. As decided, we seated everyone extra close to the flames.

The lesson came, and not ten minutes into it went by until we looked about and saw hands desperately trying to fan away the heat. We saw uncomfortable facial expressions, and all the kids trying to inch back a bit to avoid the searing waves of heat that seemed to almost smother us. We staff were lucky. We were watching the kids. We could edge back a little to make ourselves more comfortable. The kids couldn't. They had to sit still and listen. I heard one young kid say, "My leg is hot." Sparks popped and flew out of the fire, scaring us all. It lit up every face as the dark night descended. In a deep, loud, intimidating voice, the bold preacher hollered at the crowd, driving home every minute of the exposure to the blazing inferno with a lesson from Luke 16:19-31...

> *Do you think, if that godless rich man who gave Lazarus the back of his hand were alive today he would reject obeying the gospel? Do you think he would hesitate even for a moment? No, he wouldn't! He was so miserable in Hell that he wanted just a drop of water to cool his tongue! Just a drop of water would have brought him comfort! How miserable and thirsty and hot do you have to be to fill up on just a drop of water? Here's an idea; do you all feel the heat? Now everyone extend your arms to the flame. Come on, I know it's hot, but you can do it. You guys and gals on the front row can barely stand it, right? NOW IMAGINE MUCH, MUCH HOTTER THAN THAT FOR ALL ETERNITY!...[pause] That's right! That ungodly rich man will never get another chance to obey Jesus again, but you have a chance tonight.*

The children's eyes were as wide as onions. Looks of horror adorned their faces. Gasps of unbelief could be heard. The sermon soon ended, and the fear-stricken crowd was asked to stand. This they did gladly, shaking their legs, and moving back from the inferno. The invitational hymn was sung, and yes, many more than usual were baptized. It worked!

Young, timid, impressionable minds were taken down to the river and baptized. Others came forward, confessing their sins. These flexible minds, like most good Christians, were scared into obedience, threatened by this judgmental monster in the sky they served. A few of them, the older kids, would lose this fear immediately after camp was over. Some of them would take it with them for the next few weeks or months, and some of them would forget about it as the years went by, but some of them might have forever been steered away from thinking for themselves because of this and similar forms of fear-based conditioning.

I am ashamed of myself for having helped to promote an agenda of fear and torment as I once did, for having squashed rationality with the dread of terror. I regret it deeply and wish I could take it back. I only hope any damage I did to those young minds will one day be healed, and that the fear to reason freely will be overcome.

The Dangers of Fundamentalism (Part II of IV)

"Sitting Behind the Tarp, Wasting Time"

What I am about to share may seem funny to you. It may seem ridiculous, but it is quite serious and real. The story you are about to hear is true and was one of the most bizarre examples of fundamentalist paranoia I have ever personally encountered.

For the summer of 2003, my church's youth group loaded up to once again enjoy a refreshing and biblically educational blast at Camp Hensel, our yearly place for a summer camp get-away. Bear in mind, I was already an atheist undercover by now and still planning how and when I would make my final departure (which turned out to be less than 3 months later) from the ministry.

Camp was always fun. But one thing amiss this year was the swimming and lifeguard arrangements. The laws that bound the camp stated that a lifeguard had to be present with the number of swimmers we were going to have. We had trouble getting the two lifeguards we preferred (one guy and one gal), so my cousin, a well-accredited, very experienced lifeguard was about to help us out since we were in a severely tight spot and needed the help. Then the problems began.

The elders of this congregation of the Church of Christ were very uncomfortable with the fact that only one male lifeguard was going to be watching over males and females. Partly, from a fundamentalist's perspective, I can understand their inflexibility. Ideally, if you are a believer, worried about causing someone to lust after someone else, a lifeguard should be of the same sex as the swimmers they are watching. Okay, not a bad requirement for a Church of Christ camp. But they didn't stop there.

The Church of Christ is about as wacky as they get when it comes to modesty. In fact, they almost resemble a church camp from the 19th century when the girls had to swim in ankle-length dresses. The following precautions were put in place and supported inflexibly by the men of the congregation...

1) The boys and girls must be separated into different swim groups. Fair enough. Unnecessary, but if this was all that was done, I would never have written this article.

2) The boys and girls had to agree to sit down in the back of the trucks and cover themselves up with their towels on the ride to and from the swimming hole! Naturally, the girls got the worst end of the stick here. The counselors went so far as to make sure that the girls were already back in their cabins by the time the boys were even allowed to dress up and head to the trucks to get to the river. I observed as a girl in one of the trucks, being brought back with the rest of the girls to their cabins from the swimming hole, got excited and shook her arms in the air, laughing with the other girls. At that moment, a counselor yelled at the passing truck she was in, "Sit down and cover up, girls!" Several more counselors followed suit in reacting to their playful gestures by verbally scalding them as though they had exposed themselves at a topless bar! Some counselors went after a few of the girls and threatened them with expulsion from the camp if they dared let go of their towels again, lest any poor, unfortunate boy look upon them and lust, earning him a one-way-ticket to Hell! Heaven forbid a girl shake her arms and risk accidentally jiggling her breasts, inducing "animal passions"!

3) The boys and girls were required to wear knee-length, baggy shorts, plus a one-piece swimsuit underneath a dark colored t-shirt that could *not* be taken off even after they got to the river! Even though the boys would be swimming separately, the shirt was too important! The worry seemed to be that a patch of cold river water would harden a girl's nipples and cause a man to lust upon seeing the girls on their way back to the cabins, even though the boys weren't even around to see anything! Heaven forbid we drop our guard against nipples because nipples are intrinsically evil—even when seen through a swimsuit, a black t-shirt, and in summer temperatures!

I think the modesty bill has been paid by now, don't you? But those running the camp didn't agree with me when I told them that separated swim groups and one-piece swimsuits should be easily good enough to guarantee no "lust of the eyes" (I John 2:15). Berating campers for playfulness as was done was unnecessary. The girls had done nothing wrong. Under my calm demeanor, I was mentally yelling at the top of my lungs at the director's idiotic paranoia. My words were to no avail. They continued planning out their maddening fundamentalist rules for modesty. I was brushed aside when the more careful elders made a ruling that if a child came anywhere outside of a cabin with shorts just a hair under the prescribed length, they were disciplined and told they would be sent home if any other violations of the dress code were found.

But all of this *still* wasn't enough! The elders decided that my cousin – the lifeguard – to ensure that he did not lust upon the girls he would be watching, had to be seated **almost a half-mile away from the river, behind a 12 x 20 foot army tarp, attached to two trees, blocking any view of the water**! No, I'm not joking or exaggerating. This area where the lifeguard was to sit was up a slight hill. So not only was the river too far away for a lifeguard to see anything accurately, but it was just about out of view all the way because of the elevation of the ground, not to mention that totally obstructing view from behind the tarp! This made it impossible to see the water at all.

How was the lifeguard supposed to do his job of watching the water, you ask? Well, the elders discussed this, and they determined that the lifeguard would be sitting with only a view of a tiny patch of ground somewhat close to the river, but a ways away from the swimming area. Should someone begin to drown, a certain young girl was instructed to run up to this tiny patch of ground and jump up and down and yell as loud as she could for help. The lifeguard was then supposed to see this girl, jumping and yelling for help and come running down the good distance from his seated area to the river, jump in, and then save the drowning girl.

Mind you, identifying a person from this distance away would make it extremely difficult to pick out the features or gestures of any particular person needing help, and almost impossible to hear a cry or yell, leaving a lifeguard to ask, *"Is that a child playing in the distance, jumping up and down, or a girl trying to get our attention, calling out for help?"* This is *assuming* the children playing around a drowning child even managed to notice someone drowning. Many drownings don't make a scene. The person just slips under water and doesn't come up again! That playful children should be expected to responsibly look out for their peers in a lifeguard capacity in a river with a current is complete and utter folly! The time that it would take, (should the other children even notice a drowning child in dark, murky river waters) to relay the information to the appointed girl, so she could run up to the tiny patch of land where she was instructed to go and jump up and down, screaming for help, waiting for the lifeguard to notice her (*if* the lifeguard managed to notice her at all!), and begin his minute-or-onger trip down to the water's edge (running at a very good speed), would probably take about ten minutes or better—long after an oxygen-deprived brain would have been hopelessly damaged or the person died! The insanity, the absurdity, the sickness of this situation is mind-blowing! If it were not so serious, it would be hilarious!

Anyone who knows anything about life-guarding knows that there is training involved and certain rules that must be followed. A lifeguard is responsible for their allotted section. Every few seconds, a head count of how many people above and below the water must be done to properly do the job. Now this implies that the lifeguard must be in close enough proximity to the water to actually see it! Not surprisingly, my cousin, being an exceptionally recognized and well-accredited lifeguard, refused to work under these absurd instructions set by the church.

As it turned out, no one drowned. Everything went alright, but had things gone wrong, it would have been disastrous for everyone…for the owners of Camp Hensel, who tried to comply with all state laws (and expected us to see to it that we did our part faithfully), for the church leaders involved, some of whom were just following the orders of the elders, not to mention some devastated, grieving parents, who would not be happy to learn of their child's death! It could have been a nightmare, but we got lucky, and it wasn't.

If I had it to do over again, I would report the directors and elders of this church group to the owners of the camp for violating the law. In my cousin's place, two part-time, young, male lifeguards that they managed to get last-minute ended up just where my cousin would have been—behind that stupid tarp, well away from the water's edge! When I brought it up to the men that I strongly objected to this, the line they gave me was that "technically," the laws that bound the camp said a lifeguard had to be "present," but not necessarily "present at the water," as that was not stated in so many words. This, of course, was a woeful manipulation of the law. I wish I had made the move to stand up and report this dangerous abuse of regulations.

On one particular trip, as I was heading back from the water, I beheld that damn green tarp again, and the two young, inexperienced lifeguards sitting behind it, twiddling their thumbs, unable to do their jobs because of the religious nuts that ran the place. I was angry about this, and from the looks of it, so were they. I could only bring myself to apologize to them for the elders not letting them do their jobs the way they knew they should have been able to.

I believe religion in any form is very often detrimental, but fundamentalism, for reasons already given, is much worse. It manages to bring out the very worst in mankind.

The Dangers of Fundamentalism (Part III of IV)

Bible Heist '96

A year before I began attending the Church of Christ, I was given a keepsake Bible from an old friend who had moved away. It was a version of the Bible known as The New World Translation of the Holy Scriptures, a Bible translation not well recognized among many churches, and certainly not among the Church of Christ. When I began attending church, I took with me this special Bible. Then, one Sunday morning, it was nowhere, not at church and not at home. I looked and looked, and no one knew where it was. I had it one Sunday morning for Bible class, then it disappeared completely. I just assumed I'd misplaced it at church, but going through every shelf of books there, it was nowhere to be found. Finally, upon my conversion, mother and grandmother bought me another one, a very expensive New King James Version which I grew to love, but I never knew what had happened to that old one. Eventually, I gave up thinking about it.

Several years later, I was at preaching school and that old book had fallen to the back of my mind. Then something troublesome came to my attention; my preaching brethren, three of whom had a big part in converting me and with whom I had become good friends, were not beyond stealing! Yes, stealing!

I have personally known some very determined men and women of God through the years, eccentrically devout people, but few of them were so determined that their actions became criminal in nature like these guys did. The three preachers I am thinking of right now conspired together to commit theft. What did they steal? They stole a huge stack of New International Version Bibles from a small church we preaching students were invited to come and speak at. Two of them played look-out for the one who actually picked up the stack of books (from his waist to his chin in height!) and loaded them into the back of none other than the church van that brought them there!

Why did they do this? Because our radical sect of the Church of Christ felt that this translation (the NIV) was deceiving and evil. The brotherhood vigorously spoke out against it and had for years. These men were so consumed with this belief that it drove them to steal an entire arm's load of Bibles that must have been worth more than a few hundred dollars—stolen, ironically, by preachers who preached against stealing! What's more, these preachers never even bothered to replace the stolen Bibles with ones of different translations that they thought would better convey the message of Christ. The two other preachers who were with the thief who actually carried off the books told me about this without the slightest hint of shame, and several other young men from preaching school heard about it too. No one took issue with it beyond making a few awkward grins and looking the other way. I confronted my friends regarding it and they didn't even bat an eye. As they saw it, even theft is not too big a price to pay when a soul can be saved from the fires of Hell!

This brought back to mind my old missing Bible from years earlier. I thought that if this bunch was in the ends-justify-the-means business of soul-saving, it wouldn't be beyond them to have taken my old Bible. I came right out and asked one of them if he took it, and he wasted no time telling me that he had. He explained how he feared for my soul. I remember hearing, "Those Jehovah's Witnesses would have eaten you alive with that translation. You were a new convert then. I didn't want you to be deceived by a heretical Bible translation, so I put it on ice." He didn't even apologize! In his eyes, I could see that he actually looked for my approval in the action he took! I didn't think to ask him why he didn't just come to me and hand me a better translation to use and tell me why I should be weary of the one he decided to steal from me, nor did I think to point out that the Bible he destroyed was special because it was from a friend, a keepsake! I just let the matter drop.

If I had confronted him on this, he would probably have quoted Acts 19:19, emphasizing the urgency to get rid of literature that was an affront to God's word, *"Many of them also which used curious arts brought their books together, and burned them before all men: and they counted the price of them, and found it fifty thousand pieces of silver."*

Historically, Christians have not been vocal in speaking out against burning books they consider contrary to their teachings. In fact, I know of at least one pamphlet in the Church of Christ that actually encourages members to burn certain "liberal" translations of the Bible (any translations that point out in a footnote that the Hebrew word, "alma," used in Isaiah 7:14, does not mean virgin made this list!)

Was I angry? Yes, I was angry, but I let it go somehow. I suppose this was because I too was absorbed in the same doctrinal nonsense my preaching comrades were and believed the NIV was heretical as well as they. This in no way justified holy theft, of course. I protested vehemently, but that was all, and I suppose my lack of willingness to name names and expose them right then and there came from this state of theological saturation.

I am tempted to name names now and expose these religious extremists for who they are, only I fear that it would be pointless. I should have reported the men to the school director. I should have taken a stand and shown those frothing zealots the fruits of being too missionary in their conduct. If only I had possessed the strength to stand up at the time for that defrauded church, for decency, and for the preaching school that aimed to produce faithful preachers. I failed, and for that I am sorry.

What if I had mustered up the courage to oppose them back then? I thought about turning them in, but I recollected I Corinthians 6:6, "Dare any of you, having a matter against another, go to law before the unjust, and not before the saints?" The belief that the church was somehow above the secular world and more precious to God also played a part in my remaining silent on this issue.

Thinking back on this today, I am still stunned. Even in this long-distant age, far removed from those closed-minded Christians who burned entire libraries to the ground in order to squelch the fear of religious opposition, the desire to suppress contrary knowledge or beliefs is still alive and well! It is shocking to observe throughout history how the most esteemed sources of "good" are found to produce some of the greatest of evils.

The Dangers of Fundamentalism (Part IV of IV)

Riding With Terrorists

There is a scientific principle called Like Aggregation. It states that objects of similar size and weight will aggregate towards one another or join together, this being due to currents and winds, the response of the objects to magnetic fields, and other factors. This effect is something we take for granted, but we see it every time we observe a wad of cat hair or a clump of dirt lying around.

It is very interesting to see a spiritual side to this principle at work in the lives of people, as well as inanimate objects. As human beings, we find that those who think like us, act like us, are comfortable and willing to associate with us, and will side with us in arguments, tend to gravitate toward us. This is why street thugs, choirboys, and presidents don't mingle and hang out together at shopping malls.

In 1997, during my last year at preaching school, I saw this principle at work like I never had before. On the way home from a lectureship in Denton, Texas, we students were making reference to the powerful preaching we heard while at the lectureship when the subject of abortion chanced to come up. This led to the subject of Eric Rudolph, the famous abortion clinic bomber and domestic terrorist. He was first becoming recognized back then, and we soon found ourselves talking about his crimes, when out of the blue, one very vocal preaching student said, "I honestly can't condemn him for what he did!" It was like someone dropped a pistol! There was the usual stunned moment of silence as the students began to look around at each other and then back at the speaker to clarify what had been said. "Honestly, murderers need to die. Abortionists are murderers. I can't condemn this guy at all for what he did."

I was unprepared to see one of my own brethren defend the likes of this monster. I said to him again, this time with a partial grin on my face as though I knew he was about to cop to pulling my leg. "Seriously..." With not the slightest of hesitation or anything but a serious, almost angry expression on his face, he said, "Does it look like I'm kidding?" I realized then that he wasn't, and at this point, just waited for some of the other guys to jump in and tell him what a nut he had become. No one did. Looking to see why, I glanced over the bus seats and got a load of the facial expressions of others. To my amazement, I beheld what appeared to be nods of approval, maybe a few disturbed looks, but not one horrified expression in the bunch.

I seemed to be alone. No one else saw this as a terrible sign of a dangerous dogma. I can remember thinking to myself, "I am riding with potential terrorists! These people are not that far removed from Subway-bombing Jihadists!" Of course, I quickly put the thought behind me, assuming perhaps they were speaking out of anger and not serious reflection. This didn't seem likely though, since even when I described the agony of having to undergo multiple painful skin-graphs and reconstructive surgeries, loss of hearing, loss of sight, chronic pain, missing limbs, and any number of other injuries that come from incendiary devices like explosives, I got no reactions from them. They seemed unphased, able only to think about the heavily influential anti-abortion materials we had been fed. This was probably the first red flag that went up in my head, showing me just how dangerous any religiously motivated ideal can be.

Even being consumed in the very same radical dogma they were, I still found this disturbing. I was apparently the only one who was truly appalled. My brethren would never have had the courage or the desire to do what Rudolph did, but they couldn't fault him for it either. What was so sad was that they didn't realize how they had stooped to the level of the desert-roaming radical groups they claimed to oppose. In effect, they became Christian terrorist sympathizers who entertained the idea that maybe God was using Rudolph to extend the arm of divine justice on those "godless baby-murderers" who worked in abortion clinics. "Thus saith the Lord, my servant Eric Rudolph shall bring justice…" Scary indeed to think about! The Bible doesn't say this, but it might as well have in the minds of these believers. It is the cauterizing lesson of humanity—if no one is around for us to hate and oppose, we eventually become what we once hated and opposed most fervently!

In my first home church, I was asked to march in several anti-abortion rallies, but never did. The whole idea seemed a bit radical to me, but as a young, Christian man, I found that the proponents of abortion rallies argued their case well, "Joe, why won't you march? If we can intimidate just one young girl into staying away from the slaughterhouse so that her child lives, we've saved a life. God wants you to do that!" I once thought to respond, "Well, we could handcuff ourselves to the doors and that would stop people too!" They quit trying to convince me to join them after a while, but listening to their boasting from pulpits on how they had such huge turnouts at the rallies was still disgusting. You never saw the eyes of believers light up with hatred as when standing outside a Planned Parenthood facility!

As I look back on these events, I remember how grandma's old saying went, "Birds of a feather flock together." Life dictates that you won't have to wait long for someone to show their true colors. People's convictions make them act like they do. The things they say, the rash statements they make, those with whom they side in arguments are all signs of their indubitable selves. And the fruits of that nature can be clearly seen; Rudolph's deeds are right in line with the beliefs of many Christians, one of those being that God wants abortionists to pay for their sins in blood (Genesis 9:6). A lot of believers might disagree on how to go about shedding this blood, but that is a minor detail in comparison to the big picture. Be it government or vigilante justice (whichever happens to come through quickest for the believer's holy cause), they want action here and now! God hates "hands that shed innocent blood" (Proverbs 6:17), even though, ironically, when all the hype is cleared away, the Bible itself is found to be a book that allows abortion (see Genesis 38:24; Exodus 21:22-23).

I hold Jesus accountable for the manufacture of Christian monsters of every mold. The greatest shortcoming of Jesus was that all throughout his ministry he never once spoke out about the fact that every sincere believer is only one notch away from stepping into life-threatening radicalism. The Christian fundamentalist mindset is dangerous. It devalues life and appreciates one that exists only in fantasy. It enslaves the rational mind, empowering an otherwise conscionable individual to do inhumane things with feelings of integral justification, or at the very least, it creates support and sympathy for those who so act.

The Follies of Faith (Part I of II)

Jesus said, *"If ye have faith as a grain of mustard seed, ye shall say unto this mountain, Remove hence to yonder place; and it shall remove; and nothing shall be impossible unto you."* (Matthew 17:20)

I don't agree with a lot of what Jesus says, but I partly agree with the above verse. Jesus is right. Faith is a very powerful thing, more powerful than we stop to realize. Hebrews gives us a list of other great works of faith…

> *4. By faith Abel offered unto God a more excellent sacrifice than Cain, by which he obtained witness that he was righteous, God testifying of his gifts: and by it he being dead yet speaketh. 5. By faith Enoch was translated that he should not see death; and was not found, because God had translated him: for before his translation he had this testimony, that he pleased God. 6. But without faith it is impossible to please him: for he that cometh to God must believe that he is, and that he is a rewarder of them that diligently seek him. 7. By faith Noah, being warned of God of things not seen as yet, moved with fear, prepared an ark to the saving of his house; by the which he condemned the world, and became heir of the righteousness which is by faith. 8. By faith Abraham, when he was called to go out into a place which he should after receive for an inheritance, obeyed; and he went out, not knowing whither he went. 9. By faith he sojourned in the land of promise, as in a strange country, dwelling in tabernacles with Isaac and Jacob, the heirs with him of the same promise: 10. For he looked for a city which hath foundations, whose builder and maker is God. 11. Through faith also Sara herself received strength to conceive seed, and was delivered of a child when she was past age, because she judged him faithful who had promised.* (Hebrews 11:4-11)

Faith is an incredible thing, but I don't think this list is fair. It mentions only positive things from a Judeo-Christian standpoint that were products of faith. I think, to be fair, we need to focus on some of the many more negative things faith has been primarily responsible for producing…

By faith, radical Muslims fly plains into buildings. By faith, suicide bombers explode themselves around sidewalks full of people, or on school buses full of children. By faith, large groups senselessly riot over the publishing of stupid Mohammed cartoons and call for the life of the artists that produced them. By faith, Jewish and Arab teens throw rocks at each other, stab each other, and get together in mobs to beat their enemies to death with makeshift blunt objects, in the absence of a gun. By faith, dedicated Muslim families place their babies and young children in front of U.S. tanks as they roll through town, trying to clear out terrorist cells.

By faith, Nick Burg had his head sawed off by extremist Muslims while videotape rolled and caught his silenced screams and gasps for breath, after which his severed head was placed on top of his lifeless body. By faith, Muslims, Jews, and Christians gather in large numbers to assemble at the Wailing Wall, nodding and praying, rocking back and forth, in adoration of a God who sits by and lets the never-ending Holy Land dispute go unresolved, allowing the respective religions to remain bitter enemies for centuries, even amidst the desperate cries of some of their representatives for the violence to stop. By faith, a Muslim man is moved to throw acid in his sister's face, disfiguring her, because she was raped and is no longer a virgin. By faith, a Somalian man, a follower of an ancient Coptic faith, or an older version of Christianity or Islam, brings his young daughter to the village elders to have her clitoris removed before she reaches maturity to ensure that she will never be tempted to know sexual pleasure, and therefore, be tempted to cheat on her husband with another man. Other men like him have their daughters infibulated (infibulation: the sowing up of the girl's labia majora to prevent promiscuity) for the same purpose.

By faith, a number of Christians on December 31 of 1999 quit their jobs, loaded up their cars with toilet paper, bottled water, canned goods, and Bibles, in fear of computer systems crashing because of the supposed Y2k bug. By faith, some preachers behind this told their congregations that this would be the beginning of the "antichrist" and his reign of terror, as he reset all computers and began to takeover everything, thus beginning "the tribulation period." By faith, Christians have awaited the return of Christ for centuries, gathering outside of their houses on rooftops, selling their possessions, waiting to be raptured up to heaven.

By faith, U.S. courts refused patents to atheist organizations who publicly declared their intentions to speak out against Jesus and the church. By faith, green wood was used to fuel the fires of stake burnings to ensure that the impenitent heretic burned slower and suffered more before expiring. By faith, a working-class, divorced mother of two breaks her arm at a local Pentecostal assembly, after a crowd of fellow idiots spin her around by her arms to "get rid of demons," when they drop her accidentally. By faith, a number of charismatic preachers end up in the obituaries due to snake bites. By faith, a woman is encouraged to leave her husband and break up her marriage as a preacher tells her she had no right to get remarried. By faith, another woman in the same situation is caused to worry endlessly whether or not God will forgive her for staying with a man after she has been divorced and has remarried.

By faith, monks, priests, and Catholic church officials are prevented from marrying or enjoying any conjugal benefits. By faith, a number of young, baptized men go to their fundamentalist fathers and ask what can be done to keep from masturbating. Since it is a temptation they cannot escape from, they urgently seek counsel on how to deal with it. By faith, men entering the ministry, if they are not married by a certain point in time, consider castration for the same reason (I have actually seen this being discussed as an option!) By faith, a Church of Christ Scientist family refuses to medicate a child when he is sick, allowing the child to die. By faith, a strict father charges into his son's room and smacks him in the face, and tells him to, *"Shape up and be a man!"* and *"Be the man God wants you to be!"*, destroying his child's respect for him and his religion.

How long can this list become? Much longer than it is, for sure. Faith is the motivating factor in an untold number of negative things. What little good can come of it is either delusional, rare, questionable, or superfluous. But the list I made a theist could respond to. I know how I would have responded to these points as a minister. I could wax quite eloquent doing so, pointing out that Bible faith, properly applied, is good and spiritually profitable. But for every explanation I would get, entire groups of believers would have their own explanations for what they believe is spiritually valuable.

For starters, I'd have pointed out that God wants us all to work and not futilely wait for the coming of Christ (2 Thessalonians 3:10-14), that God does not encourage berating children and how this father was too hard on his son, "fathers provoke not your children to wrath." (Ephesians 6:3). I'd have said that medicine should be used per the principle of I Timothy 5:23, and on and on I could go, justifying my version of Christianity. But matching my contention that my faith – correctly applied – produces good fruits, another religious leader, a believer in some other faith, will have a different take on things.

A radical Muslim will defend his exhaustive methods to rout his enemies, the Jews, whom he thinks have taken his land, and such a one might go so far as to include a justification for throwing acid in the face of a woman who lost her virginity before marriage. A believer in older Christian and Muslim traditions will defend cliterodectomy and infibulation as sacred traditions, similar to circumcision. Such a leader might even point to alleged reduced infidelity rates among their women, or point out that taking pleasure away that is never known to a person (such as when the practices are carried out on young girls) will not be missed. A snake-handling pastor will defend their handling of snakes based on Mark 16:9-11. A conventional dispute with the pastor will not change his take on the scriptures, and it will be just another religious division in an already divided religious world. No one will have solved anything, and faith will still be the root cause of these evils, justified or unjustified. This makes faith a bad thing, a thing so easily abused and capable of being misdirected that the negative applications of it far outweigh any good that comes from it.

Of course, faith goes beyond mere dogma, beyond some bland rule book. Religious faith is personal, irrational, and captivating, grafted deeply into the heart of the individual who has it. It makes man capable of what he otherwise wouldn't be capable of, and this is why it so very often can and does result in folly.

The Follies of Faith (Part II of II)

Faith is a personal thing, a psychological thing, and even when believers are a part of the same religion, there tends to be a side of them that understands that God is somehow communicating with them on a personal level. Faith, and the so-called "inner-leadings," nudgings, and wooings of God for a person to do this or that are far too strong to ignore. That is to say, believers not only hold to the guiding authority of the Bible, but believe God leads the believer individually. Most Christians are crazy about the idea that God directs by the Holy Bible, and most won't deny that God exerts a direct influence upon the heart in a mysterious and unknown way.

For instance, God might "lead" a Christian to put their child in a private school as opposed to a public one, or God might providentially "urge" the believer to attend a certain type of church with a certain type of atmosphere. Of course, God ends up "wooing" every religious person to do this or that, and every other contradictory and mutually exclusive thing, depending on which religious sect the person is from. To deny God the power to tickle your heart a little is "boxing God in," as I remember several preachers telling me. So most modern Christians consider God to be operational doctrinally by the Bible alone, but personally by a more nebulous inner-leading.

These inner-leadings can become downright bizarre. Take, for instance, the case of Rolando Del Campo. Twelve years ago, Rolando's wife was experiencing an intensely difficult labor. When the possibility became likely that his child may not survive, Campo pleaded with God in prayer that if he would allow his daughter to live, he would crucify himself fifteen times. The daughter lived and he has fulfilled his vows—almost! To date, he has been crucified (yes, nails and all!) some twelve times. He was "led" by God to make such a sacrifice. Most modern, sophisticated Christians find such behavior bizarre. They might even quote Colossians 2:23, which speaks against asceticism as a form of godliness, but try telling this man he was vainly hurting himself. Try cracking open a Bible and sitting down with him for a study and showing him how pattern-istic God is, and how he wants us all to conform to the words of a lambskin-covered holy book. Your message will not get through. His world of faith opened up when he found his daughter healed. It was all the vindication and proof he needed for his understanding of Christianity to be validated.

Maybe harming our bodies, the temples of God, is ordinarily to be considered bad, but for him, God was demanding he fulfill his rash promise, just like Jephthae was apparently required to offer up his own daughter to the Lord in sacrifice (see Judges 11), and like Isaiah, who was commanded to prophesy naked for one year (Isaiah 20:2), even though the rest of us must always wear clothes, given the provision of Genesis 3 and Paul's warning to dress modestly (I Timothy 2:9). So you see how faith is not a strictly biblical thing. It is a psychological thing, a quest for answers and self-worth in the absence of it. One need not have a deep understanding of the Bible to have faith experiences with what they consider to be "True Christianity." Of this, there can be no doubt. You can quote the Bible all you want, but in the end, it's the experiences that matter.

If that's too drastic an example, consider what happened on an ordinary morning in my home town of San Antonio, Texas. It was just business as usual at a local Mexican taco house when the Virgin Mary appeared on a frying pan. The entire restaurant was astonished and shared in extolling this holy experience as a true miracle. It seemed as though the image of Mary was carved onto the pan, but the two restaurant owners swore otherwise. They even called reporters and it became a news story. It is an experience they (and now the world, unfortunately) will never forget. This would be laughed off by so many people, but it is no laughing matter for so many Catholics worldwide with just the right kind of faith to look for and expect these sorts of things. Mary is very creative in where she chooses to appear: under a Chicago Highway, on a tree, a tent, a mosquito net, a patio deck, etc. Just let imagination run wild, and some time or another, the Blessed and Holy Virgin will be descending and making an appearance in your neck of the woods—*if* you have faith in her!

The religiously drugged world is moved to tears by men and women of great faith, by sobbing masses of pious souls, who burn incense and carry eerily decorated crosses and gory crucifixes down the streets in a parade of self-inflicted mourning, but I am not impressed at all. Why are the faithful doing these things? Why are they so feverishly putting themselves out for the sake of their heavenly caretaker? Because their deity is a monster, the same abuser of mankind who manages always to leave humanity in the dark about what he really wants from us concerning extra-biblical matters of faith. A man who must be crucified fifteen times before a deity will agree to save his child's life – even though it costs that deity absolutely nothing to do so – is an unscrupulous being. No matter what type of sacrifices God demands of his many believers, he always appears totally intent on watching us mortals put on dazzling displays of faith, and then maybe...*just maybe*...he will answer our prayers and bless our lives.

A Response to "You were never really saved!"

So I was never really saved, aye?

Then what am I to make of that shock, that feeling of inexplicable joy when I first looked in the mirror on that memorable night I confessed Jesus and made the decision to give my life to him? How is it that I actually saw myself as a different person? "Jesus answered, Verily, verily, I say unto thee, Except a man be born of water and of the Spirit, he cannot enter into the kingdom of God." (John 3:5)

What am I to make of that feeling, that indescribable feeling that I was indeed a new creation, forgiven of my sins? "Therefore if any man be in Christ, he is a new creature: old things are passed away; behold, all things are become new." (2 Corinthians 5:17)

What am I to make of all those nights I stared up at the stars and prayed, cried and prayed, being in awe of creation? "The heavens declare the glory of God; and the firmament sheweth his handywork." (Psalm 19:1)

What am I to make of my sudden change in behavior, my desire to improve my life after the biblical pattern, to stop cursing and partying, to put away the conduct of "the old man of sin"? (Colossians 3:10) "Either make the tree good, and his fruit good; or else make the tree corrupt, and his fruit corrupt: for the tree is known by his fruit." (Matthew 12:33)

What am I to make of that inner conviction I had to study the Bible, "the sword of the spirit, which is the word of God" (Eph 6:17), and to commit it to memory? "Study to shew thyself approved unto God, a workman that needeth not to be ashamed, rightly dividing the word of truth." (2 Timothy 2:15)

What am I to make of my longing to know the truth, my desire to worship and accept a higher power like I'd never experienced before? "Ask, and it shall be given you; seek, and ye shall find; knock, and it shall be opened unto you" (Matthew 7:7)

What am I to make of my improved consciousness of "sins," my awareness of failure before an almighty God? "If a man therefore purge himself from these, he shall be a vessel unto honour, sanctified, and meet for the master's use, and prepared unto every good work." (2 Timothy 2:21)

What am I to make of that overpowering sensation that I had a purpose, a divine purpose, one I never knew I had before? "For we are his workmanship, created in Christ Jesus unto good works, which God hath before ordained that we should walk in them." (Ephesians 2:10)

What am I to make of that sense of confidence I gained as a believer, the willingness to take on the world and win? "I can do all things through Christ which strengtheneth me." (Philippians 4:13)

What am I to make of that sense of calm, the "peace that passes all understanding," with which I was so familiar? "And the peace of God, which passeth all understanding, shall keep your hearts and minds through Christ Jesus." (Philippians 4:7)

What am I to make of my acquired compulsion to preach, an inner burning I had never known? "Then I said, I will not make mention of him, nor speak any more in his name. But his word was in mine heart as a burning fire shut up in my bones, and I was weary with forbearing, and I could not stay." (Jeremiah 20:9)

What am I to make of my reliance on prayer, on fasting, on meditating in the Psalms and in the Book of Job when tragedy struck? "when ye fast" (not if!) (Matthew 6:16) "But the end of all things is at hand: be ye therefore sober, and watch unto prayer." (I Peter 4:7)

What am I to make of my longing for increased wisdom and faith after every trial of faith and every turbulent ordeal? "Yea, and all that will live godly in Christ Jesus shall suffer persecution." (2 Tim 3:12)

What am I to make of my heartfelt prayers for wisdom, prayers offered to the Father in the spirit of Solomon, who asked for wisdom above all things? "To know wisdom and instruction; to perceive the words of understanding;" (Proverbs 1:2)

What am I to make of my hope that God would use me as his vessel by putting me in a position of power where I could influence the world with God's love and revelation? "Also I heard the voice of the Lord, saying, Whom shall I send, and who will go for us? Then said I, Here am I; send me." (Isaiah 6:8)

What am I to make of my continual prayers to God that I would not be led in the way of temptation, but be given only what would never lead me away from him? "And lead us not into temptation, but deliver us from evil: For thine is the kingdom, and the power, and the glory, for ever. Amen." (Matt 6:13)

What am I to make of being moved to tears as I read the emotional words of Jesus as he said, "O Jerusalem, Jerusalem, thou that killest the prophets, and stonest them which are sent unto thee, how often would I have gathered thy children together, even as a hen gathereth her chickens under her wings, and ye would not! Behold, your house is left unto you desolate. For I say unto you, Ye shall not see me henceforth, till ye shall say, Blessed is he that cometh in the name of the Lord." (Matthew 23:37-39)? Is feeling for the Jewish people and being moved when the people of God go astray a mark of a fake believer?

What am I to make of my "looking for and hasting unto the Day of God, wherein the heavens, being on fire, shall be desolved and the elements shall melt with fervent heat," (2 Pet 3:12) and my longing for "a city which hath foundations, whose builder and maker is God." (Hebrews 11:10)? Is this the mark of an infidel?

Have any of the sentiments I have expressed here shown an impenitent man who never understood what biblical spirituality is about? Does it still appear that I was "never really saved," that the Christian cause was never important to me? Do these words sound like something that would come from the mouth of an excuse for a preacher who never cared about a thing in the ministry besides money? Or, is it time to concede that for a number of years in my life I *did* indeed understand and walk the Christian walk as faithfully as any man, and then chose another walk?

This piece was written in response to those many zealous believers who tirelessly insist that I was never really a Christian, that I was never genuinely "converted," that I never possessed a true love and conviction for the Bible and Christianity. These examples bear impeccable witness to the fact that if anyone was ever "saved," I was (as far as the term goes). I understand the deepest depths of the Christian experience and know what it means to give my whole life to this cause with the greatest love and devotion. But people change. Their beliefs change. That happened to me. As a minister, a lot of people really wanted to know what I had to say, but it seems that now, since I have become wiser and have come to understand more about life and the Bible, the people who once looked up to me for guidance and edification have suddenly lost interest in anything I have to say. That is their loss.

CHAPTER 23
The Sacred Writings of Saint Sarcasticus

Bizarre, Ironic, and Humorous Reflections from the Word of God

"Fools are my theme. Let satire be my song."
- Lord Byron

"Does it make you feel big and important to spit on the only begotten son of God, who temporarily died for our sins?"
- Timothy Omachi

Joe E. Holman is...Saint Sarcasticus!

Questions for God

Hello God. It's Joe Holman, your ex-servant with yet another list of questions for you – questions you will, no doubt, add to my extensive list of blasphemies, reproaches, and mortal sins, which will further serve to guarantee my damnation – but a man must have answers, right? None of your representatives here on earth (the scholars and theologians whom you have appointed to make you look logically credible in the eyes of skeptics) can provide me with the answers I seek, so I would like to get them straight from the horse's mouth, if you don't mind.

As you know, Lord, I am a troubled soul, a rigidly dogmatic and militant atheist, headed straight for the burnt-black depths of the merciless Hell you created. I desperately need your help and salvation, but I need these questions answered before that can ever happen. The first set of questions concerns your existence.

For one, I am confused, oh Lord, about this whole creation scheme. I mean, you are a perfect being, which means you lack nothing, right? So why did you bother creating anything in the first place? I thought a perfect being would have no needs or wants. Apparently that's not true of you since, for some reason, you became discontented with the peacefulness of being alone in the quiet chasm of nonexistence that surrounded you. It was just you – perfect, holy, and lonesome – evidently not knowing what to do with yourself for a googol eons before time began. I think I understand how that could get boring. I mean, you can only create so many angels, galaxies, and diverse kinds of creatures, until eventually, you're bored out of your mind, right? Is this what it was that changed your thinking to suddenly decide to create a big, bustling universe? Let me reiterate: you don't have to be sorry for being bored in your position. Since you are the all-knowing God, no knowledge is hidden from you, which to me, would make for a lot of pronounced boredom.

Somehow, someway, you are made up of three persons: the Father, the Son, and the Holy Spirit, but you three certainly can't talk to one another since you are all one and share the same knowledge. You can't really talk to the angels or us humans down here either because you know everything we are going to say before we say it. So naturally, you can't ever find any meaningful conversations to get into. That's okay, though. Correct me if I'm wrong, but you shouldn't really want conversation because, as God, you know all things, and no one can give you knowledge that you already have, right? I'm afraid I must raise the same question in regard to praising and worshipping you.

Why do you need praise? Why worship? Why do you need to hear constant flatteries from lesser beings who are beneath you? What do you get out of this? Is worship just another form of a heavenly "high," some sort of divine masturbation? Well, I suppose your Bible does answer this question for me, at least indirectly; it says you are a jealous God (Exodus 20:5), meaning you long for ceaseless attention and adoration; but jealousy is a bad thing, isn't it? It's a human flaw. How is this a positive, perfect, and holy attribute of yours? Jealousy always accompanies obsession. If you were human and expressed the same insatiable need for such relentless, self-obsessive, self-glorifying worship, I'd think you had more issues than a newspaper, and can you blame me? I can deal just fine with obsessed, neurotic humans, but an obsessed and neurotic god? That's too much. A god with human frailties is quite a scary thing.

Moving on, in all of eternity's silence before you decided to create this universe, did you ever wonder, even for just a second, how you came to exist? Please tell me, did you create yourself? I don't see how you could have created yourself because that would make you temporal and not eternal, and a thing cannot be its own first cause now, can it? If you didn't create yourself, but existed eternally, then aren't you limited in power because you exist apart from your own approval? I mean, you didn't have any choice but to exist, did you? You must also be powerless to commit suicide because if you did, you would cease to be eternal, no? So it seems fair to say that you are powerless in these regards, a slave to your own existence. I'm only asking because I can't fathom this whole eternal god thing.

Every second grader asks their parents, "Mommy, who created God!" You and the scholars say that you were never created, but that you "always were." Well, forgive me for sounding uncouth, but isn't the phrase "always was" up for grabs? Can't we atheist philosophers just as easily postulate that the matter within the universe has always existed rather than jumping to the idea that some farfetched god has always existed? If that is the case, why should I accept your existence as being eternal and not the universe itself? What logical reason do I have to say that a god "always was" and not just stop and say that "matter always was"? I mean, you have to admit, jumping to a far-out conclusion that a mysterious, spooky deity created everything from nothing is a pretty big leap. I've never seen you, nor had any real experience with you, and so saying "I always was" has no significance and doesn't alleviate my curiosity about the problem of your origins at all. I could be wrong, but doesn't it make actually *more* sense to explain the origin of the universe on matter that we know exists instead of trying to explain it as the work of some god that we don't know exists?

All the theologians and scholars that believe in you are going out of their way to try to prove your existence to the world. They are taking everything from rocks to wristwatches and saying that since everything shows evidence of design, then there was a "Great Designer" who originally designed all things (that designer being you, of course). Hold on just a minute though, lord! If this is true, and all design in the universe is evidence of intelligent design, then your designing mind is also complex, and therefore, requires an even greater designer! So your scholars have solved nothing. Help me out here, oh mighty one.

Life is tough for us atheists. Let it be clear that we would worship you, if only we could establish your existence, but here, you really can't blame us—even you must admit that there is no way to tell you apart from a being who doesn't exist. Think about it for a moment: you are omnipotent (all-powerful). You are omnipresent (infinitely present). You are also omniscient (all-knowing), and you are supposedly omnibenevolent (all-good). This is hard to take in. You have absolutely no limits to define your being. In order for earthlings to understand a thing, it must be understood to have limits. I mean, everything we can define, we define because of limits; I am 6'4" and not 6'3" or 6'5". I have brown hair, and not jet black or blonde hair, and on and on we could go. The same applies to every person, place, and thing in the universe. We comprehend the universe by limits, but since you have no limits, there is therefore no distinction between you and a being who is non-existent, mythical, nonsensical, or completely illogical and untenably incoherent. You defy all logic, all thought, and all perception down to the smallest detail, and then you expect us to accept you as factual (existent) by way of reasoning and logical thinking? This just isn't happening! Please help!

Then I find other logical problems like the omnipotence vs. omniscience dilemma. How can you be infinitely knowledgeable and infinitely powerful at the same time? For example, let's say I am thirsty for either a glass of tea or a chocolate malt. Being an all-knowing deity, you know for sure which of the two I will choose as my beverage; you know that I will choose the chocolate malt. Now let's just say that you choose to exercise your omnipotence and force me to drink the tea instead of the malt; at this point, your two attributes (omniscience and omnipotence) clash; since you foreknew that I would drink the chocolate malt, you are powerless to make me drink the tea, and if you decided to force me to drink the tea anyway, you would be falsifying your own foreknowledge (because despite your foreknowledge, I drank the tea instead of the malt). So it seems to me that you might be a very powerful being, but not infinitely so—in my humble opinion, of course.

This second set of questions is in regard to your setup and planning in the Garden of Eden. First off, where did this talking snake come from (Genesis 3:1-7)? Since you created all things and only things good (2 Chronicles 19:7; James 1:12), from whence came Satan? If Satan always existed as an evil co-deity with you, then you are not omnipotent because in that case, you would not be the only eternal deity. If you created Satan to become evil, then you violated your own word by creating an evil thing, when supposedly, you cannot break or contradict your word (Titus 1:2; John 10:35). If Satan was originally created as an angel and later fell from grace, then why did you create a being that you knew would fall away? Are you not then responsible, at least in part, for his error like a negligent parent would be responsible for injury incurred on a child by leaving a knife in a child's playpen?

Please tell me why you put taboo fruit in your perfect paradise garden when you knew that your beloved primal pair of humans would eat of it and die? I'm confused already, but it gets worse; you created an angel who became the prince of the demons, and one primal couple that you knew would choose to eat the forbidden fruit, and thus, be condemned to death and Hell forever. You knew when you created man that he would fall from grace. You knew that I would become an atheist, yet you allowed all us sinners to live in the first place, knowing that we will one day writhe in agony, with blood-curdling screams, as we forever roast in the inferno of Hell. How could you do this?

I know you've had the freewill idea going for quite a while now, and you've been filling the heads of your mini-crusading, good soldier theologians with it to try and explain why terrible things happen in life, but tell me: is freewill really free? How can you say that we have freewill when we mortals cannot step out of the infinite maze of the cause and effect system which undercuts all human decisions and goals? I can't find a way out of this quandary. Since you know all things, isn't our every action and reaction as obvious to you as our favorite movie script is to us? Even if you somehow choose "not to know" some future events, as a few of your scholars have suggested, this would eliminate you from the role of God, since a God must, by definition, be infinite in all aspects, including foreknowledge. If you were concerned with allowing man freewill in the garden, why couldn't you have simply allowed Adam and Eve to exist without knowing evil—and what they didn't know, they wouldn't have chosen, would they? So freewill was never even an issue. You don't need the presence of evil to have freewill.

This brings up another question. How could Satan fall from grace in a sinless environment? If one must be tempted to sin, and Adam and Eve had to have Satan to sin, then who tempted Satan? If there was no sin in heaven, and yet an angel chose to become evil, what will prevent the same thing from happening to us when we get there? If sin can just "pop up" when and where there is none, what are we to do if we make the wrong choices in heaven, or perhaps succumb to some overwhelming sense of lofty heavenly pride? Maybe this was what happened to Satan? Heaven doesn't sound too comforting now! Forgive me, lord, for sounding presumptuous. It may be that you really wanted evil there or just allowed it for some higher purpose than a mere peabrain mortal like myself can understand, but how can that be with an omnipotent being? Beings with infinite power aren't limited to having to choose between a few limited options. Forgive me for thinking that a perfect being could make a way to create a world where nothing went wrong and everything was to that being's liking.

Maybe there's something wrong with me, but I thought that perhaps you were unable to eliminate evil, or perhaps you were unwilling to eliminate it, or maybe you were both unwilling and unable? If you are unable to eliminate evil, then you are not all-powerful, and if you are unwilling, then you are wicked. If you are both unable and unwilling, then you are both impotent and wicked. Since you are supposedly both willing and able to vanquish evil, why does evil exist? Questions, questions, but maybe I shouldn't jump the gun. Maybe, for instance, you allowed evil to enter the world to test the faithfulness of our souls? Only problem with this is, you already knew who would pass and who would fail the test without a test of any kind, so it's all pointless. Maybe you allowed evil to enter into the world to teach us lessons about life, but that doesn't really work either because you are omnipotent and could have taught man every lesson he ever needed to know a thousand different ways. You could even have made souls to be born with this knowledge.

Maybe you allowed evil to dominate the world to show us the love of salvation in the afterlife, but then that's sort of creating a problem to solve it, don't you think? Why not just show us love in the afterlife in the first place? Why bother with this material world business anyway since heaven and spirituality have been the real deal all along? Plus, isn't unleashing an arsenal of evils on a world of unsuspecting, helpless victims, and then promising to make up for it in some illusive afterlife sort of like a deadbeat dad giving his kid a black eye and then promising to take him to Disneyland to make up for it?

Isn't killing your disobedient children with death a little too strict anyway? If you were a father on earth, Child Protective Services and the law would be all over you! Not to mention, I just can't figure out why you created debilitating diseases like Spina Bifida, Caudal Regression Syndrome, Cancer, Diabetes, the Diptheria germ, Muscular Dystrophy, and Scleroderma (to name just a few of the many life-altering, death-causing, sin-cursing diseases and conditions you so gracefully sent our way). I also scratch my head wondering why you included the animal kingdom in mankind's curse. If indeed we are not animals, why must they suffer and die? They committed no sin. Their kind ate no forbidden fruit. Here's one that's got me all tied up: why did you create animals that prey on one another – fang, tooth, and claw – and why did you create parasites like the tapeworm? If tapeworms could, would you expect them to thank you every time you blessed one with a warm, luscious, human stomach to live in? I am confident that believers will continue to praise you for making the great white shark, but I suspect they will wait until they get to shore first. Is this really the way you wanted things to be?

While we're on the subject of right, I must ask how, lord, in the realm of morals and ethics, you dictate what is "good" and what is "bad"? Do you do a thing because it is "good," or is a thing "good" because you do it? If I say that you do a thing because it is good, this makes morality higher than and independent of you. In effect, it takes you off the moral necessity market because people can now bypass you and go straight to the morals without any god-belief at all. On the other hand, if I say that a thing is good because you do it, then I face the problem that anything you do I am committed to saying is good, no matter how atrocious that act might be. Such is the case with many of the things in your Holy Bible which seem quite inhumane and downright barbaric—forgive me for being so blunt.

Before we get off this morality point, I must ask if it is true what some learned men say who try to defend your conduct when they say that you are neither moral, nor immoral? If this is true, then are all your commandments arbitrary? Do you tell us not to murder simply on a whim? I mean, come on! If you are neither moral, nor immoral then your morals for us have no basis in fact or principle whatsoever. So they must be just randomly selected guidelines and nothing more, right? If this is not the case, and the morals you give us are based on your divine, higher morality, then we are back to the same question with which we began: do you do a thing because it is "good," or is a thing "good" because you do it?

Why did you order Moses to instruct the people to invade the Midianites' homes and kill every man, woman, child, and animal, to keep alive only the virgin women for those horny, Jewish soldiers (Numbers 31:15-18)? If anyone did this today, they'd be given the lethal injection in no time flat, but evidently you would disagree with such a reaction, and instead, be proud of these uncultured barbarians as you were proud of your servant David. Like you, he murdered anyone who crossed him (2 Samuel 4:12; I Chronicles 20:3), but make no mistake about it; you still hold the world record for the most murders, the 2004 tsunami being a case in point, though you still haven't broken your old record set back in the days of Noah's great flood in which you slaughtered the entire world, humans, plants, animals, and all, except for 8 people (1 Peter 3:20). As far as catastrophes go, it's been a while since September 11, 2001 when you decided to punish America because of the nation's rampant homosexuality and abortion. I mean, if it hadn't been for that tsunami, people might have started to think that you were softening up! I know that at this point, you are getting ready to send me to be sodomized by a demon on the shores of the Lake of Fire and Brimstone for eternity, but like I said, a man must have answers, right?

I have a question as to the merits of eternal damnation for disbelief. If you damn a person to Hell for not believing in you, how is this a just act, seeing that a person can only believe what they find to be true, and if that person only pretended to believe in you when they didn't, they would be hypocrites—and we know you don't want that sort of service (Matthew 7:1-5)! If, for some twisted, unthinkable, insane, out-of-this-world reason I did want to invent a Hell of my own to put powerless, tattered souls into, it would only be temporary to rehabilitate them, but not so with you! Once there, you never let them out. Why lord?

Well, lord, I have a good many other questions I would like to ask, like why you preferred the company of lower life forms, such as reptiles and amphibians, to that of humankind for billions of years before you created us—your prized creation. On a side note, why did you give the gecko the ability to grow new arms and legs, but not us? Also, why did you allow sea turtles to live for 200 years, but we only get to live about 70 nowadays? Do you care more about them than your blessed and best creation, man? Surely not, right?

The last big item I would like to inquire about is atheism. According to the Bible, you condemn me for being an atheist. Regardless of any moral virtue or uprightness of character I might have, you believe that I should burn in a lake of fire for eternity. This is a very discomforting thought indeed, but let me just come right out and ask: are you an atheist, God? I think you are. You don't pray to anyone at all. You worship no higher authority than yourself. You can only swear by yourself because you can swear by no one greater (Hebrews 6:13). You don't go to church, you haven't confessed Jesus, repented of your sins, or been baptized in Jesus' name. You humble yourself before no one, you are not religious, and you alone say what is right and what is wrong for you. You affirm very plainly in your word that "There is no God besides me" (Isaiah 44:6), thus, leaving no room for the possibility that a higher being than you can exist, and what's more, you punish people with eternal misery for not believing in you as the final authority in the cosmos.

You trample on the fallen, crushing the souls and destinies of your wayward, disobedient children who dared to step out of line. So it seems to me that you are not only an atheist, but a galactic dictator, a super-communist, a tyrannical Father Time, a despot like no other, more vicious, dogmatic, and militant that Stalin could ever have hoped to become in a thousand lifetimes. If I'm an atheist like you are, shouldn't a father be proud when he has a son who is like his father? It sounds like we think alike (well, to a very small extent!) So why, Lord, am I going to burn in Hell forever for being an atheist when you yourself are an atheist? Is this yet another case of "do as I say, not as I do" parenting?

I'm afraid there are other ways in which you show yourself hypocritical. The Bible is said to be a book that condemns abortion and recognizes the sanctity of unborn life, but then you don't have any problem killing the unborn to hurt someone else for ticking you off (2 Samuel 12:14; Hosea 13:16). I think I'm getting a double standard here. Are you really no different from the typical, desperate hostage-taker who will resort to whatever terror he can cook up to force his demands? Evidently not. Getting back to atheism, you know just what it would take to convince me of your existence, removing even the slightest of doubts in my mind. Why don't you provide this proof?

Well, lord, as usual, you've been pretty silent here as I've expressed my thoughts. In fact, I haven't heard a peep out of you yet, ever! I guess I'll never get the answers I want. I have no choice but to continue on my lonely road searching out truth in philosophical naturalism. In all honesty, I am not terribly afraid of you or this Hell place you made because, to me, you have demonstrated irrationality in every area of thought, and with irrationality comes erratic behavior; for all I know, you might change your mind tomorrow and find pleasure in saving atheists for being honest with themselves and their intellects, while getting a kick out of damning to Hell the redneck, backwoods, Bible-thumping, fundamentalist Christians who believe in the tall tales that you put in your holy book—who knows, right? Since you are, by definition, an unknowable being, is there any point in even trying to figure you out? Well, enough writing. I'm going to enjoy a cold Dr. Pepper or something.

A Petition to Re-instate Heretic Burning

Dear Mr. Congressman,

It is times like these when those of us who are conscionable, those of us who are proudly counted among the righteous must stand up and fight the tides of godlessness and moral evil in our great Land. As are many, I am concerned with the course our society is taking, and if you will join me in this fight, we can come together and work to promote change, change to that which is good and right. Call us old fashioned, call us behind the times if you so choose, but should you charge us with believing in righteous virtues of the past, then we are guilty as charged. We believe in the authority of the Holy Bible, along with the unlimited power of the Holy Roman Catholic Church.

I and my colleagues look back to a time when the Church was in full power and controlled the governments of almost every major nation of the world. It was during this wonderful time that dangerous democracy and unlimited freedom of expression had not yet unleashed their disasters on an unsuspecting world like they have in America today. Look at what freedom of expression has given our world: pornography, religious division among the confused Protestants, ignorance among the secularists about our true teachings, abortion, loose morals, and horrible sexual impurities on every level of society. These never became a problem when theocracy and religious authoritarianism was in play. It is when people are left to their own judgments that they are cut loose to draw their own faulty conclusions about life's grave issues, and when this happens, mass hysteria and moral chaos abounds. This cannot be ignored.

What also cannot be ignored is the fact that recent church sex scandals and unsubstantiated allegations of child molestation by our priests have been magnified and exaggerated to the point of absurdity. Not only have these offending priests been found to compose barely a microscopic fraction of God's priests, but as C.S. Lewis pointed out, if indeed the sexually strenuous life of devotion and abstinence had been the cause of these abuses, as some have claimed, then the abuses would have subsided by now in this age of sexual liberation, but they have only gotten worse year by year. I will remind you that it was the Church that fought this ungodliness and weakening of moral standards in past generations, and we are not about to give up that fight now.

Mr. Congressman, I ask you sincerely **which is better, liberty that kills or law enforcement that saves**? I think you will agree with me that laws to save are much better than the alternative. We discipline our children and use parental authority to control their decisions. We stop and imprison a murderer or rapist without their say in the matter. We commit a psychologically unstable person against their will to an asylum. We do not allow suicide even when a person's own life is in danger of ending by itself. We impose morality, objective morality to guide and do what is right, and not what is merely wanted by selfish, men-following masses. We need to start imposing morality on a good number of other issues.

The type of laws and punishments I am trying to get passed are the same ones the Roman Catholic Church had several centuries ago; they concern (a) various laws and edicts of the Catholic Church that will be binding on all men and women, (b) the bringing back of a banned book list, (c) punishments and torture methods from the periods of the Inquisition and the Crusades. I know this will seem a bit extreme, especially since our nation has been known as a nation of freedom for so long, but what must be remembered is that what we have come to call freedom and liberty is really nothing more than the toleration of sin and blasphemy against God. Such evil makes God froth at the mouth with righteous indignation and prompts his unleashing of terror on our planet. We need holiness, piety, and repentance, not fun and games. And again, I ask you, which is more beneficial for mankind, liberty that kills or law enforcement that saves?

The Holy Roman Church has been guiding the affairs of men long before any itinerant Protestant or Unitarian ever came on the scene. Good Christian people must recognize her, the Blessed Mother Church, as the ultimate authority. We can see to that. Since we are a nation that is for and by the people, my goal is to help them see that the Bible, the book America claims to so love and trust, actually teaches Church-based authoritarian principles.

In Matthew 16:19, our Lord told the Apostle Peter, *"And I will give unto thee the keys of the kingdom of heaven: and **whatsoever thou shalt bind on earth shall be bound in heaven: and whatsoever thou shalt loose on earth shall be loosed in heaven.**"* By this, the Lord makes clear that the holy Apostles had Christ's authority for the loosing and binding of eternal matters, which means access to heaven. This applied to forgiveness of sins and man being accepted by God. The Apostle John makes this quite clear. *"Then said Jesus to them again, Peace be unto you: as my Father hath sent me, even so send I you. And when he had said this, he breathed on them, and saith unto them, Receive ye the Holy Ghost. **Whose soever sins ye remit, they are remitted unto them; and whose soever sins ye retain, they are retained.**"* (John 20:21-23). Could it be made any clearer that the Apostles, the chosen of the Lord, had power to forgive sins, as Jesus did, along with the blessed Father in heaven? Men were given the power of God. What men? The men who were the leaders of the church under Christ, the Apostles.

Ephesians 2:18-19 says, *"Now therefore ye are no more strangers and foreigners, but fellowcitizens with the saints, and of the household of God. And are **built upon the foundation of the apostles and prophets**, Jesus Christ himself being the chief corner stone; In whom all the building fitly framed together groweth unto an holy temple in the Lord."* What men today carry the authority of Christ? The descendents of the men who guided that sacred institution that has always existed, going back to the first century, those who are built upon the foundation of the apostles and prophets. Does this apostleship continue today? Yes! Peter said so himself. Notice the beloved apostle's words...

> *Wherefore **I will not be negligent to put you always in remembrance of these things**, though ye know them, and be established in the present truth. Yea, I think it meet, as long as I am in this tabernacle, to stir you up by putting you in remembrance; Knowing that shortly I must put off this my tabernacle, even as our Lord Jesus Christ hath shewed me. **Moreover I will endeavor that ye may be able after my decease to have these things always in remembrance**.* (2 Peter 3:12-15).

Peter, speaking by God's inspiration, states that he will keep us in remembrance of the Word of God. But did you notice what he says then? He tells us that he would do so in life *and* beyond death! This demonstrates both Peter's authority from God and his guidance of the Church. This could only be done one way—by initializing apostolic succession. After Peter's decease, he could guide the church through his God-appointed successors down through every age.

Of course, Peter was not the only Saint of God to lay down the Law of the Lord. We have many examples of the beloved Apostle Paul. Notice his attitude in dealing with one who had committed sexual sin in the church at Corinth.

> *For I verily, as absent in body, but present in spirit, have judged already, as though I were present, concerning him that hath so done this deed, In the name of our Lord Jesus Christ, when ye are gathered together, and my spirit, with the power of our Lord Jesus Christ, **To deliver such an one unto Satan for the destruction of the flesh, that the spirit may be saved in the day of the Lord Jesus.*** (I Corinthians 5:3-5).

Paul makes it clear that it would be only right for him and the Corinthians to deliver this sinful man unto the powers of Satan for "the destruction of the flesh, that the spirit may be saved in the day of the Lord Jesus." Did you notice that? Paul says it is fitting to do damage to the flesh to save the soul! I ask you, what is heretic burning or beheading? Only methods to save a foolhardy soul from eminent damnation. Paul was no libertarian. He was a Saint interested in only the soul, as we should be.

What was Paul's methodology in handling a heretic liar named Elymas, who practiced damnable black magic, a thing accursed by the Church? I assure you Paul did not tell Elymas that practicing soul-damning magic was his business and no one could tell him what to do. Instead, Paul gave him a chastening touch of reality;

> *But Elymas the sorcerer (for so is his name by interpretation) withstood them, seeking to turn away the deputy from the faith. Then Saul, (who also is called Paul,) filled with the Holy Ghost, set his eyes on him, And said, O full of all subtilty and all mischief, thou child of the devil, thou enemy of all righteousness, wilt thou not cease to pervert the right ways of the Lord? And* **now, behold, the hand of the Lord is upon thee, and thou shalt be blind, not seeing the sun for a season**. *And immediately there fell on him a mist and a darkness; and he went about seeking some to lead him by the hand.* (Acts 13:8-11).

Paul blinded this man to save his soul and the souls of others he was deceiving. And, let's not forget what Paul said concerning Hymenaeus and Alexander, two disciples that turned heretic. *"Of whom is Hymenaeus and Alexander;* **whom I have delivered unto Satan, that they may learn not to blaspheme***"* (I Timothy 1:20). Just as with that sinful Corinthian we spoke of earlier, Paul here punished ungodliness by physical means. Paul also demonstrated the Church's authority by securing the faithfulness of cities. Titus 1:5 gives us Paul's instructions to Titus. *"For this cause left I thee in Crete, that thou shouldest set in order the things that are wanting, and ordain elders in every city, as I had appointed thee."* Don't let some wayward Protestant tell you there is no authority in the Bible for setting up bishops over cities. As we have seen, there is!

In Acts 5:1-11, we read of how his holiness St. Peter dealt with unfaithfulness and disloyalty to the church. God, through Peter, often required that men pay the ultimate price for their sins;

> *But a certain man named Ananias, with Sapphira his wife, sold a possession, And kept back part of the price, his wife also being privy to it, and brought a certain part, and laid it at the apostles' feet. But Peter said, Ananias, why hath Satan filled thine heart to lie to the Holy Ghost, and to keep back part of the price of the land? Whiles it*

*remained, was it not thine own? and after it was sold, was it not in thine own power? why hast thou conceived this thing in thine heart? thou hast not lied unto men, but unto God. And **Ananias hearing these words fell down, and gave up the ghost: and great fear came on all them that heard these things.** And the young men arose, wound him up, and carried him out, and buried him. And it was about the space of three hours after, when his wife, not knowing what was done, came in. And Peter answered unto her, Tell me whether ye sold the land for so much? And she said, Yea, for so much. Then Peter said unto her, How is it that ye have agreed together to tempt the Spirit of the Lord? **behold, the feet of them which have buried thy husband are at the door, and shall carry thee out. Then fell she down straightway at his feet, and yielded up the ghost: and the young men came in, and found her dead, and, carrying her forth, buried her by her husband.** And great fear came upon all the church, and upon as many as heard these things.*

Peter wasted no time in setting an example of those who defied the will of the Church. Remember this: *"And great fear came upon all the church, and upon as many as heard these things"* (Acts 5:11). As we can clearly see, God uses fear to terrorize his people into submission. If you sin against God, he might kill you! That doesn't sound politically correct today, but it is biblically correct.

The judgmental Protestant masses are so quick to point out the torturous pain inflicted by methods we used to secure faithfulness in times past. Starvation, beheadings, the rack, water torture, burnings at the stake, hangings, etc. Yes, pain, excruciating pain, is the idea behind these fierce enforcers of truth, but what can be compared to the salvation of souls? No amount of pain can outweigh the value of an eternal soul being snatched from the fires of Hell. *"And others save with fear, **pulling them out of the fire**; hating even the garment spotted by the flesh"* (Jude 1:23).

The soul of an ungodly rich man once cried out from purgatory to God's mediator of the Old Testament, *"Father Abraham, have mercy on me, and send Lazarus, that he may dip the tip of his finger in water, and cool my tongue; for I am tormented in this flame."* (Luke 16:24). Today, the church watches over the souls of men and gives them the forgiveness they can only receive through her mediation. If only we could secure their final salvation by enforcing the Lord's will in this life.

Speaking of enforcing the Lord's will, we must now consider another avenue of the Church's responsibility. Let us take a look at Romans 13:1-7, where Paul tell us;

> Let every soul be subject unto the higher powers. For there is no power but of God: the powers that be are ordained of God. Whosoever therefore resisteth the power, resisteth the ordinance of God: and they that resist shall receive to themselves damnation. For rulers are not a terror to good works, but to the evil. Wilt thou then not be afraid of the power? do that which is good, and thou shalt have praise of the same: For he is the minister of God to thee for good. But if thou do that which is evil, be afraid; for he beareth not the sword in vain: for he is the minister of God, a revenger to execute wrath upon him that doeth evil. Wherefore ye must needs be subject, not only for wrath, but also for conscience sake. For for this cause pay ye tribute also: for they are God's ministers, attending continually upon this very thing. Render therefore to all their dues: tribute to whom tribute is due; custom to whom custom; fear to whom fear; honour to whom honour.

There is no doubt that Paul is discussing the role of government, but notice what powers Paul declares it right for the government to possess; those who resist her receive damnation; those who do what is right will receive her blessings and not her punishments. And then the government is called *"the minister of God to thee for good."* Finally, it says *"he beareth not the sword in vain."* How much clearer could Paul make it that a government is to be obeyed at all costs as God's moral agent? In ages past, the Catholic Church was in full power and enforced her will with unbelievable veracity. Today, she is criticized for what she once did, but I ask you to show me where in the Bible she did wrong? We have learned from Paul that a government that does the will of God rules with God as his minister, his servant. Do we have any right to object to God's counsel? Do we have any right to turn away his ministers? No, we don't.

Now suppose all Roman Catholic Christians composed the government of America. Would not the balance of power throw the Christians in a position where they would have to enforce their Lord's will? It might be wrong in the eyes of the law to torture and kill someone for being a homosexual now, but based on the Christian principles we have studied, we must do all that is within our power to enforce the Lord's will. Again, I remind you that the Lord would want you to take away freedom from a mentally ill person, a suicidal person, a kidnapper, or a killer. He wants us to discipline our children by making them do things against their will, and to discipline them when they don't do what we tell them to do—if with children, why not with the souls of men who are children of God? The obvious and most unavoidable answer is that we should impose God's teachings at any cost. If indeed the Lord must be followed, and if indeed we should give our lives to do His will, then why should we limit our evangelism to the freedom of choices of people who don't know what is best for them? Where does the Bible teach freedom of expression? Where does it even passively imply it? It doesn't! As the Church, we must do what God wants us to do—guide the souls of men into the truth. Like good parents in the Lord, the church must guide her children to heaven, that greatest home above the clouds to which we all strive to go.

In conclusion, Mr. Congressman, I am maintaining that the real Lord's will must be done, not mine. The Church is right. I am not. I must follow the Bible and the Church, regardless of the will and traditions of men. It is high time for God and government to once again join hands and lead this nation on the path it should go. Call it tyranny or oppression, call it dictatorship or even papal slavery, but we will call it salvation. I am looking for your support to help guide this nation back to the pure and right ways of God. With your help and with God's, we can accomplish our goal a little faster.

Sincerely,

Christopher "Arentyougladimnotreal" Mabry
Chairman of the Golden Age of Priests Society

The Charlatan Letter

A Manipulation Manual for Psychics and Televangelists

First, when prophesying, always speak in vague generalities. Never give specific dates or times of the events you prophesy about unless you have alternate meanings for the bullshit you are peddling, and then *only* if you are extraordinarily led to do so and are sure your listeners are gullible enough to buy into it. When selling a prediction of any kind, stay with issues like entertainment, dating, people, and promises of good times ahead. Never give a negative prediction, only positive ones—this way you don't get called on the carpet for anything bad happening should you happen to get a negative one right. If you are of the Christian persuasion and want to deceive your congregation by predicting the second coming of Jesus, never give a specific time, only "seasons" when the Lord shall return. If you do make the mistake of giving a date for the end of the world, and nothing happens, just say that you miscalculated and that your prophecy was wrong because you didn't figure in the right biblical dates in your timetable. This has worked for centuries, keeping religious dupes coming back for more. If that doesn't fly, tell them that we are told to try the spirits to see whether they be of God (I John 3:4), and you mistakenly made a false prediction of the Devil. This way, no matter what, the error is not God's. Intimidate them and warn them that we must still keep looking for Jesus to come back, and for "signs" of the end.

Second, keep the authority over your people strong and do not give doubt a chance to creep in. Warn your followers that the slightest notion of doubt is evil and blasphemous to the core. The Devil *himself* is trying to lead them away from the path of righteousness, and most of all, to prosperity. Keep the skeptics as far away from your meetings as possible. Should any sneak in, have your beefy security dudes forcibly escort them out immediately!

Third, if you are a mystic or psychic, speak mysteriously and illusively. If you are making predictions for a person, and you ask the listener if he knows a "Jeremy," and he says he doesn't, just cryptically say, "You will." Be authoritative. If you are called on an error, insist that it is true (i.e. If they say something like, "I'm telling you, I don't have a brother!" Then you say, "I'm sorry, sir, but, yes, you do!"). Never give an inch. Hold out and let them fill in the gaps, and before you know it, they'll be suggesting possible meanings and giving you the clues to rip right into their bank accounts!

Fourth, if you are asked by parents what is wrong with a sick child, boldly say, "I'm getting something about the chest." Then wait for them to give more details. Remember, the chest is the same area as the stomach and all the major organs. If anything is wrong, it's probably in that region, so just rub your chest area and say, "I'm getting something right in this area." If they get checked out by a doctor, you might get lucky and there really is something wrong, but if they say the doctor didn't find anything wrong in the area, ask them to have the doctor look again, or have another doctor take a look at it. This way, even a little phlegm in a person's lungs will give cause for concern, and you'll be hailed as a true prophet who might have saved the person's life! If, in the rare case, they go through the trouble of checking out the person again and find nothing wrong in the least, and insist that you are not a true prophet, tell them God has answered your prayers in leaving not so much as a trace of the harmful bacteria that once was there. Praise God!

Fifth, during every service, always have security quietly ready to remove amputees and victims of deformities from your revival or healing ceremony. Remember to have the people with minor problems up front by the time they get there so you can "heal" them. Keep the amputees and seriously crippled people in the rear of the building so you don't have to deal with them. Make sure you have plenty of your own wheelchairs ready to dispense. Offer them only to mildly disabled people to sit down in so you can hoist them up out of it and let them stand briefly to show that you are "a true miracle worker." If you are approached by a family of an amputee or deformed person seeking healing, say a quick prayer over them, "As great as your faith, be it unto thee." (Matthew 15:28), then quickly (and discreetly) escort them out of the building without explanation and have security not let them back in. This way, no one sees that you are a fake.

Sixth, always promise pie in the sky when it's over. No matter how bad it gets, it'll be better some day. Sometimes you'll have to do this because you might not have any off-hand pranks to play on them. Be positive always. Never show defeat or depression. Be a professional. Make useless fluffy statements like, "God has a plan for your life!" "God loves you." "Everything's going to be alright!" "You have a positive energy about you!" and "Lay hold on your anointing." Say it with enthusiasm like it actually means something!

Seventh, if you are of the Christian persuasion and desire to run a snake handling church, when you handle snakes and they bite you and you live, say "Glory to God, I lived." If you die, instruct your patrons to say, "It was just God's will that he die." So either way, you look credible in the eyes of your fool parishioners. However, you might ought to use non-poisonous snakes that just look real mean!

Eighth, if skeptical folks accost you for evidences of your miracles, just tell them that evil, depraved people seek after a sign and then quote

Matthew 12:39. If you are a psychic or mystic, tell your skeptical inquirers, *"I'm sorry, folks. The spirits have their own affairs and wills too. It's not as though they sit around just waiting to please us with signs and cute little wonders. They are only concerned with bigger, spiritual issues, and even then, they sometimes don't respond for reasons all their own."* Then turn the conversation on them, *"I'm detecting a dark energy within you. Please, you must pray with me. This energy must leave your home soon!"* Or, if they are more on the intelligent side, you might try putting up a general smokescreen, *"I'm sensing a lot of pain in your life, sir!"* Get creative. If they appear angry and resentful, say, *"It's okay. God understands. It wasn't your fault."* If they don't break down and open up to your sharp routine, just pat them on the back, and say, *"God will listen when you're ready,"* Then see them out and tell them you've got other business.

Ninth, if you have any older prophecies or predictions that you or your associate prophets made that did not come true, and want to save face, just say, "There is still time." But remember to get with your associates so everyone has the same game-plan regarding your explanations. Be sure not to contradict each other. If you went the dangerous route of foretelling of impending doom on a group or individual for sins they committed, and no bad thing happened to them, you can either say that there is still time, or that they repented and God decided not to push them. It's a failsafe either way.

Tenth, if you try to heal someone and they don't get better, blame it on them and make them feel stupid and unspiritual. They just didn't have enough faith because they didn't pray hard enough. One has to believe in this stuff for it to work, you know. Anytime a healing fails, rely on that. It is always the person's fault, never God's fault. Don't forget to remind them that only God heals, not you. God has wisdom we know not of. He may decide not to heal someone if he chooses not to, and particularly, if they complain and whine to the minister who healed them that the healing is too limited or taking too long! Keep the upper hand!

Eleventh, to appear to be speaking in tongues, always claim it is a tongue of angels so that no one can find out that you are not speaking a real language, but a bogus language containing no grammar or syntax. Have clever, practiced phrases ready to spout off as "unknown tongues." It is very easy to speak in tongues once you learn the basics; to create them, take common words repeated senselessly together (i.e. see-my-tie-tie-my-tie, eat-my-son-tan-my-son, bleed-the-rug-wholly-with-fresca). This, said very fast, and accented with a foreign-sounding inflection, sounds like, "say ma taa tay ma taa, ea my sone, tawn ma sone, blay de roge ho lay wee frascaa!" Now mix it up and learn to rearrange the words and inflections. In no time, you'll get fast at it and it will become a cinch. Then, before you know it, you'll be praising the Lord just like a hillbilly pastor of an Assembly of God Church in Kentucky!

Twelfth, the more exhausted people are, the more irrational they are, and the more likely they are to part with their money. Proclaim that spirituality is made up of lots of exhausting physical activity…Staying up late at retreats, running around the church building, rolling in the aisles, jumping up and down, dancing around in a frenzy, and reverberating to music is true spirituality. No one has control over themselves if God moves a person to do such things. To biblically support this belief, refer to how Saul was made to prophesy by God (I Samuel 10:6-11). If you are a psychic or mystic, instead of a high energy celebration, be somber. Tell your believers that to get rid of their pains, phobias, and negative energies, they must bury their demons in the ground ten miles from your establishment. Have them give you the money to purchase and ship sacred spell casting materials from Jerusalem (Not really. The city just sounds holy and this way you can ask for more money for ordering "special and sacred" materials!) Then, with the materials (which you bought at your local grocery or arts and crafts store only a few blocks away), set up a sacred and drawn out ceremony to kick off the burying of the "sacred" materials that contain the negative energy. Bury them, and then assure your suckers that time will help make their lives even happier as the evil energy residue dissipates.

Thirteenth, if you want to run a church to make money, make sure that the music is running high and the atmosphere is charged with excitement. Never attempt to rile up a crowd without good musicians to spice things up. Keep the lights low to maintain that spiritual/mystical feeling in the air. This will convince your crowd of simpletons that God is in their midst. To avoid lawsuits that could rob you of your precious money, always have strong men standing ready to catch people who pass out due to your "laying on of holy hands." On a side note, this is a perfect opportunity to smack the foreheads of those who look exceptionally stupid. Just reach out and say, "God has an anointing for YOU…" Then smack them on the forehead with your palm as hard as you can (while making it look real and sincere, of course). The person probably won't be hurt or disturbed by it, but if the person is, you can blame the act on the Holy Spirit. Benny Hinn does it all the time. He is an expert. Learn from him.

Fourteenth, and most importantly, emphasize the financial offering at each and every meeting. Whether it be God or the sacred spirits, they need money, and so do you to keep doing his work! Stress that without money, God could not work in the world. God hates people who don't tithe! Never let your church forget that! Remind them of it night and day. Besides, money is there to test us; if a person will give money to you to do the Lord's work, then that person is worthy. If not, that person is evil and corrupt like the rich, young ruler (Matthew 19:16-22). Hey, you're a good soldier of God, and you deserve riches. Abraham was rich (Genesis 13:2).

Fifteenth, sell plenty of gimmicks like prayer shawls, anointing oil, prayer cloths, holy water (that wonderful stuff that comes straight from your "holy" kitchen faucet), and incentive plaques and gifts (offer them *only* with hefty contributions!) Even Paul sent cloths he prayed over to heal believers (Acts 19:11-12).

Remember, the biggest intent behind all of this is to keep the money coming. That is why we are preaching and prophesying. This trade must keep us wealthy. We don't want to have to sell our yachts now, do we? If you can't at least drive a new Lamborghini every year, then is this scheme really worth it? And don't feel bad that we are playing off the ignorance of the masses. They should know better. Like any business, we are just giving our customers what they want.

Christian McDumb Takes a Stand!

Christian McDumb, attorney at law, may seem like just another dime-a-dozen litigation lawyer from the South, but he's much, much more! Author of "One billion and one reasons why Archaeopteryx is just a bird and Lucy is just an ape," "The Face of Jesus on Mars," and "The Verdict Is In: T-rex was on the ark," McDumb holds a "BS" degree in precisely that. He is making waves in the world today. As a proud defender of the Intelligent Design Movement (a.k.a., creationism), he donates his time and abilities to skillfully bootlegging his Lord Jesus Christ into the classrooms of America through the court systems of our land.

McDumb's greatest joys are when states like Kansas (which happens to be his favorite state) accept creationism, and when science textbooks have disclaimers put on the front of them that deride evolution and science. McDumb boldly writes "scientific" pamphlets that use big, scientific-sounding words, like "probability," "hypothesis," "postulate," and "irreducible complexity," and he is always careful to leave the word "God" out of these pamphlets so that they have a better chance of being seen as scientific by an infidel judge.

McDumb was crushed, devastated in fact, when the ID movement suffered a great setback in Dover, Pennsylvania in 2005. He and Pat Robertson didn't know what to do with themselves when that dark, dark day came over our nation. But he hasn't given up! McDumb is stubborn and has a gift from God for not knowing when to quit.

He is a smooth operator. He says things like, "Teach your children they come from monkeys and they will act like monkeys." He makes arguments against evolution, like, "If evolution is true, why are monkeys still around today?" He understands perfectly well that evolution must be fought, for if not combated, it will lead to homosexuality, the most heinous and blasphemous sin in the eyes of all his friends—white, churchgoing Republicans over the age of 45.

When McDumb gets wound up, it's hard to slow him down. He's a sharp cookie, making powerful arguments in debate. Atheists run from him like Mercedes-driving sophomores from Virginia Tech. He tells them: "You haven't found the missing link yet!" Then he asks tough questions like, "What good is half an eye?" McDumb knows his stuff, especially about halves and monkey-men. "Show me an ape/man, Mr. Evolutionist! You can't, can you?" He thinks that if evolution were true, there would be half-ape/half-men everywhere...and half-mosquitoes/half-elephants, half-crocodiles/half-zebras, and half-gnats/half-brontosauruses. This subject is deep for McDumb and it took him the better part of a year to struggle through the issue of why there isn't a half-broccoli/half-pregnant woman, but that's another matter. So the next time you DON'T see a half-mollusk/half-eagle, you'll know why! It's because God created everything in wholes. If the cosmos had evolved, there'd be halves of every combination of things in the universe!

McDumb is open-minded too, just as he is intellectually keen; he goes before a judge and argues passionately that ID is not about God or religion in any way, and then he stresses that the designer of the universe could have been anything…but not an alien race or any non-eternal entity because that only begs the question of who created them, so he's right back to assigning God as the creator! Well, alright…so McDumb *is* trying to get God into the classrooms, even though he says he's not, and is only trying to teach an alternative scientific theory!

Now McDumb says he's open-minded, but he can't be too open-minded; he tells the judges and the large audiences he addresses that he just wants all sides of the debate to be heard, that he wants more information put out there so that everyone can make an informed decision about their origins, but when asked if he'd like Astrology to be taught alongside Astronomy, he said no because that doesn't agree with his beliefs.

Well, okay, so maybe McDumb isn't always fair or consistent, but God loves the McDumbs of this world anyway—the McDummies, as they are called. McDummies are not ashamed to defend The Nazarene through devious means. They are good soldiers for Jesus. They'll tread right into the heart of enemy territory to bring victory for the Lord, so they really don't care if anyone likes them or not, especially non-churchgoing scientists in white coats with real degrees.

As for McDumb, he will persevere. The spirit of Michael Behe carries him on. He sleeps with a copy of Darwin's Black Box under his pillow at night. McDumb's heroes, Sean Hannity and Michael Medved, pave the way for him. What would Jesus do without the McDummies of this world?

Give Me the Secular Nation

Give me the secular nation. I want to be free. Allow me my mind and please let me be.

But so many people want a different sort of place, a Christian nation where saints and bishops set the pace.

Where laws are made and edicts passed; defy these statutes and you won't last!

The women here love walking the Christian walk, but since it's a Christian nation, they shouldn't contribute or even talk.

Not many like going to church by the hearse, but if you think this is bad, it gets much worse!

Blue law weekends, can't buy very much on the Christian holy day, and remember, kids, no movies on Sunday!

"A" is for "adulteress," as it says on your chest. Your sin is known, you cannot protest!

Prohibition is back, no alcohol to relax or unwind. Strict parenting enforced, "Touch yourself and you'll go blind!"

Arrested for heresy, put back in the stocks, out in plain view where everyone mocks.

A nation of good soldiers, obeying God's every command, committing heinous acts to purify the land.

Weddings, organs, the sound of church bells, and always a reminder of what awaits the infidels.

Be careful what you say, be careful what you do, there's a judgmental eye staring right at you!

A nation on fire, zealously watching the flock—under penalty of law, God you will not mock!

Astute harassment, downright abuse, a witch-hunt brewing, the sinner to the noose.

Holier than thous, science rejection, for unbelievers no police protection.

Back to the dark ages, freedom choked out, the golden age of priests returns, the pious walk about.

Freethinkers locked up, the church's mind eased. They are in the dungeon, so Jesus is pleased.

"Dust off the rack," say they, "We've got to stop the sin." Torture and pain can make a man give in.

No, no thank you, I prefer the nation like the one I see, where people can think, where I can be me.

God and government, they only start with the letter "G." No other connection should be there, you see.

So give me the secular nation. I want to be free. Allow me my mind and please let me be.

CHAPTER 24
Hats Off to the Real Jesus

A Final De-conversion Milestone

"There is more to be learned from a zoo than a monastery."
- *Peter Watson*

"Take what is useful, reject what is useless, and add what is uniquely your own."
- *Jeff Johnson*

In previous pages, I have attacked my former lord and savior. I have attacked his religion and the pieces of literature that testify of him, but here, I will do no such thing.

About two years ago, I reached what I consider to be a final milestone of de-conversion. Religious indoctrination never really leaves you. You divorce yourself from it, you renounce your allegiance to it, but the etchings that remain on your heart and mind are there to stay. I took time to reflect on why this would be. The conclusion I came to was that the spirituality that comes from religion doesn't really come from religion, but from the individual in whom it awakens spiritual concerns. Love for truth is not taught, only stirred up from the still reservoirs of the human soul, the mind. Likewise, the esteem of truth, the love for truth, comes from within. To experience truth is to feel a connection, a "clicking" of an assortment of related facts, and it is a most beautiful thing to experience. To take this beautiful thing and apply it to humanity at large is the beginning of spirituality.

The Bible and my Christian years played a big part in developing and passing along the spirituality that defines me today. That spirituality is and will always be a part of me. Although my worldview has changed, the vestiges of that tearful journey still remain.

When I look into the Bible's stories, I find many appalling and reprehensible things. And yet through it all, I am surprised at what I see. Bible stories are alive to me, almost like they were my own. Like all narratives produced by a puzzled humanity, they are samplings of the human experience. I can see them playing out in the theatre of my mind with near perfect clarity.

I see an anxious Jacob, running from his brother, Esau, spending many a lonely night in Bethel. I see him years later, with butterflies in his stomach, worrying frantically about what the reaction will be of his estranged brother, whom he is preparing to meet. I see a teary-eyed Joseph who escapes to his inner chamber to let out the hurt of seeing his brethren whom he had been separated from for so long. I see an old Eli leaning back in a chair, staring off in the distance. He sees a messenger hastily running towards him who informs him that the Philistines have stolen the ark of God. His heart broken in utter despair, he falls backward in his chair and breaks his neck.

I see an angry, dejected Jephthae, thinking of the right words to express his disgust at the leaders of the Israelites who beg him to return and fight on the side of God's people after having rejected him many years earlier. I see a distraught, humiliated Samson, begging to be avenged of God for the loss of his eyes, as he finally makes peace with the fact that he will die in the process of his vindication.

I see a pain-stricken Job sitting against a wall, scratching his sores with a broken piece of pottery. With his head facing the ground, he tends to the red and swollen outbreaks on his body. I see a sobbing King David, having been called out by the prophet Nathan for the sin of adultery, refusing to eat, praying for God to save the life of his young son of Bathsheba whom God cursed. When he hears of the child's death, he resigns himself to God's will, rises up, and begins to eat, as his perplexed servants look on.

I see a joyous David, dancing and leaping with all his might before God and the people as the newly recovered ark of God is carried through the city. His wife, Michal – Saul's daughter – watches her husband through a window afar. As he returns home, she says to him: "How glorious you were today, O King, to parade yourself around, exposing yourself, like some degenerate!" With spiteful sarcasm, David replies: "You're just saying that out of jealousy because God made me ruler of His people instead of your father. So if you think this is vile, get ready! Because I am going to be even more vile than this, and all the young ladies in my kingdom will hold me in great honor!"

I see a fearful Elijah, his nerves frayed, running from a threatening Jezebel who swore to kill him. He runs away into the wilderness and sits under a juniper tree, and out of weariness, begs for God to take his life. I see a burnt out Jeremiah, his arms folded, saying "I will not speak the word of the Lord anymore," and then buckling under the pressure of his convictions: "but his word was as a fire in my bones. I was weary with forbearing and could not stay."

It was through the Bible that I learned character, that I learned self-confidence, that I learned to employ reason, and to explore my world. For me, the Bible was the doorway to becoming more than I was. I became more than I was, but then I became more than the Bible.

I was through seeing fictional connections between Old and New Testament stories, and I was no longer afraid of a tormenting, fiery Hell, but I could see the humanity in these passages like I could from the mythical tales of every religion worldwide. I can read a novel, a comic, or watch a good movie to let me relive certain segments of the human experience, or I can read the Bible. Bible stories are special because they arouse in me the same strong sense of purpose that the creators of the stories themselves seemed to feel. For us, mastering the human experience and coming to terms with ourselves is the closest thing to an objective purpose we will ever have. My time as a believer gave me the tools to fulfill this purpose—to achieve mastery in understanding the human experience. So, at last, I am ready to face the Jesus I rejected.

I imagined myself facing the wall at my desk in my apartment, busy with the task of making some final proofs of this work. Jesus appears behind me, his arms folded, with a straight face. He says to me, "I hope you're happy. You reject my word and lead believers astray. Is this really what you wanted? I made you who you are. I even made it possible to write this book, and now you turn on me? I hope you're happy. I hope you got what you wanted." Then I turn to him and say, "You're not the real Jesus." Still standing there speechless, he fades into thin air.

In a way, Project Bible Truth has not just been about exposing biblical errors or the errors of Christianity, but about revealing the identity of the real Jesus. I now know who the real Jesus is, and he isn't to be found in any book, or in a prayer manual, or in a catechism, or in any cult publication. He isn't a deity, he wasn't born of a virgin, and he never ascended to the clouds—except in the hearts and minds of a creative searcher, who created a myth to inspire his people or to teach them lessons.

The real Jesus is a victorious hunter, a persuasive voice, a display of force, a great conqueror. He is the message of good triumphing over evil, eloquence in word, and resolute moral steadfastness. The real Jesus is a soldier who stops to give a bottle of water and a sandwich to a malnourished villager. The real Jesus is the glorious shouts of the winning team. He is the strong man's display of power, the craft of the trickster's hands and well-timed moves. The real Jesus is brilliance, foresight, and overcoming determination, the unwillingness to give up or to surrender.

I look inside the Bible to see what Jesus stood for, but I can also look outside of it to see the same things. Jesus stood for spirituality – powerfully in teaching – but even more powerfully in principle—in what his identity represented. The valid and important teachings of Jesus and his character are not identical to the insipid messages of ecclesiastical, evangelical eggheads, who, through monopolization of power and ego, spread the net of oppression—something Jesus Christ would decry. Spirituality is inherent in all human drama. It is a message every human gets and a language every person speaks. True spirituality is about exhilaration, about pride, about youthful vitality and old-aged wisdom, but most of all, it's about loving and being loved. Through this turbulent, painful journey, I can now see a Jesus who stands for these things. To that Jesus, my hat goes off!

www.ministerturnsatheist.org

www.ionianspirit.net

www.debunkingchristianity.blogspot.com

www.ingramcontent.com/pod-product-compliance
Lightning Source LLC
Chambersburg PA
CBHW031131160426
43193CB00008B/97